Collaborative Software Design

T0293076

Get the eBook FREE!

(PDF, ePub, Kindle, and liveBook all included)

We believe that once you buy a book from us, you should be able to read it in any format we have available. To get electronic versions of this book at no additional cost to you, purchase and then register this book at the Manning website.

Go to https://www.manning.com/freebook and follow the instructions to complete your pBook registration.

That's it!
Thanks from Manning!

Collaborative Software Design

How to facilitate domain modeling decisions

Evelyn van Kelle,
Gien Verschatse, and
Kenny Baas-Schwegler

Forewords by Diana Montalion
and Trond Hjorteland

MANNING
SHELTER ISLAND

For online information and ordering of this and other Manning books, please visit www.manning.com. The publisher offers discounts on this book when ordered in quantity.

For more information, please contact

    Special Sales Department
    Manning Publications Co.
    20 Baldwin Road
    PO Box 761
    Shelter Island, NY 11964
    Email: orders@manning.com

© 2025 Manning Publications Co. All rights reserved.

No part of this publication may be reproduced, stored in a retrieval system, or transmitted, in any form or by means electronic, mechanical, photocopying, or otherwise, without prior written permission of the publisher.

Many of the designations used by manufacturers and sellers to distinguish their products are claimed as trademarks. Where those designations appear in the book, and Manning Publications was aware of a trademark claim, the designations have been printed in initial caps or all caps.

♾ Recognizing the importance of preserving what has been written, it is Manning's policy to have the books we publish printed on acid-free paper, and we exert our best efforts to that end. Recognizing also our responsibility to conserve the resources of our planet, Manning books are printed on paper that is at least 15 percent recycled and processed without the use of elemental chlorine.

The author and publisher have made every effort to ensure that the information in this book was correct at press time. The author and publisher do not assume and hereby disclaim any liability to any party for any loss, damage, or disruption caused by errors or omissions, whether such errors or omissions result from negligence, accident, or any other cause, or from any usage of the information herein.

 Manning Publications Co.
20 Baldwin Road
PO Box 761
Shelter Island, NY 11964

Development editor:	Karen Miller
Technical editor:	Charles Schafer
Review editors:	Adriana Sabo and Dunja Nikitović
Production editor:	Andy Marinkovich
Copy editor:	Julie McNamee
Proofreader:	Jason Everett
Typesetter:	Tamara Švelić Sabljić
Cover designer:	Marija Tudor

ISBN 9781633439252
Printed in the United States of America

To Roger, Beasty, Lulu, and Mr. Noodle,
our cats who were absolutely no help at all.

brief contents

contents

             *Getting stuck in a polarity   312 ▪ Managing a polarity as
             facilitator   314 ▪ Letting the group manage the polarity   321*

    10.4   Collaborative software design catalysts   324

    10.5   Chapter heuristics   324

    10.6   Further reading   324

11   *Communicating and documenting decisions   326*

    11.1   Formalizing a decision   327
             Finding the consequences   327 ▪ Capturing the decision   332

    11.2   Spreading the knowledge through the company   335
             Communicating decisions   335

    11.3   Keeping the decision alive   338
             *The modeling process as a whirlpool   339 ▪ Don't fall in love
             with your model   343*

    11.4   Collaborative software design catalysts   345

    11.5   Chapter heuristics   346

    11.6   Further reading   346

12   *Collaborative modeling beyond software design   348*

    12.1   Moving toward understanding the context   349
             *Focusing on customer needs   349 ▪ Connecting business strategy,
             product, and software architecture   350*

    12.2   Collaborative modeling beyond software design   355
             *Different roles, different modeling needs   355 ▪ Customer
             journeys and EventStorming: A love story   359
             Aligning capabilities with your strategy   360*

    12.3   Moving toward implementation   362
             *When to go from collaborative modeling to coding   362
             From collaborative modeling to code   365*

    12.4   Collaborative software design catalysts   373

    12.5   Chapter heuristics   374

    12.6   Further reading   374

             appendix A   376

             index   378

forewords

I was lucky. Early in my software engineering career, I worked on teams where collaborative modeling and collective reasoning were the norm. Whenever we didn't know what to do, we whiteboarded. Sometimes, we were a group of engineers solving a technical problem. More often, we were a cross-functional group that included business and product people, technology implementers, software users, UX designers, a vendor or two, and/or subject matter experts from other teams.

Thinking well together, synthesizing expertise, and learning from each other were critical to our success. We understood, from painful experience, that "all models are wrong, but some are useful." This doesn't mean that people make inaccurate models. This means that modeling is the cultivation of shared understanding, not the production of an artifact.

A model conveys a point of view. Modeling integrates relevant points of view into something useful. My teammates and I knew that to design a solution, we had to understand the problem. We had to be in the room where the modeling happened.

Our success depended on creating conceptual integrity, which Fred Brooks said "is the most important consideration in systems design." We liked to solve hard problems and take on hard challenges. To meet those challenges, we never had the luxury of being 10x individuals. We had to be 10x teams.

Over the years, I've seen processes that support conceptual integrity break down. As relational complexity in our software systems increases, roles and teams are increasingly siloed. Problem thinking is decoupled from solution thinking. Wars break out between product and tech. Decision-making is progressively hierarchical. The self-organizing aspiration of Agile turns into "We hate Agile, now what?" As a systems architect, this breakdown has made "modernization" and "transformation"—things many organizations want and need—a Sisyphean effort.

Jay Forrester, a pioneer software system scientist who taught at MIT, said that organizations can usually identify their problem spots because people are busy fixing them.

Alas, their fixes often make the problem worse—"pushing it in the wrong direction," Forrester said. Referring to this counterintuitive phenomenon, he stated, "The known and intended practices of the organization are sufficient to create the difficulties being experienced." He also discovered that, inevitably, organizations blame the wrong causes for their problems.

We are, in my experience, pushing things in the wrong direction. Creating and maintaining conceptual integrity is more important than ever. Yet we are fighting for control of software design and blaming each other for causing the problems. I see fewer teams demonstrate the critical learning-together skills they need to design relationally complex software systems. Our lack of collaborative software design is creating many of the difficulties we experience.

I understand, to some extent, why this happens. When I contributed code to monolithic software, I could envision the relatively synchronous context in which users engaged with it. I could follow established best practices. The scope of what we needed to understand seemed vast but was boxed nicely into a codebase or two.

Now, everything I work on is a system of software parts interacting with and structured by other software. The same information structured for one context (on a desktop web browser) needs a different structure for another context (when asking Alexa). Information systems change quickly. The paradigm is shifting around us, and we are all scrambling to figure out what to do about it.

We are lucky. In *Collaborative Software Design*, Evelyn van Kelle, Gien Verschatse, and Kenny Baas-Schwegler help us develop, or discover, these critical skills. They know from experience that social skills are the "hard skills." Our biggest blocker is rarely "We don't know enough about Kubernetes," but instead, "How do we think well together?"

Fortunately, they've written a book that helps us transform the social dynamics that hinder sustainable software design. When I've felt out there on my own, I've learned from them, tested their teachings in the real world, and improved my professional impact as a result.

You'll learn how to structure, participate in, and facilitate collaborative experiences that generate significantly better software outcomes. You'll understand the social dynamics that are currently blocking our ability to think well together. This understanding will help you navigate change, make effective decisions, and model effective thinking practices in your organization.

Through their BigScreen examples, you'll see that your pain is not unique. We are all experiencing the painful limitations of our current approaches. This book offers us approaches that help alleviate our pain.

You might be surprised that a book with no code samples can improve code quality. By illuminating the most common impediments we face as knowledge workers, this book helps you avoid them. And, it encourages you to provide leadership by experience and example in situations where shared knowledge is key to your success.

—Diana Montalion,
systems architect and author of Learning Systems Thinking

Have you ever been to a workshop that not only created a desirable result but even made you all feel energized and wanting to get started realizing what you as a group had created? Maybe you even had a newfound respect for people who were not like you at all and worked on things you didn't even think necessary. Or perhaps you've been to one where you pretty much felt that the whole thing was a big waste of time? Not only did it not produce anything valuable, but people even got angry at each other due to conflicts nobody even knew existed.

I suspect many of you have experienced both and everything in between, and you've probably never quite understood why workshops sometimes are great and sometimes a trainwreck. It was perhaps more or less the same people, and even though the topic was different, it couldn't have been that. Sure, some people get attached to their tools and their ideas, so much so that they don't even want to hear of anything else, but when responsible adults come together as employees, they leave their personal views behind and focus on the greater good. Surely. Unfortunately, that is often not the case, and some take serious offense to either not being listened to or having their ideas trashed by others. Ideas and design are often deeply personal artifacts, after all.

All of this is perfectly normal, both the good and the bad, and it happens all the time everywhere. But I bet the workshops that were very productive and people enjoyed being part of—proud of even—were probably run by people like Gien, Evelyn, and Kenny, the authors of this book. Seasoned and clever facilitators and managers of not only the process of doing a workshop, using some tool like EventStorming, Example Mapping, or User Story Mapping, but also recognizing and dealing with perfectly normal human behavior and group dynamics as mentioned previously. The latter separates the good from the great and may be the key difference between a workshop that people enjoyed or hated. We all know that happy people are more likely to work well together and produce greater results than people who are at each other's throats and stuck in fight-or-flight mode. A truly collaborative working mode—and the likelihood of good designs—is only possible when people regard each other as peers.

Software development is inherently a sociotechnical enterprise, where we come together as social beings working with technology to create new things. For that to have good outcomes, we need to optimize the social and technical aspects jointly. Focusing only on one, or both but separately, will not create optimal results. That is only possible when both are considered at the same time. Classical systems thinking does this. Is joint optimization possible just by being aware of it? No, if people don't see themselves as true peers, as equals, truly collaborative work is next to impossible as rank, power, competition, submission, complacency, and such interpersonal conflicts get in the way. As most organizations today are dominated by autocracy and competitiveness instead of equality and democracy, we need help to develop fertile ground for creative working mode. For that, you need facilitators and coaches who can help create the jointly optimized system necessary to make people see each other as peers and collaborators.

This book provides many of the tools, techniques, heuristics, and perspectives, particularly the social and psychological ones, that every manager should have in their tool-belt, especially those facilitating a workshop. Gien, Evelyn, and Kenny are all experts in the field, with a collective breadth of knowledge that surpasses most. With their help, you'll have all the means required to not only help people produce better results but also have a better time at work.

—TROND HJORTELAND,
IT ARCHITECT AND SOCIOTECHNICAL PRACTITIONER

preface

You might wonder how three very different individuals end up writing a book together about something they are all passionate about. What is it about collaborative software design that can bond different backgrounds, specialties, interests, and personalities?

In our own contexts, we were all doing collaborative modeling to help organizations move toward sustainable and qualitative outcomes. Numerous EventStorming sessions with various organizations led us—individually—to similar challenges and questions like these: How can we increase shared understanding of the problem, remove ambiguity in language, make decisions together, and deal with conflict? What it mostly came down to was this question: How do we facilitate collaborative software design?

So, there you have it—three individuals with specialties in decision-making, behavioral science, Deep Democracy, and software architecture faced with the same struggle in the end: being humans. We all met in the same community and started to reflect on our observations. Our most important conclusion was that what bonds us is that all of us look at the world from a sociotechnical perspective, where technical choices have social and cognitive consequences, and vice versa. We're dealing with a system in which all perspectives need to be balanced and jointly optimized. Only then can a group of people come to sustainable decision-making and quality outcomes. We see more and more people and organizations moving toward, and benefiting from, this sociotechnical perspective. Unfortunately, it's not all sunshine and rainbows. Acting in line with this perspective comes with numerous challenges, unknowns, and uncertainty.

The three of us found ourselves in more and more conversations and discussions on how to deal with the struggle while reaping the benefits of a sociotechnical perspective. In these discussions, we—more than once—didn't necessarily agree with each other. Navigating our own conflicts helped us structure our thoughts and enrich our experience, which made us all better in the end. These emerging and growing learn-ings, experiments, and observations were piling up to a point that we wanted to share our insights so others can learn from them. We started to create talks, have workshops, and write blog posts. In fact, our first collaborative blog post was about polarities, where we settled the very important matter of how to hang your toilet paper roll (under or over). It turned out there was a monster among us who just didn't care!

The sociotechnical perspective is more and more present, but the challenges that come with it will always be there. That is—in our humble opinion—the beauty of humans; they will always bring new, surprising, and challenging social dynamics to the table. We made a career out of it—or at least made it a huge part of our careers. And now, we turned it into this book that we sincerely hope will bring you new perspectives and inspiration to start experimenting in your own context.

acknowledgments

First and foremost, we are all active members of the Domain-Driven Design (DDD) community. We extend our immense gratitude to everyone we've met through community events, conferences, open spaces, and workshops. This community stands out for its inclusivity and openness, embracing discussions that reach beyond software design to encompass broader topics that influence it—topics we delve into in this book. The journey began with Eric Evans, who more than 20 years ago authored a seminal book, *Domain-Driven Design: Tackling Complexity in the Heart of Software* (Addison-Wesley, 2003), and has continued to ensure DDD evolves and remains open to change. As he recently stated, "Domain-Driven Design is not done!" This philosophy is alive and well in the vibrant communities and conferences found around the world. Our thanks go to the event organizers, who dedicate their time to nurturing a community keen on learning and improvement, enriched by everyone's shared wisdom and knowledge.

Within the DDD community, we were lucky to connect with Diana Montalion and Trond Hjorteland. Their early and valuable feedback was crucial in establishing the right foundation for this book. Their exceptionally kind and supportive forewords have genuinely moved us. And we can't wait to start reading the book they are writing themselves about systems thinking and open sociotechnical systems in IT, which is a big part of our own thinking!

We'd like to extend our heartfelt thanks to the team at Manning who helped bring this book to life. First, a huge thanks to Michael Stephens for giving us the nudge to embark on this project. Karen Miller, your guidance and sharp insights were invaluable in keeping us on the right path, helping us navigate feedback with clarity. Charles Schafer, your technical expertise added great depth to the book, and Andy Marinkovich, thanks for helping us get it through production. Finally, to Jason Everett, for ensuring every detail was ready for print—thank you all who we worked with directly and also everyone at Manning who we didn't work with directly but are just as important!

Our reviewers have provided essential input and feedback, shaping the book you're reading. We are just as thankful to those who offered their insights anonymously; their contributions have been invaluable. To all the reviewers: Alessandro Campeis, Amr Gawish, Anu Nagan, Ashley Eatly, Avraham Poupko, Chris Allan, David Paccoud, Diana Montalion, Evita van Duin, Fernando Bernardino, George Onofrei, Gregorio Piccoli, Helen Mary Barrameda, Jacqui Read, Jaume López, Jeremy Chen, Jose San Leandro, Kim Falk Jørgensen, Lora Vardarova, Marc Roulleau, Marco Heimeshoff, Matthew Skelton, Mirsad Vojniković, Neeraj Néma, Nitin Stephen Koshy, Rich Allen, Rui Liu, Ruth Malan, Sander van der Kint, Seb Rose, Shane Montague, Shawn Lam, Simon Mellor, Stefan Hofer, Sune Lomholt, Susanne Kaiser, and Vanessa Baas-Schwegler, your detailed and thoughtful feedback, freely given, has been indispensable. Without the support of everyone mentioned, this book would not have been possible.

As a community, recognizing and appreciating the significant contributions made by individuals, both visible and unseen, is essential. Many of these contributors, some of whom you may not yet know or may never know, prefer not to be in the spotlight. Yet, they have profoundly influenced us with their engagement and feedback as reviewers. It's vital that we never underestimate the value of those who operate behind the scenes. These individuals dedicate much of their free time to improving and sharing their knowledge, not on stage but through rich conversations across various online platforms. Their contributions are the backbone of our community's strength and depth, serving as a powerful reminder of the importance of recognition and gratitude. Acknowledging the unseen work and wisdom shared in these quieter exchanges underlines the collective effort that fuels our progress and learning.

Acknowledgments: Evelyn van Kelle

Writing a book can trigger some serious imposter syndrome, and trust me, it did. Without the incredible people in my support system, I would not be where I am today. I can't express enough gratitude to them for making me feel good enough when I can't get that from myself. It means the world to me.

To my parents and brother, who have been an incredible foundation and safety net.

My mom is my biggest cheerleader of all—from cheering me on as a little girl dancing on stage to watching videos from my talks and bragging about my accomplishments, even though the content sometimes feels like abracadabra. Thanks for always being there for me and using your sixth sense to see right through me and know what's really going on.

It was my dad who taught me the important skill of seeing the forest through the trees. He's one of the reasons I thrive in chaos. During my life and while writing this book, I frequently hear his voice in my head asking, "So, what's this about?" forcing me to focus on the bigger picture. Thanks for asking the hard questions and always believing in me.

To my closest friends, who, in their own words, don't always know what I'm doing or writing about exactly but are always super proud of me—thanks for listening and nodding to my writer's block frustrations, rants, and excitement throughout this process and far beyond it. I consider myself extremely lucky to have friends like you.

I owe a lot to the most brilliant mentors I was lucky enough to cross paths with in my career. Maureen Blandford, thank you for gently pushing me out of my comfort zone, being my safety net, offering me tough love, and adding new swear words to my vocabulary. Effy Shkuri, thank you for teaching me to always give first and the importance of sincere personal relationships. A huge thanks goes out to Chris Baron for the unlimited trust and for supporting my personal growth and development, making it an essential part of my career path.

Special mention also goes to Nick Tune and Mathias Verraes for motivating me and giving me the opportunity to do my first solo talk on cognitive bias at one of the most brilliant conferences I know: DDD Europe. Following Nick on the main stage was indescribably terrifying, but it gave me the confidence to continue on this journey.

Entering a technical environment as a social scientist is scary. I would not have stayed and enjoyed it for this long if it wasn't for my favorite shorts-wearing, OCD-triggering, though brilliant group of men that felt like home from the very beginning. You have been there for me and supported me (with Kit Kats) in so many ways while I am trying to make my way in this sociotechnical wonderland. Paul, Kenny, and João, you are stuck with me.

Last but not least, I have to mention my cat Rodney (or Roger, actually). My ray of sunshine disguised as a cranky cat. He was no help at all, but a constant factor of fluff and warmth and a source of great content for my talks.

Acknowledgments: Gien Verschatse

I was not part of the original plan. This book should have stated, "By Evelyn van Kelle and Kenny Baas-Schwegler." I met Evelyn at NewCrafts on May 16, 2019, and although I am not good at making a good first impression, I think I did okay that day. I don't remember when I met Kenny for the first time, but it was a long time ago. We kept running in the same circles, and over time, we got to know and appreciate each other. Two years ago, they asked me if I was interested in helping them write this book; they felt I had interesting things to say on the subject. I said yes or okay—I'm not sure anymore which one. Writing a book has always been a dream of mine. To be fair, when I was little, I dreamt of writing about monsters, not shadows. Still, I will be forever grateful to both of them for dragging me into this. Their kindness and enthusiasm for my never-ending feedback are admirable.

I also want to express my gratitude to my colleagues at Aardling, who patiently allowed me to huff and puff about this endeavor. And writing a book *is* quite the endeavor. I also want to thank Felienne Hermans, Mathias Brandewinder, and Caroline van Even. Their belief in my professional abilities and, more importantly, in me as a person has given me the confidence and strength to keep going. Besides them, there are a lot of people I feel thankful to for their support and friendship. I'm not going to try to name them all. I want to finish this book. Nevertheless, they know who they are.

Last but not least, I would like to thank Shanna Demol. She has known me since I was four years old. She supported me in everything I did, and this book was no different. She (incorrectly) claims that my job is a bit like Chandler's job from *Friends*: nobody really knows what I do. Despite that, she will buy this book and put it on her bookshelf, just so she can brag about what an amazing thing her friend managed to accomplish. And, yes, this is my way of checking if she opens it.

Acknowledgments: Kenny Baas-Schwegler

I cannot express enough gratitude to my cats, Lulu and Mr. Noodle, and to my intelligent and beautiful wife, Vanessa. Their mention in this order reflects our shared love and the significant role our cats have in our lives—they are indeed our everything. It is Vanessa's transformative impact that has been most critical, enabling me not only to author this book but also to evolve into the individual I am today. Much of the knowledge in this book is thanks to her.

When I began diving into collaborative modeling and came home filled with questions about the social dynamics I observed, Vanessa always had the insights. She has been my mentor and coach, guiding me to engage with social sciences, one of her fields of expertise. Her encouragement led me to develop interests in anthropology and Deep Democracy, greatly improving my facilitation skills and personal development. Each time I facilitated a session, discussing it with her afterward was something I cherished, as she always provided fresh perspectives for me to consider. Bringing her to one of the sessions turned it into a significantly enriching learning experience.

I wish for a broader recognition of those who work quietly behind the scenes, like Vanessa. They are the insightful, forward-thinkers who are years ahead in their understanding. Their subtle yet profound contributions are incredibly valuable and deserve greater acknowledgment.

I also owe an immense debt of gratitude to my family, without whom I could not have grown into the person I am today. Their support throughout my upbringing has been invaluable. A special thanks goes to my mother, who, as a single parent, raised my brother and me with incredible endurance and strength. Her example taught me the true meaning of resilience and determination. And I want to thank my brothers, whose unwavering support reassures me they will always stand by my side.

My heartfelt gratitude goes out to everyone who has supported and contributed to my professional growth. A special acknowledgment goes to Ruth Malan and Rebecca Wirfs-Brock, who have been monumental figures in the software industry for me. The insights and knowledge I've gained from them have been invaluable.

I'm incredibly thankful for having the opportunity to collaborate with Krisztina Hirth, Andrea Magnorsky, Marco Heimeshoff, Zsófia Herendi, Tobias Goeschel, Diana Montalion, Ruth Malan, Dawn Ahukanna, and Maxime Sanglan-Charlier within the Virtual Domain-Driven Design community. Working together has sparked an amazing flow of ideas and has been a source of constant learning and inspiration for me and shaped that community.

A huge thank you also to Marijn Huizeveld, Max Fedorov, and Nico Krijnen for their collaboration in the Domain-Driven Design NL meetup. Their dedication and energy have greatly contributed to the vibrancy and growth of the community.

My profound gratitude also goes to João Rosa, Pim Smeets, Paul de Raaij, Sjoerd Westerhof, Edo Poll, and Wesley van de Pol. Alongside Evelyn, they have been pivotal in shaping and advancing our Domain-Driven Design and collaborative modeling training and workshops and have exponentially grown my knowledge of it!

And last but not least, thank you, Evelyn and Gien, for your collaboration on this book. I learned a lot from working with you; thank you for sticking with me along the way.

about this book

This book aims to enable software teams to independently collaborate with stakeholders, understand their needs, and let this understanding guide their software architecture. This approach to collaborative software design is primarily aimed at those in technical leadership roles who can enable those teams, such as IT consultants, IT architects, tech leads, principal engineers, staff engineers, and those closely associated with teams. It also targets individuals responsible for managing software teams or their overarching strategies, such as CTOs, VPs of engineering, and engineering managers.

Who should read this book?

The content is valuable for anyone involved in software design and participating in collaborative efforts. It provides knowledge on why certain collaborative modeling sessions unfold as they do and offers tips on how to help unlock and enhance these sessions without needing to lead them directly. We have introduced these practices to a wide variety of roles included in designing, building, and running software, not limited to those previously mentioned. This includes developers, testers, product owners, product managers, user researchers, and business analysts.

How this book is organized: a roadmap

This book is organized into 12 chapters, each addressing a specific topic on collaborative software design. All chapters use a fictional company called BigScreen to illustrate the concepts we're addressing in the chapter. Starting from chapter 2, each chapter has exercises to put the theory into practice. The chapters end with a section called "Collaborative Software Design Catalysts," which contains practical tips and tricks that can be used right away so that the book offers immediate benefit. The chapters are as follows:

- *Chapter 1: The need for collaborative software design*—This chapter introduces key concepts, the fictional company BigScreen, a brief history of software development, and the themes of the following chapters.
- *Chapter 2: What is collaborative modeling?*—This chapter describes collaborative modeling and demonstrates our favorite collaborative modeling tools.
- *Chapter 3: Using collaborative modeling for design and architecture*—This chapter explains the difference between design and architecture. It describes what heuristics are and how you can use them to design software systems.
- *Chapter 4: The ingredients of collaborative modeling*—This chapter teaches you how to successfully implement collaborative modeling in your company.
- *Chapter 5: Facilitating collaborative modeling*—This chapter describes the skills required to facilitate collaborative modeling.
- *Chapter 6: The influence of ranking*—This chapter teaches you what ranking is, how it affects your software design, and how to facilitate it during a collaborative modeling session.
- *Chapter 7: The effect and opportunities of cognitive bias*—This chapter discusses cognitive biases, the effect of biases on your software design, and how you can counter cognitive biases via facilitation.
- *Chapter 8: Resistance and conflict resolution*—This chapter discusses conflict and resistance, how conflict shows itself during collaborative modeling, and how a facilitator can use collaborative modeling to move toward conflict resolution.
- *Chapter 9: Making sustainable design decisions*—This chapter explains what a decision is, how to set up a decision-making process, and the role of a facilitator during this process.
- *Chapter 10: Managing unsolvable problems*—This chapter explains what a polarity is and how you can use a polarity map to manage it.
- *Chapter 11: Communicating and documenting decisions*—This chapter showcases a few techniques to formalize a decision and how to communicate it across the company.
- *Chapter 12: Collaborative modeling beyond software design*—This chapter shows how to use collaborative modeling in other contexts, such as business strategy, user research, and code implementation. It also showcases a few tools/techniques that are well-suited for those contexts.

The chapters are structured in a specific order and build on the knowledge from the previous chapters. To get the most out of this book, skipping chapters isn't recommended. However, should you wish to skip chapters or read the book out of order, know that a concept previously introduced has a reference to the chapter it was first introduced in to make it easier to look up a concept you are unfamiliar with.

liveBook discussion forum

Purchase of *Collaborative Software Design* includes free access to liveBook, Manning's online reading platform. Using liveBook's exclusive discussion features, you can attach comments to the book globally or to specific sections or paragraphs. It's a snap to make notes for yourself, ask and answer technical questions, and receive help from the author and other users. To access the forum, go to https://livebook.manning.com/book/collaborative-software-design/discussion. You can also learn more about Manning's forums and the rules of conduct at https://livebook.manning.com/discussion.

Manning's commitment to our readers is to provide a venue where a meaningful dialogue between individual readers and between readers and the author can take place. It is not a commitment to any specific amount of participation on the part of the authors, whose contributions to the forum remain voluntary (and unpaid). We suggest you try asking the authors some challenging questions lest their interest stray! The forum and the archives of previous discussions will be accessible from the publisher's website for as long as the book is in print.

about the authors

EVELYN VAN KELLE is a behavioral change consultant who helps organizations and teams in designing and maintaining sociotechnical systems. With a background in social sciences, she believes that sustainable organizational change and transformations can be achieved by focusing on human behavior. She helps leadership and teams analyze and explain behavior and then use that knowledge to change environments in such a way that desired behavior can flourish. Evelyn loves to share her knowledge by speaking at international conferences and meetups. Apart from that, she loves food and everything related to it—preferably in the good company of friends and family.

GIEN VERSCHATSE is an experienced consultant and software engineer who specializes in domain modeling and software architecture. She's fluent in both object-oriented and functional programming, mostly in .NET. As a Domain-Driven Design practitioner, she always looks to bridge the gaps between experts, users, and engineers. As a side interest, she's researching the science of decision-making strategies to help teams improve how they make technical and organizational decisions. She shares her knowledge by speaking and teaching at international conferences. When she isn't doing all that, you'll find her on the sofa, reading a book and sipping coffee.

KENNY BAAS-SCHWEGLER believes in collaborative software design where "every voice shapes the software." Using a Domain-Driven Design and Team Topologies approach, he facilitates clearer communication between stakeholders and software creators through collaborative modeling and Deep Democracy, decoding complexities, resolving conflicts, and ensuring software remains agile to business demands. In his roles as an independent software consultant, tech lead, and software architect, he catalyzes organizations and teams toward designing and building sustainable and resilient software architectures.

about the cover illustration

The figure on the cover of *Collaborative Software Design*, titled "Cantinière," depicting a woman who carries a canteen for soldiers, is taken from a book by Louis Curmer published in 1841. Each illustration is finely drawn and colored by hand.

In those days, it was easy to identify where people lived and what their trade or station in life was just by their dress. Manning celebrates the inventiveness and initiative of the computer business with book covers based on the rich diversity of regional culture centuries ago, brought back to life by pictures from collections such as this one.

The need for collaborative software design

This chapter covers

- Understanding the need for collaborative software design
- Discovering how collaborative modeling improves design decisions
- Exploring a brief history of software design
- Recognizing collaborative software design as a catalyst for better design decisions

Great technical teams working closely with well-meaning business stakeholders can still deliver software that fails to meet an organization's needs. We see it every day. Software teams become too focused on finding solutions without fully appreciating the context of the organization. Business stakeholders can be reluctant to voice their concerns in technical sessions. Tensions escalate, and conflicts go unresolved.

Effective software requires effective collaboration, and just like every other aspect of software development and design, collaboration is a skill you have to learn and practice. Visual collaboration tools can be a key strategy in doing so because they can clarify assumptions and foster improved collaboration between development teams

1

and stakeholders. But tools alone can't guarantee effective collaboration; someone needs to guide people during collaboration: a facilitator. Fortunately, there are techniques and practices you can use to facilitate effective collaborative design, whether you're a project leader, a business stakeholder, or anyone in a team that is involved in building software.

In this book, we'll guide you toward making sustainable design decisions with the goal of developing quality software systems. We'll also help you improve collaboration with stakeholders through collaborative modeling. *Collaborative modeling* is a visualization technique to analyze complex and conflict-laden decision-making processes with all relevant stakeholders and decision-makers to create a shared understanding. We consider everyone involved in the software creation process a designer, highlighting that any designer can learn and facilitate collaborative modeling sessions. Even if you don't envision yourself as a facilitator, this book will demonstrate how collaborative modeling enhances communication. You'll learn how your involvement can contribute to better dialogue and understanding through collaborative modeling. In figure 1.1, you can see an example of a collaborative modeling session.

Figure 1.1   A collaborative modeling session in which a group of people are visualizing their conversation, enabling them to make better design decisions through shared understanding

Collaborative modeling is applicable outside of the software industry, but in this book, we're concentrating on its use within it. There's a growing trend in which teams are becoming more independent in designing, building, and running software systems. If we don't enable software teams to develop a shared understanding with stakeholders through collaborative modeling, how can these teams be expected to design, build, and run software that is effective, resilient, and ready to evolve with changing organizational needs?

1.1   Design decisions gone wrong at BigScreen

Welcome to BigScreen, an imaginary company grappling with the challenge of redesigning and modernizing its software system. While BigScreen is a fictional organization, its challenges mirror those in real organizations we've worked in and advised for. Various companies have sought our assistance over the years to address the same problems BigScreen is encountering, and we'll share how we enabled them to overcome these challenges through the adoption of collaborative modeling. Although this book recounts our experiences consulting for companies and leading collaborative modeling sessions, it's important to understand that anyone in any organization can step into the role of a facilitator if they choose to, as well as learn from what we've done, regardless of their job title, as long as they have the support to do so.

BigScreen is an international cinema chain with 80 cinemas located in 12 different countries. With streaming services becoming more and more popular, the company was seeing a decline in cinema visitors, which led to a couple of initiatives to counteract this decline. One of those projects was the modernization journey of the software system. BigScreen wanted to create a campaign called "Anytime, Anywhere," which would allow customers to purchase tickets wherever they were.

There was just one problem—their software architecture wasn't adaptable enough to implement the vision of this campaign. The user interface (UI) wasn't mobile-friendly, and it was so intertwined with the backend that it wasn't possible to make it mobile-friendly. BigScreen also wanted to create a native mobile app for their customers—also not possible because the business logic spanned both frontend (UI) and backend. The company decided to modernize and refactor the current system.

1.1.1   Understanding the landscape

Before we dive into BigScreen's modernization and refactoring attempt, we're going to have a look at the software system and the development team in more detail. The development team consisted of 15 developers, a tester, an architect, a product owner, and a team lead. Five years ago, the company made the switch from a *waterfall development* approach to an *Agile* way of working. Instead of focusing on projects with long delivery times, the team started focusing on feature delivery because they wanted to be able to get feedback from the users more quickly.

As for the software system, it has been around for 15 years. As you can see in figure 1.2, the codebase became completely interconnected, making it difficult to understand, maintain, or upgrade. This type of system, lacking a clear architecture and boundaries, is often referred to as a big ball of mud (BBoM; http://laputan.org/mud/). The original design of the system is now unclear, especially because the architect who initially designed it is no longer with the company. Over time, the system has grown through numerous patches, quick fixes, and features added in a rush. With no testing framework in place, the team is hesitant to alter any significant functionality within the system, such as the seat allocation code, due to fear of unintended consequences.

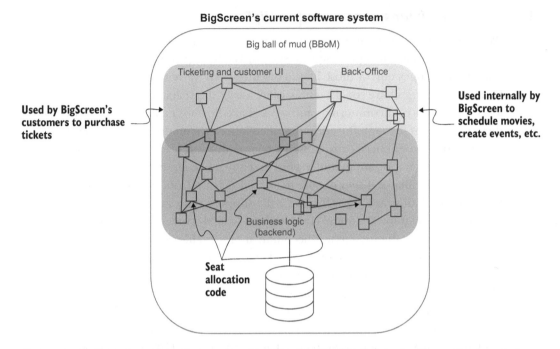

Figure 1.2   BigScreen's current software system highlights how the ticketing, back-office, and business logic sections are intertwined, showcasing a clear absence of defined boundaries. This overlap leads to functionalities within the codebase being shared across these blurred lines, complicating efforts to segment and modify the software. Such a setup means that alterations in one area of the system could trigger a domino effect that affects other parts of the system.

The system itself consists of two important parts, which the company called ticketing, where customers can purchase tickets for movies and events, and the back-office, where internal users can schedule movies, create events, and analyze movie performance. The customers have a profile where they can add movies to their watchlist, write reviews for movies and events they attended, and track upcoming movies and events.

1.1.2   *BigScreen's attempt at refactoring*

When we as a team of three were hired by BigScreen, their goal was to get help for the development team to redesign the system so it would be able to handle the "Anytime, Anywhere" campaign the company wanted to roll out. We were invited by Meera, the CTO, for a preliminary conversation. In discussing the team's current efforts to refactor their architecture, we discovered the following problems:

- Two developers could not agree with the proposal of the architect and wanted a different approach, which resulted in a very stressful situation for the software architect and the rest of the team. One developer disregarded the design of the architect altogether and just started implementing their own.
- Due to the countless debates between the two developers and the software architect, the other team members didn't fully understand the design. Because of

the tension rising in the team, they didn't want to bring this up again, so during implementation, they implemented things incorrectly. A lot of the code had to be rewritten as a result.

- Following industry trends, the company adopted an Agile approach for the development team without fully understanding the methodology, hoping that this would improve the current situation. When the previous software architect left, they didn't hire a new one for a couple of years because of a misconception of what "no upfront design in an Agile environment" means. The architecture suffered a great deal during that time because no one was paying attention to it.

1.2 BigScreen: How collaborative modeling helped to improve design decisions

In our conversation with CTO Meera, it became clear that the problem wasn't just about modernizing and refactoring the system. Users in the back-office struggled to make informed decisions because data was either inaccessible or not formatted properly. For instance, the system's handling of movie playtimes was inadequate. Normally, movies are set to show for two months, but this period might be adjusted based on the movie's popularity, either extending or shortening the available viewing time in cinemas. The back-office feature designed for this task didn't meet the users' needs. As a workaround, they had to rely on developers to run database queries, export the data to Excel, and then proceed from there. Decisions to extend a movie's run had to be manually entered into the back-office as `scheduling a new movie`, leading to inaccurately stored data and inaccurate performance metrics. Gathering comprehensive performance data across all theaters was cumbersome and rarely undertaken due to the effort required.

We dug a bit deeper into their approach to understand how they collected information on the functionalities required by their back-office users. It turned out that only the product owner, Ralph, was involved in gathering user requirements. After talking with the stakeholders, Ralph would write a user story for the developers with the implementation details instead of the user requirements. This translation often led to incomplete or incorrectly implemented features.

As often happens during our interviews with clients, we discovered that a rigid architecture isn't the company's only or biggest challenge. Merely modernizing and refactoring the system is likely to lead to the same problems. The problems with the current software architecture are directly linked to their software development process. A significant challenge is the lack of collaboration between stakeholders and the software development team. Instead of direct communication, there was only a single hand-off at each step of the process, with developers working in isolation. This method meant the team lacked a shared understanding of user needs and the architecture's design. As a result, developers often make assumptions and resort to quick fixes to meet user demands, which only makes the BBoM bigger. Initially, we aimed to focus on redesigning the architecture, but we soon recognized the necessity for a broader strategy to support the company.

1.2.1 Our approach for BigScreen

Based on our combined experience, we agreed with CTO Meera to help the software development team with the redesign of the system *and* to teach them how to make sustainable design decisions that aligned better with the business via collaborative modeling. We discussed the following approach:

- Participating in the team's SCRUM sessions, such as daily stand-ups, backlog refinements, retrospectives, and other routine meetings
- Initial interviews with a couple of the team members to get a better understanding of the conflict in the team and to gain their perspective on it
- Three kickoff sessions that focus on the context and bigger picture of the company, as well as how that relates to the current state of the software architecture
- Twelve follow-up sessions to investigate the pain points with the back-office and come up with a strategy for creating a new design that aligned with the "Anytime, anywhere" campaign to improve the quality of the features delivered
- Sessions would span a time period of three months

Collaborative modeling can bring a lot of benefits when it comes to sustainable design decisions:

- Creating and maintaining a deep and shared understanding (and a shared language) of the domain
- Creating alignment on the mental models between stakeholders and the software team
- Directing conversations through visualization
- Exploring alternative views or needs from the domain experts
- Gaining a shared understanding of the design decisions
- Making informed decisions by tapping into the collective wisdom of the people attending the session
- Reaching group consensus

Now, as with many other techniques, collaborative modeling involves certain tradeoffs. First, achieving the full benefits of collaborative modeling requires buy-in from stakeholders. Without their participation, especially those with domain expertise, it's difficult to confirm your understanding of the business problem, leading to alignment within the development team(s) but not with stakeholders. Second, higher management often sees collaborative modeling as a significant commitment because it pulls 5 to 20 people away from their regular duties for participation, making the long-term benefits challenging to measure and leading to the following frequently asked question: How much faster will the teams be able to deliver features because we use collaborative modeling? The answer is complex, as delivery speed depends on more than just alignment problems and architectural rigidity. Finally, collaborative modeling isn't a one-stop solution for all design and decision-making problems, and it won't solve all the challenges faced during software development immediately.

Throughout this book, we'll share stories from our collaborative modeling sessions at BigScreen, emphasizing the benefits they offered in meeting BigScreen's goals. But before we get into those details, we'll skip ahead and show you the architecture we ended up with.

1.2.2   *The new architecture*

After the initial interviews, 3 kickoff sessions, and 12 follow-up sessions, we settled on a new architecture that has two major improvements, as shown in figure 1.3. First, this architecture has a clear boundary between the ticketing application and the back-office. We also found a better name for the back-office, *planning and scheduling* (PaS), because the back-office can mean many things. Separating ticketing and PaS allowed the software team to deploy the two systems semi-independently from each other, making it possible to gather feedback from and adjust the features for the internal users faster.

Second, a clear distinction between client and server was introduced, and all business logic was moved server-side for the ticketing system. This makes it possible to create a dedicated mobile app that can use the server side as well, which previously wasn't possible. Finally, a separate service for scheduling movies was introduced containing the business logic both systems relied on, avoiding duplication in the two applications.

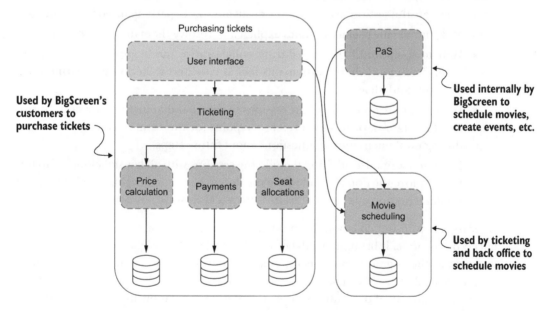

Figure 1.3   The new BigScreen architecture. The ticketing and customer UI is now separated into the ticketing system and the user interface system. The backend, which previously was a mess, has clear boundaries again. The back-office logic is now located in PaS. The shared business logic between ticketing and customer UI, the back-office, and the backend has its own dedicated boundary—movie scheduling.

We collaboratively designed this new architecture, drawing from the diverse ideas of two developers who initially had conflicting views on how to update the system, together with the original architectural concepts from an architect who had left the company. Throughout multiple collaborative modeling sessions at BigScreen, the stakeholders and every team member, including those two developers, voiced their ideas and proposed solutions. Chapters 5 to 11 will provide detailed insights into these sessions.

With a broad array of stakeholders present, including crucial decision-makers, the sessions successfully avoided turning the developers' disagreement into a personal problem, which had been a challenge previously. The aim was to find the most beneficial strategy for the organization, a task made easier with the decision-makers present in these sessions. The resulting architecture brought together the best suggestions from the developers and the insights of the previous architect, which were further enriched by the team's collective learning from resolving their conflicts. This collaborative effort led to more streamlined decision-making and less need for later adjustments. In terms of software architecture, it allowed the team to take full ownership, removing the need for an architect outside the team and leading to less refactoring due to wrong assumptions, increased team engagement, aligned mental models, and well-defined boundaries. As consultants, our job was to do the following:

- Organize the session in a way that ensures everyone leaves with a clear understanding of the redesign process.
- Facilitate the session to achieve consensus among all participants on the redesign.
- Make hindering social dynamics explicit and resolve them during the session.
- Wait to speak until the end during collaborative modeling sessions, creating an environment where participants feel at ease and valued when sharing their thoughts and ideas.
- Document the outcomes of the sessions in a format that includes version control and timestamps, providing a reference point for the team in case of challenges during implementation or questions about future steps.
- If needed, organize additional modeling sessions with all key stakeholders to further explore the domain and refine the design based on insights acquired during implementation attempts. The aim is to quickly resolve any confusion.

BigScreen kept using collaborative modeling internally because the company experienced the benefits it brought. Collaborative modeling gave BigScreen a better way to understand the organization's needs, enabling developers to create better solutions for the users. Because the stakeholders were now actively involved in the development process, the quality of the features improved as did the relationships between the software developers and domain experts.

1.2.3   A brief history of software design

Part of our job as consultants is to facilitate collaborative modeling sessions between engineers and stakeholders. During these sessions, there is a lot of individual and group behavior that results from the interaction between people. We refer to that behavior as *social dynamics*. We've noticed that most engineers and developers struggle with these social dynamics when introducing collaborative modeling in their teams or organizations. This makes a lot of sense because most engineering education programs don't include much social sciences instruction. We believe those struggles are one of the main reasons most engineering teams aren't successful at starting collaborative modeling.

We think one of the causes has something to do with where we, as an industry, came from. Twenty years ago, the Waterfall model was the de facto standard for most companies developing software. The Waterfall model splits the activities of building software into small sequential parts. It was developed by copying the manufacturing and construction industry's project management method. Waterfall was successful in that industry because it gave the client certainty of costs and time; however, as a downside, it left little room for changes. This model was introduced in the 1970s when most computer programmers created, edited, and stored their programs line by line on punch cards. Changes after the design were costly and took time, so the Waterfall model made sense.

1.2.4   The Agile theater

Winston W. Royce, in his 1970s paper titled "Managing the Development of Large Software Systems,"[1] was the first to write down a detailed diagram of the process without calling it Waterfall, which you can see in figure 1.4. However, he also felt it had significant flaws stemming from the fact that testing only happened at the end of the process, which he described as "risky and invites failure." Fast-forward roughly 50 years, and we still base most of the software development approach on the same diagram. Yes, companies did transform to an Agile way of working by splitting up the work into smaller batches and delivering those smaller batches to the users faster so they were able to adapt quickly to the users' feedback. Still, we observe that it's usually an Agile theater, implementing SCRUM in the development teams, but keeping the hierarchies and the idea-to-production value chain in place; only the development teams are doing Agile development, whereas the business side of the company maintains a very Waterfall mentality, like the situation BigScreen is in.

We believe this mindset is the result of how software engineering is perceived or misunderstood by people who need software to run their organizations. These organizations want to know how long it will take and what the costs are, similar to the manufacturing and construction industries. They let architects gather the more technical requirements and design the system, and then let those designs be built by software

---

[1] www.praxisframework.org/files/royce1970.pdf.

teams. When someone without an understanding of Agile software development with a Waterfall mentality wants software to be built, they will perceive any Agile artifact—such as collaboration—as a waste of time. That person sees it as a waste of time because, in their mind, they just need to give a list of requirements to calculate the costs and estimate the work, and then let it be built.

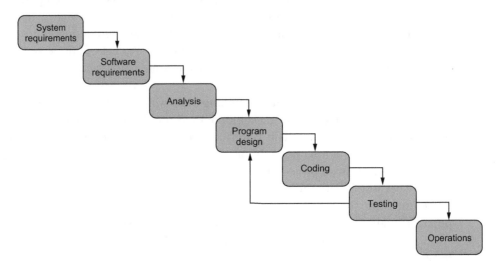

Figure 1.4   Detailed diagram of the Waterfall process

One of the main differences between designing and building in the manufacturing/ constructing industries and the software industry is the rate at which requirements change. For example, if we want to construct an office building, we can gather requirements and design the building up front. During construction, hardly any changes are needed in the design. There might be adjustments, but the main purpose and functions of the building scarcely change after design. This is different from most software systems we develop. As soon as a user interacts with a new feature of the software system, that feature might be exactly what they want, might have potential but need improvement, or might not be what they want at all. Usually, it's the latter two because we're building a solution for the needs of our users, which hasn't been built before. Unlike constructing office buildings, a practice refined over many years with established good and best practices, in the software industry, we're mostly designing and building software that hasn't been built before. If it had been built before, we could just copy and paste it or just buy it off the shelf. So, you can expect a lot of new insights once users interact with our software. Most of the time, when building software, we can only see a clear solution in retrospect.

Building software requires a different approach to design than we use in manufacturing and constructing. Designing software requires taking an Agile approach to architecture, which involves collaborating on design, experimenting, following emergent design principles, prototyping a solution, and enabling the engineers building the software to understand the problem.

When organizations start to work in an Agile way, most of them don't know what to do with the software architects, and, usually, the software architects keep designing and gathering requirements in a Waterfall way, which can create a bottleneck for the development teams. The teams either are forced to wait on the software architect or start building the software without designing the software architecture because it's not considered Agile. This is what happened in BigScreen—the software architect left, leaving the company without any software architecture knowledge in the team. However, a key aspect of Agile also means that the team has the knowledge to take ownership of their software architecture.

1.2.5 *Enabling teams to do collaborative software design*

When teams take control of their software architecture, they bypass the potential blockers in the flow of development that come from depending on an external architect. However, eliminating architects outright could leave a substantial gap in architectural knowledge within the team. It's important, then, to provide support that enables teams to make architectural decisions independently. Collaborative modeling stands out as an effective method for this purpose because it's straightforward, it's easy to engage with, and it promotes working together on the software architecture.

Engaging in collaborative modeling brings to the surface the social dynamics we've mentioned before. We've personally faced challenges where discussions stalled, decisions cycled without advancement, or a supposed consensus led to delays because, in reality, there was no broad agreement. For instance, at BigScreen, we saw disagreements between two people over the architecture bring progress to a standstill. Managing these social dynamics during collaborative modeling is vital for reaching well-supported design decisions. These are decisions that harness the collective knowledge of the group, maximizing the decision's effect and earning the backing of the entire team. This critical aspect of dealing with social dynamics in collaborative modeling isn't discussed or taught enough in software architecture.

The software architect, acting as a facilitator, can significantly change these social dynamics. As individuals already engaged in the organization's software design, they are well placed to serve as enablers. They can catalyze teams and the broader organization to embrace Agile methods in designing software. Software architects can facilitate teams in making design decisions, provide advice, and avoid imposing designs on them. This is accomplished by initiating collaborative modeling sessions with teams, thus allowing them to collaboratively design software with stakeholders. This approach shortens the feedback loop from requirements to deployment, enabling quick, timely, and reliable value delivery to users. The software architect acting as a facilitator isn't enough. The architect should also teach the teams about collaborative modeling so that the team isn't reliant on the architect anymore and the team can run these collaborative modeling sessions on their own. When teams are capable of designing software independently, it removes the bottleneck of software changes and frees the software architect to focus on maintaining alignment within the team and with the organization's vision and goals, thereby enhancing the agility and efficiency of the software development process.

We won't need to enable teams to start collaborative modeling; starting within the team itself can often be more beneficial because it allows team members to make mistakes and learn in a less risky setting. Successes achieved internally can motivate other teams to adopt similar practices and eventually encourage stakeholder participation.

As we write this book, we're at a pivotal moment in the software industry as we transition from software architects designing the architecture to teams taking ownership and doing software architecture without an external software architect. Now you might think, I'm not a software architect, so will this book help me? Rest assured, it will. The concepts discussed are applicable within any software team context. We've successfully introduced these practices to a wide range of roles, not just to software architects, including software engineers, testers, product owners, product managers, CTOs, engineering managers, user researchers, and business analysts. Anyone involved in the software development process is seen as a designer, capable of both facilitating and participating in collaborative modeling. However, as long as someone in the session has experience in software design and architecture, anyone can lead collaborative modeling sessions. Thus, everyone is capable of enabling their teams and others to undertake collaborative modeling and manage the associated social dynamics. The goal is to enable software teams to collaborate with their stakeholders, understand their needs, and allow this understanding to shape their software architecture, which is the essence of teams engaging in collaborative software design!

1.3   *Collaborative software design as a catalyst for better design decisions*

This book is about looking at software design in a new (or different) way. Collaborative software design isn't just from a technical perspective but also from a business perspective, all while taking into account the social dynamics that affect both collaborative modeling sessions and design decisions. This is what makes this book different; we didn't find many books on software design and architecture that talk about the effect and opportunity that social dynamics have when we need to adapt when a company strategy or business strategy changes. From experience, this is valuable and relevant information, which is why we ended up writing this book. In this section, we'll give you an overview of what to expect in the coming chapters.

1.3.1   *Collaborative modeling, design, and architecture*

As mentioned earlier, we see it as vital for teams to take ownership of their collaborative design decisions—a lesson learned from less-than-ideal experiences. We experienced frustration when provided with an unrealistic solution by an architect from above (in the famous ivory tower meme). Our valuable suggestions, unknown to the architect, were overlooked. This led to software that failed to satisfy us or our stakeholders, a situation similar to what BigScreen faces today. Our goal was to shift this dynamic; we aimed for teams to reach their highest potential and to develop software that they and their stakeholders could be proud of. Collaborative modeling became the key to initiating this change. We witnessed the method's capability to unlock a team's full potential and guide us toward better models and solutions.

Figure 1.5 offers a visual representation of a collaborative modeling session, similar to the session photo shown earlier in figure 1.1. Chapter 2 dives deeper into what collaborative modeling entails, discussing the various tools used within the modeling space. Throughout this book, we share stories from our collaborative modeling sessions at BigScreen, using a range of tools designed for different needs. We provide insights into our firsthand experiences with collaborative modeling tools, including the Business Model Canvas, several types of EventStorming, Example Mapping, domain message flow modeling, Wardley Mapping, Domain Storytelling, and others.

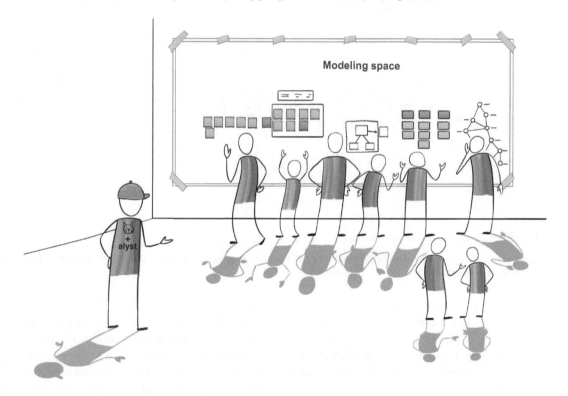

Figure 1.5   A visual representation of a collaborative modeling session

Figure 1.5 also features the facilitator as the catalyst, enabling the group to make sustainable design decisions. Chapter 5 dives into the facilitator's role and the essential competencies and skills needed for collaborative modeling. Continuing in figure 1.6, we see the same facilitator next to a table with the heuristics toolkit on top, which chapter 3 discusses in detail. Throughout the book, we'll share some of our heuristics, hoping to inspire you when creating your own. Also shown on the table are various collaboration styles that a facilitator might employ to guide the group's efforts, as discussed in chapter 4: Together Alone, Split and Merge, Small Group Diverge and

Converse, Liberating Structures 1-2-4-All, Ensemble, Fish Bowl, Anarchy!, Guerilla, and The Secret Modeler.

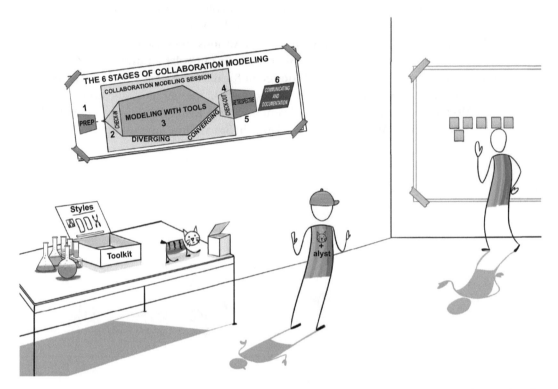

Figure 1.6 A visual representation of the facilitator and the tools needed for a collaborative modeling session. On the wall, you see the stages of a collaborative modeling session.

Together with all the principles and practices mentioned throughout this book, the heuristics toolkit and collaboration styles act as the chemicals the facilitator uses to manage the social dynamics of collaborative modeling. Mixing these chemicals appropriately is crucial to align with the group's needs and to structure the sessions effectively. Facilitating collaborative modeling involves numerous decisions: choosing the appropriate chemicals for the group, determining the most suitable style, using the right heuristics, and so on. This requires many skills and figuring out the best way to combine them. All of these considerations require careful preparation, foresight, and flexibility. A misstep in mixing these chemicals can disrupt the group dynamic, akin to a chemical reaction causing an unintended explosion, potentially leading to significant group tension. Collaborative modeling sessions can be intense, and the incorrect mix of tools and styles can profoundly affect participants in a personal way.

This is the reason we're writing this book—to guide you in effectively selecting and blending these chemicals yourself. We'll provide you with the fundamental chemicals, but it's essential for you to explore which chemicals work for you and experiment with using and mixing new principles and practices, heuristics, tools, and styles. Getting comfortable with these tools and trying them out in a safe environment allows for learning from mistakes without serious consequences.

1.3.2 Collaborative modeling ingredients and potential benefits of facilitation

Collaborative modeling sessions are designed to be fluid, letting us tweak the approach by introducing different chemicals as needed. Although the sessions are dynamic, collaborative modeling has several ingredients and stages to guarantee the effectiveness of each session and its follow-up activities. In chapters 4 and 11, we'll explore these ingredients in more detail. We try to avoid calling collaborative modeling a process because the dynamic of collaborative modeling is nonlinear, so we see it more as a framework of stages. We'll cover the stages for preparing a session, conducting a check-in, leading the session, performing a check-out, holding a retrospective, and communicating and recording the outcomes and results in various ways. This approach is depicted on the poster shown earlier in the top-left corner of figure 1.6, similar to a periodic table poster in chemistry labs. Essential chemicals and ingredients are integrated into the stages, ensuring the collaborative modeling group can successfully develop their shared understanding.

1.3.3 The effect of social dynamics on collaborative modeling sessions

Facilitators mix specific chemicals to handle the complex social dynamics within a group, such as social rank, cognitive biases, conflicts, and polarities. These dynamics can disrupt the progress of a session, blocking the group from moving forward and making well-informed design decisions. Observing these hidden dynamics is compared to shining a flashlight on the group that shows the shadows, as depicted in the model in figure 1.7. If not properly addressed, these shadows can prevent the group from using its collective potential, knowledge, and wisdom to create a shared understanding and come up with sustainable decisions. Addressing these shadows can be challenging for a group, which is where the facilitator comes in, making the group aware of these shadows and assisting them where needed in tackling them. Ignoring these underlying shadows allows them to intensify and become demons that emerge and form significant barriers within the group, significantly affecting the outcomes.

Chapters 6 through 10 are dedicated to observing these shadows and providing strategies for facilitating the group to manage them. Topics such as conflict, ranking, cognitive bias, resistance, and polarities are examined, with techniques offered for addressing these social dynamics and the unseen aspects within the group. Facilitators must understand that groups may not always be ready to confront their shadows. Although you might observe what's holding the team back, the decision to address these problems rests with the team itself.

These shadows can also influence us as facilitators if we aren't careful. For those who naturally lean toward solving problems, it can be frustrating to see a group avoid confronting their problems. It's important for us to manage our own shadows to stay as neutral and provide the high-quality facilitation the group needs. Losing too much neutrality as a facilitator can inadvertently strengthen these shadows, turning them into demons and preventing us from effectively assisting the group. We'll delve deeply into observing the various shadows present within ourselves and in the group in chapter 5. Addressing these shadows successfully hinges on our ability to create a psychologically safe environment where they can be tackled. This book will extensively cover this topic, and you'll find discussions on it throughout most chapters, highlighting its critical role.

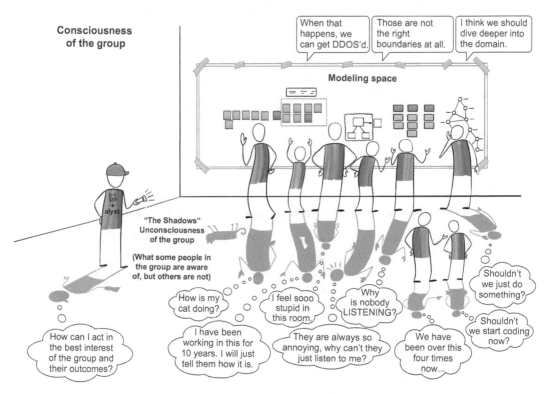

Figure 1.7 Lurking in the group's shadows, called the unconsciousness of the group, are a lot of social dynamics, such as ranking, cognitive bias, conflicts, and polarities, that can block the flow of a session and stop the group from moving forward and making sustainable design decisions.

1.3.4   *Collaborative decision-making*

The shared model that emerges from collaborative modeling sessions becomes a key tool for teams and stakeholders to engage in collaborative design decisions. These decisions can involve changes to the business model or strategies for constructing solutions. Chapter 9 will go into greater depth on decision-making theory and how to enable collaborative design decisions to ensure that decisions are supported across the entire group. This doesn't imply that all group members must be present for each decision or have decision-making authority, but it's critical to involve participants in the process to ensure they are on board with the decisions made. While the ideal scenario involves everyone in decision-making, practical time constraints might not always allow for this.

Addressing the follow-up of making collaborative decisions, it's also essential to formalize these decisions for future reference and clarity. Chapter 11 discusses how architectural decision records (ADRs) and diagramming serve as a documentation tool for capturing all aspects of architectural decisions, including the context, the decision itself, and its consequences, to avert future confusion and facilitate sustained decision-making. Yet, it's important not to focus too much on documentation. The real outcome of a collaborative modeling session isn't just the visual model produced but the shared understanding and collaborative design effort it generates. This collaborative approach is what leads to the design and development of software that is both sustainable and capable of adapting to the organization's evolving needs.

This introduction, along with the combined mental model from figures 1.5 to 1.7, which we detail in the appendix, provides an overview of the discussions to be found in this book. Note that this book isn't the definitive resource on collaborative software design but rather an initial step for digging into this topic.

Summary

- Collaborative modeling is a visualization technique to analyze complex and conflict-laden decision-making processes with all relevant stakeholders and decision-makers to create a shared understanding.
- Collaborative modeling creates and maintains a deep and shared understanding of the domain, directs conversations through visualization, enables exploring alternative views, and creates a shared and sustainable design decision.
- Collaborative modeling requires buy-in from the stakeholders if you want to gain all benefits, and it's also perceived as a "big investment" by higher management.
- Most companies didn't change to an Agile way of software development, ending up with a so-called Agile theater where design is still being done up front.
- Software architects can be the enablers of change to Agile architecture by using collaborative modeling.
- Software architects need to understand and learn how to facilitate the social dynamics that are a big and important part of developing a software system, and they can negatively influence decision-making.
- Collaborative modeling can help bring social dynamics challenges to the surface, where they can be dealt with. This will lead to better design decisions and clarity in a team.
- Through facilitation, we can become the catalyst for change in bringing software architecture ownership to the teams.

What is collaborative modeling? 2

This chapter covers

- Recognizing the importance of a shared understanding of the business problems
- Analyzing stakeholders to be involved in collaborative modeling
- Discovering the different kinds of collaborative modeling tools

In this chapter, we delve into the essence of collaborative modeling and its pivotal role in software development. Understanding the business problems is essential for software development teams, but that's just the beginning. We advocate that software development teams actively engage in the design process and make collaborative design decisions because their technical expertise significantly enhances the software's capability to address user and business needs. In addition, the user journey and business process should be jointly optimized to get the most value out of building that software. That is the true potential of collaborative modeling.

For those unfamiliar with collaborative modeling, we'll introduce some of our favorite tools, offering a glimpse into their practical application. Even if you're a seasoned collaborative modeler, we'll provide insights on the different tools and when we use one over the other. We end the chapter with the characteristics that make a tool fit for collaborative modeling in software design, what makes a tool less effective for collaborative modeling, and what the difference is between diagramming and collaborative modeling.

2.1 *Understanding the business problems*

As mentioned in the introduction, we believe teams are too focused on finding solutions instead of understanding the business problems. By *business problems*, we mean the various needs of our users and stakeholders. Stakeholders are individuals or groups, either within or outside the organization, who are invested in the outcome of solving these business problems. Their needs can range from overarching purposes and objectives to specific goals, tasks, customer and user journeys, business processes, constraints, and any challenges they face. We categorize all these as business problems. Here are a few examples:

- Customer needs, such as the need to go to the movies with friends or immerse yourself in a movie
- The broader experience of a *customer journey* when purchasing a ticket at the cinema's kiosk
- The goals and tasks in a *user journey* when interacting with our products, such as reserving seats for a movie or having the best seats available
- User needs of the back-office system, for example, having automated weekly insight reporting into ticket sales
- Business pain points in which management is worried because of a decrease in ticket sales
- A pain point of the data team who gets corrupted data from the database and therefore can't make correct forecasting models

Most of the time, we see software development teams try to understand what the business needs, they are already thinking about how this translates to a feature request that fits in the existing software—instead of analyzing the problem. This is a remnant of the early days of software development. Thirty years ago, companies didn't depend so heavily on software. Most of the business problems a company faced weren't related to software. Nowadays, some business problems exist because we use software. BigScreen's "Anytime, Anywhere" campaign is only relevant because the company sells tickets online.

We've evolved from small software applications that support and automate the business to software being a key component and product to succeed as a company. An important part of a software engineer's job is to make sure that parts of the software system can evolve together with the company. Most software isn't created in isolation anymore either; there is already existing software even if it isn't easy to detect. So, software engineers need to make sure that the overall functionality of the system doesn't change while the individual parts evolve.

2.1.1 *What problems are we trying to solve?*

Companies must change, or they will run out of business. When companies change, the software system needs to change too. If we look at BigScreen again, one of the major problems is that the company can't reach its modernization goals because of the software system. The company wants its customers to be able to purchase a ticket "any-time, anywhere" but because of how the software system was built, that isn't possible. When we're trying to solve business problems, we can't do this in isolation anymore—we need to understand the context in which we're solving the business problems. Here are a few example questions to give us a better understanding of the context:

- What industry are we working in?
- What is the domain that we're working in?
- What does the market look like?
- What is our company's position in this market?
- What are the key value propositions that we're offering our customers?
- What are the key goals of the company?
- How is the company going to achieve those goals (often referred to as company strategy)?
- How can the software help to achieve those goals?

We've encountered many teams who were responsible for creating a software system and could not answer these questions because they didn't know the context in which they were solving the business problems. Fortunately, there are visualization tools that can help you do this, for example, the Business Model Canvas, which we'll look into later in this chapter.

Certain areas of the organization couldn't use the software system to help them do their jobs because it didn't fulfill their needs or wasn't adaptable enough. Of the many possible reasons for this, one reason we see often is that the stakeholders don't always understand what software can do (this is fine, as it isn't their job to understand that). Software can do a lot of things—even things that humans can't—so we need to understand the organization and its capabilities to gain a deep understanding of how it works. For example, if we take a stakeholder's request at face value for a "spreadsheet to know how many tickets a movie has sold each week since it was released," we'll miss a lot of opportunities at that moment. We need to dig deeper to understand what the business is trying to achieve. Imagine having the following conversation with Nala, one of the stakeholders responsible for scheduling the movies in the back office:

> Nala: We need to know how many tickets a movie has sold each week since it was released, and we need to be able to export it.
>
> Us: That's great, we can do that. Do you need that for all theaters or per theater?
>
> Nala: We need that per theater. We want to know how well a movie is doing in a given theater.

Us: That is interesting; what do you do with that information if I may ask?

Nala: Oh yeah, sure! Movies have a fixed period they are running in the cinema, but if they are still performing great, we extend that a week or maybe even a few weeks.

Us: Does this only happen once?

Nala: No, we reevaluate this after a few weeks, together with all the other movies playing. We could extend again, even though that rarely happens.

Us: I didn't know that, thanks! One more question . . . you mentioned you need an export for that; which format? How will you be using that export?

Nala: Excel would be nice. We want to make a chart, so we can see the evolution.

Us: We could create those charts for you on the page. We can even create functionality for you that makes it possible to extend the playtime for a movie in a specific theater on the same screen and send out a notification for that to the marketing app.

Nala: Oh, that would be great; that would save us a lot of time. It is very cumbersome to have to update all of that manually every time.

Amazing, isn't it? With just a few extra questions, we now understand that they don't really need an overview of how many tickets a movie sold each week in an export; instead, they want to be able to decide whether or not a movie should stay in a specific theater and how long they can postpone reevaluating that decision. We call this a *complicated problem.* Complicated problems are ordered, have predictable outcomes, and have a solution although they require expertise to understand them. In our scenario, this means that the stakeholder knows how to decide to extend the playtime of a movie at this point in time. They have been doing it for many years, and we want to make it easier for them by automating (parts of) that process.

"At this point in time" is an important part here because the business is always looking for differentiators. The company wants to stand out in the market and change its processes to get a competitive advantage (or for other reasons) but isn't sure how. This leads us to complex problems.

Complex problems are characterized by high uncertainty, unpredictable outcomes, and the absence of fixed solutions. These problems demand exploration and collaboration with stakeholders to unearth potential solutions.

Take, for instance, the challenge of boosting attendance at a local cinema. On the surface, it might seem simple: offer discounts, screen popular movies, or upgrade the cinema's amenities. Yet, a deeper examination reveals its complexity. Stakeholders may observe unexpected spikes in attendance on certain days, but the reasons remain elusive. Are the attendance spikes driven by a specific movie premiere, a local event, a recent change in the snack offerings, or a mix of these factors?

Addressing such challenges in software design demands a different approach because the solution isn't always evident, there are many unknowns, and we're trying to discover how this could work. We need to come up with different ways—that is, different models—in which this could work. We need to probe different models to be able to create adaptable software systems. For example, a system might integrate with social media analytics to track movie trends or sync with local event calendars to predict attendance surges. Such a system should be adaptable, enabling the cinema to experiment with various pricing or promotional strategies and swiftly adjust based on feedback.

If we don't focus on the problem we're trying to solve, we don't know this. It's important to know whether your problem lies in the *complex* or *complicated* domain[1] because you'll need different approaches and different collaborative modeling sessions. Essentially, if a problem's cause and effect become clear only in hindsight, it's a complex problem.

> **NOTE** The Cynefin framework refers to the decision-making framework created by David Snowden. It helps the decision-maker make sense of the context in which a decision must be made and how to approach finding a solution. It has five domains: clear (all is known), complicated (there are known unknowns), complex (there are unknown unknowns), chaotic (little to no knowledge), and confusion (we can't determine the context). A problem starts in confusion because we need to categorize the problem that we are dealing with. Once the domain has been determined, as we gain more knowledge, a problem can move from chaotic, via complex and complicated, toward clear. Most of the problems we try to solve with software reside in the complicated or complex domain.

Addressing these challenges requires a deep understanding of the context and the problems at hand. Collaborative modeling serves as a tool to grasp this context and the business landscape. In the subsequent sections, we'll delve deeper into the essence of collaborative modeling and its role in problem-solving.

2.1.2   *What is collaborative modeling?*

You're actively engaging with the stakeholders to understand their problems better, which is a step in the right direction, but simply talking to the stakeholders isn't enough—you want to collaborate with them. So, in a very broad sense, we can define collaborative modeling as "a visualization technique to analyze complex and conflict-laden decision-making processes with all relevant stakeholders and decision-makers to create a shared understanding."It's not innate to software development (https://mng .bz/0Ggp) and is sometimes referred to as *participatory modeling.*[2]

Let's take a closer look at the definition of collaborative modeling, starting with "a visualization technique." Modeling itself isn't visual by default. You can build up a mental model of the problem by having a dialogue with each other, as we showed in the previous section. There are a few challenges we have to deal with if we aren't visualizing.

[1]   Kurtz, C. F., & Snowden, D. The New Dynamics of Strategy: Sense-Making in a Complex and Complicated World, 2003. *IBM Systems Journal,* https://ieeexplore.ieee.org/document/5386804.
[2]   Basco-Carrera, L., Warren, A., van Beek, E., Jonoski, A., & Giardino, A. "Collaborative Modelling or Participatory Modelling? A Framework for Water Resources Management," 2017. *Environmental Modelling & Software,* 91, 95–110.

First, there is a limit to what you can remember. In her book, *The Programmer's Brain*, Felienne Hermans talks about our cognitive processes and their limitations, and she offers techniques to deal with those limitations that will help us become better programmers. One of those techniques is creating visual or explicit models of the code with tools such as dependency graphs and state tables. Although the book mostly focuses on the technical aspect of programming, those same cognitive processes and their limitations are there when we're trying to understand a business problem. Similar to code, creating visual models of the problem, for instance, with EventStorming as shown in figure 2.1, will help us become better at understanding it. Don't worry yet about the notation; we'll follow up on that later in the chapter.

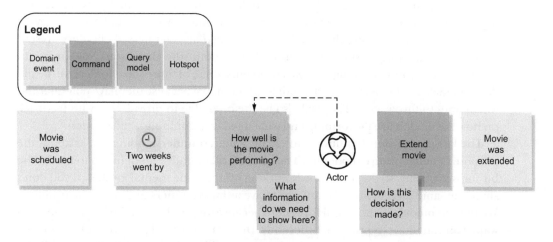

Figure 2.1 Visualization of the conversation with the business stakeholders at BigScreen on extending movies using EventStorming. domain events are business-relevant events that happen in a conversation. We'll go more in-depth on how EventStorming works later in the chapter.

Second, people misunderstand each other. Even worse, we often don't realize that we're misunderstanding the other person because we're using the same words for different concepts. When we visualize our mental model of the problem, those misunderstandings will come to light sooner.

Analyzing complex and conflict-laden decision-making processes, applied to software development, means we model the business problems and analyze the context in which those problems occur. As mentioned in the previous section, complex problems focus on discovery and have a high uncertainty because we're not yet sure how they could work. This is where collaborative modeling shines. It's a cheap way to create different models of the problem and validate them for their usefulness. You can throw different scenarios and edge cases at them and see where the model breaks.

That doesn't mean collaborative modeling isn't effective for complicated problems, but just remember that collaboration can be expensive. When dealing with complicated problems, you can analyze the problem in smaller panels of experts. When you model with a small subset of the involved people, make sure you bring information back into the shared model of the people building the software to mitigate the risk of diverging the shared understanding of the domain. You might recognize that feeling when you thought you understood each other, happily started working on some code, and later found out that you weren't on the same page after all.

It's also important to know that conflicts will arise when you're modeling together. "Conflict-laden" in this context means opposite ideas or interests, disagreement, and controversy. Although conflict is normal, people should not experience any type of barrier to expressing their knowledge because when they do, they will hold back. Chapter 8 is dedicated to the conflict-laden aspect of collaborative modeling and how you can deal with that during collaborative modeling.

Knowledge resides in the minds of people, but not all knowledge is inside one mind, unfortunately—it's scattered across multiple minds. We want to have all relevant knowledge when modeling the problem, so we need all relevant stakeholders present during the modeling session. We'll go in-depth about who those stakeholders are in section 2.2.2. If you're tackling complex problems, some of those stakeholders will be the decision-makers who decide which models to try out first because they have potential and which ones to throw away. They will also be the ones able to provide you with feedback on how the models are performing and what needs reexamining or adaptation.

The last part of our definition, "to create a shared understanding," talks about the purpose of collaborative modeling. The goal of collaborative modeling is to model the business problems so that everyone is working off the same mental models. If you don't share the same mental models, you can't have a shared understanding of the problem. We refer to models in the plural form here because, depending on the information you want, you can model a problem differently. Different tools will give you different information and a different perspective on the same problem. Later in this chapter, we'll dig a bit deeper into what those tools have in common and when to use which tool.

2.1.3   *Exploring business problems using collaborative modeling*

When exploring business problems through collaborative modeling, the focus of the modeling must be on discovering the domain and not the specific collaborative modeling tool that is being used. In collaborative modeling, *domain* refers to the specific area of knowledge or expertise that is being explored or modeled. The domain represents the subject matter or part of the organization that we together with the stakeholders are trying to understand and represent through collaborative modeling. Using collaborative modeling to understand the domain is also called *domain modeling*.

While many tools are available for collaborative modeling, not all of them are suited for collaboration. Good collaborative modeling tools have a minimal learning curve. You can explain the tool while you're modeling with the stakeholders. EventStorming, for example, uses different colored sticky notes. Each color has a specific meaning; for example, a blue sticky represents commands in the domain. If you want to introduce a new color, you can quickly add a sticky to the legend with the concept it represents. During a session, you're working toward deeper insights into the domain, so things are always moving around on the whiteboard. With a good collaboration tool, you can do this efficiently. Sticky notes are easily moved, swapped, and so on. Domain discovery will span multiple sessions, which means that you need to be able to adapt or re-create parts of your model easily. We'll go over a few of our favorite tools later in the chapter.

During the collaboration, pay attention to the words that the stakeholders are using. Dare to ask what they mean when they are using a word that could be ambiguous. Sometimes, a single word contains multiple concepts. When you find a word like that, introduce a new one to capture one of the concepts. In BigScreen, we talk about showing movies, but that captures a lot of things. Theaters play all sorts of things these days: operas, documentaries, movies, and so on. Is it important to know the difference? Is it *always* important to know the difference? Other times, there is more than one word for the same concept. Try to create an agreement on which word will be used from now on.

Let's go back to the conversation we had with the domain expert in BigScreen. We made a lot of assumptions in that conversation. One of the big assumptions we made is that the playtime of a movie stays the same, but is that true? What if they extend a movie for two weeks, but it will only be playing on Tuesday and Thursday? Another assumption is that all movies can be extended. What about events such as opera nights or premieres? Should we allow extensions on those? In figure 2.2, you can see these assumptions made explicit.

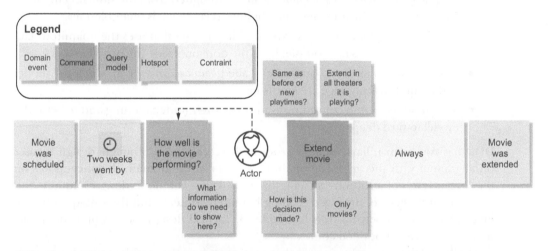

Figure 2.2   Visualization of the assumptions we made when a movie gets extended. We used a red sticky as hotspot to show that a movie will always get extended and added its meaning to the legend. We also added our assumptions in the form of questions/remarks.

We want to make extending movies as easy as possible for our users while also helping them avoid mistakes. Discovery of deeper insights only happens when you're engaged, curious, and not afraid to ask a lot of questions.

2.2   Domain-Driven Design and collaborative modeling

Collaborative modeling is often spoken about in the context of *Domain-Driven Design* (DDD). Domain modeling was already a recognized topic, but no one discussed what exactly it was or good ways to do it. DDD attempted (and succeeded) in giving us a *framework* to talk about good ways to design domain models and use those models in our software systems. A framework[3] (e.g., the Cynefin framework described earlier) in this context is a topology that makes you look at things from different perspectives so you can make distinctions and do things in different ways. Let's take a closer look at what DDD exactly is.

2.2.1   What is Domain-Driven Design?

DDD is a discipline rooted in the belief that creating good software systems for problems in the complex domain can't be done without a deep understanding of the business problems you're trying to solve in the domain. It has a set of principles for designing software to guide that belief and a lot of patterns, tools, and techniques that enable us to follow these principles, which are described here:

- To create a software system for a complex domain, all stakeholders involved need to share a deep understanding of the domain itself. Creating that shared understanding is guided by the domain experts.
- To improve understanding, the stakeholders communicate with each other in a language, the *ubiquitous language*, which is designed from the domain language. Unlike the domain language, the ubiquitous language is unambiguous.
- The shared understanding is expressed in a model that uses the ubiquitous language and captures the complexity of the domain inside the problem space.
- The design has explicit boundaries, called *bounded contexts*, in which the model and ubiquitous language are consistent.
- Stakeholders should continuously improve their understanding and refactor the model toward deeper insight.

DDD has two main pillars: *strategic design* and *tactical design*. Strategic design focuses on alignment with the organization and discovery of the domain. It concentrates on the higher levels of a software system, that is, activities you do to design solutions and create an architecture, such as designing bounded contexts and their ubiquitous language. We'll go deeper into this in chapter 3. Tactical design focuses on code implementation of each bounded context.

   Having a DDD mentality means that understanding the problem comes first, and creating a solution for that problem through software only happens when you understand the problem you're trying to solve. Just as collaborative modeling isn't a silver bullet, DDD isn't one either. It simply gives you a model and language to talk about a different mindset toward creating software systems.

2.2.2   Who are the stakeholders?

We've already mentioned that collaborative modeling should involve all the relevant stakeholders in a domain. That doesn't mean you shouldn't invite nonrelevant

---

[3]   Kurtz, C. F., & Snowden, D. "The New Dynamics of Strategy: Sense-making in a Complex and Complicated World," 2003. *IBM Systems Journal,* https://ieeexplore.ieee.org/document/5386804.

stakeholders, however, and we even advise it when possible because they can give different insights. Now, you might wonder who those people are exactly. In collaborative modeling, there are four stakeholder categories: domain experts, users, development team, and customers. As shown in figure 2.3, a stakeholder can be part of one or more categories.

Domain experts
Users
Development team
Customers

Licensed under https://creativecommons.org/licenses/by-sa/4.0/

Figure 2.3   This Venn diagram illustrates the interrelationships between four primary categories of stakeholders in a project or business context: Domain Experts, Users, Development Team, and Customers. Each category is depicted by overlapping shapes, indicating that stakeholders can simultaneously fulfill multiple roles. For example, a stakeholder may possess the specialized knowledge of a Domain Expert while also being a Customer of the product or service. This visual aid helps to identify the complex positions stakeholders may hold and the potential for shared interests and expertise among them.

First, the *development team* builds software to solve the business problems. That team should at least have software engineers who take ownership of the software they make and gain a shared understanding of the domain. The teams gain that understanding from domain experts. The *domain experts* are people who understand or are experiencing the business problems. *Customers* are the stakeholders who purchase the product or service the company is offering. *Users* are the stakeholders who use the software system the development team is creating. There are a few common misconceptions about these categories:

- The domain experts are always users.
- Customer is synonymous with user.
- The development team members aren't customers, users, or domain experts.

MISCONCEPTION 1: THE DOMAIN EXPERTS ARE ALWAYS USERS

The domain experts can be anyone from your customers to any of your colleagues in the company. They don't have to use the software system that you're building. In BigScreen, if you want to know your company's strategy or vision, or you want to know the key goals of the company for the next two years, your domain expert resides in higher management—your CEO, CTO, or CFO. They are the people who determine the modernization strategy, its budget, and so on. They don't use the ticketing system nor the back office; they aren't users, but they have valuable information that will influence how the team builds the system.

If you want to change the online ticket purchasing because 50% of your customers don't finish buying a movie ticket online and end up at the register in the theater, then your domain experts are your product owner, your user experience (UX) designers, the customer help desk, and perhaps even the customers themselves—anyone who has relevant information about the domain.

MISCONCEPTION 2: CUSTOMER IS SYNONYMOUS WITH USER

Customer and *user* aren't interchangeable; they are two different categories. In BigScreen, we have customers who aren't users and vice versa. The back office, for example, is only accessible by employees of BigScreen. These people are our users, but they aren't our customers. BigScreen also organizes private events. Other companies want to do something special for their employees and contact BigScreen to book a private movie viewing with drinks. This isn't done via the ticketing system but is managed by BigScreen's employees via the back office. These companies are customers that aren't users.

MISCONCEPTION 3: THE DEVELOPMENT TEAM MEMBERS AREN'T CUSTOMERS, USERS, OR DOMAIN EXPERTS

Employees of BigScreen, which includes the development team, also like going to the movies. This makes people from the development team also customers, which is a very good thing. It gives the development team the opportunity to test the ticketing system in their own lives and look for shortcomings and improvements they can make. Developers using their own products is a practice referred to as "eating your own dog food."

When we create internal services or libraries, the users are people inside the development teams. In BigScreen's new architecture (refer to chapter 1, figure 1.3), there is a service called Movie Scheduling, which will be used by developers, making them also users of this service. Domain experts can also be part of the development team. Here are two examples:

- For domains that are very complex by nature, such as biology or chemistry, domain experts are often trained to become programmers or product owners.
- If we look at streaming services such as Netflix, an important business problem is the video streaming itself, which requires highly complex specialized software.

For these scenarios, people on the development team are considered domain experts. Another way that developers become domain experts is through time. The longer developers work in a specific domain, the more knowledge they gain about the domain. In time, they become domain experts themselves.

If you want to better understand who your stakeholders are and the expectations you have of them, you can perform a stakeholder analysis using the four categories shown for BigScreen in figure 2.4. They can help you answer questions such as these:

- Do we want to inform your stakeholders?

- Do we want them to participate but not help decide, or do we want them involved in the decision-making?
- Do we have gaps in domain expertise?

The outcome of such an analysis can help you decide what type of collaborative modeling session is needed when talking to a specific group of stakeholders and help you manage expectations for each group. Setting the right expectations and knowing when *not* to invite a stakeholder will create a better engagement between you and the stakeholders. There is nothing more disengaging than being invited to a meeting and leaving it feeling like you wasted your time. If a domain expert knows that their presence will be helpful and that they in return will gain valuable knowledge by being in your session, they will be enthusiastic, which will result in better participation.

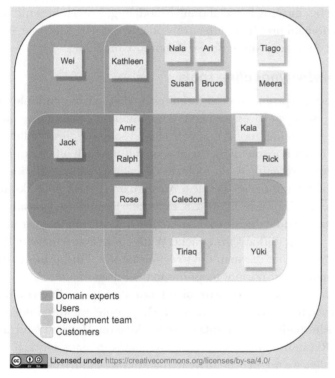

Licensed under https://creativecommons.org/licenses/by-sa/4.0/

Figure 2.4   This diagram showcases a simplified stakeholder analysis for BigScreen. Wei is a marketing user researcher and domain expert. Kathleen is the operations BA who serves as both user of the back office and domain expert. Nala, Ari, Susan, and Bruce are back-office users from the Operations and Marketing department. Developer Jack has been with the company for a while and possesses deep domain knowledge, alongside Rose who also loves to go to the movies, making her also a user and customer. Amir (tester) and Ralph (PO) are domain experts who also use and troubleshoot the application behind the scenes as support. Kala and Rick are part of the development team, alongside Caledon who also loves going to the cinema and is also a user and customer. Yūki is one of the customers of the Marketing department, who plans events for her company at the cinema. And Tiriaq is one of the many customers Wei contacts for user research. Meera (CTO) and Tiago (COO) are important stakeholders but are neither one of the four main types, so we placed them on the outside.

2.2.3   Why DDD and collaborative modeling go hand in hand

As previously mentioned, DDD encompasses a set of patterns, principles, and tools. Importantly, it doesn't prescribe explicit rules or methods. For instance, while DDD emphasizes the need for a deep, shared understanding of the domain, it doesn't dictate the exact means to achieve this understanding.

Enter collaborative modeling, a visualization technique tailored for analyzing complex domain problems. This approach provides visual tools that enable stakeholders to foster that deep, shared understanding. Furthermore, collaborative modeling aids in designing the ubiquitous language derived from the domain language and design models, as well as in identifying explicit domain boundaries.

There are tools tailored for both the strategic and tactical phases of design. In essence, collaborative modeling serves as a practical application of DDD principles. Some even argue that by engaging in collaborative modeling, one is inherently aligning software design with domain problems, effectively practicing DDD. However, it's worth noting that DDD isn't obligatory when using collaborative modeling.

2.3   Different collaborative modeling tools

Grasping complex business problems often requires modeling from multiple perspectives. To model different perspectives, we need to use different collaborative modeling tools. No collaborative modeling tool is a one-size-fits-all solution, silver bullet, golden hammer, or whatever metaphor you might use in your culture; each offers a unique perspective of the problem, abstracting the complexity of reality to address specific needs.

For instance, one of the authors resides near Amsterdam. To visit the Rijksmuseum, we might refer to the map shown in figure 2.5, especially because we typically use the metro. Using this map, we could decide to board metro line 50 at Bijlmer Arena, transfer to line 52 at Zuid, and get off at Vijzelgracht. While we're aware that the Rijksmuseum is adjacent to this station, the map doesn't indicate this. Furthermore, the map doesn't provide alternative transportation options to the Rijksmuseum.

Amsterdam is renowned for its extensive bike lanes. Perhaps cycling could offer a quicker route? However, to determine the fastest cycling route, we would need to consult a different map. Alternatively, we might consider taking the Metro to Zuid and then renting a bike to the Rijksmuseum, necessitating a look at both maps. Heck, if we don't value our time and wallet, we might even drive to the Rijksmuseum, frustration guaranteed! This would require yet another map.

In essence, to determine the most efficient route, we must consult multiple detailed maps. Each map serves as a model for a specific mode of transportation, and a combination of these maps is essential to devise the optimal solution.

Another observation is that we present various solutions to the problem, enriching our understanding of the problem at hand. For example, we suggested driving as an option for those less concerned about time and cost. This can spark a discussion on the value of time and money in specific contexts, aspects not explicitly mentioned or clarified in the original problem statement. This underscores the importance of employing diverse collaborative modeling tools. By doing so, we can generate multiple models that offer deeper insights and varied perspectives on the problem, as well as provide a range of potential solutions.

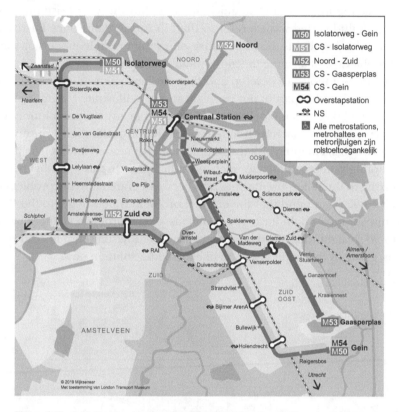

Figure 2.5 A metro map for the city of Amsterdam, showing how to get from one station to another. It doesn't directly tell you the fastest route to the Rijksmuseum; for that, you need to use other maps that tell you how far each station is to the Rijksmuseum.

2.3.1   *Collaborative modeling in the problem and solution space*

As mentioned a couple of times already, it's important to have a deep, shared understanding of the problem. We can't repeat that enough! Think of this as the *problem space*—the area where we explore and define the challenges that we and the stakeholders face. Within this space, we do collaborative modeling to create models that help us grasp the problems. These models then guide us when we're coming up with solutions. For example, when figuring out our route to the Rijksmuseum, we used maps from this problem space to help design our journey.

In section 2.1, we emphasized the importance of testing our models. During our design phase, collaborative modeling allows us to design multiple models. Within the solution space, we might implement and experiment with several of these models to determine which one is most effective.

Take the journey to the Rijksmuseum as an example. We could have multiple routes or methods to get there. By weighing the pros and cons and analyzing each, we can narrow down the best options. However, the true test comes from real-world applications. For instance, biking might seem the quickest route, but there's a twist: my bike gets "borrowed" (a light-hearted way we refer to theft in Amsterdam) once I arrive at the Rijksmuseum. This highlights the importance of testing multiple models or solutions for a single problem to determine the most suitable solution.

Over time, the solutions we develop and that our customers adopt can evolve into new challenges or become part of our problem space, as illustrated in figure 2.6. Let's continue with the biking example. While biking might be my chosen solution, I could encounter new problems, such as frequent stops due to traffic lights on my chosen route. To address this, I might revisit the original map (or model) and update it with my bike route, noting potential obstacles such as traffic lights. In this way, what began as a solution (biking to the Rijksmuseum) has now been integrated into the problem space. However, always keep in mind that the original problem is how to get to the Rijksmuseum, and our solution might have new problems, or the problem changes by adding the need to go straight to Rotterdam after visiting the Rijksmuseum instead of going home. Thus, going by car might just seem like the better solution now.

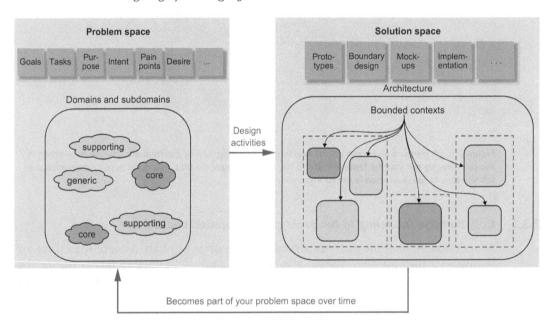

Figure 2.6   **The problem space is where we use collaborative modeling to make models of the user/business needs, which can be goals, tasks, purpose, intent, and much more. The solution space is where the output of our design activities is placed. We perform a variety of design activities to go from the problem space to the solution space. With collaborative modeling, we iterate on our design to improve our models to solve the needs of the problem space.**

Different perspectives on the problem space and the solution space

Different perspectives on the problem space and the solution space already exist in the industry and can cause a lot of confusion when you jump into the rabbit hole of searching for the explanation for the two concepts. For this book, it's important to understand the separation of the two spaces and that we use similar and different collaborative modeling tools for different purposes in both spaces. In the next chapter, we'll dive more into the two spaces and how they will help drive our design. You can also go to the "When & Why to Explore the Problem Space" blog post (https://mng.bz/KZgP) by Indi Young that explains the topic more fully and differentiates the spaces even more.

We use various collaborative modeling tools tailored for different situations in both the problem and solution spaces. It's worth noting that some tools are better suited for one space over the other. As mentioned in the introduction, we'll share stories from our collaborative modeling sessions at BigScreen, and we use different tools in each story. However, our primary goal in chapters 6 to 11 is to ensure that you grasp the key takeaways and lessons from those chapters, rather than getting bogged down in the intricacies of each tool.

To that end, we'll now offer you a brief introduction to the tools we used in each chapter, giving you just enough context to follow the narrative. For those seeking a deeper understanding, each chapter includes additional resources and recommended readings detailing that specific tool's functionalities. It's important to note that the tools we discuss aren't exhaustive, nor do they represent the entirety of our toolkit or the tools that are out there used by others. In addition, the tools are all created to work independently, and you can combine them during a session or switch tools during collaboration when you feel the need to.

For a more comprehensive exploration of the tools and when to combine them, Kenny, one of our authors, is curating a Leanpub e-book titled *Visual Collaboration Tools: For Teams Building Software* (https://leanpub.com/visualcollaborationtools/). This community-contributed e-book delves into these tools, providing step-by-step guides accompanied by real-world stories. While the book is available for free, any contributions you make will be directed entirely to scholarship projects promoting diversity in tech.

Now, let's return to our case study at BigScreen. We'll delve into some of our most frequently used collaborative modeling tools, focusing on the "Anytime, Anywhere" campaign. This initiative aims to empower customers to purchase tickets on the go. BigScreen aspires to modernize its ticketing system, enabling mobile app purchases. However, the existing monolithic system poses challenges. While our instincts as software engineers might drive us to immediately address the monolith, it's crucial first to understand the campaign's underlying motivations in the problem space. This foundational understanding will undoubtedly shape our subsequent decisions.

BUSINESS MODEL CANVAS

As mentioned earlier in this chapter, we've encountered many teams responsible for creating a software system that could not answer questions about the company they worked for. Yet, context is key. Having a shared understanding with the business will help teams make decisions, prioritize better, and, most importantly, think with the company and come up with ideas that will achieve success for this company. You can create a shared understanding with the business by discovering the company's strategy. A strategy includes a *business model*, which is a plan for what the company needs to succeed. Many tools are available that are designed to describe the business model of a company. One tool, *Business Model Canvas* (created by Alexander Osterwalder) is our favorite because it's simple and easy to use, yet it gives a good understanding of what a company needs to succeed. There are four sections in the canvas: offerings, customers, infrastructure, and finances (figure 2.7).

Adapted from the Strategyzer "the business model canvas"
https://www.strategyzer.com/library/the-business-model-canvas
Licensed under https://creativecommons.org/licenses/by-sa/4.0/

Figure 2.7   The four sections of the Business Model Canvas tool. This canvas gives us an understanding of what we offer, who we offer it to, what we need to do to succeed, and what finances we have.

OFFERINGS

When we fill in the Business Model Canvas, we start with the offerings. Offerings only have one subsection, *value propositions*. Value propositions take a central place in filling in the canvas, which is why we often give it a different color. As you can see in figure 2.8, it also sits in the middle of the canvas. The value propositions are important because these are the reasons that customers choose us instead of a competitor. Thinking about the value propositions first makes it easier to fill in the other sections. You can find the value propositions by looking at the marketing strategy of your company and asking the following questions:

- What are we offering the customer?
- Why would they use our products/services?

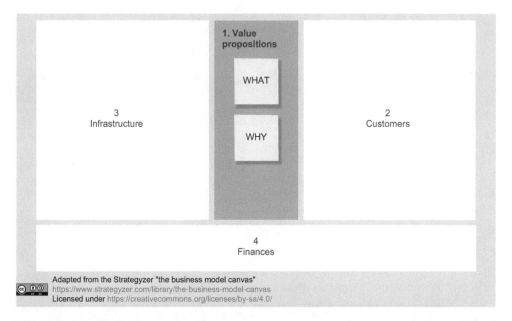

Adapted from the Strategyzer "the business model canvas"
https://www.strategyzer.com/library/the-business-model-canvas
Licensed under https://creativecommons.org/licenses/by-sa/4.0/

Figure 2.8   The offerings section of the Business Model Canvas is given a different background color because the value propositions take a central place in the canvas.

CUSTOMERS

The customers section has three subsections: *customer segments, customer relationships,* and *channels.* The customer segments subsection can be very high level: business-to-consumer (B2C), business-to-business (B2B), or low level: students, food industry, pharmacies, and so on. You don't have to pick a level, just make sure you have a good understanding of who your customers are.

Next are the customer relationships. You can think of the customer relationships with the following question: How do we offer our value propositions to our customers? It's important to understand that you don't have a single relationship type. You might have a different relationship with your B2B customers than with your B2C customers. A few examples of relationship types are direct or indirect contact, self-service, or personal assistance.

The last subsection is channels, which you can think of as follows: What channels do we use during those relationships? Keep the different phases of a customer in mind when finding the channels: prospects, onboarding, active users, and so on. Figure 2.9 captures the keywords to remember when filling in the customers section:

- WHO are we offering the value propositions to?
- HOW do we offer the value propositions to the customers?
- What ENABLES us to have these relationships?

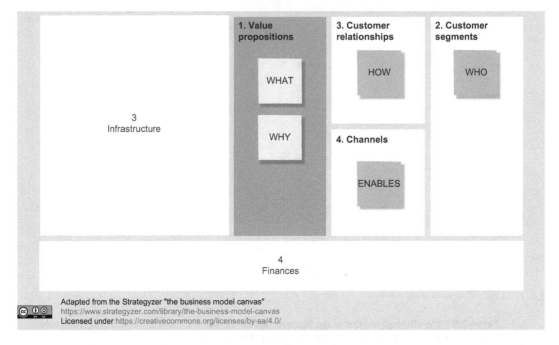

Adapted from the Strategyzer "the business model canvas"
https://www.strategyzer.com/library/the-business-model-canvas
Licensed under https://creativecommons.org/licenses/by-sa/4.0/

Figure 2.9   The customers section of the Business Model Canvas tells us more about who our customers are, how we communicate with them, and which channels we use for that communication.

INFRASTRUCTURE

Next comes the infrastructure, which also comprises three subsections: key activities, key resources, and key partners. We want to emphasize the *key* here in each of the titles: companies have a lot of activities, resources, and partners. Don't try to sum them all up; instead, focus on the most important ones we need to offer our customers as our value propositions. Figure 2.10 shows the short sentences you can use to remember how to fill in the infrastructure section:

- *Key activities*—WHAT DO WE DO to make our value propositions possible?
- *Key resources*—WHAT DO WE NEED to do those activities? Don't forget the less visible resources here, such as people, their knowledge, and intellectual property.
- *Key partners*—WHO DO WE NEED to work together with to do those activities?

FINANCES

The last section, finances, is interesting, but it doesn't often contain any information that can help the development team with decisions or priorities. This is why we marked it in gray in figure 2.11. The section answers two questions: What does it cost (cost structure), and how do we pay the costs (revenue streams)? A company has many costs, so try to focus on the most important ones and those that take up the largest chunks. Sometimes that will be surprising because we don't always think about certain costs, such as legal fees. Lawyers are quite expensive in some countries. The revenue streams

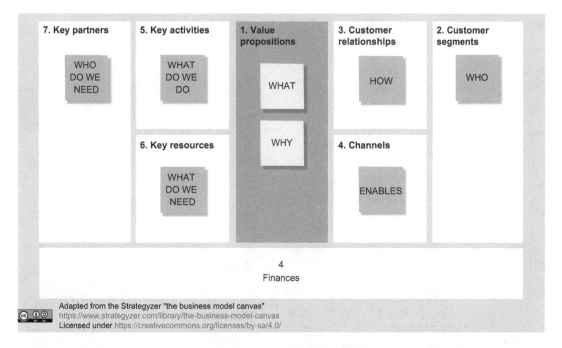

Adapted from the Strategyzer "the business model canvas"
https://www.strategyzer.com/library/the-business-model-canvas
Licensed under https://creativecommons.org/licenses/by-sa/4.0/

Figure 2.10 The infrastructure section of the Business Model Canvas gives an overview of the key activities the company performs, as well as the most important resources and partners we need to perform those activities.

are pretty straightforward, and most people in the company know how their company makes money or at least they know the most important revenue stream. There is an opportunity here to discover new revenue streams, although that is rare. If one of your key resources is a piece of software that was difficult to create, and you know that this will stop being a differentiator soon, you could look into selling it to competitors.

HOW TO USE BUSINESS MODEL CANVAS

The Business Model Canvas is a good icebreaker for starting collaborative modeling with the business. It focuses on the company and the key aspects of its strategy. The Business Model Canvas shows the domain experts that you and the development team have a keen interest in understanding the business better. It's further removed from software and feature discussions with the domain experts, yet it gives the development team important information on the company. We try to fill in the Business Model Canvas together with the development team. Afterward, we invite one of the domain experts to validate our understanding.

For BigScreen, we did the same. We started with the value propositions: fun outing, easy to reach, comfortable movie experience, affordable for everyone, and a wide range of movies. We found these by digging into previous marketing campaigns. Then, we tried to get a sense of our customers and the infrastructure needed to support the propositions. We briefly tried to sum up the most important costs and revenue streams. The Business Model Canvas was incomplete, but we filled it in as best we could. Afterward,

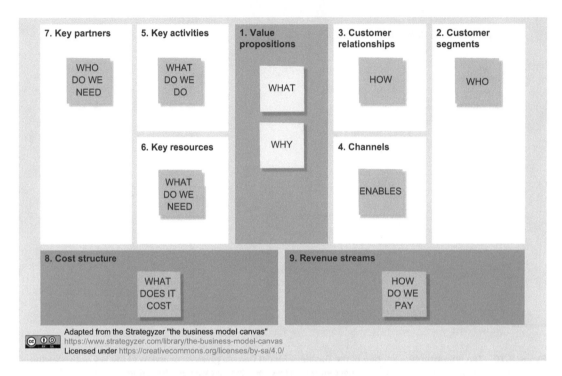

Adapted from the Strategyzer "the business model canvas"
https://www.strategyzer.com/library/the-business-model-canvas
Licensed under https://creativecommons.org/licenses/by-sa/4.0/

Figure 2.11   **The finances section of the Business Model Canvas contains the cost structure and the revenue streams. It tells us the biggest costs and the main revenue streams.**

we spoke to the CTO, Meera, for about an hour to fill in the gaps in our knowledge (don't worry, we didn't write out the entire conversation):

Us: So, we looked at previous campaigns, and we think the value propositions for BigScreen are fun outing, easy to reach, comfortable movie experience, affordable for everyone, and a wide range of movies.

Meera: Yeah, those are pretty good. I am not sure about the wide range of movies though, and, well, the latest campaign is missing, the "Anywhere, Anytime" one. It's a really important one; it has to succeed. Every other movie theater offers this already, and we noticed that we are losing our mobile generation.

Us: Okay, let's first focus on the missing campaign. Who is the mobile generation?

Meera: Oh, right. People between 18 and 30 years. Those generations were raised with a mobile phone. Hence the name. If they notice they can't buy tickets with their mobile phone, they find a movie theater where they can do it. You have to understand, it's not just about right now. Part of that group will start working soon, so they will have a bit more money to spend, or they will get married and have kids. So, they are our future customers for our themed events.

Us: Themed events?

Meera: Yeah, we organize themed events targeting a specific customer segment. For example, for parents with young kids, we organize Sunday-Funday events. They happen once a month. They are a huge success; we are always sold out in every city.

We adapted the Business Model Canvas during our conversations with the feedback and additional information we were receiving from Meera, which improved our understanding of the information. The CTO also felt that we appreciated her taking the time to talk to us about this and that we find understanding the business model important. We updated the value propositions and marked "buy a ticket anytime, anywhere" in its own color because this is a value proposition that isn't possible right now. The other ones we marked in a different color because we're successful as a company in offering these value propositions. We created a legend, as shown in figure 2.12, to capture the meaning of the colors on the canvas.

We also added the "mobile generation" explicitly to the canvas because that is the language that they use to talk about a specific customer type. We changed the language we used when filling in the canvas whenever it was appropriate during the conversation; for example, the business still talks about "movie tapes" even though they work with digital files now, so we captured this term in the key resources. This way, we can start creating our ubiquitous language from the domain language.

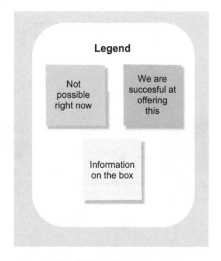

Figure 2.12   The legend of the BigScreen Business Model Canvas. Try to capture the meaning of the different sticky note colors that you use by creating a short legend for each color.

We also discovered during the conversation that BigScreen has contracts with public transportation to stop in front of their movie theaters because they want their theaters to be easy to reach. We added public transportation as a key partner. You can see the finished Business Model Canvas in figure 2.13.

Exercise 2.1: Your own Business Model Canvas

Whether you're building in-house software to support the company's activities or developing software to sell, your company will have a business model that you can capture with this canvas. Try filling in the canvas with your team for your own company. If your company is very large, such as a bank, take a part of that company that you belong to as input. Afterward, use it as a conversation starter with the domain experts inside your company. Remember, the Business Model Canvas is nice-to-have documentation, but the main focus is the conversation itself. Listen to the language the domain expert is using, and capture it in the canvas.

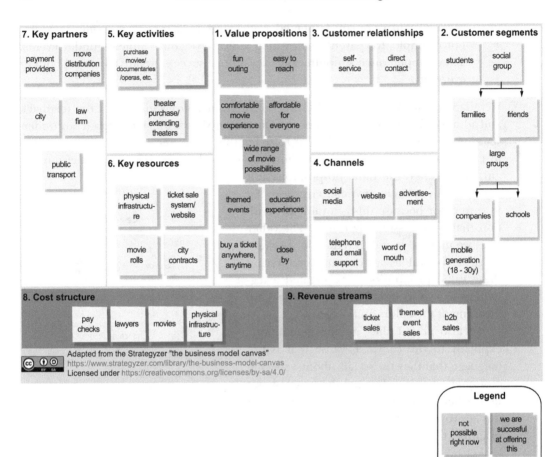

Figure 2.13   The finished Business Model Canvas for BigScreen. It captures the domain language and knowledge of the domain experts we discovered while validating our understanding of the business model.

2.3.2   EventStorming

Now that we have a grasp on our business model, we turn to EventStorming to visualize the entire process of purchasing a ticket. We refer to this as a *flow* rather than a customer journey or business process because it's the combination of both and more that delivers value to the customer. EventStorming facilitates the rapid creation of a shared understanding, leading to fresh insights.

EventStorming stands out as an adaptable collaborative modeling tool. One of its strengths is that participants can dive in and grasp the concept during a session, even without prior knowledge. This empowers the participants to convey their understanding of the narrative. As such, it's an ideal tool for intricate, cross-disciplinary discussions among stakeholders from diverse backgrounds. The essence of EventStorming's effectiveness lies in its ability to provide just the right amount of structure to collaboratively generate knowledge and solutions.

DIFFERENT TYPES OF EVENTSTORMING

Alberto Brandolini introduced EventStorming within the context of DDD as a tool to foster a shared and deep understanding of a domain. In his e-book, *Introducing Event-Storming: An Act of Deliberate Collective Learning*, available on Leanpub (https://leanpub .com/introducing_eventstorming), he describes three types of EventStorming:

- *Big Picture EventStorming*—This method encompasses the entirety of a business line or domain and usually engages 30 to 40 participants. For example, at BigScreen, we could conduct a Big Picture EventStorming session covering the complete domain of showing a movie. This would span from acquiring the movie rights, scheduling its screening, and facilitating ticket reservations, all the way to the actual day of the screening.

- *Process Modeling*—Multiple teams can work together to map out both the current (as-is) and desired future (to-be) customer journeys and business processes. For example, at BigScreen, we might first conduct a session to understand our existing movie planning process and then immediately transition into designing the envisioned future process.

- *Software Design EventStorming*—Software development teams can tailor their design and implementation to specific business scenarios. For instance, at BigScreen, after conducting a to-be process session, we can delve deeper into designing how this process would integrate within our software architecture.

We refer to figure 2.14 for guidance on when to use each type of EventStorming, depending on the problem space and solution space. It's worth noting that many discussions about EventStorming often focus on software design or aggregate design without specifying the type because Brandolini initially used EventStorming for software design and expanded to other types later. For a comprehensive understanding, we recommend reading his book on Leanpub.

In figure 2.14, we've shown overlapping types to indicate that during a session, you might transition from one type to another. For instance, a session might begin with Big Picture EventStorming to capture a broad scenario, such as onboarding a customer. However, if the core problem is identified in a specific segment, such as screening the customer, the focus might shift to Process Modeling. Similarly, while modeling a business scenario as-is using Process Modeling, the team might transition to designing the desired future to-be state.

You might question the term *software design* instead of *process design*. The journey typically starts with process design and culminates in software design. To avoid confusion among stakeholders, it's often best not to specify the type in session invitations.

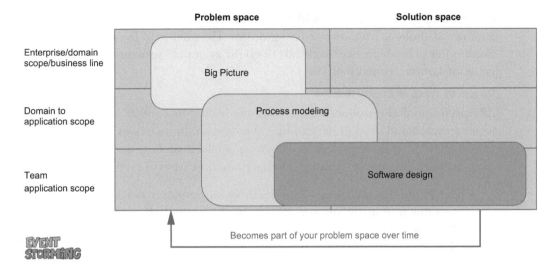

Figure 2.14   When to use each type of EventStorming. For modeling the problem space of an enterprise, domain, or business line, we use Big Picture. Designing the solution space of a stakeholder needs to be done with Software Design. For everything in between, we can use Process Modeling. On the left side, you see the different scopes of an organization where these types are typically used.

PREPARING FOR AN EVENTSTORMING

Whether you conduct EventStorming in person or online, the essentials remain the same: enough modeling space and orange stickies. However, it's important to note that the inherently chaotic nature of EventStorming often leads to heightened interaction and discovery during in-person sessions. While online sessions can still foster these interactions and discoveries, they demand a more structured approach and explicit facilitation. One potential challenge with online tools is that they might pose a steeper learning curve, potentially hindering participants from easily expressing their knowledge. Therefore, it's advisable to allow participants to familiarize themselves with the online tool prior to the session, ensuring they're comfortable using it. We added a blog post by Alberto in Section 2.5 later in this chapter if you want to know more about online EventStorming.

STEP 1: CHAOTIC EXPLORATION

Every EventStorming session often starts with what's termed a *chaotic exploration* of a given scenario or set of scenarios. In the realm of EventStorming, a *scenario* refers to a sequence or set of business activities or processes that are being explored or modeled. It's essential to understand that while *scenario* implies a singular sequence, EventStorming can simultaneously tackle multiple scenarios. These can later be organized into distinct swimlanes for clarity.

   We start a chaotic exploration with every participant writing down all the domain events they can think of for the given scenario. A *domain event* represents a significant occurrence within our scenario that holds business relevance. This relevance is determined by what our stakeholders deem relevant. For example, within the BigScreen context, domain events such as "Tickets are Purchased," "Ticket are Paid," and "Seats are Reserved" are seen as relevant. On the other hand, technical occurrences such as "Database Connection Lost" or "DDOS Attacked" aren't seen as relevant to the stakeholders. Such technical aspects might be discussed later, once we finish modeling out the scenario enough and have a clear understanding of the problem.

Note that domain events are phrased in the past tense, as they reflect events that have already happened. A common initial hurdle for participants is to distinguish between *actions*, which are often about the future or the present, and *events* that have already occurred. This distinction can be a bit confusing, especially for those new to this or those who've spent years modeling processes. Yet, it's a crucial part of EventStorming. As facilitators, our job is to help participants understand this difference, making sure they focus on events rather than actions. If they struggle to find the right past tense words, let them know that the most important thing is to write down their thoughts. We can always refine and adjust these details later.

After participants have noted down all the domain events they can recall from the scenario, they place them on the modeling space, as illustrated in figure 2.15. This figure showcases a typical outcome of the chaotic exploration phase in Process Modeling. A fundamental principle of EventStorming is that the modeling space serves as a timeline, progressing from left to right in this context. Given that domain events signify occurrences that have transpired over time, participants are instructed to arrange these events chronologically on the timeline. For instance, as depicted in the figure, "Movie is picked" precedes "Spots are picked" in the sequence of events.

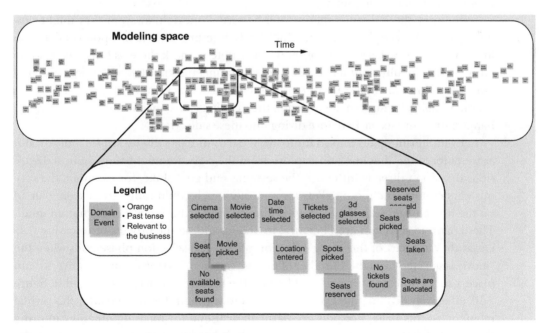

Figure 2.15   An example outcome of the chaotic exploration step in EventStorming, where everyone used domain events to model the scenario for themselves

Each EventStorming session is unique. For instance, the session depicted in figure 2.15 began in a rather chaotic manner. Participants were asked to independently identify domain events and position them on the timeline based on their understanding. In contrast, some sessions might follow a more structured approach, where participants collaboratively arrange the stickies in sequence and engage in discussions about specific domain events from the outset. Both approaches are valid. The primary goal at the beginning is to capture everyone's interpretation of the scenario through domain events. In this context, the focus was on the ticket-purchasing process.

The figure also includes a distinct legend that defines a domain event. Maintaining an updated legend is crucial. While EventStorming has a foundational set of color-coded concepts, it's acceptable to modify these colors or introduce new concepts like wireframes or mock-ups, as long as these changes are accurately reflected in the legend.

STEP 2: ENFORCING THE TIMELINE

Now that everyone has put their understanding of the scenario on the board, it's time to refine the timeline into a shared narrative. This step involves enforcing the timeline, which means we remove any repeated events and work together to create a single, meaningful timeline. It may sound easy to just put our domain events in order, but by asking the group to build one timeline, individual perceptions start to blend with others' perceptions. This can bring up some unclear areas and disagreements on certain parts of the timeline that need to be addressed. These disagreements are actually useful. If we handle them well, they help us learn and build a shared understanding. We'll explore this more in chapter 8.

Sometimes, these disagreements can't be sorted out right away, or they might slow down the whole group's discussion, which leads to getting stuck in one point of the timeline. In these cases, we use a neon pink sticky note to mark these as hotspots. *Hotspots* are areas of difficulty, conflict between people, or missing knowledge. It might also be a point where the timeline splits into different branches, as shown in figure 2.16 when a "Payment failed." The goal of enforcing the timeline is to concentrate on finishing the happy path of the scenario before diving into these side effects.

In EventStorming, it's important to avoid narrowing our discussion too quickly. But as we enforce the timeline and explore from the start, we might venture into discussions that don't directly influence the session's end goal. Take, for example, the various ways customers choose tickets for a movie, which could range from seeing an ad on the home page, searching for upcoming movies, or having a specific film in mind. These paths to selection aren't central to understanding the process of reserving tickets, as they are part of the movie selection phase. The selection phase ends when the "movie is selected" and the "number of tickets is chosen." To focus our narrative, we can place a sticky note and on a vertical line on the modeling space, as depicted in figure 2.16, effectively dividing the EventStorming into segments before and after this pivotal moment. At this stage, hotspots are particularly useful for focusing on and capturing the essential dialogue. Scoping in this manner is crucial for maintaining focus on the primary objective of the EventStorming session.

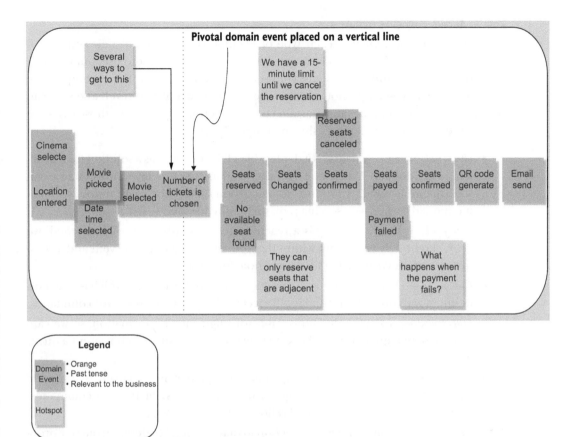

Figure 2.16 Example of how to proceed with enforcing the timeline in EventStorming where the groups merge all of their own models into one timeline of the scenario. We added a pivotal domain event where we can now decide what is inside our storyline and what happened before.

In figure 2.16, we've simplified the scenario to make the process clearer; a real-life EventStorming session typically involves many more sticky notes. However, this streamlined version provides a general idea of how EventStorming usually unfolds. In chapter 6, we'll delve into a more comprehensive example of Big Picture EventStorming, particularly focusing on ranking. This will be closer to what you can expect in your own experiences. It's important to remember that company culture plays a significant role in how these sessions progress, especially in resolving conflicts that arise. A culture that encourages open communication, respect for diverse viewpoints, and a collaborative approach to problem-solving will greatly enhance the effectiveness of EventStorming. Such a culture helps to navigate disagreements constructively, allowing for a more productive and insightful session. If you do EventStorming within an organization that doesn't have that open communication, this book will definitely help you still make such a session worthwhile!

STEP 3: ADDING CONCEPTS ITERATIVELY

While enforcing the timeline, each type of EventStorming can add new concepts if needed in the form of stickies. These extra concepts aren't a must to use, but they can help you categorize and make some conversations more explicit. Depending on the context you're in, you might not even use these extra concepts; however, a session can become blocked at times because certain concepts weren't clarified. In those cases, we can use the following concepts, as shown in figure 2.17:

- *(External) System*—A system is a deployable IT system used as a solution for a problem in the domain. When we've finished making the timeline consistent, we can start mapping systems around domain events. Per Alberto Brandolini's book mentioned earlier, we use a big pink sticky note for this.
- *Policy*—In essence, a policy is a reaction that says "whenever *X* happened, we do *Y*," eventually ending up within the flow between a domain event and a command/action. We use a big lilac sticky note for these.
- *Command*—This represents an instruction given in the domain, which is an action or intent with no certainty that it will succeed. We use a blue sticky for commands.
- *Query model*—To make decisions, an actor might need information, so we capture these in a query model. We officially use a green sticky to represent a query model.
- *Actor*—An actor or agent is a group of people, a department, a team, or a specific person involved around a (group of) domain event(s) or triggers commands. The official color to use is a small yellow sticky.
- *Constraint*—A constraint is a restriction we have or need to design from our problem space when we want to perform a command. The official color to use is a big yellow sticky. When we go from Software Design to aggregate design the yellow stickies can turn into aggregates, which it was originally called. But we rather not discuss aggregates in front of the stakeholders.

Now for some groups and for some people, all these colors can be overwhelming, together with their meaning. We've added the final result of the EventStorming and examples of the concept in figure 2.18. You can also find more information freely available on the ddd-crew EventStorming Glossary & Cheat Sheet (https://mng.bz/9d9x), and we can't mention enough the importance of reading Alberto Brandolini's book on Leanpub for more in-depth examples of when and how to use these extra concepts.

One vital thing to understand is that the concepts just mentioned have names that might be confusing in your context. We once tried to explain the word policy in an insurance company. We can tell you that didn't end well. Change the names of the concepts as necessary in your context. For instance, *action* can be used instead of *command, information* instead of *query model,* and *business rule* instead of *constraint.* You can also decide not to use some or all of the concepts, as long as you keep your legend up to date! You can use different color stickies, which is very handy when one color isn't available. You can add your own concepts, such as lines between the concepts, as shown in figure 2.18. EventStorming is adaptable to the needs of the session's goal, and the core concepts are the domain events set out in a timeline and the marked hotspots. Then you can add concepts as needed with the goal to discover and design a shared understanding of the problem.

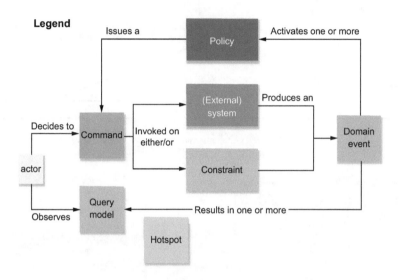

Figure 2.17   All the EventStorming concepts. The lines represent how these concepts interact with each other in the flow. Only Process Modeling and Software Design types use all the concepts and the way they interact. Big Picture often only uses domain events, actors, external systems, and hotspots. Remember, you can always change the naming or add new concepts to the legend.

Exercise 2.2: EventStorming your own context

You don't need stakeholders in your session to do EventStorming. As an exercise, either with your team or just yourself, model a scenario in the software that you're working on now. Of course, without stakeholders, it won't be a collaborative modeling session, so you won't build up that shared understanding, but it's a great trial run, and you'll be surprised at the discovery you'll make in your team and see how aligned your team is. Just doing chaotic exploration and enforcing the timeline is usually enough for a lot of great insights and even more questions. Don't be afraid to experiment, but make sure you do so when it's safe to fail, for instance, within your team and not with stakeholders where you might not get a second chance!

Figure 2.18 is the final result of our Process Modeling EventStorming at BigScreen, with all the Process Modeling concepts that EventStorming offers. We could discover and dive into many more branches, but the key here is that we create a shared understanding as a group about the process. Now, we can decide how to move forward. As mentioned, go read the *Visual Collaboration Tools: For Teams Building Software* book for a much more detailed description of all the EventStorming types, or just buy Alberto's *Introducing EventStorming: An Act of Deliberate Collective Learning* e-book as we did on Leanpub.

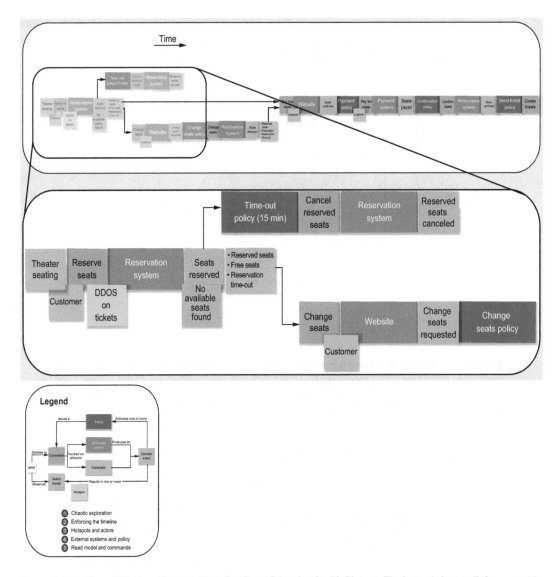

Figure 2.18   The result of our Process Modeling EventStorming for BigPicture. The legend shows all the concepts EventStorming brings that can make the story clearer.

2.3.3   *Example Mapping*

While EventStorming shines at modeling one or several scenarios in one timeline or process, it doesn't shine so much at discovering several use cases happening at a certain moment in that scenario, timeline, or process. For instance, when the system reserves seats for our ticketing purchase, many constraints can keep the system from finding tickets to reserve for a movie. If we look back at figure 2.18 where there is a command saying "Reserve Seats" and two domain events called "Seats Reserved" and

"No available seats found," we know there are constraints that either give you "Seats Reserved" or "No available seats found" because there can only be one ticket per seat, or we can only reserve seats that are adjacent seats for a single reservation. Usually, at this point, we go into several examples trying to discover what constraints there are. As another example, when we're designing a new flow, we might find ourselves locked into a discussion in EventStorming, going into several scenarios, and discussing different what-if scenarios; in this case, we should switch to another tool—Example Mapping. Example Mapping visualizes the different examples and use cases that can happen at a certain moment in time.

During his time at Cucumber, Matt Wynne introduced Example Mapping in this blog in the Behavior-Driven Development (BDD) community (https://mng.bz/jXYz). With Example Mapping, the goal is to discover *acceptance criteria,* which are the business requirements the implementation needs to meet. But we can also take constraints discovered during EventStorming as input for Example Mapping. It has a much lower threshold than EventStorming because all you need to do is discuss concrete examples happening during a certain point in the timeline and then visualize these in a structured way to discover new acceptance criteria. Next, let's make this clearer with the user story of reserving seats.

STARTING AN EXAMPLE MAPPING

Our discussion began by differentiating between EventStorming and Example Mapping, and understanding when to opt for one tool over the other. It's essential to recognize that Example Mapping is a standalone tool; there's no prerequisite to conduct EventStorming before delving into Example Mapping. The primary requirement for Example Mapping is a use case or user story provided by a stakeholder.

To start Example Mapping, jot down the user story or use case on a yellow sticky, as illustrated in figure 2.19. Directly below this, list any known rules on blue stickies. Following this, capture specific examples related to these rules on green stickies. For instance, for the rule "Only 1 ticket per seat," you'd detail clear examples on the green stickies. While we've used an online tool in this example, in-person sessions typically employ index cards. This choice is strategic: index cards can be effortlessly rearranged on a table, facilitating a dynamic discovery process.

DISCOVERING NEW RULES

As you can see in figure 2.19, we visualized the examples. To make the example more explicit, we advise making a drawing of the example if you can. In this case, we drew a cinema room with the seating arrangement. Now, most of the time, the first examples are pretty straightforward. But as soon as you start discussing more complex rules, you'll discover more what-ifs. You can find our final result in figure 2.20. While drawing the "only adjacent seating per row" examples, someone created an example showing two reservations that are adjacent to each other, but have one chair open in between. From here, we start discussing if we want to have one chair in between or not. Ralph, the product owner, then says no, we want to let people pick their own chairs, but we do want to fill up the entire room. Leaving one seat in between isn't optimal because there

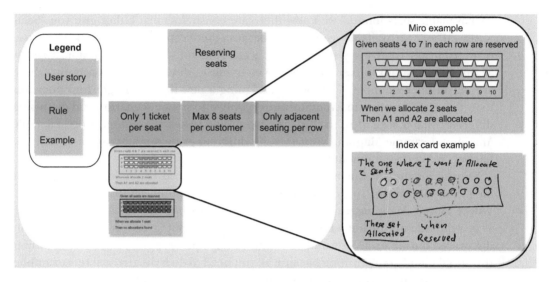

Figure 2.19   An example of how to start an Example Mapping. With a user story and the rules, we explore the first concrete example of the rule. On the right side, you can see how to do it either using a virtual board such as Miro or using index cards in a physical setting and drawing with a dry-erase marker on it. From here, we can discuss and find new examples.

aren't a lot of one-person reservations. So, from here, the No Orphan Seats rule gets discovered, and examples for that rule are created. From here, as you can see in figure 2.20, more examples pop up, and more rules get created.

It's important that we have a diverse set of people in the room. In the BDD community, they call it the three amigos—developer, product owner, and tester. You should have at least all the relevant stakeholders in the room, as well as the entire team. The more diverse set of people, the more different insights you'll get. Having a person with testing experience in the room who will challenge the scenarios or can come up with edge cases especially helps during this discovery.

Another important thing for Example Mapping is that everyone can write examples, and as you create more examples, even the obvious ones, and discuss them together, you need to make more rules to handle these examples. A general rule of thumb is as follows: you think it, you write it! We spread out the rules horizontally while categorizing the examples that explain the rule underneath. Another general principle is that if you need more than three examples to explain a rule, or you validate more than one option in the rule, you can probably discover a new rule.

SPLITTING UP USER STORIES

Sometimes, we choose to skip or not delve into a specific example because the risk seems low. Often, not all the necessary knowledge is available right away, or we go into too much detail too soon. So, we use a red sticky note or index card to note down things we need to follow up on after the session. We can also organize the rules by priority from a product perspective or group together rules that are related and affect

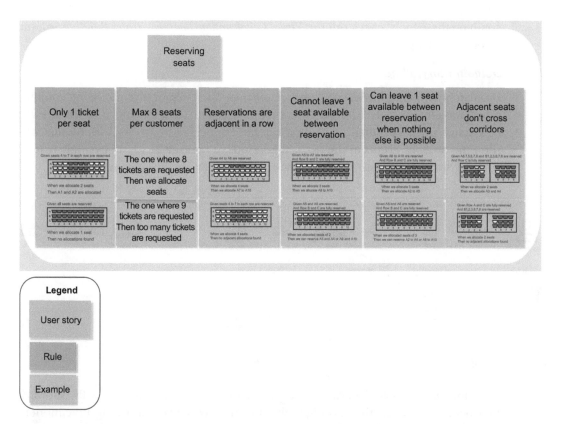

Figure 2.20 The final result of our Example Mapping, showing we discovered and decided on new rules. We also discovered new concepts, such as there is a corridor, for example.

each other. In a scrum-like development process, user stories or product backlog items are the smallest units of work to include in your sprint backlog for development.

They need to be small, but a common challenge for teams is figuring out how to break these down into the smallest workable units. By categorizing the examples—whether they involve several rules that need to be built together or just one on its own—we can further divide our user stories. Example Mapping is a powerful tool for breaking down larger stories into smaller ones, which helps reduce the feedback loop through smaller, more manageable stories. However, it's crucial to timebox discovery to 20 minutes, or else the story is still too confusing. After that 20 minutes is up, you can separate the rules that are clear from the rules that still need more clarification before they can be Example Mapped in the next section.

COMBINING TOOLS DURING A SESSION

We already mentioned that EventStorming and Example Mapping, just like all the tools covered, are two separate tools that we can combine during a collaborative modeling session. If we do so, we can take the constraints that we captured as input, and we won't have the yellow sticky. The rest stays the same. To see more examples of how to combine these tools, check out the *Visual Collaboration Tools: For Teams Building Software* e-book on Leanpub mentioned previously.

2.3.4   *Domain Storytelling*

Domain Storytelling has become very popular in the collaborative modeling community. It was created by Henning Schwentner and Stefan Hofer as a more structured way of telling a story. This method uses pictograms connected by arrows, with numbers to show the order of events in the story. Take a look at figure 2.21 for an example from a Domain Storytelling session on the BigScreen's ticket reservation scenario.

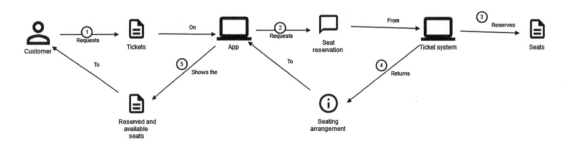

Figure 2.21   BigScreen's Domain Storytelling with legacy system

We appreciate this tool because it captures the story clearly and visually, showing how people work together. As highlighted in the "Why EventStorming Practitioners Should Try Domain Storytelling" blog post by Schwentner and Hofer (https://mng .bz/WE84), there are similarities between EventStorming and Domain Storytelling. Remember, no tool is perfect. What we find most useful about Domain Storytelling is how easy it is to record a conversation as it happens. This way, the group can talk about the story and decide what is important to include. The tool's visual style is straightforward, which helps everyone understand what has been recorded.

While it might seem at first that the tool's icons are too rigid for quick, spontaneous whiteboard sessions, the tool actually offers a lot of flexibility. The set of icons can be changed to fit the specific (sub-)domain you're working on. It's a good idea to agree on what each icon means during your workshops and add it to the legend.

WHAT MAKES DOMAIN STORYTELLING SHINE

Domain Storytelling allows a facilitator to start modeling conversations quickly and easily. The clear pictograms and diagrams are almost self-explanatory, enabling the drawing of discussions for instant validation and a shared understanding. You can either draw these on a whiteboard or use a digital tool for online sessions. The authors of Domain Storytelling have created an open source tool, Egon.io, which is great for quickly sharing your screen and getting started.

A unique aspect of Domain Storytelling is how it clearly shows the level of cooperation in business processes. It's easy to see the interactions between different participants, such as people, groups, or software systems. This feature is a key difference from Event-Storming, where showing cooperation in a timeline of events isn't as clear.

Domain Storytelling usually focuses on a single scenario, whereas EventStorming can cover multiple scenarios in one session. For instance, in figure 2.21, we focus on the process of buying a ticket. In EventStorming, this could be expanded to include what happens if a purchase fails, using different swimlanes for different scenarios.

Groups often prefer to explore every detail of a scenario, a tendency we call the Deep versus Wide approach. Balancing these approaches is vital for a successful session. However, people often lean toward one approach, which can split the group. We'll talk more about managing this balance in chapter 10.

For groups that tend to focus on details, Domain Storytelling can help broaden their perspective. It allows you, the facilitator, to stay focused on one scenario without going into too much depth. When new scenarios come up in Domain Storytelling, you can make notes for later exploration, keeping the current session focused.

MODELING WITHOUT THE CURRENT SOFTWARE LANDSCAPE

Domain Storytelling works by capturing the interactions in a scenario as numbered steps. These interactions, whether they are between people or systems, are shown using pictograms. They represent conversations or objects and can be placed anywhere in the modeling area. The numbers on the steps guide us through the story. It's important to think about what we're modeling. In our example, we modeled the current process as it is, including the existing software systems. However, Domain Storytelling also allows you to break away from the current software setup and focus on what the story is really about. Let's look at how this approach changes the diagram.

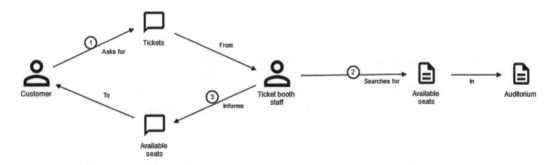

Figure 2.22 BigScreen's Domain Storytelling without the legacy systems

In figure 2.22, we took out the legacy systems to focus solely on what our customers really want. This approach of modeling a scenario without mentioning any software systems leads to a completely different discussion with your stakeholders. It's especially helpful when working with people who might not know the names of the systems or call them something else. If you find that the conversation is getting too caught up in the specifics of the current software implementation, try leaving out system names altogether. This can help clear any confusion and guide the discussion back to the core objectives of the business.

2.3.5   *When to use what tool*

Many people often ask us when they should use which collaborative modeling tool. To help answer this, we've put together table 2.1, which provides an overview of the tools we've discussed, highlighting their strengths and weaknesses. It's based on our own experiences with various collaborative modeling tools. Use this table as a starting point, and feel free to adjust it or create your own as you become more familiar with these tools.

Another key factor to consider is the group's experience with collaborative modeling. For those new to collaborative modeling, it's best to start with a simple tool that can yield quick results. When we first began with collaborative modeling, we applied it in the solution space. This doesn't require inviting additional people; you can simply take a user story or request and, for instance, use Example Mapping with your team. Starting in a familiar environment helps you safely experience the benefits and power of collaborative modeling. Remember, for Example Mapping, all you need is a business rule and the following question: Can you give me an example?

Table 2.1   **An overview of the collaborative modeling tools, their strengths, and their weaknesses**

Tool	When to Use	Strengths	Weaknesses	What Space
Big Picture EventStorming	When modeling or designing an enterprise, business line, or domain	Adaptable, and quick to learn Chaotic nature gives a lot of insights	A lot of people in one room, requires a lot of experience facilitators Only works with a timeline	Problem Space
Process Modeling EventStorming	When modeling or designing a story, process, or timeline	Adaptable, and quick to learn Chaotic nature gives a lot of insights	Difficult concepts to grasp Can feel like a high time investment Only works with a timeline	Problem Space and Solution Space
Software Design EventStorming	When designing software for stakeholder needs	Adaptable, and quick to learn Chaotic nature gives a lot of insights	Difficult concepts to grasp It can feel like a high time investment. Only works with a timeline	Solution Space

Table 2.1　An overview of the collaborative modeling tools, their strengths, and their weaknesses (*continued*)

Tool	When to Use	Strengths	Weaknesses	What Space
Example Mapping	When you want to discover different examples and rules for a scenario	One of the simplest collaborative modeling tools to start with Can formalize acceptance criteria from the discovery	Lacks visualization of the process or storyline, which can make people discuss invisible things	Problem Space and Solution Space
Business Model Canvas	When you need information on the context: the company and its strategy	The business often knows this tool already because it's a popular tool in business management.	The tool is further removed from the software, and it's harder for the development team to understand its importance before they have worked with it.	Problem Space
Domain Storytelling	When modeling one specific scenario, process, or timeline	No learning curve, instant documentation	Structured approach that can lower the amount of discovery	Problem Space and Solution Space

2.4　*Collaborative software design catalysts*

You might be thinking, "What now? How can I start applying what I've learned in this chapter?" Don't worry, we've thought of that. At the end of each chapter, you'll find a section called "Collaborative software design catalysts." These are practical tips, suggestions, and practices that you can begin using right away, regardless of your current position in a team or your current software development life cycle. They're designed to give you quick benefits from the insights in this book, even if you're not modeling collaboratively, and get a jump start on applying these ideas. Let's start by introducing the first two:

- When discussing a business problem, for example, in a refinement or similar meeting, consider using domain events to map out the conversation on a timeline. You can do this on your own or get help from the group.
- When discussing business requirements with stakeholders, introduce a helpful rule: "You think it, you write it." This encourages people to visually express their ideas, contributing their thoughts to the collective understanding. It's an effective way to ensure everyone's mental models are shared and understood by the group.

2.5   Further reading

- *Discovery: Explore Behaviour Using Examples* by Gaspar Nagy and Seb Rose (Create-Space, 2018)
- *Domain-Driven Design: Tackling Complexity in the Heart of Software* by Eric Evans (Addison-Wesley Professional, 2003)
- *Domain Storytelling: A Collaborative, Visual, and Agile Way to Build Domain-Driven Software* by Stefan Hofer and Henning Schwentner (Addison-Wesley Professional, 2021)
- "EventStorming in COVID-19 Times" blog (https://mng.bz/x25Y)
- *Gamestorming: A Playbook for Innovators, Rulebreakers, and Changemakers* by Dave Gray, Sunni Brown, and James Macanufo (O'Reilly Media, 2010)
- *Introducing EventStorming* by Alberto Brandolini (Leanpub, https://leanpub.com/introducing_eventstorming)
- *Learning Domain-Driven Design: Aligning Software Architecture and Business Strategy* by Vlad Khononov (O'Reilly Media, 2021)
- *The Programmer's Brain* by Felienne Hermans (Manning, 2021, www.manning.com/books/the-programmers-brain)
- *Visual Collaboration Tools: For Teams Building Software* by Kenny Baas-Schwegler, Krisztina Hirth (Leanpub, https://leanpub.com/visualcollaborationtools/)
- "When & Why to Explore the Problem Space" blog (https://mng.bz/KZgP)

Summary

- Teams often prioritize solutions over understanding user and stakeholder needs, leading to missed insights into the broader business challenges.
- Understanding business problems requires analyzing user needs, stakeholder concerns, and system limitations before proposing software features.
- Software's role in businesses has evolved from support to a central component, necessitating adaptive development to align with company growth and market changes.
- Collaborative modeling is essential for tackling complex problems, involving stakeholders in visualizing and analyzing decisions to achieve a shared understanding.
- Effective problem exploration through collaborative modeling focuses on domain understanding, questioning assumptions, and using accessible tools to facilitate stakeholder engagement.
- Collaborative modeling and Domain-Driven Design (DDD) synergize to deepen the understanding and design of domain models, prioritizing shared knowledge among all stakeholders.
- Stakeholder roles are diverse, with distinctions between domain experts, customers, and users; effective stakeholder analysis is key for targeted engagement.

- Misconceptions—such as equating domain experts with users or misunderstanding the roles within software development—underscore the need for clarity in stakeholder involvement.

- DDD's principles guide the strategic and tactical phases of software design, with collaborative modeling serving as a practical toolset to apply these principles, though not mandatory.

- Different collaborative modeling tools offer unique perspectives on complex business problems, each tailored for specific scenarios and needs.

- Collaborative modeling tools are essential in both the problem space and solution space, helping to create shared understanding and test multiple solutions through visual and interactive tools.

- The Business Model Canvas aids in understanding a company's strategy and business model, focusing on offerings, customers, infrastructure, and finances.

- EventStorming facilitates a rapid, collaborative understanding of business processes, enabling stakeholders to map out and analyze scenarios with a focus on domain events.

- Example Mapping helps in breaking down user stories or use cases into actionable tasks, identifying acceptance criteria and constraints through structured example-based discussion.

- Domain Storytelling provides a structured approach to capturing and visualizing business processes and interactions, highlighting cooperation and communication within scenarios.

Using collaborative modeling for design and architecture

This chapter covers

- The relationship between collaborative modeling, design, and architecture
- Heuristics and their usage during collaborative modeling
- Driving the design by understanding the business

The previous chapter gave you an idea of what collaborative modeling is and how it can be used to truly understand business problems before diving into solutions. We explained the relationship between Domain-Driven Design (DDD) and collaborative modeling, and described some of our favorite collaborative modeling tools. So, we've got the basics right. At this point, you're probably wondering how collaborative modeling can be used to create an actual design and architecture. That's exactly what we'll cover in this chapter.

We'll continue with our BigScreen example and take you further on their journey. We start with defining design and architecture, which is crucial if we want to move to the solution space. We'll also dive into the difference between design and architecture, as well as how you can benefit from doing both collaboratively.

58

All of these activities take place in a bigger system in which we live and work. It's not just about getting the technical details right, such as the structure of the software system, the work that needs to be done, or even the best technology for the challenge at hand; it's also how the organization structure, social structure, and our cognition affect these activities. Those aspects together form the sociotechnical system that balances social, technical, and cognitive aspects. To succeed, you'll have to optimize all aspects together because they heavily affect each other. In this chapter, we'll provide an introduction to sociotechnical systems.

Definitions are great, but putting those definitions into practice is a whole other ballgame. We'll also further explain the need for collaborative modeling in design and architecture. We'll explore how bad design decisions can affect social dynamics and (implicit) architecture, and which consequences can follow from these bad decisions. One way to drive the design and collaborative modeling sessions is by using *heuristics*, which are simple rules to make quick decisions. This chapter will explain what heuristics are and how and when you can use them. We'll share some of our own favorite heuristics and invite you to start your own heuristics journal at the end of this chapter.

This chapter concludes with more insights on how to drive design by understanding the business. This is where we really move toward solutions. We'll dive into bounded contexts and why boundaries are designed through collaboration.

3.1   *What is software design and architecture?*

In the previous chapter, we discussed how the goal of collaborative modeling is to foster a deep and shared understanding of the problem. We aim not only to share our individual mental models of the problem but also to understand the diverse perspectives and ultimately create a shared understanding of those models. *Models* is plural here because, depending on the information, a problem can be represented in various ways. Donella Meadows puts it like this in *Thinking in Systems: A Primer*:

> *Remember, always, that everything you know, and everything everyone knows, is only a model. Get your model out there where it can be viewed. Invite others to challenge your assumptions and add their own.*[1]

This notion of everyone having a model, whether you spend a lot of time and energy on modeling or no conscious time at all, is inevitable.

Similarly, when it comes to software design and architecture, the presence of some form of design, whether good or bad, is unavoidable. Bad design is very real. Bad design can manifest from a lack of design decisions, isolated decisions that no one truly grasps, or decisions that exist but haven't been explicitly stated. Often, we observe that these problems are caused by design decisions that are based on incorrect models or misunderstood concepts. This leads to an implicit design and architecture.

---

[1]   Meadows, *D. H. Thinking in Systems: A Primer*, 2008. London: Chelsea Green Publishing (p. 172).

When faced with such implicitness, software development teams might resort to workarounds because they need to navigate the murky waters. However, these workarounds only introduce more complexity into an already intricate environment. To prevent this added complexity, we stress the importance of making design and architecture explicit. The key is to model collaboratively, ensuring a shared understanding and eliminating as much implicitness or ambiguity as possible. By doing so, we can effectively manage the complexity introduced by the people within the system, that is, in the sociotechnical system.

3.1.1   The importance of meaning and definitions

Language is crucial in collaborative modeling because if we don't have a shared understanding of what a word means, that misunderstanding ends up in our decision-making. It reminds us of *Friends* episode "The One Where Underdog Gets Away" (Season 1) where Monica and Rachel walk out of their apartment. Monica says, "Got the keys," and Rachel replies, "Okay." Neither has the keys, and they are locked out of their apartment. As the episode shows you, language ambiguity can lead to all sorts of negative, time-consuming, and frustrating situations. Language ambiguity is everywhere, so we're always keen on removing it in collaborative modeling sessions. "What do you mean with . . .?" is a question we hear ourselves ask very (very) often. Now we wouldn't call ourselves DDD practitioners without finding it essential to define these words and create our ubiquitous language for this book.

Of course, those definitions might not be how you would describe those concepts or use the words we use. We would be surprised if our description matches what is used across the entire software industry because language is fluid and constantly changing. Nevertheless, keep in mind that we designed our definitions in the context of this book, our ubiquitous language.

You can agree with it or disagree with the definitions, and that's perfectly fine. In fact, we believe that definitions should be continuously challenged and evolve where necessary. We can all learn from that process.

Now, we'll elaborate on what we mean by *design*, *architecture*, and *sociotechnical system*. Let's start explaining *our* definition by seeing how implicit architecture and design can create more accidental complexity in our BigScreen company.

3.1.2   What is software architecture?

The previous chapter highlighted how BigScreen reaped the advantages of collaborative modeling in understanding its business problems. Through EventStorming, the team delved into the current ticket-purchasing process, which offered invaluable insights for their "Anytime, Anywhere" campaign. Understanding how the business operates with the existing software system is important for this team because they are afraid of altering the reservation code due to lost knowledge. Throughout the session, a recurring theme was the team's astonishment and questions about how the software system evolved to its present state. This isn't a unique observation; we've seen numerous instances where individuals were taken aback by certain design decisions.

It's becoming increasingly common for software teams to encounter such surprises, and perhaps you've experienced this yourself. While there were specific, contextual reasons for these past decisions, the recurring surprise underscores a gap in knowledge or communication. We posit that the industry's shift toward Agile methodologies in the past 5–10 years, a transition BigScreen also underwent, might be a contributing factor.

As mentioned in chapter 1, we've observed that many companies often find themselves in an "Agile theater;" that is, they might implement Agile frameworks such as Scrum or Kanban, or even use a scaling framework, yet they retain their traditional hierarchies. We're not criticizing these frameworks; in fact, we've employed them ourselves and recognize their value when applied in the right context for the right reasons.

Following industry trends, BigScreen also transitioned to an Agile approach for its development team. However, the team didn't fully grasp the methodology's nuances. One major misconception they held was the belief that up-front architecture and an Agile approach are inherently at odds. This misunderstanding fostered significant emotional baggage among the development teams, who began to view the architect and the overarching architecture as limiting factors. As these teams shifted to iterative development, delivering features every sprint, the architect and the practices surrounding architecture became a bottleneck. This led to the rise of terms such as "ivory-tower" architect. It's essential to note that being perceived as a bottleneck, or being labeled an ivory-tower architect, isn't solely or even primarily the architect's fault, especially in BigScreen's case. The company's existing hierarchy persisted, and this structure still held the same expectations of the architect as it did in the past.

In response to this conflict, teams began to sidestep the architect to ensure they could deliver on their commitments. This led to a situation where the teams and the architect found themselves with competing objectives. However, these teams weren't adequately trained or well-versed in software architecture, as it wasn't a primary focus in the waterfall approach they were accustomed to. As a result, they didn't initiate explicit design activities, which left them oblivious to the ramifications of their design decisions on the software architecture. We believe that software teams—not a software architect outside the team—should own the software architecture. However, before they can do that, they should be enabled and trained in software architecture before firing the architect!

Even when coding, you can make pivotal design decisions. The act of coding makes a developer do software architecture. For example, you're tasked with modifying an integration with another system. While coding, you decide to alter a specific name that triggers a series of changes across the systems involved. You've made a significant design decision. While a mere name change might not alter the fundamental structure of the software systems, it introduces complexities and dependencies that ripple through the architecture. This perspective on software architecture aligns with the views of Grady Booch, who is internationally recognized for his contributions to software architecture and is the creator of the Unified Modeling Language (UML).

> **DEFINITION**   *Software architecture* represents the significant design decisions that shape a system, where significance is measured by cost of change (www .bredemeyer.com/whatis.htm).

BigScreen is consistently involved in decision-making processes that shape the system at various levels of the organization. While transitioning from waterfall to Agile isn't directly making design decisions, these shifts certainly affect the manner in which design decisions are approached and executed.

Design decisions, regardless of their scale, have the potential to affect the fundamental shape of software systems. The essence of these decisions lies in their significance. Booch has associated significance with the cost of change. Thus, when a design decision is made, architectural considerations should factor into the potential cost of implementing that change and its influence on the fundamental structure of the software. This fundamental structure is the foundational layout and organization of the software system. Alterations to this structure can affect the degree in which a system can be divided into smaller self-contained units (*modularity*), which affects its ability to undergo modifications (*changeability*), and its capacity to adjust to new functionalities or requirements (*adaptability*).

In the context of BigScreen, the cost associated with altering the design is substantial. The current software system poses challenges in adapting to the new "Anytime, Anywhere" campaign requirements. The company aspires to modernize the ticketing system, enabling customers to purchase tickets through a mobile app. However, integrating this feature into the existing software isn't cost-effective. Ideally, a good architecture should ensure that the introduction of new features doesn't slow down the system or escalate costs, maintaining both its changeability and adaptability. Yet, the inherent challenge lies in the unpredictability of the future and the probability of new features needing to be added, making software architecture a complex endeavor.

3.1.3   *What is software design?*

By using collaborative modeling as introduced in chapter 2, the teams started to understand the business problems. Having a model of the current situation that includes the wisdom, perspectives, and knowledge of the entire group created an overview and insights into how processes affect each other. BigScreen could start moving toward a design to modify the software system. Modifying your current system to what you want is where design activities come in. As mentioned in chapter 2, we use design activities to go from the problem space to the solution space. We'll provide more in-depth examples of these design activities later in the chapter. For now, we're using these design activities to create a plan to modify the current software systems to end up with the new desired systems. That is how we define *software design*, which includes all the design activities aimed to modify the current software systems into a preferred one.

DEFINITION *Software design* refers to the design activities aimed to modify the current software systems into a preferred one (www.bredemeyer.com/whatis.htm).

Design activities often culminate in a plan to modify software systems. Within this plan, we formulate design decisions. However, not every design decision holds equal weight or significance for our software architecture. As Booch aptly puts it, "All software architecture is design, but not all design is software architecture." This distinction is crucial to grasp. Software design is a given; whenever we make alterations to software systems, we're inherently engaging in design. The real question is, which of these design decisions have the potential to alter the foundational shape of the software system, that is, the software architecture? Later in this chapter, we show you examples of software design done within BigScreen by designing boundaries (section 3.3.1), as well as how that software design leads to a new software architecture.

If a design decision doesn't affect the core structure, then it's not a matter of software architecture. In such cases, there's no need to invest time and effort in software architecture considerations. If the change is merely tweaking a portion of the code without causing ripple effects throughout the system, then explicit architectural design decisions aren't necessary; you can simply implement the change.

Software architecture, however, encompasses more than just the software system itself. It's embedded within a broader ecosystem, being built by a team of people, used by individuals, and integrated into the organization's structure. Design decisions— whether they pertain to the team, the organization, or the manner in which people work—have continuous and interconnected effects. Given the interconnected nature of software systems and the broader ecosystem they exist within, it's crucial to make sustainable design decisions that account for long-term effects and adaptability. We'll talk more about what makes a design decision sustainable in chapter 9.

One of the most significant benefits of collaborative modeling, especially when aligned with company goals and strategy, is its ability to help teams concentrate on the right priorities. With a clear model of the present situation, we can envision and design the future with the following questions in mind:

- What does our ideal future look like?
- What steps should we take to reach that state most effectively?
- Where should our investments go?
- Which areas should our development teams prioritize?
- Is our current team structure equipped for the impending changes?
- How will these changes affect the cognitive load of our teams?

These are all critical strategic questions that leadership teams must address. Having a clear understanding of where you currently stand—your starting point—provides invaluable insights into answering these questions.

3.1.4   *What are sociotechnical systems?*

To enable teams to focus on parts of the software systems that are in line with the company strategy and goals, the bigger mental model needs to be created and shared with all involved. Certain teams may still focus more on specific parts of the system, but at least the effects and dependencies are known and can be designed for.

When we talk about *systems*, we don't mean purely technical systems; we mean the system as a group of interacting components, for example, the team, the people in the team, and the software systems they use and build. To be more specific, sociotechnical systems are networks of interrelated components where the different social, technical, and cognitive aspects interact. A technical decision will have social and cognitive consequences, and vice versa. Balancing these aspects is hard, but necessary.

A sociotechnical system provides us with a holistic framework for understanding and organizing intricate work environments. Rooted in the foundational work of Emery et al., the term *sociotechnical system* encapsulates the intricate interplay between human dynamics, technological tools, and the broader environmental context,[2] as you can see in figure 3.1. Today, as we navigate increasingly complex workspaces, this interplay between social practices, technology, and cognitive processes becomes even more pronounced. These elements are deeply intertwined, and any attempt to optimize one while ignoring the rest only amplifies systemic complexity. For instance, a technological decision can reshape team dynamics and increase cognitive demands, as new tools necessitate new skills.

A notable example of focusing on one aspect while overlooking others is seen in how many companies have adopted open-plan office spaces. This move was influenced by the benefits observed in communication, collaboration, equality, health, and cost in other organizations with similar environments.[3] However, simply shifting to an open-plan layout often means just optimizing the physical system, while neglecting to jointly optimize structure, people, and task systems in a sociotechnical system. Studies reveal that most companies making this transition mainly realized cost reductions, but the other four expected benefits often didn't improve as anticipated. Those companies that did achieve all the benefits managed this by involving their employees in the design of the open-plan space. By doing so, they effectively jointly optimized all four systems in the sociotechnical system. The physical system was improved through the workspace alteration, the people system evolved as employees influenced the social dynamics in the new space, the structural system benefited from teams reorganizing based on their communication needs, and the task system was enhanced due to the new interaction methods. The connections and mutual dependencies within a sociotechnical system are depicted in figure 3.1.

---

[2]   Emery, F. E., Trist, E. L., Churchman, C. W., & Verhulst, M. *Socio-Technical Systems, Management Science Models and Techniques*, 1960, vol. 2. Oxford, UK: Pergamon (p. 83–97).

[3]   Wright, J. *The Good, the Bad, the Open-Plan: Creating Environments for Collaborative Knowledge Work*, 2019, Lean Agile, https://vimeo.com/374629143.

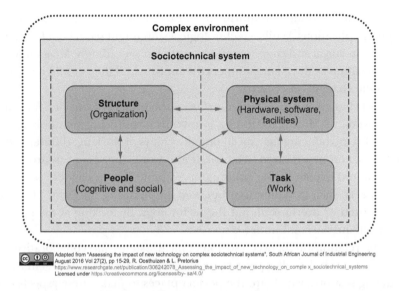

Adapted from "Assessing the impact of new technology on complex sociotechnical systems", South African Journal of Industrial Engineering
August 2016 Vol 27(2), pp 15-29, R. Oosthuizen & L. Pretorius
https://www.researchgate.net/publication/306242078_Assessing_the_impact_of_new_technology_on_comple x_sociotechnical_systems
Licensed under https://creativecommons.org/licenses/by- sa/4.0/

Figure 3.1   A sociotechnical system is the relationship between the technical system (the tasks and the physical system) and the social system (structure and people). When designing software, we often forget about the effect of the social system.[4]

Sociotechnical might seem like a modern buzzword, but its origins date back to the post-World War II era. During this period, scientists investigated work systems in coal mines. They found that organizations where teams were responsible for control, coordination, and the primary goal of coal extraction were more efficient than those where teams focused on specific tasks, such as digging or detonation. In these latter organizations, the responsibility of control and coordination fell to the managers.

Emery's later research in Norway provided deeper insights. Organizations without a hierarchical structure for control and coordination, known as "design principle 2 (dp2)," outperformed those where these responsibilities were held by management, termed "design principle 1 (dp1)." A hallmark of dp2 organizations was the teams' active involvement in shaping their structures through participatory design sessions. This approach enabled them to quickly adapt to external changes, unlike the slower response seen in dp1 structures.

This research underscores the significance of optimizing various aspects collaboratively for success. Prioritizing one element, such as efficiency, can inadvertently affect other system components, negating potential benefits. Technological decisions carry social and cognitive implications. For instance, the evolution from early mobile phones to smartphones transformed not just communication but also our societal behaviors and culture. Similarly, in development teams, introducing a new technique or process, such as Scrum, alters team dynamics and relationships. This change demands

---

[4]   Oosthuizen, R., & Pretorius, L. "Assessing the Impact of New Technology on Complex Sociotechnical System," 2016, https://mng.bz/lM0R.

immediate cognitive adjustment, requiring individuals to understand the new workflow and its broader implications. While a technological shift might seem beneficial, it's crucial to anticipate its social and cognitive effects and plan accordingly. Most importantly, the shift must be done by the team members themselves, and they should have the control to discard the changes if necessary.

We see a lot of change initiatives and transformation projects. Consider, for example, the DevOps movement. Moving to DevOps is not only introducing new tools and methodologies but also introducing new social practices, ways of working, different communication patterns, and new desired behavior. It also works the other way around when organizations intend to change the culture, for example. There's a lot of focus on the more social aspects, such as values, mindset, and emphasizing the "why." The work is often being ignored or overlooked, not the technology. By looking at the system as a whole, you can create the conditions for success.

So, what's the relationship between sociotechnical systems and collaborative modeling? The short answer is that all aspects of sociotechnical systems are present in collaborative modeling sessions, which are the perfect places to make these aspects explicit and balance them out. Collaborative modeling sessions depend on the knowledge and behavior of the people involved. When facilitated properly, they also trigger the right conversations about software, architecture, processes, relationships, and underlying challenges. Collaborative modeling sessions expose group dynamics and cultural norms, which influence the process of creating software. Many signals—both weak and strong—tell you something about the culture within a group of people, a team, or an organization. Collaborative modeling is the perfect setting to clarify these signals. This is also why we believe it's so important to have proper facilitation during these sessions. It's almost a full-time job to pay attention to these signals and see how they affect the group.

3.1.5 *Design decisions and collaborative modeling*

Design decisions are a critical part of design and architecture. As mentioned, collaborative modeling enables making (design) decisions, taking into account all aspects of sociotechnical systems (technical, social, cognitive). All design decisions made will affect the architecture and social dynamics within a group. Again, this is why it's so important to think in terms of sociotechnical systems instead of focusing on one part of the puzzle.

Collaborative modeling can help you make good design decisions that will result in the best possible solutions. When all domain experts and relevant stakeholders are present, it's easier to identify possible decisions, their tradeoffs, and their value. It's also the perfect place to make design decisions explicitly, so you won't end up with a black box and/or *implicit architecture*. But that's the ideal world; now, let's dive into the consequences of bad design decisions and how they affect your group dynamics and architecture.

CONSEQUENCES OF BAD DESIGN DECISIONS

Remember our fictitious company called BigScreen? The company faced challenges including the product owner (Ralph) being involved in gathering user requirements, arguments between developers, and tension in the group, which resulted in one of the developers just starting and implementing his own design. One of the biggest problems was that the team wasn't kept in the loop regarding design decisions. This led to wrong implementation, delays, and rework. When design decisions go wrong, it often results in what we call an implicit architecture. We see three main reasons for this:

- Design decisions are being made, but they aren't made explicit (often with time pressure).
- Those implicit design decisions weren't understood by everyone.
- Implicit design decisions can't be communicated.

As stated in the introduction of this section, there is no such thing as *no design*. As in the BigScreen example, someone may decide to just start and implement whatever they see fit. Or maybe someone makes design decisions in isolation that affect the architecture big time. What's interesting here is to look into why there are no decisions being made. Hesitation to make decisions can be a signal that people are suppressing knowledge. Maybe it's not safe enough to speak up in the group, maybe the group has learned that making a decision is followed by more work, or maybe the environment isn't safe to fail in. A lack of design decisions being made doesn't have to mean that (technical) knowledge is missing in the group. It can be, of course, but there's a good chance that social and cognitive factors are influencing these patterns as well. Treating your environment like a sociotechnical system (refer to section 3.1.4) will help!

When design decisions are being made, but they aren't explicit, it's valuable to look at certain social dynamics within a group. Bad design decisions can heavily affect both the implicit architecture and social dynamics in a group. Ranking, which will be further discussed in chapter 6, is a good example of this. We usually see that the person higher in rank (e.g., CTO, CEO, architect, but also developers who are in the company the longest or know the most) makes a decision that eventually lacks buy-in from the group. Because that person is perceived to have a higher rank, many people choose to stay quiet and work with—or around—the decision. This could result in conflict, polarities, and people ignoring the decision when implementing the design.

The same happens when design decisions are being made, but not everyone understands them. It might lead to lower buy-in, and groups will find themselves cycling back to those decisions over and over again. Be mindful that these sorts of decision-making processes will likely initiate resistant behavior: sarcastic jokes, gossiping, or communication breakdown, for example. These resistant behaviors indicate there is something lingering in the shadows of the group. When not dealt with properly, this will grow and hinder progress. We'll discuss resistance and how to manage it further in chapter 8.

Hopefully, it's clear now how bad design decisions can affect the social dynamics in a group and how that influences the (implicit) architecture. Some very negative consequences also become visible when implementing the design, including the following common ones:

- Not being able to add new functionality
- Adding new functionality takes much longer
- Longer push-to-production time
- More bugs because developers need to write hacks

Our take on technical debt

Technical debt is often perceived negatively, typically linked to implicit architectural decisions. However, this perspective may be overly narrow. Technical debt isn't merely about *cruft*, which is poorly written or redundant code. Rather, we view technical debt as a result of a conscious, explicit architectural decision. This happens when you knowingly introduce less-than-ideal design and code to deliver value more quickly. In doing so, you create a debt, similar to a financial obligation, that needs to be repaid over time. It's essential to distinguish between cruft arising from technical debt and that which comes from implicit design, possibly due to a lack of skill or awareness. With an explicit decision, you're looking ahead, including stakeholders in the decision-making process, and acknowledging the potential risks and consequences. In contrast, implicit architectural decisions lead to unintended cruft, which can bring unexpected risks and consequences. Such scenarios often cause frustration, especially toward developers, when efficiency begins to suffer. In the end, cruft is inevitable, but recognizing cruft as part of technical debt, especially when it's deliberate, makes it less difficult to manage.

This is what you want to avoid and that starts with making better design decisions. Collaborative modeling is a good starting point to make explicit which decisions need to be made, how these decisions could possibly affect the architecture and social dynamics, what alternative views are available, and what it takes for people to go along with a decision.

3.2   *Heuristics for collaborative modeling*

The previous sections explained what software architecture and design entails, why we need to approach this from a sociotechnical perspective, and design decisions in collaborative modeling. In this section, we'll dive a bit further into some of the (group) processes that you can encounter during these sessions. For example, did you ever get the feeling during a (collaborative modeling) session that you're stuck and don't know what the next step should be? That's a common state in most sessions we've been a part of. Discussions on where the boundary should be, removing duplicate stickies because someone assumes it's a duplicate, and conversations that go in completely different directions are all examples of situations that can occur during collaborative modeling and that require a decision to make progress. What do you do in these kinds of situations? Through experience, you build up simple rules—*heuristics*—that can help you make decisions. When talking about heuristics, we like to use the following definition:

> **DEFINITION** A *heuristic* is a simple rule to help you make a (quick) decision.

Note that heuristics are based on experience. You've learned what works and what doesn't from experience in facilitating collaborative modeling sessions. Some heuristics are more universal and are effective across groups; others are group specific. As a facilitator, it's important to keep your box of heuristics flexible and open for suggestions. Heuristics can make you feel more comfortable and secure in situations that aren't comfortable and secure. They can guide you, based on experience, to the next step. In this section, we'll dive into heuristics and how to use them during collaborative modeling sessions.

Remember that the practices and techniques outlined in this book are intended as guidance. The same is true for heuristics. Think of them in the same way you would approach a cooking recipe. You might not follow the recipe exactly; you could add more garlic, for example, if you have a preference for a stronger garlic flavor. Similarly, in each session you facilitate, it's necessary to adjust the "ingredients" to ensure its success. Heuristics can provide enabling constraints and inspiration, but the specifics will differ for each session. It's important to initially use heuristics from others as they are, much like following a recipe for the first time, before modifying them to suit your own needs. In this section, we'll present some example heuristics that have been gathered over the years.

3.2.1 What are heuristics?

Heuristics help us make progress. Based on previous experience and learning, we've gathered some sort of toolkit that we can use in particular situations. You can imagine that this could be very useful during collaborative modeling sessions, but it goes beyond that area. For example, when I go to the supermarket to buy groceries, I use heuristics, such as "Get nonfrozen stuff before frozen stuff." This is a very simple example, but it helps me tackle the problem of buying groceries in an optimal manner. Collaborative modeling sessions are much more complex than buying groceries, of course, and heuristics are even more useful there. As mentioned, heuristics are simple rules to make quick decisions.

A very important aspect of the definition of heuristics is the focus on decision-making. Heuristics work in situations where a decision is needed. Are we putting this boundary here or there? Are we going to discuss this diverging topic together or in a smaller group? When facing situations like this, heuristics help us make quick decisions. Note that a decision implies conscious action. A decision without action is just an intention. We'll dive further into decisions and decision-making in chapter 9.

Another important thing to note here is that using heuristics doesn't necessarily provide worse results than you would have when doing a deep and detailed analysis of the situation. Think about an emergency room; doctors use heuristics to determine if your situation requires immediate and urgent action, or if you can wait. They simply don't have time to complete a deep analysis of your situation. Instead, doctors use heuristics they gained from previous knowledge and experience, which provides them with proper results.

The same goes (to some extent) for collaborative modeling sessions. No matters of life and death here, but the time constraint is similar. During these sessions, there's usually no time to do a deep analysis before making a decision. Based on what you know and have experienced in the past, you know that it's probably best to do A (or B, or C) in that particular situation. It enables decision-making and therefore progress, which is what's needed at that moment. Different situations and goals require different types of heuristics. Let's explore these types and dive into some examples.

DIFFERENT TYPES OF HEURISTICS

Heuristics aren't extensive rule-based phrases, but short sentences and reminders that help you take the next step in tackling a problem. Based on experience, you've learned that in situation A, it might be helpful to do B, unless C is the case. Or, it might help to try X before Y in situation Z. For example, if it's raining outside, it might be helpful to bring an umbrella, unless there's a very strong wind too. This has a lot to do with common sense, but it's how heuristics work. They live in people's heads and are very often used unconsciously. Imagine how much groups, teams, and organizations could benefit from collecting, documenting, and sharing all the heuristics that exist within a group of people. When thinking about our BigScreen company, a heuristic might be "If I want to buy a ticket via the app, it might be helpful to have my credit card information at hand."

We use three types of heuristics (https://dddheuristics.com/):

- *Design heuristics*—Heuristics we use to design software
- *Guiding heuristics*—Heuristics that guide our use of other heuristics (i.e., meta-heuristics)
- *Value-based heuristics*—Heuristics that determine our attitude and behavior toward design (or the world) and the way we work

Because we're talking about design and architecture, you can imagine that the design heuristics are crucial. When designing a system or architecture, you have to solve various specific problems. Because most of us do this more than once, a lot of design heuristics are probably already lying around and (un)consciously being used when designing. Here are a couple of design heuristics that we regularly use: "Align with domain experts on boundaries," "Design bounded contexts by looking at the humans during a big picture EventStorming," and "Align bounded context with the domain experts." The list of (personal) design heuristics is constantly growing and evolving, and we try to share them with others as much as possible.

THE BOUNDED CONTEXT PATTERN

We mentioned the bounded context pattern when we explained DDD in the previous chapter. If you're not familiar with a bounded context, Eric Evans describes the pattern as a boundary (typically a subsystem, or the work of a particular team) within which a particular model is defined and applicable (see Evans's book, *Domain-Driven Design: Tackling Complexity in the Heart of Software* [Addison-Wesley Professional, 2003]). He described the pattern because he observed that large projects often have multiple models due to varying user needs, independent team approaches, or different tool sets. Combining distinct models can lead to buggy software and communication confusion. A bounded context ensures clarity by providing a boundary where terms and concepts have unambiguous meanings, preventing model mix-ups and allowing independent evolution.

Let's think about one of the most crucial parts of collaborative modeling sessions: designing boundaries. It's also a very hard part. A lot of the conversations during the sessions revolve around boundaries. Where do we put them? What's in, what's out? Who's responsible for this? Where are the dependencies? Very often, this is a conversation around designing bounded contexts. We work out how design heuristics work for BigScreen in section 3.3.1, where we'll do an extensive deep dive into design heuristics. Heuristics are very useful here, especially design heuristics. One design heuristic that can help here is "Find the natural boundaries in the domain." It gives you a starting point in making decisions and moving on.

What hopefully stands out to you is that heuristics can be used to drive the design and handle smaller design decisions. They can help tackle specific problems within a potential bigger design problem. That's why heuristics are so valuable during collaborative modeling sessions; they are pragmatic and focused on a specific problem at hand, which helps the group in taking the next step instead of circling back to recurring topics without making decisions.

The guiding heuristics are used when we're approaching a problem and feel the need for structure. What do we need to do now? What's the next step? How could we use all the heuristics we have at hand to make progress? We use them when we need some sort of plan that guides us in our endeavors and comforts us that we're doing the right thing. That feeling, or need, very often arises during collaborative modeling sessions—especially when you're facilitating a session.

HEURISTICS FOR THE FACILITATOR IN COLLABORATIVE MODELING SESSIONS

Following are some example situations that you can run into during collaborative modeling sessions where heuristics are very helpful:

- You sense that not everything is said that needs to be said within the group.
- You sense that some people aren't comfortable speaking up, increasing the risk of suppressed knowledge.
- Discussions, conflicts, or polarities start to arise.
- You sense frustration during a Big Picture EventStorming session because the storyline doesn't seem to get structured enough.

The first three example situations can be very uncomfortable and frustrating because they are mainly implicit, can be sensitive, and can hold back progress. When encountering situations like these, one of our go-to heuristics is the following:

GUIDING HEURISTIC   Do sensemaking to test your assumptions.

Sensemaking is a low-key, nonjudgmental exercise to get the group's perspective on a certain topic. It will trigger conversations and allow the minority or alternative perspective to be brought up. We'll dive into sensemaking in more detail in chapter 4. Arising conversations on alternative perspectives trigger another heuristic:

GUIDING HEURISTIC   Ask the group who feels they can relate to or recognize even a part of what was just discussed.

People often recognize parts of alternative views. By making that explicit, the conversation will feel safer and easier.

During a Big Picture EventStorming session it is also common to find these situations. After the chaotic exploration part of Big Picture EventStorming, you can have 100+ Domain Events on your paper roll. Now what? How do you structure that in a nonfrustrating way? Let's clarify with an example conversation from one of our sessions that starts after everyone put their stickies on the brown paper, and we start enforcing the timeline:

> Us: Okay, so the next step is to enforce a timeline here. We have all these Domain Events on stickies, and now we have to create one logical timeline out of them. This also includes getting rid of the duplicates. We'll leave it up to you to decide how you want to do this.
>
> Ralph: Right, so how many days do we have to do this? Ha ha!
>
> Wei: Maybe we can start with the end and work our way backwards?
>
> Rick: We could, but the essence and challenges are in the middle part. I don't really care about the last part to be honest. It's about getting the middle part right because that's where our real problems are.
>
> Ralph: That's not true Rick. Maybe for you it is, but I'm stuck in pointless meetings about that last part more than I would want. Plus, starting in the middle doesn't feel right.
>
> Us: Is there anyone who feels they can relate to or recognizes even a part of what Ralph is saying?
>
> Susan: I do. I know the marketing part at the end is not the most technical and probably not the most interesting for many people here, but there are a lot of dependencies we have to deal with there. So, for me, it would be very valuable to dive into that part.

Ralph: It's absolutely interesting. For everyone here. I think we could all learn a lot from what you put on the brown paper.

Rick: Ok, never mind. I'll shut up then . . . let's start there then, since it's so important. Which Domain Event is first?

Wei: This feels off. It feels a bit condescending to be honest, Rick. The point of us being here is to get to a shared understanding, right? So that means we have to address all the parts of this process and that they are equally important.

Us: Who might partially agree with this statement?

Everybody raised their hand.

Us: Okay, so if we all partly agree with that, then we suggest we divide this process. We can make a first division in stickies. We do that by identifying two Domain Events that are key. Once we have them, we can move all stickies either to the left or right of that particular event. That way, we can create subgroups who can work on parts of the timeline. No worries, we'll converge every 15 minutes so we all stay aligned. Is that okay for the group? Great. Which Domain Event would be a good candidate to start with? Any suggestions?

This is a common conversation during collaborative modeling sessions. As facilitators at the end, we use one of our heuristics. The heuristic we often use in this case is the following:

GUIDING HEURISTIC　　Indicate emerging pivotal events.

We use these pivotal or key events to start sorting and structuring the Domain Events. These events are very important to the group and mark a key point in the flow: only when this happens can other events happen. Domain Events can be placed left or right from a pivotal event, which can unblock the group and get them started in sorting and structuring the timeline.

These are just a couple of examples. There are many more, and the list grows as we gain experience. You might encounter a problem in which more than one heuristic seems to fit. In that case, you're dealing with competing heuristics.

3.2.2　Competing heuristics

Heuristics are very useful, but they can also be competing. Two or more heuristics can be valid and useful at the same time. When that happens, the *competing heuristics* push you in different directions and give different outcomes, even though they are both valid options. What to do then? Let's illustrate with an example from an EventStorming session. When doing Big Picture EventStorming, usually there are more than 10 people in the room working on the same paper roll. Starting to enforce the timeline can be challenging with a big group of people. Effectiveness and the number of insights might go down, some people may turn quiet, and the group might feel they aren't making progress. Two heuristics are valid here:

GUIDING HEURISTIC   Create different groups between pivotal events.

GUIDING HEURISTIC   Add minority wisdom to the group.

Splitting up the group and enforcing the timeline between pivotal events will work in terms of progress and speed, and adding the full and minority wisdom to the group works in terms of completeness. We need the full group for this. It also allows everything to be said by creating a safe space where everyone can share what they want to share. There are also tradeoffs, however: splitting up the group might mean we're not including minority wisdom in all parts of the timeline, and adding minority wisdom might mean we don't finish the timeline. We want to do both—finish the timeline and add minority wisdom to all parts of the timeline—meaning our two valid heuristics are competing. What are we going to do? In this particular case, our heuristics gained nuance as our experience grew. Splitting up the group is the way to go, as long as we converge as a group every 30 minutes or so to walk through the timeline centrally. By doing so, we allow alternative perspectives to be added. By asking "Who can somewhat relate to this?" often during this convergence, we try to add the minority wisdom as much as possible to the subgroups. This is an example of how heuristics can evolve over time, especially competing ones that recur from time to time.

DIVERGING CONVERSATIONS

Here's another example to illustrate these competing heuristics: negotiating boundaries during a collaborative modeling session. A huge part of collaborative modeling is about boundaries: What's in, what's out? How do they relate? Do we need to design for dependencies? Because people usually have a stake in the decisions around boundaries—it affects them and their work—conflicts arise pretty easily. People or groups of people disagree with each other for various reasons that may or may not be about the content itself. As a facilitator, you have to deal with that. Two heuristics that are both valid in this situation are the following:

GUIDING HEURISTIC   Discuss conflicts with the entire group.

GUIDING HEURISTIC   Split and merge during diverging conversations.

These are both valid heuristics, but they compete with each other. Discussing the conflict with the entire group will take time and therefore slow down progress, with a risk of not achieving the desired modeling outcomes for that day. On the other hand, it might result in mutual understanding and trigger long-awaited conversations that needed to take place to really move on. Is it worth it to invest time in that? The other valid heuristic—"split and merge during diverging conversations"—will result in the bigger part of the group continuing with the model, which increases the chances of achieving the desired modeling outcomes for that day. The subgroup can dive into the matter at hand and share their insights later with the entire group. There's a risk here when it comes to mutual understanding regarding the subgroup and the entire group, so what are you going to do?

From experience, you might find that when there are only two or three people in a specific conflict, it's better to split, discuss, and visualize the conflict in a subgroup before coming back to the group. Or you might find that when a social dynamic seems to be causing the conflict, rather than the boundary itself, it's more valuable to discuss the conflict with the entire group and even add some sensemaking exercises. What we're saying is that a set of heuristics is never complete. You might start with a more general one and, after time, add more heuristics to make it more nuanced in a way. You can be flexible when using the guiding heuristics.

3.2.3 *How to use heuristics*

As previously noted, a heuristics toolkit is a personal thing. While heuristics can be shared, they are greatly influenced by your own preferences, knowledge, and experience. Ultimately, there is immense value in learning from your own experiments, trial and error, and personal reflections. Therefore, we recommend that you take time to plan before each session. Write down a few heuristics from others that you might want to apply in the upcoming session, focusing on one or two to integrate into your facilitation. Gradually incorporating these heuristics can be very effective. We also suggest starting a heuristic journal. After every session, whether you participate or facilitate, take a moment to record your observations and experiences. What did you notice? How did the group dynamics unfold? From these insights, you can develop your own heuristics, which will evolve and become more intuitive over time. Initially, you may find yourself referring to your journal often during sessions. However, as you gain experience, you'll likely find that certain heuristics become second nature to you.

> **Exercise 3.1: Get started with using heuristics**
>
> To get you started and encourage you to adopt the new habit of starting a heuristics journal, we'll provide some of our own heuristics at the end of every chapter. Another important insight from this section is that heuristics can drive the design. Using design heuristics can help you with designing boundaries, for example. In the next section, we'll explain how design heuristics can be used to make design decisions by continuing with our BigScreen journey.
>
> To get started with your own heuristics journal, try to capture personal heuristics you use during sessions. These can be collaborative modeling sessions, programming, workshops, or any other. Reflect on decisions you make to maintain flow and get to the next step. Write them down, and reflect on them some more and attempt to generalize them. You can use the heuristics we provide at the end of the chapters as inspiration.

3.3 *Driving the design by understanding the business*

In the previous chapter, we explained how to get better at understanding the business and the business problems. To understand the business better, we create models of those problems through collaborative modeling with the domain experts. Now, the hard part is finding a fitting and sustainable design and architecture.

Let's start with some bad news: there is no perfect solution and no one way to model a system. We know, it's difficult to read this; it took us a long time to accept this too. To be honest, on a bad day, we're still desperately looking for that perfect model, and we believe that's normal, if you really think about this part of the job we're performing. It has fancy titles, such as software designer, senior architect, and so on, as well as fancy (-ity) words such as flexibility, scalability, and extensibility, to describe the system's characteristics we're trying to achieve. Honestly, a more fitting job title would be *clairvoyant.*

- *Why do we need flexibility?* Because companies change, and the system has to change with them.
- *Why do we need scalability?* Because companies grow, and the system has to grow with them.
- *Why do we need extensibility?* Because the companies evolve, and the system has to evolve with them.

You get the idea. So why would clairvoyant be a better description? Basically, we're trying to predict the future. We don't know how companies will change, we don't know what will change, and we don't know when this change will happen. There is a lot of uncertainty when creating software systems, and the only certain thing is that there will be change, which is why there is no perfect solution or correct way to model a system.

And now for the good news! Many great people in our field have done research into software architecture and its characteristics. One of the important things to do in a software system is create explicit boundaries. You can achieve that by dividing the business model into smaller parts. Breaking the business model into smaller parts is often referred to as *modularity.* There are different levels of modularity in a system, but here we'll talk about the creation of deployable units. A *deployable unit* is a component of the system that can be tested and deployed to production independently, for example, a microservice. Before we can create our deployable units, we need to design boundaries for the business model. Modularity is so important because it's both a characteristic and an enabler of other architecture characteristics. This is why you have to investigate and explore how you can break up your business model into smaller parts. In this section, we'll dig a bit deeper into that.

3.3.1 Designing boundaries

In chapter 2, we mentioned that we go from the problem space to the solution space by performing a number of design activities. If we zoom in on those design activities, we're doing a number of iterations on our bounded contexts. We do a variety of design activities to work toward this deeper understanding of where the boundaries are in our software system. Designing the first boundaries, Iteration 1 in figure 3.2, relies on intuition. While heuristics are specific mental shortcuts with identifiable patterns, *intuitions* are more general feelings or judgments. But intuitions might sometimes be the result of internalized heuristics, which you apply unconsciously, while drawing the first bounded contexts.

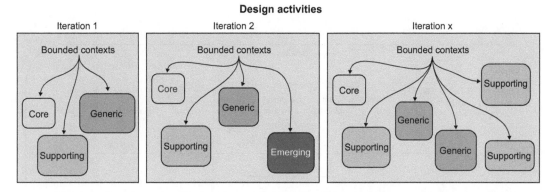

Figure 3.2   Zooming in on the design activities, we can see that this is an iterative process where we design toward a deeper model. In each iteration, the model captures more of the complexity of the domain. Sometimes, we can identify the bounded context as the Core, Supporting, or Generic domain, and sometimes one emerges that we can't identify yet (Emerging).

The more experience and heuristics you use, the better your intuition will become. In other words, the collection of heuristics that you unconsciously apply during that first iteration will grow. But don't worry, we're giving you an intuition starters kit called "Find the natural boundaries in the domain" to help.

INTUITION STARTERS KIT

"Find the natural boundaries in the domain" is a high-level heuristic, which encapsulates several other heuristics, as shown here, in the intuition starters kit. When starting out on your own, this high-level heuristic isn't useful on your own because you are still building your intuition. That's where the intuition starters kit heuristics that you can apply to find the natural boundaries. The more experience you have designing boundaries and using heuristics, the more heuristics you'll apply when you say "Let's find the natural boundaries."

> **DESIGN HEURISTIC**   Find the natural boundaries in the domain.

The intuition starters kit includes the following heuristics, which will allow you to be successful in using the "find the natural boundaries in the domain" heuristic:

- Split according to the language
- Split according to the departments
- Split according to the actors

Let's apply the intuition starters kit to BigScreen. In figure 3.3, you can see a small part of the Big Picture EventStorm of BigScreen.

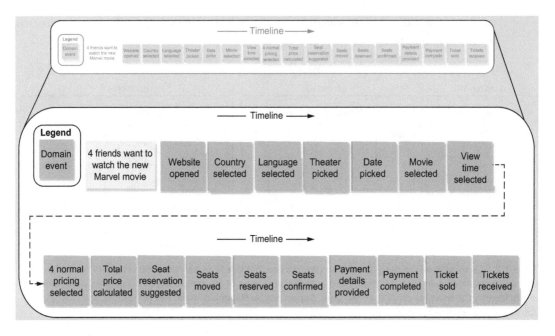

Figure 3.3   A small part of the EventStorm on purchasing tickets with a legend. The output of an EventStorming session, which happens in the problem space, will be used as the input for our design activities. Those design activities will give us bounded contexts for our solution space. (Note: An EventStorm normally appears on just one line as shown at the top of the figure here, but to fit the page and make it readable, we set the EventStorm on two lines.)

We created two bounded contexts in our first design iteration (figure 3.4): Movie Scheduling and Ticket Purchasing. To create these boundaries, we applied design heuristic "Split according to the language." When we look at the language, we notice that movie scheduling talks about how our users search for a movie. Once they pick a specific movie, in a specific theater, at a specific day and time, they start the process of purchasing tickets. So, until we have our Domain "Event 4 Normal Pricing Selected," we're searching for movie scheduling. Before that, a ticket didn't exist. So, we split the EventStorm right before Domain Event "4 Normal Pricing Selected," where the concept of a ticket exists, and we create two boundaries.

Of course, we could have picked heuristic "Split according to the departments" or heuristic "Split according to the actors" from the starters kit and had a different starting point, or we could have applied all three at once and gotten a lot more bounded contexts (which is what you do when you have a lot more experience). The important thing is that you pick one, apply it, and start your second iteration. A lot of participants in our collaborative modeling sessions fall into the trap of starting to discuss what bounded context there can be instead of modeling them out in iterations. They ask each other,

"How many bounded contexts should we have?" or "What should they be, and are they correct?" This leads us to a guiding heuristic to use during your design activities:

GUIDING HEURISTIC   Pick some boundaries to start with and iterate.

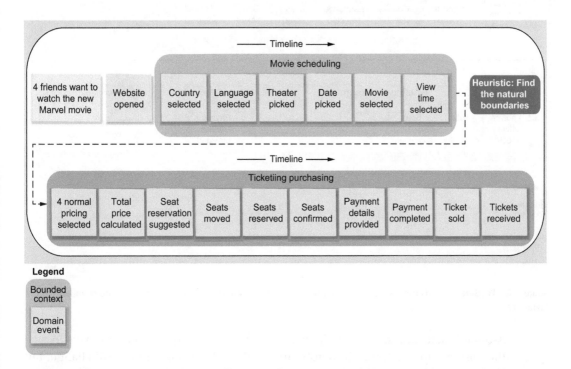

Figure 3.4   BigScreen's natural boundaries. We picked one of our heuristics from our intuition starters kit and applied it to the EventStorm, creating two bounded contexts: Movie Scheduling and Ticket Purchasing. This way, we have a starting point to dig deeper with other design activities.

So that is what we did in BigScreen. If we dig a bit deeper, we notice the Payment Details Provided and Payment Completed events. Remember our business model canvas? We said that payment providers are key partners, so these events don't happen in our system, but in the system of the payment providers. We have to communicate with that external system and translate their ubiquitous language into our language. This is true for all communication that happens with external systems, so a good design heuristic is the following:

DESIGN HEURISTIC   Communication with external systems happens in a separate bounded context.

In figure 3.5, you can see how the BigScreen EventStorm looks when applying that heuristic.

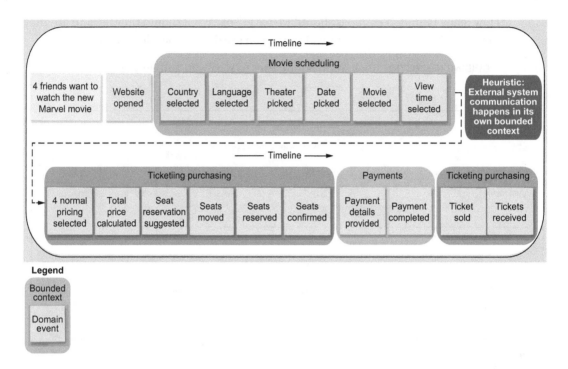

Legend

Bounded
context

Domain
event

**Figure 3.5   BigScreen's external systems communication is encapsulated in a new bounded context called
Payments.**

As mentioned earlier, while designing the boundaries of our system, we have to take
the business and its future into account. We don't know how things will change, but
the business has a better understanding of that. The company might not know how it
will change but can see the potential value of some business processes. This leads us to
another design heuristic:

DESIGN HEURISTIC   Optimize for future potential.

Understanding the future potential is something you need to learn from your domain
experts. You can optimize for the future, but only the domain experts can tell you if
this has potential from a business perspective.

If we look at BigScreen again, where would the future potential be? We had two ideas
for that: where the prices get calculated and where the seats get allocated. We spoke
with the business and explained how we could change the pricing model and the seat
allocations model in the future.

For the pricing model, right now, BigScreen doesn't offer subscriptions yet, but the
idea is floating around in the office. Some theaters are struggling because there aren't
many movie viewers, and even the blockbusters aren't doing well. We're unsure how

subscriptions would work, but we do know that there could be multiple subscriptions similar to the ticket pricing, and the domain experts told us it's worth testing subscriptions in those theaters that aren't doing well. So, first, we put that in a different bounded context: Price Calculation.

Second, the system suggests seats to the customers. Right now, this is a very simple flow that doesn't take the customers preferences into account, and we told them we could change that. If we change the seat allocations algorithm to take customer preference into account, we wouldn't have to perform it so often, *and* customers could purchase tickets quicker because they don't have to change seats. We want to start collecting data on this to be able to analyze how often customers change their seats. The domain experts liked our suggestion but said this wasn't something we should try to do this year because the "Anytime, Anywhere" campaign was more important. We agreed, but we introduced a bounded context called Seat Allocations, to make sure we could implement this easier when the time was right.

We also changed the name of the Ticket Purchasing bounded context to Ticketing because the logic inside this boundary now focuses on creating and sending out tickets to our movie viewers and not on purchasing a ticket. We now have five boundaries in total, as shown in figure 3.6.

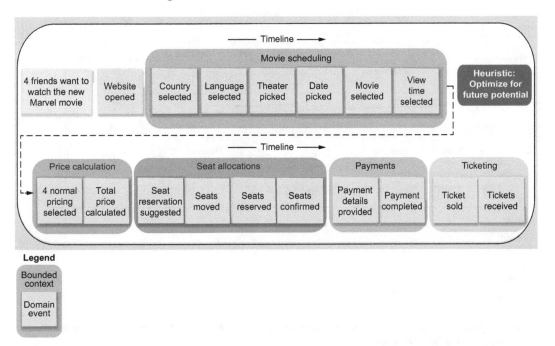

Figure 3.6   BigScreen's future potential bounded contexts: Price Calculation and Seat Allocations. We also renamed the Ticket Purchasing boundary to Ticketing because the business logic inside this boundary is about creating and sending out tickets.

Introducing a separate boundary for price calculation means more communication happening between bounded contexts because Seat Allocations, Ticketing, and Price Calculation have a dependency on each other. We have another design heuristic in our toolkit that pushes us in a different direction:

DESIGN HEURISTIC   Split bounded contexts based on how it would happen in a paper world, without using software.

In a "paper" world, before we digitized ticket purchases, you went to the cinema and purchased your tickets when you arrived. Calculating the price was done manually with premade tickets, similar to the ones from those rolls you get when entering a raffle. With this heuristic, we would not separate the Price Calculation from the Ticketing bounded contexts. We only have two bounded contexts called Ticket Purchase and Seat Allocations, as shown in figure 3.7. These are the competing heuristics we spoke about previously.

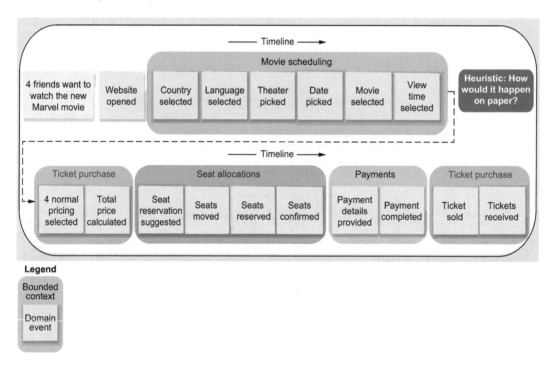

Figure 3.7   **BigScreen's paper process bounded contexts. Price calculating and ticketing are one bounded context instead of two, called Ticket Purchase.**

How do we select one of the options now? First, we see if we have any other design heuristics in our toolkit that could help us decide. Second, we look for the tradeoff that both designs give us. If we pick the design in figure 3.7, there would be fewer dependencies between bounded contexts, but Ticket Purchase would have more internal business logic and dependencies, increasing the local complexity of the bounded context. If we pick the other one (refer to figure 3.6) there is a higher global complexity in the system because we have more dependencies between bounded contexts, but less local complexity for both bounded contexts. Which tradeoff is better? That depends (sorry)—we would need to dig deeper into the teams, the business, and so on to answer that question. One thing's for sure, though, we can't answer that question on our own.

Exercise 3.2: Your current bounded contexts

In the previous chapter, you created an EventStorm for one of your own scenarios. In this exercise, you'll use the output of exercise 2.2 to apply the intuition starters kit. Apply the heuristics from the starters kit to your EventStorm by drawing boxes around the stickies that fit together. Give the boxes a different color for each bounded context, as we did in our examples from BigScreen.

When you've applied the heuristics, try to find names for the bounded contexts that you discovered. Look at the stickies inside the boundaries to come up with a fitting name.

3.3.2 *Why boundaries are designed through collaboration*

When designing boundaries, there are a lot of different perspectives that you need to take into account. In our BigScreen examples, we mostly focused on the business value. We didn't think about the user experience, the technical constraints, and so on. We still need to put on a lot of different thinking hats to come to a good design. One person can't do this on their own, which is why designing boundaries also happens in collaboration. We can approach these modeling sessions a bit differently though. We start with a few iterations on the design with just the people who are directly involved in creating the software system. Afterward, we can validate the outcome of those iterations with the other stakeholders. We take their feedback and start iterating again. Slowly, a better model will arise throughout this process because we gain insights and a deeper understanding.

So far, we've used EventStorming as a tool to design the boundaries. There are different tools that you can use here too. If you want to know how commands and events will flow through the system, you can use a *domain message flow diagram* (figure 3.8), which is based on Domain Storytelling but specific to bounded context design.

Context mapping will give you another visualization, which mainly focuses on the models, language, and team communication between bounded contexts (https://github .com/ddd-crew/context-mapping). All those visualizations will give you new insights and new tradeoffs to consider when designing. A design is never finished, but you have to start building it anyway at some point. In chapter 10, we'll go into that polarity between designing and implementing.

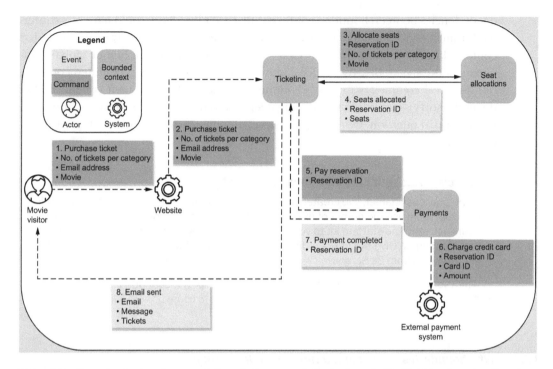

Figure 3.8   Example of a domain message flow diagram, a modeling tool created by Nick Tune based on Domain Storytelling but specific to bounded context design. You can learn how to use this tool at https://mng.bz/Ddyg.

3.3.3   From design to architecture

Many people think that designing your bounded contexts is the only design activity needed to create the architecture of a system, but nothing is further from the truth. An architecture is more than the bounded contexts. This isn't a book on architecture, so we won't go into a lot of detail here, but we do want to show you the relationship between bounded contexts and deployable units (and sneak in some more heuristics for your journal).

Looking at the current architecture of BigScreen's software system in a bit more detail (figure 3.9), we can see that it has multiple domains, a single bounded context, and one deployable unit.

Taking the newly designed bounded contexts in mind, a possible architecture could be as shown in figure 3.10.

Notice that deployable units and bounded contexts don't have a 1:1 relationship. Depending on the size or the dependencies, bounded contexts can align with a deployable unit, but they are different concepts. Bounded contexts are linguistic boundaries, where deployable units are boundaries of deployment. You can have multiple deployable units for one bounded context, but we don't advise that. If you create multiple deployable units from a single bounded context, those deployable units will have a high chance of being changed together because the logic elements inside a bounded context are dependent on each other. On the other hand, you can put multiple bounded contexts into a single deployable unit, often nowadays referred to as a modular monolith (the rebranding was needed because, in the past, people didn't implement the monolith architecture correctly, so that got tainted). Don't make a deployable unit too big though, or you'll start losing adaptability and scalability.

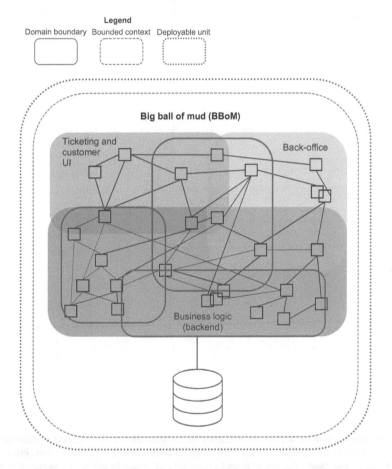

Figure 3.9   Detailed current architecture of BigScreen. This architecture has a single bounded context, which is Big Ball of Mud, and a single deployable unit. This type of architecture is referred to as a monolith. A monolith isn't a bad architecture style, but the problem is that we're lacking a clear architecture and boundaries. If we put the domain boundaries on top, you can clearly see the problem.

Sometimes, changes affect multiple bounded contexts, so you deploy the bounded contexts that change together. This leads us to another helpful design heuristic:

DESIGN HEURISTIC   What changes together, gets deployed together.

This heuristic is derived from a more generic heuristic. We use this more generic heuristic when we look for bounded contexts: "The business logic that changes together, stays together." Another heuristic that you can apply when looking for bounded contexts is the following:

DESIGN HEURISTIC   What changes together, stays together.

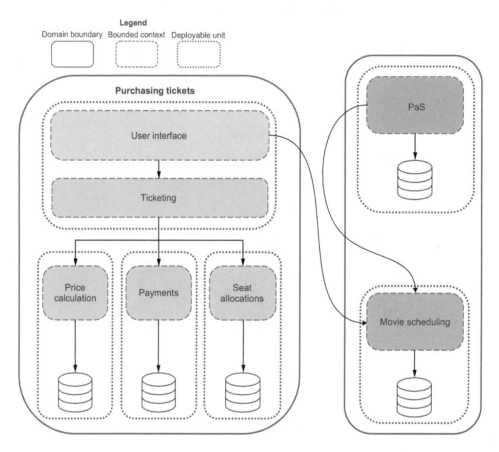

Figure 3.10   New architecture for BigScreen, designed via collaborative modeling. This architecture captures the complexity of the domain with multiple bounded contexts and deployable units. Price Calculation, Payments, and Seat Allocations bounded contexts align one-to-one with a deployable unit. User Interface and Ticketing are two bounded contexts in one deployable unit. PaS and Movie Scheduling are a single domain but are in two deployable units. This architecture makes the "Anytime, Anywhere" campaign possible.

We split Ticket Purchase into two different bounded contexts—Price Calculation and Ticketing—because it was more valuable to the business to have the pricing separate. While creating deployable units, we can decide to deploy them together, as long as it makes sense. If two years from now, we're still deploying them together, we can decide to merge the bounded contexts (this is also a heuristic).

One last thought before we move on to the next chapter: during this exercise, we focused on a very small part of the business. Big Picture EventStorming stays at a very high level. Because of that, the bounded contexts and architecture are simplified. Should we build the actual system of BigScreen, we would stay much longer in the problem space and dive much deeper into understanding the problems. We would also spend a lot more time on designing the bounded contexts before we used the design as input for the solution space.

3.4 Collaborative software design catalysts

- During a meeting, it's beneficial to ask the following: "What do you mean by *X*?" where *X* represents a business-specific term. A lot of confusing communication can be resolved by creating a shared understanding of domain-specific concepts.
- During collaborative modeling, it's beneficial to make assumptions, questions, and conflicts clear by jotting them down on a sticky note.
- Aim to extract and clarify people's heuristics from their assumptions, questions, and suggestions for a good design. This practice of making heuristics explicit can be a valuable part of the process.

3.5 Chapter heuristics

As mentioned, we'll start collecting our personal heuristics at the end of every chapter. These can serve as inspiration for you to start your own journal. Feel free to use, edit, and complement them as you please.

Design heuristics: heuristics to solve a specific problem

- Split according to the language.
- Split according to the departments.
- Split according to the actors.
- Communication with external systems happens in a separate bounded context.
- Optimize for future potential.
- Split bounded contexts based on how it would happen in a paper world, without using software.
- What changes together, gets deployed together.
- What changes together, stays together.
- If we're still deploying the bounded contexts together after two years, we merge them into one.

Guiding heuristics: heuristics that guide our use of other heuristics (i.e., meta-heuristics)

- Do sensemaking to test your assumptions.
- Ask the group who feels they can relate to or recognizes even a part of what was just discussed.
- Indicate emerging pivotal events.
- Create different groups between pivotal events.

- Add minority wisdom to the group.
- Discuss conflicts with the entire group.
- Split and merge during diverging conversations.

3.6 Further reading

- *Adaptive Systems with Domain-Driven Design, Wardley Mapping, and Team Topologies: Architecture for Flow* by Susanne Kaiser (Pearson Education, 2024)
- *Architecture Modernization: Socio-Technical Alignment of Software, Strategy, and Structure* by Nick Tune with Jean-Georges Perrin (Manning, 2024, www.manning .com/books/architecture-modernization)
- "Are software patterns simply a handy way to package design heuristics?" by Rebecca Wirfs-Brock (PLoP '17: Proceedings of the 24th Conference on Pattern Languages of Programs)
- *Design and Reality* by Rebecca Wirfs-Brock and Mathias Verraes (Leanpub, https://leanpub.com/design-and-reality)
- *Learning Systems Thinking* by Diana Montalion (O'Reilly Media, 2024)
- *System Design Heuristics* by Gerald M. Weinberg (Leanpub, https://leanpub.com/ systemdesignheuristics)
- *Thinking in Systems: A Primer* by Donella H. Meadows (Chelsea Green Publishing, 2008)
- "Traces, tracks, trails, and paths: An Exploration of How We Approach Software Design" by Rebecca Wirfs-Brock (PLoP '18: Proceedings of the 25th Conference on Pattern Languages of Programs)

Summary

- Software design and architecture are inevitable in development, with "bad design" often arising from implicit, misunderstood, or unmade decisions. Making these aspects explicit through collaborative modeling is key to managing complexity and ensuring shared understanding within teams.
- Language and definitions play a critical role in collaborative modeling, highlighting the importance of establishing a shared vocabulary to prevent misunderstandings and streamline decision-making processes.
- BigScreen's shift to Agile methodologies revealed challenges in adapting to up-front architecture, emphasizing the need for software teams to be trained and take ownership of software architecture to avoid bottlenecks and foster iterative development.
- Sociotechnical systems emphasize the interconnectedness of social, technical, and cognitive components within work environments, advocating for a holistic approach to optimizing workspaces and technology decisions.

- Collaborative modeling and design decisions within sociotechnical frameworks focus on inclusive, participatory processes, ensuring that technological advancements and workspace designs enhance rather than disrupt team dynamics and overall system efficiency.

- Heuristics are simple rules to make quick decisions. The three different types of heuristics help you drive the design and facilitate collaborative modeling sessions based on experience and knowledge.

- Heuristics compete when more than one heuristic is valid at the same time, but push you in a different direction. Based on tradeoffs and experience, you can decide what the outcome of both paths is and determine the best way forward.

- Heuristics evolve and increase (in numbers) over time and experience. Keeping a journal and adding to it after every session is a great way to build your heuristic toolkit.

- Considering various perspectives and using tools beyond EventStorming, such as domain message flow diagrams or context mapping, lead to insights and refinement.

- Bounded contexts and deployable units shape system architecture, emphasizing adaptability and the principle of deploying together what changes together for effective design and implementation.

The ingredients of
collaborative modeling

This chapter covers

- The collaborative modeling stages
- Sensemaking during collaborative modeling
  sessions
- The effect of using check-in and check-out
- The collaboration styles you can use during
  sessions

Our first collaborative modeling sessions didn't go so well. We were part of a development team, and as a developer, architect, and so on, we could see the huge benefit that collaborative modeling and its tools could bring us, but we had a hard time convincing other people of its power. Mistakes were made along the way, and they were ours. Over time, we adapted and discovered an approach that worked well. In this chapter, we'll share that approach with you, so you can learn from our experiences (and avoid these mistakes). We'll describe the following six stages we use to organize a successful collaborative modeling session:

1 Preparation

2 Check-in

3 Modeling with tools

4 Check-out

5 Retrospective

6 Communication and documentation

In this chapter, we'll first give a brief overview of all the stages. Next, we'll talk about the preparation that goes into organizing a collaborative modeling session. Then, we'll cover the importance of sensemaking during a check-in at the start and a check-out at the end of a collaborative modeling session. We'll teach you how to create good sense-making exercises, which you need during the modeling exercises to probe the shadows of the group. In chapter 3, we discussed the importance of modeling different options, but coming up with these options isn't easy. There are a few styles that you can use to kick-start generating options, which we'll discuss in section 4.5. No modeling session goes perfectly, so we'll also explain how to evaluate the session and create feedback loops for the following sessions.

4.1 The collaborative modeling stages

In the previous chapters, we've mentioned the collaborative modeling session many times. The session is where the actual collaborative modeling happens. But, as a facilitator, your job doesn't start at the beginning of a session nor end when the session is over. There is a lot that needs to happen before a session and after a session is finished. That is why the session is a part of a larger undertaking. Figure 4.1 shows a single flow with all the building stages. There is a good chance that you have multiple of these flows going at the same time, and each flow will be at a different stage.

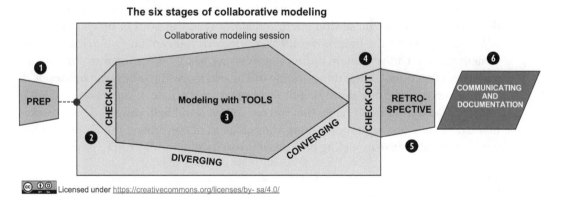

Licensed under https://creativecommons.org/licenses/by-sa/4.0/

Figure 4.1   The six stages of collaborative modeling: prep, check-in, modeling with tools, check-out, retrospective, and communicating and documentation. The collaborative modeling session is a subpart of the entire flow.

4.1.1   Why use our stages?

Introducing collaborative modeling, such as EventStorming, into a company can be challenging. Reflecting on our initial attempt at implementing it in the company we were working for at the time, it turned out to be a disaster. This was due to several reasons:

- We weren't familiar with EventStorming. We followed a session during a meetup and wanted to try this out in our company, so we had 30 minutes of experience with the tool in total.
- We invited all the people on the team to participate, who had a total of 0 minutes experience with EventStorming. We didn't give much context to why we were scheduling this, what the intent was, or what was going to happen. It resulted in a lot of shadows in the group, resistance behavior, and conflicts.
- We wanted to explore if there was a better way to schedule surgeries, which was a business process of an existing product. This type of exercise isn't fitting for a first session, which we didn't know at the time. It's very hard to let go of how something already works in software. Combine that with very little experience with the tool, and we were in a very difficult situation for a first modeling session.

It might seem that we were really setting ourselves up for failure, but at that point in time, it wasn't that obvious. Hindsight is a lovely thing to have. Getting good at facilitating sessions takes time and experience. On top of that, you need to teach a bunch of new tools to other people at the same time. Take it from us, that isn't an easy thing to do. So what should you do instead? Focus on getting to know the tools that will be used during the session. Find a few enthusiastic colleagues that are open to experimenting, and learn the tools together. Once you've done that a few times, you can put on your facilitating hat and organize a session.

People are often cautious when it comes to trying out new things. It's important that the participants leave the session energized and spread the word of how wonderful it is. Word of mouth is the most powerful advertisement you can have when introducing something new. Unfortunately, during your sessions, you'll be dealing with participants who aren't that open to new things. Some will be excited, while others will be skeptical. A lot depends on getting those skeptical people to participate in the session, which is why we created this flow of stages that you can follow. It will help you avoid the mistakes we made in our first session, meaning your chances of convincing the skeptics of the power of collaborative modeling have just improved dramatically. You're welcome!

4.1.2   The stages

Alright, let's get this flow started! As you can see in figure 4.1, shown earlier, there are six stages to the flow. We'll start by giving you a brief summary of each stage, which you can use as a cheat sheet when you're putting all of this into action. So, bookmark this page!

STAGE 1: PREPARATION

As the first stage, *preparation* refers to preparing the modeling session. During the preparation, you'll perform the following tasks:

- Define the goal.
- Find a good location.
- Determine who to invite.
- Create the agenda.
- Select the tools and material.
- Prepare the check-in, check-out, and sensemaking exercises.
- Define a good outcome.
- Prepare the space.

STAGE 2: THE CHECK-IN

A *check-in* is a moment at the beginning of the session where you focus on the participants instead of the goal. The purpose of a check-in is to make the participants comfortable and to start orienting them toward the goal of the session.

STAGE 3: MODELING WITH TOOLS

The *modeling with tools* stage is where the actual collaborative modeling happens. This stage can take many forms and have many durations, depending on the goal you set for the session. The tools you'll be using for a session also depend on the goal. It's very hard to prepare for this, to be honest, so you might not want to overdo it. You don't want to hold down the discovery by sticking blindly to the goal of the session. The session goes where the group wants it to go. Discovery is exploratory by nature because you want to examine business problems, try different designs, and so on. Sometimes, it's hard for a group to keep it going. When that happens, there are *enabling constraints* that you can try as a facilitator to get the group unstuck, a group of these enabling traits are called *collaboration styles*, and we'll dive a bit deeper into them later in the chapter.

At the end of the modeling with tools stage, you'll go into *convergence* mode. Converging here means that you'll stop the discovery part of the modeling session and start working toward summarizing the discovery and planning the next steps. The group will have to start making decisions:

- What do we explore next?
- What do we do with this information?
- Which parts of the discovery do we want to dive into deeper?

Participants will have different opinions here, but the group will still have to make decisions. There is a lot to be said about making decisions in a collaborative way, which is why we dedicated chapter 9 to this topic.

STAGE 4: THE CHECK-OUT

A *check-out* is fairly similar to a check-in. It's a moment at the end of the session where you focus on the participants again. A check-out does have a different goal from a check-in, however. During the session, conflicts may arise, and, sometimes, the tension gets really high. The purpose of a check-out is to leave this conflict and the session itself at the door when leaving the session.

STAGE 5: RETROSPECTIVE

As we mentioned in the introduction, we made a lot of mistakes when we first started collaborative modeling. One of the biggest mistakes we made was not reflecting on the collaboration that had happened. It's important to understand what went well, what could have gone better, what important knowledge the participants gained, and so on. This *retrospective* stage happens after the session is finished, and it doesn't include the entire group. We'll discuss this further in section 4.6.

STAGE 6: COMMUNICATION AND DOCUMENTATION

If the absence of a retrospective was one of the biggest mistakes we made, not communicating or documenting the sessions was *the* biggest mistake. As a facilitator, it's not your job to communicate and document the session, but it *is* your job to facilitate it. During the *communication and documentation* stage, you want to observe and keep track of whether the participants are following through with the decisions that were made and whether these decisions and their results are properly documented. If not, you want to act upon that. Advice on how to do this can be found in chapter 11.

We know this is a lot to keep in mind as a facilitator, but don't worry, as this becomes intuitive after a while. You'll spend less time preparing a session, and you'll know when to schedule a retrospective and what needs to be communicated and documented. Until that time comes, our advice is to follow the structure we provided for you.

4.2   *Preparing for a session*

The first step of collaborative modeling is preparation (aka prep). Preparation has two meanings here: prepare the content of the session, and prepare the space of the session. We'll start with digging a bit deeper into preparing the content.

4.2.1   *Preparing the content*

To have a successful collaborative modeling session, a lot of people want to understand what they can expect will happen during this session and why they were invited. The best way to achieve that is by adding an agenda when setting up the meeting. We created a template (figure 4.2) that will help you with that. Feel free to use it as is, or adapt it to something that works for you.

In figure 4.3, you can find the finished template for one of the follow-up sessions we did with BigScreen. Because we were external, we prepared the session with the development team to make sure we were on the right track. It pays off not to do the preparations alone, so invite one or two people to help you with this.

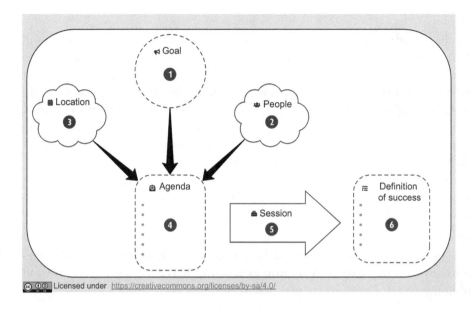

Licensed under https://creativecommons.org/licenses/by-sa/4.0/

Figure 4.2
Our preparation template for preparing the content of a collaborative modeling session

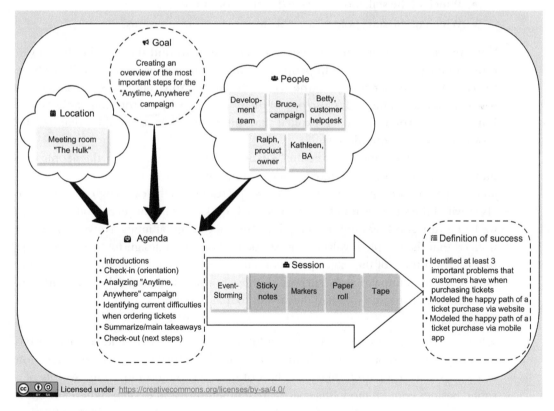

Licensed under https://creativecommons.org/licenses/by-sa/4.0/

Figure 4.3 The preparation template of BigScreen's follow-up modeling session, which we prepared together with the development team

THE GOAL

Creating the agenda is easier when you already know what the goal of the session will be, so that is where we start when filling in the template. It's tempting to try and create some excitement or curiosity when setting up the meeting by staying a bit vague on what will happen during a session (especially when it's the first time), but don't do that. Being "boring"—aka fully informing the participants—is the right way to go here. Most people already have full agendas, and it's important to inform them what we get out of the session. Don't make it too technical either. Remember, not all stakeholders in a collaborative modeling session have a technical background.

The first session we organized in BigScreen to redesign the Big Ball of Mud was focused on understanding the new campaign. We formulated the goal as follows: "Creating an overview of the most important steps for the 'Anytime, Anywhere' campaign."

THE PEOPLE

When you define a clear goal for the modeling session, you can determine which stakeholders to invite for this session. When you look at the goal of the session, ask yourself two questions:

- Which of the stakeholders have the questions for this goal?
- Which of the stakeholders are able to answer these questions?

You can use the stakeholder analysis from chapter 2 to find the stakeholders. Even though we try to invite the right people, it's important to know that this will rarely be the case. We never had a session where we didn't hear: "You would have to ask this person, but they aren't here." It's also one of the reasons why EventStorming has hotspots. With hotspots, you can make it explicit that there is another stakeholder that has the answer to a specific question.

When it came to understanding the "Anytime, Anywhere" campaign, the people who had the questions were the development team, the product owner, and the business analyst. The person who could answer these questions was the campaign manager. We also invited the supervisor of the customer helpdesk. This might seem a bit weird, but we had a very good reason for doing that. During our initial intake conversations, we noticed that the people involved were so focused on the redesign for the mobile app that they lost track of the major problems customers had right now when purchasing tickets. For the campaign to be successful, those problems needed to be dealt with too, so we invited the person who had the answer to that question.

THE LOCATION

When you organize a session, you need a lot of modeling space. An ideal location has a lot of empty walls or a long table that you can use. Unfortunately, the ideal location rarely exists, so you have to make the best of it. The two most important aspects of a room, besides enough modeling space, are temperature and oxygen. When a room is too cold or too hot, attention spans drop, which can make a difference in the effectiveness of the session.

When you're dealing with a team that mostly collaborates remotely, it's better to organize these sessions remotely as well. In that case you're very lucky, because finding a good location isn't a problem you need to solve. (Don't get too excited about this, there are other problems that might pop up, such as time zone differences, bad internet connections, bad sound, and people having small screens to work on!)

THE AGENDA

When people read the agenda of the session, they need to understand why they were invited. People like to prepare themselves for a meeting as well—that is why we send out an agenda in the first place—so make sure it's clear what is expected from them. When we created the agenda for BigScreen, we added an introduction to it. The campaign manager and helpdesk supervisor had never spoken to the software team before, so they had no idea who those people were or what their responsibilities were. A lot of companies deal with silo problems in which departments rarely communicate with one another. This is especially true in software development. Make sure you leave room for people to get to know one another, as that will make the rest of the modeling session a lot easier. We also added the topic "Identifying current difficulties when ordering tickets" explicitly, so that Betty from the helpdesk department understood why she was invited and could prepare herself for the session. We also like to send some information up front if we know we will be doing EventStorming or use some other tools, so people have a feeling for what we will be doing.

After the agenda is finished, you can schedule the meeting. When you send out the invitations, make sure that you add the goal and the agenda in the invite. We like to send out the invite at least a week before the actual session, so people have time to prepare or ask questions.

THE SESSION

In this step, there are a few things you need to do: prepare the check-in and the check-out, think about possible sensemaking exercises, and select the tools that you'll use during the session. We'll discuss the check-in, check-out, and sensemaking exercises, as well as how to prepare for them, in sections 4.3 and 4.4.

Selecting the (possible) tools that you'll use during the session is important because you need to know which materials you need to bring to the meeting. If you're organizing an EventStorming session, you need a lot of different-colored stickies and markers. If you want to fill in the Business Model Canvas, then a whiteboard with markers and a wiper are better suited. After a while, you'll know by heart the fixed set of materials you need to have when modeling. We even have an entire flight case with all the materials we use so we're always good to go! As a backup, we have some stickies and markers in our backpack. When the session is remote, you'll need an online collaborative whiteboard and your favorite videoconferencing tool instead.

DEFINITION OF SUCCESS

The *definition of success* refers to a few guidelines, specifically for this session, that allow the facilitator to assess whether they have reached the goal of the session. This definition isn't shared with the participants because we don't want our definition of success to turn into a hard objective. Our definition of success for the modeling session with BigScreen includes the following:

- Modeled the happy path of a ticket purchase via website
- Modeled the happy path of a ticket purchase via mobile app
- Identified at least three important problems that customers have when purchasing tickets

Don't turn these definitions into hard objectives, as they represent the ideal future and are just there to guide you during the session. Modeling sessions are a bit unpredictable in nature because you're never sure what topic will come up. Sometimes, the conversations diverge completely from your initial goal—and that is okay, so long as the group explicitly decided to do so. The guidelines that weren't accomplished during the session can be used as an input to prepare a new collaborative modeling session.

4.2.2   Preparing the space

When you're organizing a session, you want as many people as possible to participate in the collaboration. You want them writing stickies, moving stickies, making little side notes, asking questions, and so on. At the same time, for a variety of reasons, people are a bit cautious to participate. You can try to remove as much of the *participation barrier* as possible by preparing the space. Preparing the space for a session is different depending on whether you're having a remote session or an in-person session.

IN-PERSON SESSION

When you're having an in-person session, a good way to lower the participation barrier is by removing the chairs and tables from the room (if you're not using them as modeling space). When people are already standing up, it's easier for them to pick up a sticky and hang it on the board. When you remove the chairs completely from the room, it looks more spacious too.

> **NOTE**   Keep your participants in mind; not everyone can go hours without being seated. In addition, make sure you add regular breaks to the session.

In our early days, we had learned from our first disaster and done an excellent job at preparing the content and the space. We had prepared a beautiful PowerPoint to explain the purpose of this meeting. The stickies and markers were neatly arranged on a small table. We were particularly proud of ourselves because we hadn't forgotten about the chairs: they were neatly stacked in the corner of the room. The participants started coming in while we were doing some last-minute checks. When we turned around, all the participants were sitting down. One of them had grabbed a stacked chair and every other person in the room had followed their example. The participants were very enthusiastic: they answered all the questions and showed their own PowerPoints to visualize their business processes. They just never got out of the chairs again—no matter what we tried. We never left the chairs in the room after that, except the exact amount for those people who can't stand for a period of time.

REMOTE SESSION

Remote sessions have default barriers that you can't get rid of: all participants are physically removed from one another, some participants struggle with the tools, and so on. This makes remote sessions harder than in-person ones. The good news is that we've picked up a few tips to help you with that.

First, the online whiteboard tool should be easy to use. A few examples of popular whiteboards are FigJam, Microsoft Whiteboard, Lucidspark, Mural, and Conceptboard, and our favorite is Miro. To lower the barrier, you can prepare some easy tips that can help your participants with using the whiteboard. In figure 4.4, you can see our Miro tips. Second, make sure you have clear joining instructions when you send out the invitation. Add a link to the whiteboard you'll use during the session, with the tips and the agenda already on it. If you added an introduction section to the agenda, prepare a small introduction section they can already fill in before the session. This way, they can already practice a bit with the tool; however, always account for some extra time at the start because not everyone will have time to practice beforehand.

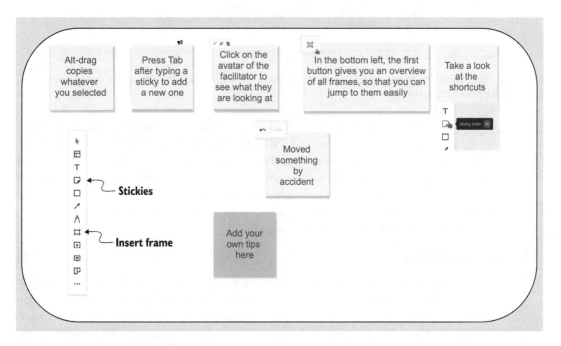

Figure 4.4   An example of whiteboard tips for the participants. These tips are for Miro specifically, but you can do this when using another whiteboard too.

Create an initial structure for the group to lower the "empty space" paralysis. When you plan an EventStorming, add some stickies to the whiteboard. Fill some of them in with events, and leave a whole bunch of blank stickies around them, as shown in figure 4.5.

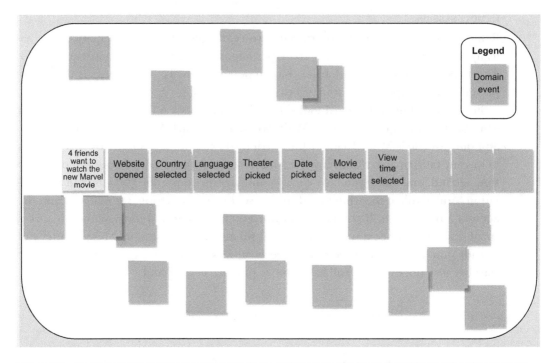

Figure 4.5   Counteract the "empty space" paralysis by adding some stickies to the whiteboard during a remote collaborative modeling session.

We try to avoid hybrid sessions in which some people are remote, while others are sitting together in a conference room. It's an added layer of complexity for the facilitators that is very difficult to deal with. If you can't avoid hybrid sessions, at least make sure the people who are in the same room each have their own laptop to participate on the whiteboard and preferably have headphones with them so that everyone is joined in the same way. Sensemaking and a good check-in also help to lower the participation barrier, which we'll discuss in the next section.

4.3   Sensemaking

Ever been in a situation where you felt something was going on in a group, but you couldn't pinpoint what it was exactly? Your gut feeling observed shadows, but you couldn't really put a finger on it. Maybe you felt tension or sensed frustration within the group. Not addressing it could really hinder conversations, collaboration, and progress. At the same time, addressing it isn't easy. Social dynamics, power dynamics and psychological (un)safety make it hard to call this out in a group. What if your assumption is wrong? What if the group wasn't feeling hindered by what you thought you observed? This is a delicate matter that should be handled in a delicate way.

As facilitators, we find ourselves in situations like this all the time: conversations and decisions that keep cycling back to one specific topic, workshops where some people keep diving into details and others want to stay more high-level, or groups beating around the bush and skillfully avoiding certain topics. These situations can lead to tension, slowing down, and healthy or unhealthy conflict.

Sensemaking helps us in getting and providing relevant insights to guide a workshop, meeting, or decision-making effort. It's also a great way to make shadows explicit to the rest of the group in a neutral, nonjudgmental way and then address them properly. In this section, we'll dig into what sensemaking is and how to use it, what benefits it brings, and how it helps address the shadows in a group.

4.3.1 Conscious and unconscious minds

Before diving into sensemaking, let's go back to our mental model. More specifically, the shadows that participants bring to collaborative modeling sessions. Although they seem more in the background at first, they heavily influence the outcomes, social dynamics, and progress of these sessions. There's more than meets the eye here as ranking, cognitive bias, assumptions, polarities, conflicts, and so on can all live in the shadows of groups and might even turn into demons when not addressed and managed properly. Negative feelings, frustration, or conflict can drag on for too long, becoming bigger and bigger until they can no longer be suppressed and ultimately turn into demons. This is where the facilitator can shine by turning on the flashlight so the shadows become visible.

Our mental model, and way of working, is of course based on other valuable work that was done far before we entered the world of collaborative modeling and facilitation. A very important and foundational theory comes from Sigmund Freud.[1] Freud created a model where he describes three levels of the mind—*conscious, preconscious, and unconscious*—using an iceberg analogy, as shown in figure 4.6. This model is at the foundation of many models we use and know today. The three levels represent the following:

- *Conscious*—The mental processes and sensations we're aware of. It's what we can see, observe, feel, notice, and see. We can think about these processes rationally. For example, feeling hungry makes you decide to get something to eat. This is the tip of the iceberg.
- *Preconscious*—Things you don't instantly know, but that you can access by association. This lives between the conscious and unconscious mind. It's some sort of storage, with thoughts and knowledge that waits around to go to the conscious level. It's about memories that you extract for a specific purpose at a specific time. For example, hearing a certain song triggers memories of your first holiday with friends, or seeing an architecture design pulls up memories and best practices from earlier projects.
- *Unconscious*—The mental processes that are inaccessible to consciousness, but influence judgments, feelings, and/or behavior.[2] Following Freud's iceberg analogy, this is the biggest and most important part that you can't see. According

---

[1] Freud, S. *The Unconscious,* 1915, SE, vol. 14. London: Hogarth (pp. 159–204).
[2] Wilson, T. D. *Strangers to Ourselves,* 2004. Cambridge, MA: Harvard University Press.

to Freud, the unconscious mind is the primary driver for human behavior. The unconscious also contains the more unpleasant parts such as anxiety and conflict.

Now let's relate this to collaborative modeling sessions. Every participant brings these levels to the session. If most of what goes on in the mind is unconscious but can heavily affect behavior, then that leaves us with a challenge. As facilitators, we need to turn the flashlight on so the shadows become visible. Lots of things in our minds are pushed and oppressed to the unconscious part because we find them unpleasant or uncomfortable, or because we've been taught to not have these emotions. The ongoing conflict you have with your manager about the modeling and design process, that one colleague that never stops talking and never listens, those people who only want to talk and model together instead of doing the actual coding are all examples of things that could live in the unconscious mind being suppressed or even oppressed during collaborative modeling sessions. At the same time, they influence how people behave. They influence who speaks and who stays quiet, who shares a minority perspective and who doesn't, where people stand in the room, the subgroups that arise, and so on. So, it might seem a good idea to address these during a session.

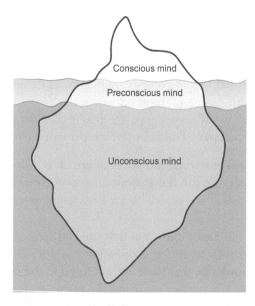

Figure 4.6   Iceberg model that describes three levels of the mind: conscious, preconscious, and unconscious

SHADOWS OR ICEBERGS?

The iceberg model is mainly about individual perspectives: the unconscious, conscious, and preconscious minds of individuals. Because collaborative modeling is about the group conscious and unconscious, we instead refer to shadows in our mental model. Figure 4.7 illustrates a group and its shadows during a collaborative modeling session. You could see the shadows as the unconscious. Another reason we prefer to use shadows is because an iceberg implies that what's beneath the waterline isn't visible. Cognitive bias, ranking, polarities, and so on *are* visible during collaborative modeling sessions; otherwise, we wouldn't be able to see them as facilitators. So, they might exist in the unconscious, but the shadows of people expose them. The shadows can be subtle and relatively light, or very dark, big, and personal.

> **NOTE** For those familiar with Carl Jung and his concept of shadows, we use it differently and more broadly here because we focus on the *group's* unconsciousness. Carl Jung's concept of shadows is about an *individual's* repressed desires, ideas, instincts, weaknesses, and shortcomings that the individual is completely unaware of.

Now when shadows get too big and dark, they might turn into demons that can no longer be (easily) facilitated. As facilitators, we're looking for these shadows as they influence group behavior. It requires the skill to turn on the flashlight in the right way so the shadows become visible. That's just the first step though. The next step is to make the shadows visible to the rest of the group and make them smaller and lighter to prevent the demons from coming out.

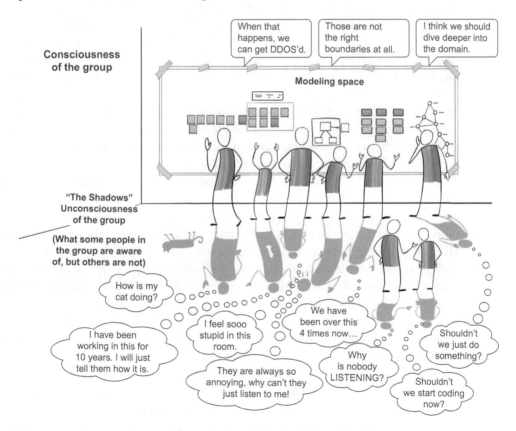

Figure 4.7   Example of shadows that live in the unconsciousness of the group during collaborative modeling

There are several techniques that can help you do that, including using sensemaking exercises, check-ins, and check-outs. Using the iceberg analogy, you would say that you're trying to lower the waterline and get more of the unconscious to the preconscious and conscious level. In our model, we try to reduce the size and darkness of the shadows by shining a flashlight on them, making those shadows fluid throughout the group. In the next sections, we'll explain how check-ins and check-outs can help you here.

4.3.2   *Opening up conversations*

What can you do when you feel like there are some potential shadows lurking but they're not being addressed properly? You have this urge to open up the conversation and shine a flashlight on the shadows to get them out because they're holding the group back. Maybe you observe a few people being very active and vocal, where others seem a bit more hesitant to share their perspectives. Your gut feeling might tell you to ask the quieter people to speak up and add to the conversation. Whatever you do, *never* put the spotlight on an individual. This might create a very unsafe environment where people won't share anything or will share what they think is politically correct.

Let's dive into an example from our BigScreen journey. Shortly after the pandemic measures were lifted, allowing us to do collaborative modeling together in a room again, most of the team was very excited about this. They planned an EventStorming session the week after, and everyone was expected in the office. It was a bit awkward at first, but after the check-in, it started to feel normal. At one point, we as facilitators noticed that some people were distancing themselves from the group and the modeling space, and they weren't adding a lot to the conversation. What was going on there?

During one of the breaks, we picked up on a conversation about physical presence and how it wasn't that exciting and comfortable for everyone in the group. As facilitators, this is your cue to bring this back into the group. To address this, we employed sensemaking. We asked the group "How comfortable are you being in the same room?" and then asked them to line up from "very comfortable" to "not comfortable at all." Turned out the group was divided, and it was causing some friction ("Why are some people distancing themselves; can't they just join us at the modeling space?") and frustration ("I'm not going to stand so close to others because my partner's health isn't that great"). By asking the question, making the division visible, and opening up the conversation, we could make some agreements that made the session comfortable for everyone. Figure 4.8 shows what that exercise looked like, where people are represented by dots on the line.

This is exactly what sensemaking can bring to a group and session. You can do these exercises at any time or moment during a session. Check-ins and check-outs are also forms of sensemaking with a specific purpose and timing, and it can tell you a lot about a group and their emotions, polarities, and opinions. In section 4.4, we'll discuss check-ins and check-outs and how to use them during collaborative modeling sessions. First, let's dive into sensemaking.

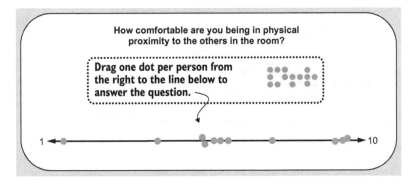

Figure 4.8 Sensemaking example exercise we did at BigScreen

4.3.3 *What is sensemaking?*

Sensemaking—as the word suggests—is about making sense of the environment. Beyond the obvious and visible. It's about getting an understanding of the group and elements in play, and giving meaning to their collective experiences. Sensemaking is very often about the unknown—the beliefs, opinions, worries, and gut feelings that live in a group. Making sense of these—structuring them—helps us act in the unknown. We test a mental model that is based on observations of behavior within a group. We create these mental models based on observations of patterns and behavior within the group and based on experience. Instead of jumping to conclusions and flying blind on assumptions, we test the mental model and make it more complete and accurate by adding data from the group. It's never about right or wrong. It's about creating a shared sense of reality and increasing mutual understanding. As mentioned, this is usually about stuff that lives in the shadows—uncomfortable feelings, conflicts, polarities, ranking, and so on that adds to the energy in a room and affects the chemistry—but is hard to grasp. By doing sensemaking exercises, you can make these things explicit and address them accordingly.

When you're in a situation that feels off, unpredictable, frustrating, or chaotic, sensemaking helps you to understand the story. Let's clarify this with a BigScreen example. We were facilitating an EventStorming session for BigScreen, where we tried to discover challenges and opportunities in the software delivery process. Over time, we felt that the discussion kept cycling back to the same unspoken problem. We decided to test our mental model by posing a sensemaking question to the group: "Do we build a standard product or custom-made solutions?" Just by posing the question and asking people to place a dot on a line with one pole of the polarity at each end of that line, we made this polarity very explicit. Figure 4.9 shows the outcomes of that sensemaking exercise.

Uncomfortableness followed. These two beliefs were highly present and important within the company, but rarely spoken about. It formed the basis of many discussions and problems in the software delivery process. Uncomfortableness slowly moved to relief and long-awaited conversations.

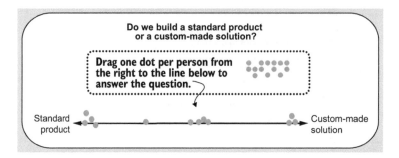

Figure 4.9   Sensemaking exercise example on what product we're actually building

Sensemaking has helped us more than once to move toward a shared understanding of beliefs and underlying social dynamics that hinder conversation and collaboration, as well as to facilitate opportunities where people can say what needs to be said without judgment.

4.3.4   Why would you do sensemaking?

Sensemaking can feel like a big hurdle to jump, especially at the start because it can often bring uncomfortableness, vulnerability, and negative feedback from the group as it's not a very common practice. On the upside, sensemaking can trigger conversations, increase mutual understanding and empathy, provide insights into why certain processes are ineffective, and tell you something about the personal relationships of the people in the room. It lessens the shadows that block effective decision-making. Sensemaking is also a very low-key, simple exercise that doesn't necessarily require a lot of time and effort unless the triggered conversations necessitate that time and effort. It can also help you make decisions on the process quickly: Do we want to continue the collaborative modeling part, or do we want to move to the coding part? This polarity can be made very explicit by a sensemaking exercise. Then, it's up to the group to decide, based on the outcome, what the next step is. Sensemaking can prevent endless discussions without decisions.

As mentioned, sensemaking can be a way to make shadows explicit and make these shadows smaller and lighter. It also helps everyone see the shadows that are there and encourages people to see other (minority) perspectives. In a lot of situations, the group might not notice the shadows that are hindering their progress. In the earlier "What are we building?" example, the group was getting frustrated and irritated, but they didn't observe the polarity that was hindering them. As facilitators, we noticed that people were talking about different things when trying to create a shared model. That's where we stepped in, created the sensemaking exercise on the spot, and opened up the conversation. The role of the facilitator is crucial here: you have to sense what's going on. You don't have to be right, but it's up to you to turn the flashlight on and give meaning to the shadows that are there. It could have very well been the case that the polarity we thought we were hearing (standard product versus custom-made solution) wasn't perceived as such by the group. That all dots would have been on the standard product side. That's fine as well because then it's settled and we can move on. So, as a facilitator, sensemaking is also a way of testing your mental models.

GUIDING HEURISTIC   Do sensemaking exercises when you get the feeling shadows are in the way.

For the people in the session, sensemaking exercises are very efficient ways of seeing other perspectives and challenging their own. It's only logical that people sometimes get stuck in what they know, become focused on a small part of the EventStorm, and kind of neglect the rest of the timeline. Or they might try to convince others of the way a certain process works because they haven't seen it any other way yet. Collaborative modeling is also about creating a shared mental model, meaning among all participants. For that to happen, we have to bring together all the individual mental models that are present. Again, sensemaking is a very helpful tool here. It's not just about lines and dots, as there are more ways you could do a sensemaking exercise. The following two figures show two examples of other sensemaking exercises that we regularly use. We added them to inspire you to come up with different forms of your own. Different forms have different outcomes and effects. Depending on what you want to achieve with the sensemaking exercise, you can decide which to use.

First, figure 4.10 shows a triangle that allows people to put in a dot somewhere in the shape. It tells you more about the individual perspectives in the group and if they align. We like to use this form when options are a bit nuanced, that is, when there is no black and white option. All options might be used, but in different frequencies. Some might be valued more than others. Seeing the division of the dots helps open up this conversation both on how it is now and what people would prefer in the future.

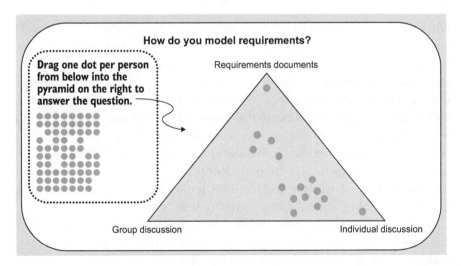

Figure 4.10   Sensemaking exercise example using three options in a triangle. Using a pyramid offers several advantages: it captures nuanced opinions by providing a middle ground, reduces polarization by avoiding binary opposition, increases the accuracy of sensemaking collection by reflecting a wider range of perspectives, and enhances engagement by better matching individual views.

The second example, shown in figure 4.11, is an interesting matrix that is a bit less nuanced than the triangle example. In the matrix, people have to make a decision. Sure, they can place their dots near the borders, but it's a bit more decisive. The options are also more contradictory, which can lead to interesting conversations on where we are now and where we should be.

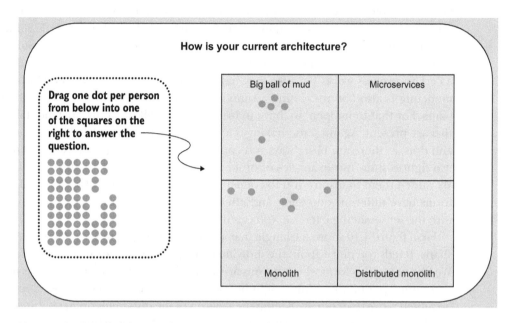

Figure 4.11   Sensemaking exercise example using a four-quadrant diagram

When doing these exercises, it's the conversation that has the most effect. The visual outcome of the exercise—how the dots or people are divided—is very interesting, but having an open conversation about what we're looking at as a group adds the most value and is transformative. As facilitators, we always ask the group if anyone wants to share something about why they placed their dot (or themselves) somewhere, or if there is anything that stands out to them by looking at the outcome. The outliers often require the most time to discuss. Perspectives seem to be very far apart, and it's interesting to understand why that is. We always try to address the outliers if no one brings them up. In our experience, the outcomes provide the group with enough conversation material. As a facilitator, you focus on getting to a mutual understanding, asking questions, listening, and achieving completeness.

So, what if you don't use sensemaking? Well, then you miss out on a lot of crucial things that influence behavior. When we don't address these things in a session, they might continue to linger and eventually even turn into demons. And demons are a lot harder to manage than shadows. If you don't do this, you also hinder the group and its progress. When conflicts or different perspectives aren't made explicit, you might end up circling back to the same conversations over and over again. Increasing frustration, tension, and delays. So whatever form you use, know that sensemaking exercises can help you in making shadows smaller and lighter. You just have to pay close attention to the signals.

SPOILER ALERT: VULNERABILITY REQUIRED

Unfortunately, sensemaking won't be very effective without vulnerability, which is also why sensemaking is so hard. By answering a question or placing themselves or a dot on a line, people show their colors. It could very well be that some are representing a minority perspective. Are they willing—and feeling safe enough—to share this with the group? Partly, sensemaking helps because it doesn't require anyone to speak up if they don't want to. We try to do the sensemaking exercises as anonymously as possible, which is easier in a remote setting because no names are added to the dots. When you're dealing with an in-person session, you can use blank stickies, but people still need to walk and put their sticky there. You can also ask them to write the number on a post-it, fold it up, and give it to the facilitator. When everyone's stickies are collected, the facilitator will put them on the boards. The point is that, even then, the minority perspective is included in the complete picture. It provides a more complete picture of the entire wisdom of the group, and a conversation can be started.

Vulnerability can be scary. Sensemaking isn't about certainty, which is exactly what we as humans love to seek. Moving away from the unknown and ambiguous situations. Sensemaking exercises can be uncomfortable, insecure, and ambiguous. That might make them pretty unattractive to actively seek. Sensemaking can force you to stay longer in those uncertain situations because it makes the shadows explicit. Sensemaking can also feel counterintuitive to the culture of some organizations. This is especially true for cultures that are driven by results and/or driven by hiding from and avoiding conflict, even more so when value is placed on leaders making decisions quickly or being deemed indecisive, for example.

Sensemaking requires you to take a step back and be complete about perspectives instead of jumping to conclusions. Doing that requires vulnerability, leading by example. A powerful question to ask in this light is "Who can somewhat relate to this?" by the showing of hands. When there is a minority perspective being discussed, people often recognize parts of that perspective. That's why "partly" is a very powerful word in this question. It enables people to show vulnerability and have open conversations that include the wisdom of the entire group.

Now, sensemaking can get you right into the midst of a conflict that has been brewing for a while, so be careful what you ask for! But no worries, in chapter 8, we got your back, where we go deeper into conflict resolution. So, until you read that chapter, keep the sensemaking to topics that aren't so sensitive.

4.3.5   *In-person or remote?*

Nowadays, we work in a mixture of online, offline, and hybrid sessions. Sensemaking, but also check-ins and check-outs, remain truly valuable techniques in all these forms. There are different ways of getting the most valuable insights per form, but the outcomes are similar: triggering conversations by making shadows explicit.

Whether you create a sensemaking exercise online by drawing a line and adding dots like the previous examples, or you ask people to stand in a line in the room, the question and outcome remain the same. Being in the same room might make it easier to have meaningful conversations because you can observe nonverbal communication better and sense the energy a bit easier. As facilitators, we noticed that it's slightly easier to observe and pick up on (weak) signals when being in physical proximity rather than behind a screen. It's easier to keep the overview of one room and group, than it is to keep an eye on every (non)verbal signal in all the small images on a screen. When doing sensemaking exercises in physical proximity, the movement itself can also tell you a lot about what's going on in a group. Who walks up to the line or paper first to take a position, who is waiting for others to go first, and who seems to follow someone else? These could be signals on psychological safety, ranking, and cognitive bias. As a facilitator, these are sometimes even more interesting than the outcome of the exercise itself. Even though this is harder to observe in online sessions, there are still things to look out for: mouse movement, camera's on or off, microphones on mute or not, who places the first dot, who speaks up first, and so on.

Although it might seem that offline sessions are a better stage for sensemaking exercises, there is added value in doing them online that you can't get offline. For example, some people feel safer in the context of their own homes. They might feel even more safe to share their opinion and perspectives because they aren't in close proximity to people they otherwise might find more intimidating. Ranking (see chapter 6) can actually be less present in online sessions. Another potential benefit is that—when desired—the sensemaking can be done anonymously. Placing a dot on a line can be done without other participants seeing who moves where. On delicate matters, this might be the preferred way of entering the conversation afterward. As mentioned, online sessions can lack the ability of observing and experiencing all nonverbal communication that's going on. Sensemaking can even replace this to some extent, as it makes emotions and opinions explicit. We tend to do more sensemaking exercises during online meetings to account for this. We focus some of the exercises more on the emotional part to make sure we get the chance to pick up on signals.

Whether online, offline, or hybrid, they all require vulnerability. It also takes some time to get comfortable with doing the exercises. We encourage you to start experimenting and trying it out. To give you one more concrete example to try, we'll explain a premortem sensemaking exercise in the next section.

4.3.6   *Premortem*

We can do all the collaborative modeling we want, but there is still a good chance our projects won't exactly turn out as we hoped or planned. It's pretty common to do a *postmortem analysis* on these projects. A postmortem comes from the medical field, where doctors learn what caused a patient's death. While this is very interesting and valuable, the patient won't benefit from it. Analyzing what went wrong in a project in hindsight is very useful, but wouldn't you rather know up front so that a project can be improved rather than autopsied?

One of the reasons projects don't turn out as we hoped or planned is that people might feel reluctant to speak up about worries, reservations, or concerns they have regarding the project plan. A decision was made, based on a lot of wisdom in the group, and quite some time was spent on it, so maybe it's better to just keep quiet. While this is a common thought, it can be very useful to do an up-front analysis of the causes of these worries and concerns. This analysis can help you prevent the early shipwreck of new ideas, projects, and plans. By making it safe to share reservations up front, you can anticipate potential shipwrecks and improve a project's chances of success. One of the formats we use for this is the *premortem exercise*. This is a form of sensemaking because you're looking for different perspectives, polarities, potential conflicts, and concerns, that is, stuff that may live in people's shadows. By doing this exercise, you make shadows explicit, smaller, and lighter.

Risk analysis is nothing new, but the difference here is that we don't look at the project asking what might go wrong, but we focus on the hindsight perspective asking what did go wrong. It's a very low-key, simple exercise that isn't too time-consuming. We start this exercise by setting the stage: ask the group to imagine they are *x* months ahead in time and, by that time, the project has miserably failed. Everyone tried their best, but we ended up with a huge failure. Next, we want to explore three questions:

- What were our initial goals?
- What actions did we take?
- What went wrong?

Everyone writes down their perspectives on stickies, and then we go over them. From an efficiency perspective, this helps us identify potential problems early on and allows us to start preparing mitigation actions. We can prioritize the risks with the group and decide how we want to mitigate them. That's great, but what's even better is that we get the chance to hear from the experts themselves and use this wisdom in our project. We're creating a safe space to share the unpleasant, uncomfortable, and very often negative thoughts and emotions that people often repress because they want to look ahead and keep a positive mindset. This is a chance to actively listen to people, let them feel heard and valued, and learn from them at the same time. This makes a premortem exercise perfect for sensemaking. It could also be a perfect exercise during the first part of a check-out. In the next section, we'll take a closer look at check-ins and check-outs.

4.4 Check-in and check-out

Imagine your team decided that an EventStorming session would be a valuable exercise. The session is planned, the facilitator is briefed, and the team is excited. You grab some coffee, enter the conference room, and chat with your colleagues. At some point, the facilitator briefly describes what is expected from you in the upcoming 30 minutes: write down Domain Events for everything you know of the process you're modeling today. You are told to write down one event per sticky and place them on the timeline in the right order, and afterwards you'll structure the entire timeline together. The facilitator says "GO!" The group looks at each other, moves around a bit, grabs some stickies and sharpies, and the uncomfortableness is painfully obvious.

Spoiler alert: we start our training on facilitating collaborative modeling sessions this way. It's super uncomfortable—also for us—and doesn't improve the energy in the group. Questions start popping up, people aren't comfortable with each other yet, and they feel like they missed an important step. We do this to make a point, not to bully trainees—although they might feel that way at first. The point we're trying to make is that starting something like collaborative modeling without a proper check-in affects the rest of that session in a negative way.

We always (always!) start our sessions with a check-in, and we always (always!) end with a check-out. It's a way of really connecting with each other, getting to know each other a bit better, and exploring common ground. Especially in collaborative modeling sessions, these check-ins and check-outs are crucial. All the aspects of sociotechnical systems are flying around, and it's really important to also focus on the social and cognitive part of such a session.

Check-ins and check-outs are a form of sensemaking with a specific purpose and time. In this section, we'll dive into check-ins and check-outs: what they are, why they are important, what they bring to the group and the facilitator, and what they could look like.

4.4.1   *What is a check-in and check-out?*

As highlighted in the earlier example, many people aren't comfortable jumping right into the content at the start of a session without first having a check-in. This discomfort is often due to wanting to know the purpose of the meeting and to get to know the other participants in the room. This helps in feeling safe and understanding the dynamics of the group. As facilitators, we stress the importance of properly preparing a check-in and check-out for every session. These are specific to the meeting and context, and they demand thoughtful preparation and active listening on the part of the facilitator. Next, we'll clarify what we mean by check-in and check-out, along with some examples.

CHECK-IN

A *check-in* happens before diving into the content. You either start a session with a check-in or do it after the introduction of the day, the agenda, and the goal of the session. It's a way of connecting with each other on a personal level by getting to know each other a bit better and getting oriented toward the goal of the session. Why are people there? What do they want to get out of it? When is it considered successful? Check-ins help people focus on the session they're in and the people they're in the session with. It's also an opportunity to connect with the content of the session by asking questions on the topic at hand, for example, Domain-Driven Design or collaborative modeling. It's a great way to see how comfortable people are with what you're going to do that session. The way we do check-ins, which we describe in this book, is inspired by the Lewis Deep Democracy method.[3]

Figure 4.12 shows an example of a check-in we regularly use. We ask people in the room to answer these questions if they want to and to the extent they're comfortable with. This is an important working agreement in every session: "You have the right to pass." We never force people to answer certain questions in a check-in or check-out if they don't want to. However, we do ask them to at least say their name when people don't know each other. When someone has spoken at the check-in, it becomes easier to start talking later on in the session.

Let's check in!

1. What motivates you to be here today?
2. Is there anything on your mind that's distracting you from being fully present?
3. What do you know about the "Anytime, Anywhere" campaign?
4. Do you have any questions regarding the campaign?

Figure 4.12   Example check-in we used at BigScreen. We start with a personal question to create more group understanding. Questions 3 and 4 focus on the session's content, ensuring participants engage and reflect on the topic at hand. Our goal is to avoid opinions on the content and instead delve into what participants know and their questions. Remember to customize your check-in questions for each session and refresh the format regularly to keep it genuine.

Another important aspect of check-ins and check-outs is that this isn't a conversation— it's sharing and dumping. Dumping might sound a bit harsh, but what we mean is that this is a monologue. Everyone gets to dump their thoughts, opinions, perspectives, and feelings, and the rest of the group doesn't interrupt; they just listen. Facilitators have an important role here to emphasize that this isn't the place for dialogue but that there will be room to react at the end of the check-in. An overview of characteristics of check-ins and check-outs is provided later in this section.

Check-ins can come in many different forms and styles. Depending on the group's size, the goal of the meeting, and the social dynamics, you can do a check-in that adds value. In smaller groups, you can take more time per person or do multiple check-ins. When groups are bigger, we like to split them up. Each group will have one facilitator who shares the insights from the separate check-ins afterward. We also choose impromptu networking (https://mng.bz/BdQl)[4], where people ask each other questions in groups of two and then share with the entire group what they've heard.

---

[3]   Lewis, M. *Inside the NO: Five Steps to Decisions That Last,* 2008, e-book, https://houseofdeepdemocracy.nl/webshop.
[4]   Lipmanowicz, H. and Keith McCandless. *The Surprising Power of Liberating Structures: Simple Rules to Unleash a Culture of Innovation,* 2014.

Performing a check-in and a check-out results in enhanced focus, more personal connections, underlying tensions made explicit sooner, and less gossiping through the grapevine. Here's an example of how important a check-in can be from our own experience and perspective: Once we facilitated a collaborative modeling session with two facilitators. We did a check-in, but it was pretty superficial, meaning the check-in questions didn't leave much room for people to share what was hindering participation or focus that day. The questions we asked were limited to weekend highlights and what people were hoping to achieve in the upcoming session. And boy did we learn our lesson that day. One of the facilitators wasn't very vocal nor assertive in guiding the group toward an outcome. This wasn't normal behavior, and it frustrated the other facilitator who said, "We are on a deadline here. We need to show our added value, and you're just standing there letting the group struggle." After a few hours, during lunch, it turned out that the passive facilitator was in serious pain. The person just got an abscessed tooth removed yesterday, and the antibiotics weren't kicking in yet. Talking hurt, so it was easier to stay quiet. Knowing that led to empathy and understanding from the other facilitator, and we made agreements on their roles during the rest of the session. Had we done a proper check-in, this probably would have been shared at the start of the day. The agreements could have been made earlier, and no one had to feel frustrated or uncomfortable. So, both for the group and the facilitator(s), doing a proper check-in and check-out is highly important.

Check-ins are also great ways to start a conversation after everyone shares their input; that is, at the moment everyone has shared what they want to share, the facilitator asks if someone wants to add something or react to something. Let's take a look at the example check-in in figure 4.13. We use this very regularly both as check-in and check-out by the way. (And, yes, they are our lovely cats, in case you were wondering.) It's a simple way of sensing what's going on in the group in terms of energy. Although it's low key, the check-in allows people to elaborate on why they chose a certain cat if they want to. It might turn out that someone had a horrible night of sleep because his child was sick and therefore chose cat number 2, or maybe someone had an amazing party the night before and that's why she chose cat number 2—same cat, different story. In both cases, the check-in serves as a way to connect with each other and increase understanding and empathy.

We encourage you to start including check-ins and check-outs as a standard aspect of your sessions. For longer sessions (4 hours or more), we account for at least 20 minutes for the check-in and 20 minutes for the check-out. Even in short meetings, a very short (one question) check-in can already add a lot of value. In that case, you could limit the time to 5 minutes and get a lot of information and context you'd otherwise not have. Relevant questions obviously depend on the meeting, but the following are some example questions that you could use and adjust to your context in your next check-in:

- Why do you want to be here?
- Why don't you want to be here?

- Which three words describe how you're feeling at the moment?
- What's the most important thing for you to achieve today?
- Is there anything you wanted to say in the previous meeting, but you didn't?
- How did you sleep, and how's your energy level?
- If we could only agree on one thing in this session, what should it be?
- Show thumbs up or down based on how you feel the project is going so far.

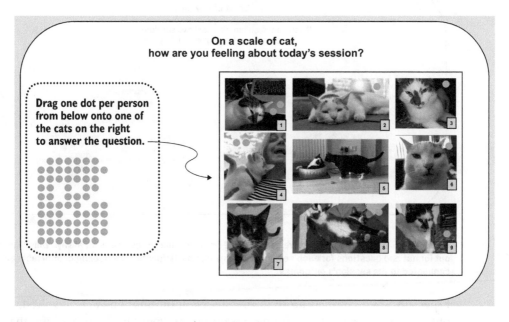

Figure 4.13   Example check-in to sense the energy in a group

CHECK-OUT

Starting with a check-in suggests that we end with a check-out, and that's exactly what we do! The goal of a check-out is to "detach" from the meeting, the content, and the group to see if there's anything that needs to be said that hasn't been said during the session. Provide a safe space to share that in the meeting and not when having drinks afterwards or days later over coffee. We want to prevent people from leaving with negative emotions lingering. If they do linger or weren't shared, this can affect someone for a while after the session. In essence, we ask people in a check-out how they are leaving the session, if there's anything left that needs to be said, and if agreements need to be made. It's also a great way to check with participants about how they experienced the sessions from a content perspective. Figure 4.14 gives an example.

Like the check-in, this isn't a conversation. It's sharing and dumping—monologue style. If a dialogue or conversation seems to start, it's up to the facilitator to remind people of the monologue style or do a climate report if it happens a couple of times (more on that in chapter 8). In the example in figure 4.14, we used stickies. This can be done both online and offline, and after everyone writes something down, we ask if anyone wants to elaborate on their sticky. A check-out can be evaluative and personal at the same time. Questions on the content can be combined with questions on energy level, for example. "How are you leaving this session?" is a very powerful question to ask.

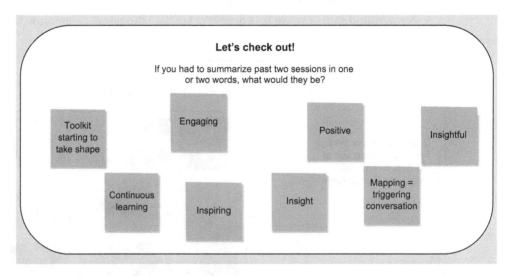

Figure 4.14   Example check-out we used at BigScreen. Similar to the check-in, always tailor the check-out format and questions for each session. This ensures participants leave feeling comfortable and connected to the session's outcomes.

Especially when conflicts arose during a session or emotions were involved, a check-out is a way to really close off one session before going to the next thing that needs attention. Not doing a check-out after an intense session might result in people holding on to negative feelings afterwards, growing frustration, and gossiping. The lack of check-out might affect the outcome of the session too. These negative emotions could be projected on the outcomes and cause the group, or individuals, to perceive the outcome and session as nonvaluable. You want to provide a space and opportunity for people to share what they need to share after a session. Check-outs are meant to do just that. Just like a check-in, a check-out also enables personal connections to be made. Because it's not a conversation but a monologue, you're more encouraged to listen to others. If any emotions, concerns, frustrations, or thoughts haven't been addressed during the session, the check-out provides a safe space to do that.

Check-outs occur in many forms and styles that you can experiment with; impromptu networking or forming a circle to step in and step out of are among our favorites. To inspire you, here are some questions you might consider for your next check-out:

- How are you leaving the session?
- Which new insight do you consider most valuable?

- What will you be doing differently tomorrow?
- What will you still struggle with?
- What should definitely be in the follow-up session?
- Is there anything you want to share/say that you didn't?

4.4.2 Characteristics of a check-in and check-out

Now that you have an idea of what a check-in and check-out are, there are some characteristics that you should know about. These characteristics help you in preparing and leading a check-in/check-out, as well as give you an idea of their structure and course:

- It's not a conversation; it's sharing and dumping.
- Monologue style is used: the person speaking can't be interrupted.
- Everyone says at least something (saying you'll pass is also fine!).
- Popcorn style is used: everyone does their check-in when they feel like it rather than pointing to people.
- The facilitator leads by example and starts the check-in/check-out.
- At the end, the facilitator gives a summary of what has been said.
- After the summary, the facilitator asks the group what the facilitator may have missed.
- The facilitator asks if someone wants to react to something that was shared.

4.4.3 Why would you do a check-in and check-out?

We hope the first part of this section convinced you of the value of check-ins and check-outs already, that is, the personal connections, the "formal" start and end of a session, and the safe space to share what participants want to share with the group. The power of check-ins and check-outs is also in their simplicity—just an opportunity for participants to share something about themselves, the agenda, or the meeting in an informal way. The questions can be superficial or more in depth, depending on the goals, group, and social dynamics.

Check-ins and check-outs provide insights into what's important to the group: emotions, energy, and potentially hindering social dynamics. We can bring the pain forward of the group if we ask the right questions, and we can make the rest of the session go faster. This is valuable to the group, as it makes things explicit and prevents shadows from turning into demons. This is also valuable to facilitators because it tells them where to pay extra attention, where to deep dive, and which conflicts and polarities exist within a group. Based on these insights, you can adjust the course of the session. In essence, it's a way to put a flashlight on and make shadows explicit and reduce their size and darkness. The smaller and lighter the shadows, the less lingering demons that can hinder progress. When it's clear which polarities or conflicts are present in a group, you can focus your check-in and check-out on them, so they come to the surface much sooner to be addressed and managed.

So, what if you don't use check-ins/check-outs? Well, you might end up in uncomfortable situations. Let's go back to BigScreen and one of their collaborative modeling sessions. The group was in a rush, the pressure was on, and the day really needed an outcome to retain the sponsorship from the management team. The group was more focused on the outcome than anything else, so the check-in got skipped from a time perspective. It wasn't the most inspiring and exciting session for BigScreen. The goal was to EventStorm a specific part on a process level. There were some disagreements in the group about this process and what it currently looked like. Our goal with that session as facilitators was to get to an agreement and remove ambiguity. Little did we know that the day before, there was a meeting on a related topic, and it wasn't a peaceful session. It started that way, but after a while, it turned into a conflict that wasn't resolved at the end of the day. During our EventStorm the next day, we felt tension; people weren't listening to each other and were trying to convince each other why they were right and the other person was wrong—no conversations, only discussions. The goal of most of the participants apparently was being right, as opposed to our goal of being complete and in agreement. Had we done a proper check-in, we could have addressed this sooner. It would have helped the group and the progress and outcomes of that EventStorm.

This example illustrates how important it is to do a proper check-in and check-out. The connection and understanding would have helped the progress and outcomes of that session. This also shows why it's so important to have facilitators who make sure to do the important tasks to make a session successful—even if it means there is less time to do the actual modeling because that time is needed for checking in and checking out. A check-out is also an opportunity to explicitly ask for what you need or to optimize follow-up. In the next section, we'll explain how you can do this.

4.4.4   *Capturing feedback through check-outs*

A check-out can also be a great way to capture feedback from the group. Both on the content (outcomes, progress, speed, expectations, etc.) and the facilitation (style, exercises, facilitators, etc.). The example in figure 4.14 is a way of capturing feedback on the content of the session. Knowing how people describe the session in just a few words provides valuable insights to the facilitators. Especially if there are follow-up sessions planned, it's very useful to include at least one check-out that captures feedback. For example, the following check-out question can help you as a facilitator prepare the follow-up session better: "Based on the outcomes of this session, what should we start with in the next session?"

Another very valuable way of capturing feedback without putting anyone on the spot, is the *Wow/How about?*[5] method. You can do this one from very small groups to huge groups because method only requires stickies and some space. On one side of the whiteboard, you write "Wow," and on the other side, you write "How about?"

---

[5]   Bowman, S. *Training from the Back of the Room!: 65 Ways to Step Aside and Let Them Learn*, 2008.

On the Wow side, people can write down what stands out for them now that the session is done. What was eye-opening, what made them rethink something, and what did they really like about the session? This can be on any topic: content, outcomes, facilitation techniques, group dynamics, and so on. On the How about? side, people can write down things they are still wondering about after the session. How about the follow-up, how about action points, how about communication with the rest of the organization, what about <specific topic>, and so on?

As a facilitator, you get a nice overview of what's going well and what should stay, and you'll get an idea about what's important for the group to cover in follow-up sessions. Figure 4.15 is an example of a Wow/How about? check-out. You can combine multiple exercises for a single check-out. We often provide two exercises: one focused on making sure people are able to detach from the session and another one to gather feedback.

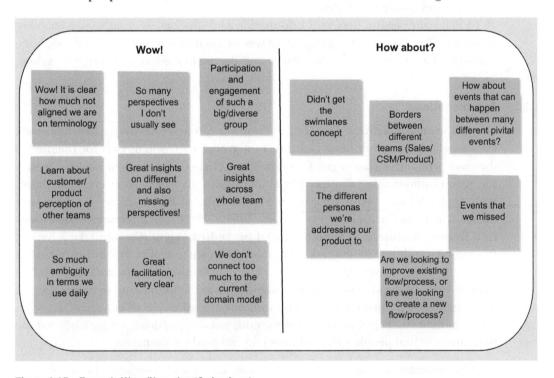

Figure 4.15   Example Wow/How about? check-out

Exercise 4.1: Design your own check-in and check-out

Now that you know more about check-ins and check-outs, it's time to design your own check-in and check-out. For one of your next upcoming sessions, try to come up with a relevant check-in and check-out. Make sure it adds something to the session, and experiment with different forms. Make sure to get the check-in and check-out on the session agenda and reflect on it afterward: What did it bring to the session, how did people react to it, and what could you improve next time?

4.5   *Different collaboration styles for modeling with tools*

In the previous chapter, we talked about the different tools you can use during a collaborative modeling session. We use these tools during the modeling with tools stage of a collaborative modeling process. The specific tool you want and expect to use is based on the type of problem you'll model. As mentioned before, EventStorming is better at modeling a storyline, and Example Mapping is better at modeling a specific moment in that storyline where business rules affect what happens next. We have the same tradeoffs when collaborating as a group during the modeling with tools stage. Adding more people to a group also means more diverse knowledge, possibly more opposite opinions, and definitely more biases. We found out that the larger the group, the harder it gets to collaborate, make sustainable decisions, get more insights, and allow the group to feel included.

To make the session flow with information and insights, we want to use enabling constraints for discovery. One important way we do that is to use a specific collaboration style in a session. In the next sections, we'll explain the styles you can use in these sessions.

4.5.1   *Together, Alone*

One of the most effective styles in our toolbox is the *Together, Alone* style, which is a well-known principle used in design sprints. In a group, everyone models for themselves the same problem or challenges. Everyone gets a chance to share their knowledge with the group without being disrupted by a discussion with others. After everyone shares their model, we can decide what to do. For example, at BigScreen, we sat down with the team in a Bytesize Architecture Session (https://bytesizearchitecturesessions.com). In a Bytesize Architecture Session created by Andrea Magnorsky, you take a look at the software architecture and ask every team member to model that out alone. After around 20 minutes, everyone shared their model of the architecture, each one valid on its own. We then decided to use one of the models as the foundation to merge the rest of the models. Eventually, we ended up with one shared model of our architecture, as shown in figure 4.16. Just make sure at the end, you also put down a legend of what the parts mean so that people who could not join can read the model.

> **GUIDING HEURISTIC**   Merge on the most complete model, instead of the one that is most accurate.

We like to employ this technique especially when we're modeling a new problem or scenario, or the group doesn't collaborate in that setting. For example, when we do EventStorming, we ask the participants to first model a timeline of events as they understand it before merging that timeline into one. Making a timeline for themselves means we did constrict the participants and gave them some structure. We constantly balance how much structure we give compared to the chaos that arises. Remember, the more unstructured chaos, the more chance we have for diverse insights.

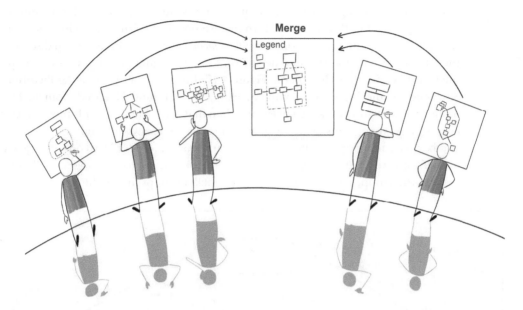

Figure 4.16   An example of using the together, alone style in a collaborative modeling Bytesize Architecture Session

> **GUIDING HEURISTIC**   Optimize for chaos over structure. We want to postpone giving too much structure to a session because the more structure you provide, the fewer insights emerge.

One thing to keep in mind is the number of people involved. If the modeling is something simple, such as a timeline in EventStorming, you can scale it up to 30+ people. If it's a model of the architecture, such as in Bytesize Architecture, it's better to keep it to the size of a team. Although it's doable to add more people, more time will be required, and you might be better off using any of the following types.

4.5.2   *Split and Merge*

During a complex, in-depth collaborative modeling session, one of our heuristics is to not have groups larger than seven people because decision-making will be much harder in such big groups. One of the styles we use a lot during these sessions is *Split and Merge*, which splits the large group into smaller groups of three to seven people. We can divide the group in two ways, either by categorizing the model or by having each group model the same problem. After splitting, we always do a walkthrough over what the other groups modeled and decide how to continue with merging the models into one.

> **GUIDING HEURISTIC**   When modeling an in-depth problem, split groups that have more than seven participants.

For example, splitting on categorization can be done when doing a Big Picture Event-Storming. For a Big Picture EventStorming, we stay in the same modeling space, but we can split the timeline using a concept called *pivotal events*. We let the group discover what these pivotal events are. We then decide on some emerging pivotal events we can put on the board as milestones to split on. Figure 4.17 shows an example of a Big Picture Event-Storming for the BigScreen company. Here, the Planning Finalized Domain Event is modeled by the group as a pivotal event. When that event happens, only then can customers start reserving tickets. Now the group can split themselves left and right of that event and begin cleaning up. We did this session with around 30 people, so once the group was divided into two groups of approximately 15, we asked them to first model another pivotal event in the group, splitting it up again into smaller groups that fit the size.

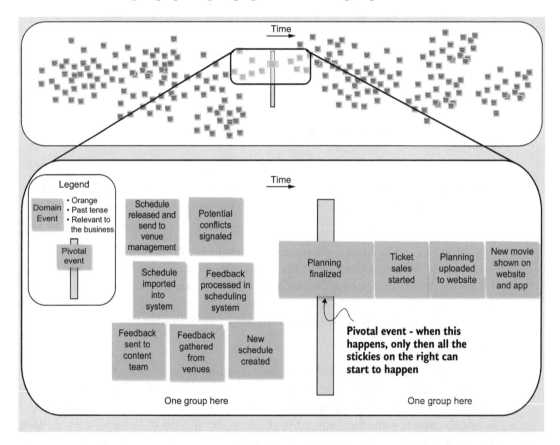

Figure 4.17   Zoomed in part of a Big Picture EventStorming showing how a pivotal event can help split the large group into smaller groups

Modeling the same problem is somewhat more straightforward. For example, we take a user story as input for an Example Mapping session. The group in total is 12 people, so we create two to three groups and let the teams self-organize based on diversity of knowledge. Each group does its own Example Mapping in isolation for a fixed amount of time. After everyone is done, the groups do a show and tell, and then we merge it together into one Example Mapping and decide what to do next.

4.5.3 Small Group Diverge and Converge

When we start to design models for complex business problems, ideas can become diverse. Splitting and merging will be complicated and time-consuming because ideas go in all different directions. When you, as a facilitator, expect this to happen, do a *Small Group Diverge and Converge* instead. Create groups of three to four people to model a design for the same problem. Then, several times during the session, share what has been discovered, and let the group go back to their own modeling space to continue. The difference here between split and merge is that your goal isn't to merge the models in the end. However, sometimes you can still end up with everyone converging to the same model. We actually prefer to enable the group with this style to create several different models for the same problem. From here, we can start to map out the tradeoffs, as shown in figure 4.18, between the models and decide what to do next, or we could even make what Morgan Jones (*The Thinker's Toolkit* [Crown Currency, 1998) calls a Pros-Cons-and-Fixes list if we want to get it all out. We'll discuss more about decision-making and the Pros-Cons-and-Fixes list in chapters 9 and 11, respectively.

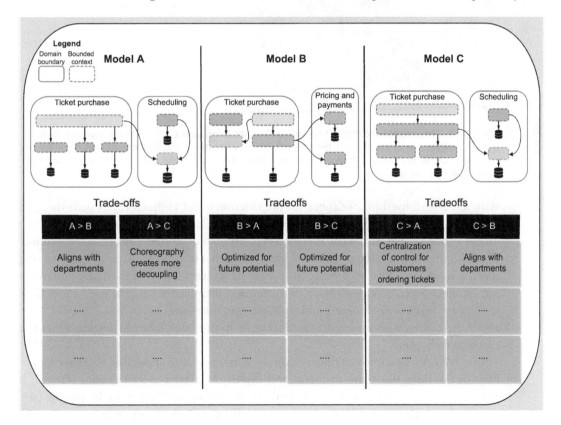

Figure 4.18 A simple tradeoff exercise filling in why one model has a better tradeoff than the other

4.5.4   *Liberating structures: 1-2-4-All*

Merging different models has its challenges in larger groups, especially if you want to focus on gaining insights and giving the least modeling structure possible. For example, during one of our exercises, we ask the participants to build a Lego duck. They get a number of building blocks in different colors but no example. Everyone builds a slightly different duck from the Lego blocks, as shown in the example in figure 4.19. Agreeing on which duck is the "correct one" is impossible, but we can synthesize the characteristics of a duck by looking at all the duck models to see what they have in common.

Figure 4.19   An example of different Lego ducks. Imagine using Lego blocks to make your own duck, would it look like one of the ducks in the picture? Everyone creates a slightly different Lego duck, based on our mental model of a duck. From all those examples, we can distill the characteristics of a duck and create a shared mental model.

With a 1-2-4-All method, we focus on the discovery and characteristics with the goal of learning from them more than merging the models per se. What concepts of the model can we leave out, what can we keep, and what models can we leave behind? When you're with a large group and want to slowly build up your model toward one specific model, we love to use the liberating structure 1-2-4-All. Liberating structures are a collection of 33 easy-to-learn collaboration techniques you can use in meetings to increase psychological safety and trust, and get more outcomes. You can read more about them at www.liberatingstructures.com or in the book listed in section 4.9 at the end of the chapter.

In a 1-2-4-All, as shown in figure 4.20, we start again with modeling together alone. Everyone tackles the same problem and builds their own model. Then, after an *x* amount of time depending on how hard the modeling problem is, we let people pair up and discuss their model. From here, we ask them to improve upon their own model with the insights from the other model or even merge them together into one model.

Again, after an *x* amount of time, we let two pairs group up together, and do the same thing. We end up with several models from multiple groups, which we share in the group. Now we can start to decide what to do, which we'll talk more about in chapter 9. If the modeling problem is hard, and the group is large, we might start this exercise with groups of four, then combine to eight, and finally share it with the group.

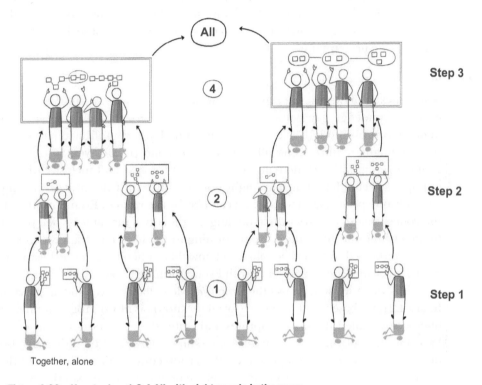

Figure 4.20 How to do a 1-2-4-All with eight people in the room

The original 1-2-4-All is about generating ideas, and we can also use it for that. For instance, we can ask the group what opportunities they see on our finished Big Picture EventStorming. Each person gets 2 minutes to generate ideas for themselves. After these 2 minutes of silence, we let people go in pairs, sharing the opportunity and similarities with each other and developing new ideas. Then after roughly 2 minutes, we let the couples become foursomes, doing the same. In this round, we asked each group to let every single person in the group pick one opportunity that stood out for them. After 4 minutes, every person will get 30 seconds to share their opportunity and show and tell them where on the Big Picture that opportunity is in the timeline. We end up with the most significant opportunities of the session, and we can start to decide which one is the most important.

A tradeoff when using 1-2-4-All, however, is that we also leave many ideas behind. We explore different models to gain a deeper understanding, but not all models go beyond exploration. Participants don't always understand that it's about the gained knowledge of modeling, and not about the end result—the model, itself. During a session, you're generating models and abandoning them. This is innate to designing boundaries or models, and many people aren't accustomed to that, especially in the beginning.

Social ranking is involved in 1-2-4-All, and we ask you to be careful doing these sessions when the culture is hierarchical and when psychological safety is low. We can mitigate a lot by determining the groups as facilitators instead of letting the group self-organize. Doing so will put you into the group dynamics of social rank, which we'll discuss more in chapter 6.

4.5.5   *Ensemble*

Sometimes we have just the right tool for tackling a problem, but there is an experience or knowledge gap between the people in the group. For example, running an in-depth process model EventStorming on an in-depth complicated part of a business process might require using all the different concepts of EventStorming. Starting EventStorming with just domain events is great for easy and inclusive discovery with multiple stakeholders. But that might not be sufficient if the process is complicated and only one person knows it. So, we can play by the rules of EventStorming, using all the concepts, and constrict the modeling. A tradeoff is that at least one person needs to understand the concept of EventStorming to not let it constrain the modeling too much. And you don't want people who know that difficult part to be busy with how to model it because their experience with EventStorming is low.

This is when we start to use the *Ensemble* style collaborative modeling. As shown in figure 4.21, it's based on Ensemble (formerly known as Mob) programming, where we one person, called the *driver*, captures and writes the conversation on stickies. Then, have another person, called the *navigator*, who decides what the driver needs to write down during EventStorming based on the group conversation. The rest of the group is having a dialogue about what to model. Depending on the experience and knowledge, we might switch these roles regularly. Facilitators are either facilitating the group discussion in the group as navigator or can take the driver role. It's also possible to permanently be the driver, and we only change the role of the navigator so that the group can focus on discovery together. The benefit is that when the other people in the group don't know how the tool works, you take away the learning curve for the group and focus on collaborative modeling. Ensemble is also the default facilitation type when doing Domain Storytelling.

A tradeoff of Ensemble is that the conversation can go either too quickly to capture or starts diverging from the use case that is discussed. We don't advise you to use it for discovery or design where the conversation diverges and becomes too much for one person to capture. There is a thin line between modeling the current situation and discussing how it should work. We advise you to spot this quickly and switch to a different type when needed. Especially when the group gets too large, say above seven, Ensemble isn't the way to go.

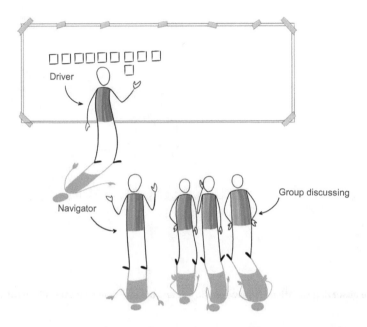

Figure 4.21 Example of ensemble modeling showing the roles and setup based on Ensemble programming

4.5.6 *Fishbowl*

When the group is too large, and we don't have enough experienced modelers in the group, we can do a *Fishbowl*. The Fishbowl collaboration style is based on the user experience fishbowl from liberating structures, which 1-2-4-All is also part of. We create one group of around three to six people who will do the modeling together for a fixed amount of time, and we let the rest of the group stand around that group only observing. The observing group can make notes or write down any insights they gain, but they can't barge into the discussion. At the end of the fishbowl style, the observing group shares the insights, and then we can see if the group is ready to do a split and merge style or a diverge and converge style.

Using the Fishbowl, you can quickly show how the modeling goes and what is expected of the exercise, which can be very important for many people. So, if you think a group is hesitant about a specific exercise, switch to a Fishbowl exercise. Sometimes, people observing can have insights that can be critical for the modeling group.

There are two variations of the Fishbowl that can help, as depicted in figure 4.22. One is to let people from the observing group step in for a timebox of 2 minutes where they can present the insight and then go back as observers. A second is that the person from the observing group can become a modeler themselves, and then someone from the modeling group needs to become an observer. We like this variation the most because the observing people can join in and take responsibility for the model.

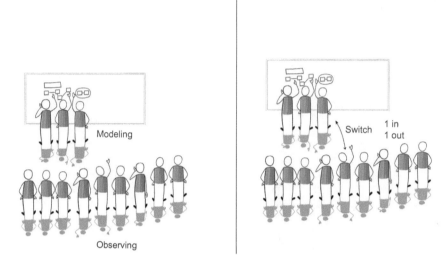

Figure 4.22   The observing variation Fishbowl on the left and the switching variation Fishbowl on the right

4.5.7   *Anarchy!*

Sometimes you deal with an experienced team that is mostly equal in knowledge and ranking and has been working together for a long time. The best way to do a collaborative modeling session for these teams is by anarchy. Anarchy style means we're not using any facilitation of the styles and tools; we let the group figure out how to do it. This implies that someone in the group has enough knowledge of collaborative modeling, and the rest of the group is quick to pick up. The main role of the facilitator then is to spot what happens in the shadows, which is more difficult with an experienced team, perhaps the hardest because the shadows are very subtle. But as mentioned before, the chaos of these sessions and self-organization will provide powerful insights and deeper models. You might believe your role as a facilitator is minimal in this case. Still, we believe even the most high-performing teams require reflection and facilitation to get all the wisdom and potential out. We used this style ourselves when collaboratively modelling this very book!

4.5.8   *Guerilla*

Guerilla modeling isn't actually a collaborative modeling style you'll use during a prepared collaborative modeling session, but it's a style to get buy-in to do collaborative modeling. So, when we have difficulty getting people together in a room or are in a meeting where we talk about complex problems but aren't doing collaborative modeling, we deploy the Guerilla style approach. We start modeling for ourselves as facilitators.

For example, one of the authors consulted a team that depended on many other teams' data for proper testing. Talking to every team gave a different perspective of the architectural landscape and where the data came from. Although a collaborative modeling session was the best way to understand that and make decisions on how to move forward with the dependencies, no one had time or interest or saw the problem we experienced as a team. So, I set up shop at the coffee corner and hung a paper roll next to it. Then, started modeling the landscape version and put out all assumptions, especially making intentional mistakes to draw people's attention. Within no time, it grabbed the attention of the other teams who passed by to get some drinks at the coffee corner. They started asking questions because they noticed the systems they were working on. I explained what I was doing and got them to do collaborative modeling with me. Just standing there for 4 hours and having people jump in and out of the session got the outcome we needed as a team to move on. Be sure to share the results with the rest of the teams as well afterward.

> **GUIDING HEURISTIC** Be the least informed person in the room. To get people engaged in the session, ask questions you know are wrong. People love to tell you that you're wrong and correct you, starting the engagement.

You can do something similar for a meeting you're in, which isn't prepped as a collaborative modeling session. For example, when talking about a complex problem for around 5 minutes, going back and forth about the storyline, share your screen and start modeling the conversation. Of course, we can only do this if we have enough ranking in the session, which we'll talk about in chapter 6. If it's acceptable, you can now begin to facilitate by asking questions and making mistakes. Within no time, you have people on board, and you might switch to an Ensemble style quickly or get everyone on that tool.

> **GUIDING HEURISTIC** Start visualizing the conversation that takes over 5 minutes. When people can't settle on a storyline or have a lot of confusion for about 5 minutes, start visualizing the storyline.

4.5.9 *The secret modeler*

The secret modeler, which was coined to us by Ben Monsoir (https:// learningwardleymapping.com), isn't at all a collaborative modeling style but more of a tactic. We get a lot of questions from people on how to start and learn to use the collaborative model tools, and one tip we give is that you can always model a conversation or meeting for yourself. Suppose you expect a particular meeting will be a good fit for collaborative modeling, but you don't have the authority to organize it. In that case, you can start to become a secret modeler. In a physical meeting, just pop out your notebook or a Bambook, which is a personal A4 whiteboard. Now just begin modeling the conversation. You can keep it simple and just use boxes and arrows to do this. Putting out a paper roll and starting to do EventStorming in a meeting isn't so secret.

But for online meetings, you can pop open Miro and have all the space you need. With the model visualized, you can ask powerful questions. Eventually, people might start noticing you as the person who always asks the most insightful questions because you just visualized the landscape of the conversation. Like Simon Wardley mentions in his blog post "On Being Lost" (https://mng.bz/67PZ), you now have an actual chessboard in front of you while the rest are playing chess without the board visible. For example, one of the authors used EventStorming during a presales meeting to model the other person's needs. Using hotspots as a powerful tool to ask questions, the author understood the problem and saw how best to help.

Exercise 4.2: Be a secret modeler

At your next meeting, where you know you'll be sitting around a table without any form of visualization going on, try to be a secret modeler. Wardley Mapping is our favorite way, but just visualizing any way you can is majorly effective! See what insights and questions pop up before and after the session that you normally won't get from such a session. It's the perfect opportunity to get some practice with any of the collaborative modeling tools before you use them in a session.

4.5.10 *How to use the styles*

Preparing what style to use won't be necessary for short collaborative modeling sessions, and you'll probably follow the same style you used before. For example, for a basic EventStorming, you'll start with the Together, Alone style. First, you let everyone write down their own stickies. Then, for the next step, enforce the timeline, everyone will merge the timeline together into one, and you can decide what to do next.

Sometimes, you'll need to use another style during a session. For instance, during a software design EventStorming, people will come up with two competing storylines. We then go back to Small Group Diverge, Converge to work out these timelines. We end up having several models for the same problem. We can now analyze the tradeoffs and decide what to do next.

> **GUIDING HEURISTIC**   Change the collaboration style when you've been using the same style for a while with the same group.

However, for a full day of collaborative modeling, you want to be more prepared to set yourself up for success. You might also use several tools during the session to get the desired outcome. For each section of the day, you can already think about what style you can use when a specific situation pops up. Especially when you're unfamiliar with one particular style, we advise you to be better prepared for what can happen. In addition, a very good heuristic to keep in mind from Sharon Bowman's *Training from the Back of the Room* (Pfeiffer, 2008) is "Different trumps same." In other words, if you've been running several collaborative modeling sessions with the same group and the same style, changing the style might bring new insights and learning.

4.6   *Retrospective*

After letting participants know what they can expect next, and everyone has checked out, we officially close the session. Sometimes, we might all end the day together, enjoying a nice cup of tea or other drinks. Before everyone leaves, we usually bring out a flipchart and ask people to share their thoughts on it. This might include what they thought went well, and any questions they still have. Or, we might create a sensemaking exercise with three scales focusing on return on time invested, content, and structure. We also tell them that this is optional and that we'll send an email the next day with more information and a way for them to give feedback. It's important to be careful about asking for feedback directly in the group to avoid putting anyone in the spotlight as mentioned earlier. People will provide feedback when they feel ready. If you push for it and put them on the spot, the feedback you get might not be accurate. We prefer quality feedback over a large quantity of potentially inaccurate feedback. Sometimes, not receiving any feedback is okay and understandable. If people don't give feedback, it could mean many things: they might be under pressure, be afraid to speak up, or perhaps thought the sessions were excellent.

Now the participants usually leave, and you end up with the persons involved in setting the meeting up. You clean up together, take pictures of the visuals when working with a physical space, and talk about how the session went. Online usually means everyone leaves the video session, and the ones left are these same people. Now we share the insights we had about the concerns, quickly evaluate what people gave for feedback, and discuss a follow-up to reflect on the session. It's time to start a retrospective of how the session went.

4.6.1   *Evaluating the outcome of the session*

The goal of a retrospective is to reflect on the collaboration that occurred. It's important to understand what went well, what could have gone better, what important knowledge the participants gained, and so on. So, the first thing you want to do as a facilitator when you have the chance is to take some time to write down your thoughts about the session. What did you observe? What topics did you hear? What is your own feeling about the session? What were the insights after the people left during your discussion with others? Doing this is vital because those first insights and feelings are the ones you might lose and be gone forever. You want to take at least a day to reflect on yourself about the session before you pick up evaluating the session. Your first thoughts are valid but can be based on bias, which we'll discuss later in the book. You want to dump these.

With all the gathered input from the session, you can make sense of what has happened and start to reflect together with the persons involved. You want to discuss what everyone thought about how the session went. What went well? What could we do better next time? What are the concerns we have for a follow-up? Is there something we need to communicate to the group? What can we do with the outcome of our premortem? It's essential to ensure all the concerns are addressed that the group mentioned. If we make a decision during the meeting, we want to ensure people can actually work on it.

We want to discuss how we can ensure that everyone can execute the decisions and how we can follow these up.

Another possibility is that we need a follow-up, perhaps because we couldn't complete the session. So, we start our collaborative modeling process and fill in the canvas. Is there something we need to do differently this time? Perhaps some unspoken shadows are left that need to be addressed before we start a new session. Are we worried about certain people in the group? Are they feeling okay? What was their feedback? Do we already need to document something or communicate it to the group?

4.6.2   *When we don't do a retrospective*

Often, we may forget to do a retrospective or decide not to do one. We might feel that the session's outcome was determined, decisions were made, and these are now acted upon. It's possible that just by doing collaborative modeling, things have already changed. People act slightly differently and are in a different state of mind because they are removed from the environment they are usually in. They were in a pressure cooker. The minute they return to work, they return to business as usual. You can't change the behavior of a group or company with just one workshop. We can do a lot in one day, but we need to break and do more to change the unwanted behavior in the organization that can keep a group or team from moving forward.

When we don't do a retrospective, we might have a short gain, and everything just after seems to go fine. But the next time you'll do another collaborative modeling session, people will start to wonder, did we actually do something with it? Did we actually change something, or will this be another worthless waste of our time and nothing happens as a follow-up. We want to know what people think about the session. We want to catch that feedback early so that we can adjust with the group to determine what's required to get the outcome they need. Sometimes, collaborative modeling just doesn't work, which is fine because there are many reasons why people aren't ready to use it. At the very least, we want to know why it didn't work for them so we can deal with the social dynamics and make it safe to fail. You'll learn more on all of these social dynamics in upcoming chapters.

4.7   *Collaborative software design catalysts*

- For your next meeting, let the participants engage in an impromptu networking check-in. As a topic for the impromptu networking, you can discuss any questions that they have on the topic of the meeting. Having some coffee and snacks during impromptu networking helps to make people more relaxed.
- At a halfway point of a collaborative modeling session, do a sensemaking exercise. Encourage participants to evaluate how confident they are that the group will reach the goals at the end of the session, by rating their confidence on a scale from 1 to 10. Invite those in the group at various points on the scale to give feedback, and decide together if we should make changes to the session.

- At the end of a meeting, initiate a sensemaking exercise. Encourage people to evaluate the effectiveness of the meeting in terms of reaching its goals by rating it on a scale from 1 to 10. Invite those in the group at various points on the scale to give feedback, and inquire what would help them move closer to a 10. This feedback can serve as valuable input for planning the next meeting.
- When you're running collaborative modeling sessions with several groups in breakout sessions, it can be challenging to ensure that everyone knows what they need to do. Before moving into the breakout exercises, start a Fishbowl style exercise with one of the groups. Have the other groups watch and write down any questions they have. After 5 to 10 minutes, stop the exercise to answer these questions. Once all questions are addressed, then allow everyone to move into their breakout groups.

4.8 Chapter heuristics

Guiding heuristics

- Do sensemaking exercises when you get the feeling shadows are in the way.
- Merge on the most complete model instead of the one that is most accurate.
- Optimize for chaos over structure. We want to postpone giving too much structure to a session because the more structure you give, the fewer insights emerge.
- When modeling an in-depth problem, split groups that have more than seven participants.
- Be the least informed person in the room. To get people engaged in the session, ask questions you know are wrong. People love to tell you that you're wrong and correct you, starting the engagement.
- Start visualizing the conversation that takes over 5 minutes. When people can't settle on a storyline or have a lot of confusion for about 5 minutes, start visualizing the storyline.
- Change the collaboration style when you've been using the same style for a while with the same group.

4.9 Further reading

- *Facilitator's Guide to Participatory Decision-Making* by Sam Kaner (Jossey-Bass Business & Management, 2014)
- *Fifty Quick ideas to Improve Your Retrospectives* by Ben Williams and Tom Roden (New Consulting, 2015)
- *Retrospectives Antipatterns* by Aino Vonge Corry (Pearson, 2022)
- *The Surprising Power of Liberating Structures: Simple Rules to Unleash a Culture of Innovation* by Henri Lipmanowicz and Keith McCandless (Liberating Structures Press, 2014)

- *Training from the Back of the Room!: 65 Ways to Step Aside and Let Them Learn* by Sharon L. Bowman (Pfeiffer, 2008)
- *Visual Meetings: How Graphics, Sticky Notes & Idea Mapping Can Transform Group Productivity* by David Sibbet (Wiley, 2010)

Summary

- There are six stages in our collaborative modeling: preparation, check-in, modeling with tools, check-out, retrospective, and communication and documentation.
- As a facilitator, it's important to prepare both the content and space for a collaborative modeling session. It helps participants understand the goals, their roles, and the desired outcomes of the session.
- Preparation of the space depends on whether the session takes place in person or remote. In-person spaces should encourage people to stand and move around most of the session, where remote sessions require a well-prepared online whiteboard.
- Sensemaking is a technique you can use to get and provide insights into perspectives, emotions, concerns, polarities, and (potential) conflicts within a group that are beyond the obvious and visible.
- As a facilitator, sensemaking helps in guiding a session or decision-making process. For the group, sensemaking helps them see other perspectives and challenge their own to come to a shared mental model.
- Sensemaking is a powerful way to make shadows in a group explicit and dive into the group unconscious. Doing this prevents seemingly minor conflicts, disagreements, or negative emotions from growing so big that they will hinder progress and outcomes of the session.
- A premortem exercise is a form of sensemaking and a way of doing up-front analysis of a failed project. The hindsight perspective forces you to think of what *did* go wrong, instead of what *might* go wrong.
- Check-ins and check-outs are a form of sensemaking with a specific purpose and time. You focus on the participants instead of the goal of a session. They can help with focus, personal connection, underlying tension made explicit sooner, and less gossiping through the grapevine.
- A retrospective is usually done with a subset of the group, that is, the people who were involved in setting up the session. The goal is to evaluate the outcome of the session and decide if a follow-up is needed.
- We described eight collaboration styles that you can use in a session, depending on what you want to achieve. The styles can be used while using the earlier described tools such as EventStorming and Example Mapping. In your preparation, you can think of the tools and style you want to use when specific situations pop up.

5

Facilitating collaborative modeling

This chapter covers

- Different stances a facilitator takes
- Fundamental skills for different stances
- Underlying skill set of the fundamental skills
- Applying facilitator skills in a collaborative modeling session
- Facilitating collaborative modeling sessions remotely

In the previous chapter, we discussed the six stages of the collaborative modeling process. By now, you've gained a solid understanding of what collaborative modeling entails, its flow, the various tools and styles that can be used in a session, and how to design software architecture using this approach.

This chapter will focus on the role of a facilitator and the different stances you can adopt during collaborative modeling. We'll detail the skills necessary to become an effective facilitator, delving into how to apply collaborative styles in a facilitation role and outlining the responsibilities of a facilitator at each stage of the process. Even if you're not aiming to become a facilitator or don't feel confident in that role, some of the skills that aid a facilitator are also beneficial for participants in collaborative modeling. Honestly, all these skills can help everyone not only become better at their job but also in their personal growth and interaction with others.

135

5.1   *The role of a facilitator*

The term *facilitator* is derived from the French word *faciliter*, which means "to render easy;" thus, a facilitator is someone who makes things easier for others. In the context of this book, a facilitator's role is to make the flow of collaborative modeling easier for the participants. While facilitators guide collaborative modeling, they don't bear the weight of the outcome. That responsibility rests with the collective group. It's essential to understand that a successful facilitation doesn't always guarantee the desired outcome. Sometimes, even if the process is flawlessly managed, the end result might differ from initial expectations. However, a different outcome doesn't necessarily mean it's unproductive or negative. As the saying goes, you can lead a horse to water, but you can't make it drink.

The essence of being a facilitator isn't confined to a specific job title. Whether you're a team lead, software architect, user researcher, business analyst, software tester, software engineer, or any other roles in an organization, you can embody the role of a facilitator. The crux of the matter is that individuals across various roles all have the potential to guide and influence. We strongly believe that most collaborative modeling sessions should feature at least one, if not several, dedicated facilitators. This arrangement ensures that someone is exclusively focused on steering the flow and dynamics of the session, enabling participants to zero in on the session's goals and results. Merging the roles of a facilitator and a participant can introduce distractions, potential conflicts of interest, and a diminished focus. Such overlaps can significantly undermine the productivity and success of the session. While it's not impossible to combine these roles, and we occasionally do, the subsequent chapters will delve into the potential pitfalls and guide you on when the presence of a dedicated facilitator is indispensable.

Now let's delve deeper into how a facilitator can adopt multiple stances during the process. They might act as an observer, coordinator, coach, enabler, counselor, or task organizer. Among these, the role of an observer stands out as the foundational stance for a facilitator that in every role is needed, as illustrated in figure 5.1. Depending on the situation, a facilitator can embrace all or some of these roles.

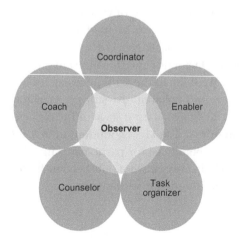

Figure 5.1   The facilitator takes on different stances. The observer stance takes a central place, which provides a facilitator with important information to take on other stances.

5.1.1 The facilitator as an observer

One of the first things we did when joining BigScreen, was assess the current situation. We wanted to understand the conflict between two developers, Jack and Rose, with regard to the redesign. We scheduled separate interviews with both Jack and Rose, so they would be more comfortable talking to us about the redesign. The stances of a facilitator apply not only to the collaborative modeling session stage but also to all the stages. Interviews can be done as part of the prep. During those two interviews, we heard things such as, "They aren't listening to me when I am explaining my point of view," and "I get the impression they don't WANT to understand my idea." We could hear the frustration in their voices when they were explaining how they got there. Their body language also changed when we started discussing this. We observed that they were mostly pointing fingers to the other person during their respective interviews.

Being an observer often extends beyond mere visual observation; it involves actively listening and engaging with individuals to understand underlying problems. In our case, interviewing became a crucial observational tool. We were fortunate with Jack and Rose, who openly shared their perspectives. However, as we expanded our conversations within the company, challenges arose.

When we sought to understand the back office's problems, we scheduled a meeting with Tiago, the COO overseeing that department. Initially, we encountered resistance. Comments like, "Sure, there are areas to improve in the back office, but the development team has provided decent workarounds," and "I don't believe addressing this should be a top priority," were common.

With our extensive experience observing individuals and groups, discrepancies became evident. For instance, while a department head might verbally downplay a problem, their tense posture or avoidance of eye contact suggested otherwise. These conflicting signals between words and body language are what we call *double signals*.

Moreover, we had concrete evidence of the back office's challenges: frequent system downtimes, delayed responses to customer queries, and a high rate of clerical errors. These weren't mere inefficiencies but significant operational problems.

From Gerald Weinberg's book *System Design Heuristics* (Leanpub, 2018, p. 41), "The incongruence insight" became our guiding heuristic. It emphasizes the importance of recognizing when words don't align with actions or other nonverbal cues, prompting a deeper investigation.

> **GUIDING HEURISTIC** When words and music don't go together, they point to a missing element.

The "incongruence insight" heuristic suggests that when an individual's words aren't aligned with their tone of voice and body language, there's an underlying element that's not being addressed. In our model, that element became a shadow. In many situations, this misalignment can indicate a lack of safety. When people don't feel secure, they might hesitate to discuss conflicts or contentious problems. The fear of repercussions or judgment can lead them to avoid the topic, hoping it will dissipate on its own.

For instance, if an employee says, "Everything's fine," but their voice quivers and they avoid eye contact, it's a sign that everything might not be as "fine" as they claim. The underlying problem, in this case, could be their discomfort or fear of addressing a particular conflict.

Creating an environment where individuals feel safe to express their concerns and address conflicts is crucial. We'll delve into the importance of fostering such a safe space later in this chapter. Additionally, strategies for effective conflict management will be discussed in detail in chapter 8. For now, our emphasis is on honing the skill of observation to detect these incongruences in individuals or groups.

Upon recognizing the discrepancy with COO Tiago's words and body language, we initially refrained from jumping to conclusions. While we had previously discussed the "incongruence insight" heuristic and its potential link to a lack of safety, it was essential not to prematurely impose this interpretation on the situation. Instead, we allowed the individuals to express their reasons.

As humans, we naturally interpret and make sense of the behaviors we observe. Completely detaching from our interpretations is nearly impossible. The key, especially in a facilitation role, is to be acutely aware of our own biases and interpretations. It's about holding our interpretations lightly, being open to them being challenged, and not letting them dictate our interactions. We'll go more in depth about how to do this later in chapters 6 and 7.

When we assume we understand someone's feelings or motivations based solely on our experiences or beliefs, we risk misjudging them. This not only can lead to misunderstandings but can also damage the trust and rapport we're trying to build. Thus, while it's natural to form interpretations, it's crucial to approach situations with an open mind and allow individuals to share their perspectives without feeling predefined. We'll discuss how to handle these judgements a bit more later on in the chapter.

PATTERNS

From the observations that you make, you'll try to detect if patterns are present. What makes a behavior a pattern? This behavior is notable for its repetitive aspect. It isn't just a one-time occurrence but happens regularly. Moreover, this behavior is influenced by cultural norms. Within a certain culture where such behavior is acceptable, or even encouraged, individuals adopt it as a standard way of handling problems. However, this behavior doesn't manifest in different contexts when faced with similar problems.

For example, one developer mentioned that in their previous company, this pattern of behavior wasn't observed. They had never been involved in prolonged arguments with someone else before. Yet, when they started working at BigScreen, they began to unconsciously adopt the practice of blaming others. This illustrates how behavioral patterns are often passed down within an organization, from established employees to new ones, either deliberately or inadvertently.

As a facilitator, we try to detect these patterns. We can use guiding heuristics again to help us with finding patterns. An example of a heuristic that helps us detect patterns follows:

GUIDING HEURISTIC   When someone says "this is how we do it here," you know you've found a pattern of their specific culture.

A pattern doesn't necessarily imply negativity. Many individuals possess patterns that prove advantageous both for themselves and those around them. At BigScreen, Caelan, the team lead, consistently ensured that they engaged in a one-on-one conversation with every team member weekly. These discussions typically lasted 15 to 20 minutes, although they could extend if problems arose. Such a pattern is immensely beneficial for a team lead. It can foster open communication, ensures that team members feel valued and heard, and promptly addresses any concerns, thereby promoting a harmonious and productive work environment.

When facilitating collaborative modeling, we're there to facilitate the process to the group's desired outcome. That's why we want to look at coherent patterns in a group—not only in the individual—because collaborative modeling is a group process. We start by observing the behavior of individuals, try to find this pattern in the group, and then try to discover whether or not this pattern is fractal.

FRACTAL PATTERNS

We didn't just observe pointing fingers and blaming each other within the development team; we also observed similar accusations from and toward the development team. Departments were criticizing other departments: "They aren't listening to what we need," and "They are just not interested in understanding how we work." We call this a fractal pattern because this type of behavior was observable throughout the company. It's innate to the organizational culture, or the team culture. A pattern is fractal when it's repetitive, not just in time, but also at every scale of an organization, similar to mathematical fractals (see figure 5.2). We named this pattern the Only Criticize the Other pattern, where everyone is pointing fingers at someone else as the guilty party and not self-reflecting on their own behavior.

Figure 5.2   A fractal triangle pattern. This triangle is repetitive at every scale. The big triangle comprises three smaller triangles. Those smaller triangles comprise three even smaller triangles. You'll find fractal patterns also in companies. Patterns exhibited by higher management will be observable on lower levels of the company.

Exercise 5.1

During your next company or department meeting, take a moment to jot down the patterns you observe. It's challenging, but try to avoid interpreting these observations through the lens of your own biases. For instance, if you notice that one of your colleagues, say Julia, frequently interrupts others while they're speaking, resist the urge to infer reasons, such as "Julia interrupts because she fears her opinion won't be heard." You can't be certain of Julia's motivations without directly asking her. Instead, record your observations factually: "Julia interrupts others #times during the session," "Julia doesn't interrupt X," or "Julia interjects when the topic is X."

What you then write down is your own thoughts and feelings about the observation, for instance, "I have the feeling she does this because she fears her opinion won't be heard." If possible, delve deeper to discern if these patterns are fractal in nature: Does anyone else exhibit this behavior? Is this "interruption" pattern pervasive across different levels within the company? Remember, it's impossible not to interpret, but being aware of your own biases is crucial for objective observation.

5.1.2   *Other stances of a facilitator*

As a facilitator, you're always an observer. After a while, it becomes innate. You'll observe a group and the interactions within that group and try to find patterns. The patterns that you detect will be used when taking a different stance during the collaborative modeling process.

COORDINATOR

The responsibility of a coordinator in an organization is to ensure others work together effectively when organizing events or activities. In the context of collaborative modeling, this means that you help to plan and design the collaborative modeling sessions. You're the person responsible for preparing the content and space. When you're internal, you have a lot more knowledge to work with, and you'll have a better understanding of what the pain points are and how to prioritize those. When you're an external facilitator, you'll depend upon the input of the teams you're working with. As we mentioned in chapter 4, we prepped the collaborative modeling sessions for BigScreen together with the development team. When we were doing this, we were taking the coordinator stance.

COACH

Just like an Agile coach, who plays a crucial role in supporting, empowering, and facilitating teams to adopt Agile practices and methodologies, your role as a collaborative modeling coach is equally pivotal in helping companies embrace collaborative modeling. As a collaborative modeling coach, you're primarily tasked with guiding, challenging, and encouraging individuals to effectively engage with collaborative modeling, which includes honing their skills in using the necessary tools. A vital initial step in assuming the coach stance involves establishing clear expectations through "contracting" with the individual or group you're coaching. This agreement should clearly define the boundaries of your support, empowerment, and facilitation, while also explicitly stating what should not be expected from the coaching relationship. Contracting can range from simple agreements such as consent for feedback during sessions to more complex arrangements, such as setting precise goals and outcomes for integrating collaborative modeling within a company.

At BigScreen, for example, we dedicated our first session to tool demonstration. We illustrated how Big Picture EventStorming functions, actively modeling the interactions among stakeholders, including adding swimlanes and pivotal events. Gradually, we shifted the responsibility to the participants. Instead of doing it ourselves, we encouraged them to take the lead: "That's an interesting point. Would you want to add a pivotal event for that? Remember to phrase it in the past tense."

> **NOTE** As you might already know, coaching is a well-established field. For those seeking deeper insights, we recommend starting with *Coaching Agile Teams: A Companion for ScrumMasters, Agile Coaches, and Project Managers in Transition* by Lyssa Adkins (Addison-Wesley Professional, 2010).

ENABLER

An enabler is a person who enables others to achieve a certain end. That end can be the goal of the collaborative modeling session, making inclusive decisions, and so on. As a facilitator, it's your responsibility to remove roadblocks for individuals or the group that prevents them from achieving that ending. We remove those roadblocks by using the skill set of the facilitator, which we'll discuss in section 5.3. For example, when doing Big Picture EventStorming, some people in the group might stay more in the back, while others will start talking through each other. In that case, we can give back to the group what is observed so that they become aware of their unconscious behavior, giving them an opportunity to improve their flow. We call that a climate report, which we'll discuss further in chapter 8.

COUNSELOR

Sometimes as a facilitator, you have to be a counselor, by supporting individuals in the group. The individual interviews we scheduled with Rose and Jack when we first arrived at BigScreen were done by looking at this problem from a counselor stance. As a counselor, you'll listen to the problems that people are experiencing. You'll help to guide them to better understand their emotions and their triggers during group dialogues. This is a big responsibility. We understand that there is a limit to what you can do as a counselor. It's important that you know yours. To help someone, sometimes the best decision you can make as a facilitator is to refer this person to someone who is better equipped than you.

TASK ORGANIZER

As we mentioned before, you're not responsible for the outcome of a collaborative modeling session. You're a task organizer, you're responsible for making sure that all tasks are picked up by an individual or a subgroup. You create a contract between you and these people and follow up to make sure that they respect this contract. The easiest way to do this is to track the to-dos on the whiteboard and take a few minutes each session to go over them and update their progress. When you're updating their progress, we also use the enabler stance to remove possible roadblocks. We ask questions such as these: "Is there anything preventing you from moving forward with this?" or "What do you need to complete this to-do?"

All of these different stances require certain competencies. In the next section, we'll dive into three important core competencies that you need to develop as a facilitator to take on all of these different stances.

5.2   *The core competencies of a facilitator*

Learning to take on different roles as a facilitator definitely takes a lot of practice. In any organization, anyone can become a facilitator if they're willing, no matter what their job is. This includes a wide range of people, from software engineers, testers, architects, and data scientists, to business analysts, UX researchers, managers, product managers, and C-level executives. It even includes roles you wouldn't usually associate with facilitation, such as assistants, cleaners, and project managers. What matters most isn't the job title, but the ability to create a collaborative environment, keep things moving smoothly, and transition groups through different parts of collaborative modeling.

Software architects, technical leads, agile coaches, and consultants are often seen leading collaborative modeling sessions. This is mostly because they have had many opportunities to build up these key skills. However, this doesn't mean they are the only ones who can do it. With the right training and experience, anyone in an organization can step into this role and make a meaningful difference when given the chance. We'll talk more about what "given the chance" means in the next chapter on ranking theory.

Competencies which are inspired by the Lewis Deep Democracy method metaskills, are broad qualities that support a range of specific skills, or skill sets. These core competencies grow through using your skill set, and getting better at them also makes your skills more effective. For a collaborative modeling facilitator, there are three main competencies and skill sets that support each other, as shown in figure 5.3. These are Compassion, developed through holding space; Neutrality, built through holding space and active listening; and Observing, developed through active listening and clear communication.

It's important to realize that the three main competencies of a facilitator—Neutrality, Observing, and Compassion—can be learned by anyone. We'll keep highlighting how important these competencies are for everyone involved in collaborative modeling. While some people might find these skills come naturally, others might need more time to learn them. Remember, these skills might seem natural, but they aren't something you're born with. They are learned, often without realizing it, over time. Let's first take a closer look at each of these three core competencies to understand what they really mean.

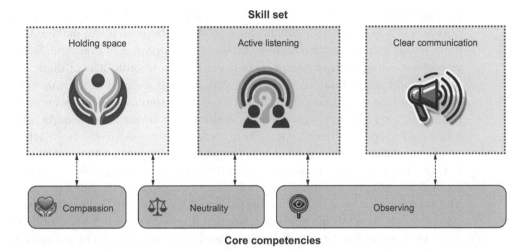

Figure 5.3 **The link between facilitation skills and core competencies. Core competencies consist of Compassion, Neutrality, and Observing, and they are fundamental yet require self-awareness and adaptability across cultures. These competencies enhance the facilitation skills of Holding Space, Active Listening, and Clear Communication, which can be improved through study and practice.**

5.2.1   *Neutrality*

This might sound confusing, but being fully neutral is unattainable. The goal of acting neutral is to ensure that everyone in the group feels they are treated equally different. *Equally different* is the idea that every culture or individual is unique, but they all have the same right to be recognized and respected for their differences. Neutrality doesn't always guarantee that outcome. The aim is to create an environment where participants feel psychologically safe to express their ideas, ask questions, voice concerns, and make mistakes without fear of punishment or humiliation. Understand that psychological safety doesn't mean a conversation is always comfortable. Some discussions that include tense conflict might be uncomfortable, but they should never border on unsafe. As facilitators, our responsibility is to support each participant in a manner that makes it safe for them to speak up, even in moments of discomfort or tension. Yet, it's essential to understand that while we aim to be neutral, we might not always achieve it. Still, the effort is crucial.

Neutrality means we must strive to be selfless and support everyone in the group equally different, genuinely, and sincerely by considering all possibilities, perceptions, opinions, and emotions. It's important to create an environment where people feel free to express views and concerns, even if we disagree with them or find them unproductive. The key is to ensure these opinions are heard and understood by the group, fostering a sense of inclusivity and understanding.

GUIDING HEURISTIC   If you feel the urge to react to opinions being made, write these down, and reflect on them after the session.

We want to be able to identify all wisdom and potential in the group. We want to support as much as possible in collaborative modeling because it will make our models more useful. As a bonus, the models will be more supported by everyone. Supporting or understanding ideas or perspectives doesn't mean we must accept them; it means we listen and understand what has been said and find a way to support that concern. For instance, we might be able to understand and listen to why someone new to the team likes to do a branching strategy for developing software. But we might not accept it in our development lifecycle of the team because we believe in fast feedback cycles.

Instead of immediately dismissing their opinion, we should understand why they like it. Listen to any perspectives and concerns the person has. It might be because the person had a lot of harsh comments on their code when exposing it to their previous team. The person might be afraid of the backlash and the resulting feeling that they aren't good enough. Now joining another team, that fear is even greater because there is no trust yet. The way for them to feel safe is developing on a branch in solitude, making sure the code is perfect for exposure to people. So, knowing that, we might come to new ways or ideas that support that safety for the person and bring us fast feedback. We might pair up with the person, making sure they get time with everyone in the team so they can feel comfortable. We might let the person work on a branch, but ask them to create a merge request every day so we can review it faster.

When not to act neutral

In certain contexts, acting neutral may not be practical or expected, particularly when you have a specific role within a team, such as a developer, consultant, architect, or when dealing with conflict resolution.

As a developer involved in facilitating collaborative modeling for your team, your input as a Subject Matter Expert (SME) on software design is crucial. You shouldn't hesitate to share your perspectives. When you do, establish what we call a "contract" with the group: seek their agreement for you to momentarily step out of your facilitator role to express your opinion as an SME. You might even use a physical marker, such as a circle drawn on the ground with painters tape, to delineate when you're acting as the facilitator and when as the SME.

In the role of a consultant, your clients mostly hire you for your expertise, advice, and experience. They anticipate and value your insights. It's essential to be transparent about your objectives, facilitate the team in acknowledging and agreeing on the current problems, and ask the team explicitly if they need advice and guidance to solve that problem.

For architects tasked with critical domain-level decisions, especially those involving risk mitigation, maintaining neutrality can be challenging. In such situations, it's effective to clearly communicate the risks to the group and underscore the urgency of reaching a decision during the meeting together.

Lastly, in situations of major conflict where there is a polarized divide between two groups, and you're part of one, neutrality may not be the best approach. In such cases, having facilitators representing each side can ensure that both perspectives are fairly considered and addressed.

DEALING WITH YOUR OWN SHADOWS

We as facilitators might be biased and have prejudices about ideas a group has, or we might have totally other ideas! Knowing our biases and prejudices is essential because if we're unaware of them, it can affect the way we react. We don't want to give the person the feeling we're against the idea. We must stay open to ideas, or people will notice and won't speak up.

Facilitators can learn a lot from the anthropology field. Anthropologists do qualitative research through participant observation to observe a culture as they are. They want to capture the culture as is, which means they need to let go of any preconceptions to let all events happen naturally. But it's also well known in the field that it's impossible to do so. So instead of focusing on making sure not to have any preconceptions, they instead spend time understanding these preconceptions and capturing them. When anthropologists write field stories about their participant observation, besides describing what happens in the group, they also describe what happens to them. Trying to suppress your own emotions and prejudices during facilitation is a losing battle. We call those emotions and prejudices the shadows within us. Ignoring and suppressing shadows will turn them into demons at some point. If we ignore and suppress these shadows long enough, they will eventually become too strong to suppress, and they will come out when it's the most inconvenient in a burst of emotion, making us lose our neutrality beyond repair.

Instead of suppressing, we must acknowledge the stark reality that we all harbor irrational beliefs and prejudices. While some of these may be influenced by our emotions, they can also stem from other sources. It's essential to confront these inner demons and understand how to address them when they surface. Address them early on, when they are still shadows, making them easier to manage. During facilitation, it's natural to occasionally drift from neutrality. However, by recognizing these moments, we can recalibrate and return to a balanced perspective. This is why we describe neutrality as a verb; we continuously monitor and address our biases, ensuring they don't cloud our judgment. This vigilance is a lifelong practice, both in facilitation and in our daily lives.

Working on your inner thoughts and emotions isn't new behavior to humanity. The ancient philosophy of stoicism already has practices to deal with shadows. A common misunderstanding is that stoics are people that don't have emotions. However, stoics have a massive understanding of their emotions and have dealt with them and reflected on them daily. That's why, in the moment, when something happens, they aren't overcome with emotions, but already understand them and come to terms with them. Coming to terms with one's emotions allows us to act seemingly emotionless in challenging situations. A common practice you can do before you a collaborative modeling session is to imagine all possible scenarios that might happen. Stoics call this *premeditatio malorum*, which helps us deal with the shadows and demons ahead. Rehearse what happens in your mind, especially feel what happens within yourself. What situations might trigger you, and what preconceptions might you have about the problem being modeled? How will that person who annoys you push you this time, and how can you genuinely listen and understand? Are there any conflicts in the group that might show up? And what does that do to you? How would you react if you didn't prepare for it? Let the demons out!

Exercise 5.2

A good exercise to help you find biases and preconceptions in yourself is to experience different cultures, especially the ones we consider to be extreme or weird. One of the coauthors loves watching documentaries on YouTube by Louis Theroux who visits these many different subcommunities of our society and gives you an inside experience. Locate and watch some of these documentaries and videos to see and experience what biases and prejudice you have. What judgements did you make about them? Would you be able to stay neutral given their opinions and the way they act? From these examples, learn how to ask powerful questions to uncover more about their culture without losing too much neutrality.

5.2.2   *Observing*

Working on neutrality gives us access to more information from communication channels. *Communication channels* refer to the various ways in which information, feelings, thoughts, and perceptions are conveyed within a group. The communication channel is a way to observe behavioral patterns that groups are dealing with that might hold them back or block the flow of collaboration. Behavioral patterns are happening in the group and in the shadows of the group, which they are unaware of but which we can help them see and deal with.

Observing extends beyond the realm of active listening. While active listening emphasizes tuning into a person's verbal and nonverbal communication (which we'll delve into later in this chapter), observing encompasses a broader spectrum that involves observing the interactions among group members, as well as identifying the dominant culture and subcultures within the group. *Group culture* refers to the shared values, beliefs, and norms that guide behavior within a group, while *subcultures* are smaller groups within the larger group, each with its distinct values and behaviors. How does one subgroup's values and behavior contrast with another's?

Additionally, it's crucial to note the positions individuals assume within the group and the dynamics of their movements toward or away from one another. Equally important is the surrounding environment, which often houses cultural artifacts. These artifacts, such as posters or symbols, offer insights into the group's culture, revealing underlying beliefs and values.

An example of cultural artifacts in the surroundings

One of the authors had an experience with a company focused on organizing their teams around business processes. In this company, numerous business capabilities were recognized as shared responsibilities among different teams. However, there was a lack of ownership for these capabilities, especially when problems occurred. These problems were reported in a ticket system and bounced from team to team, all assigning the ticket to the other team to solve it.

An interesting observation was made in the area leading from the building's staircase to the workspaces. There were doors with notes attached, requesting they be closed to avoid drafts. Yet, each time the coauthor visited this client, these doors were invariably left open. Curious, they asked the managing director who was responsible for closing the doors, and the response was that it was everyone's responsibility.

This scenario is a clear example of how behavioral patterns within IT settings can be reflected in the physical aspects of a workplace. The consistent problem with the open doors was a direct mirror of the organizational behavior, where shared responsibilities were acknowledged but not actively managed by any specific team, demonstrating what is known in organizational studies as *fractal patterns*.

Lastly, and perhaps most subtly, is the need to be observing the group's shadows. This refers to the underlying, often unspoken or unrecognized, aspects of group dynamics that aren't immediately observable. By being conscious of these shadows, we can gain a deeper understanding of the group's inner workings and potential challenges.

BECOMING FULLY CONSCIOUS: USING THE FLASHLIGHT

The way to observe the group's shadows is what we call metaphorically "using a flashlight." With the flashlight we can shed light on the unconscious part—the shadows of the group where deeper emotions live. Following are examples of the unconscious shadows:

- Losing a teammate
- Fearing speaking up because of a previous manager who always started shouting when they disagreed
- Feeling insecure when new to the group
- Making quick decisions and judgments due to cognitive bias

To observe these individual and group behavioral patterns, we must be aware of our unconsciousness. It's more than what we discussed in neutrality. It's also about our deeper emotions. How are we feeling today? Are we calm, or is something keeping us busy?

You can think of it like a rugby player that sprained their ankle, so they will find it much harder to run. The same goes with emotions, if we're upset or stressed, it will be harder to observe the shadows in the group because our consciousness is clouded. For instance, let's take not feeling welcome as an example of an emotional trigger. A lot of things can trigger that emotion. Perhaps someone isn't reacting the way we expect or is questioning every step we take. We might get emotionally distressed because of it and that can lower our neutrality. As a result, we might act on our shadows and start working hard to eliminate that feeling by forcing that person to react the way we want them to react by dictating the session and using our rank to do so. Or we might defend every step we take that is being questioned by the group. But working hard on our inner thoughts and emotions with self-reflection helped separate and eased that emotion so we could factually observe what was going on. Perhaps that person isn't feeling well today or is feeling insecure. So, we should see which is true: Are they not welcoming, or are our shadows getting in the way? And judging whether it's about ourselves or something in the group gets harder the more emotionally distressed we feel. Because, yes, we might not be welcome in a group.

So, it's crucial to stay in contact with and deal with your feelings and stress level before and during a session. There are a lot of ways to do so. Some people might do mindfulness exercises, others might do coaching sessions, or and still others may choose to go to a therapist. Sometimes quick remedies might work, such as taking some medicine to calm us down. But we would always advise looking deeper into your mental state and feel where your distress is coming from. We've mentioned using a notebook before to write down heuristics. We do the same with self-reflection before and after each session to write down our emotional patterns.

> **GUIDING HEURISTIC**   If you find yourself feeling drained or exhausted by the facilitation process, it might be an indicator that you're taking on too much responsibility or don't have enough skills yet to facilitate that specific session. Facilitation should not be overly taxing.

In the end, we're complex beings, and you need to do what will work for you because what works for one person may not work for the other. Experiment and become self-aware of how you feel and deal with situations. Discover what works for you. One important signal to watch out for when you know you're fighting your shadows is if you've worked too hard in the sessions. If you're exhausted, what is there to learn and do differently next time?

5.2.3   *Compassion*

If we truly understand our own shadows, we become equipped with a deeper insight into the complexities of human emotions and struggles. This understanding doesn't necessarily mean we've experienced the exact same challenges as others, but it gives us a foundation to approach their struggles with compassion. To understand those shadows, we require the skill of compassion during collaborative modeling. We can only give space to all different perceptions, how weird or wrong we might find them, with compassion. Compassion is feeling upset by another person's negative emotions and trying to help them deal with it if that person wants your help. Compassion isn't that you're the problem solver, the one in power to solve the problem for the helpless. Compassion is about recognizing our shared humanity. Can I recognize my shadows in the other, and vice versa? We as humans give meaning to things. Nothing is inherently right or wrong on its own, but through interaction in groups, communities, and cultures, we assign meaning to things to decide what is right and what is wrong. Compassion is about whether I can find myself in you and empathize with you.

Compassion is also a type of empathy according to the psychological field, but not every form of empathy is compassion. There are many different types of empathy, and we find the ones described by Indi Young in her book *Time to Listen* (Indi Young Books, 2022) have the most use to us in describing what compassion is for a facilitator. As a facilitator, it's essential to distinguish between what Indi describes as compassion, also known as empathic concern, and other types of empathy, particularly empathic distress and empathic listening (commonly called "empathy"). With *empathic distress*, we feel upset by another person's emotional state but aren't motivated to help that person. As you can guess, that isn't so useful for our collaborative modeling session, and we see no use for this skill as a facilitator, but it can be handy in other situations.

With *empathic listening*, we try to let the other person feel understood when experiencing certain emotions. It goes deeper than compassion as we try to connect and support that person but don't try to relieve that person's suffering. The challenge with empathic listening is that connecting and supporting every single person in the group is very hard to do in a collaborative modeling session. It will drain your energy. Does that mean that we shouldn't have any empathy at all in collaborative modeling? No not at all! There are certain situations where the group and the outcome of the group are blocked because a person doesn't feel understood, connected, and supported. In that situation, we use empathic listening as facilitators. We also try to enable the group to connect and be empathetic with each other, making it a collective thing of the group instead of people being dependent on us. We want to coach the group to connect with each other, let the group empathize with each other!

LIMINALITY

We also need to prioritize compassion over empathy because a collaborative modeling session means groups are in a liminal state. A liminal state or *liminality* is the process of transitioning between two states. An example given to us from the anthropology field is that people transition from a child to a grown-up. That doesn't happen overnight, and that gradual transition is what we call liminality. They aren't children anymore, but they are neither grown-up, so what are they? Everyone has been in liminality, and you probably have experienced that it means there is a lot of uncertainty and chaos. An example might be when your teams changed from the waterfall to Agile way of working, or you went from being a software engineer to working DevOps. Liminality can cause a lot of emotional distress to people, so it's vital to work on your compassion to help people if they need help with that liminality.

During a collaborative modeling session, groups are also in liminality. Before the meeting, people all have their mental models of the problem, that is their own concepts that give their own meaning to the problem. During collaborative modeling, we give people the space to express these mental models, but at the same time, people will be exposed to other people's mental models. Maybe our own beliefs are being challenged, so during collaborative modeling, our understanding of the problem isn't valid anymore. Still, we also don't know the new shared mental model that we can use, so it's good to experience collaborative modeling sessions yourself. What do you experience in that liminality? Can you recognize yourself in the other person? Can you recognize why people behave the way they do? Being a participant yourself together with all the knowledge we share with you in this book will make you better at being compassionate toward others.

5.2.4 *Using and learning the core competencies*

Unfortunately, our core competencies aren't so quickly learned, and you might not be able to use them depending on the context and the group you're facilitating for. They are culturally dependent and ranking dependent, as well as dependent on the people allowing you to use them. For example, it will be hard to work on your neutrality as a facilitator if you're the company's CEO. But if you, as the CEO, will facilitate a collaborative modeling session outside your own company, you can be more neutral. Another example might be that you're facilitating a group from a different country, and the cultural differences cause people stay to remain quieter or behave differently, making it harder to observe what is going on. Or, perhaps you're a woman in tech, facilitating a group of guys who don't accept your leadership. In the next chapter, we'll talk more about ranking and the effect it can have on the group and yourself.

Another aspect that might affect these core competencies is how people perceive you. How you're perceived, particularly in terms of self-esteem and charisma, can influence the effectiveness of your facilitation. Do participants see you as confident and engaging? Can they relate to your enthusiasm, stature, and expertise? These perceptions are shaped by the values and beliefs of the group members. For instance, while some might view an individual such as Donald Trump as exuding self-esteem, others might interpret his behavior as stemming from deep-seated insecurities. If group members perceive you as lacking confidence, they might be hesitant to embrace your compassionate approach and engage with the collaborative process.

However, it's worth noting that while perceived self-esteem and charisma can be advantageous, they aren't the sole determinants of a successful facilitator. The essence of facilitation lies in understanding, compassion, and the ability to guide a group toward a common goal. Awareness of one's standing within a group is crucial. Indeed, navigating the intricacies of group dynamics and perceptions can be among the most challenging aspects of facilitation. While learning from failures and being receptive to diverse perspectives is invaluable, it's not the only path to self-awareness. Continuous reflection, seeking feedback, and immersing oneself in diverse environments can also foster a deeper understanding of oneself and others.

By being genuinely curious about others' viewpoints and fostering an environment where diverse opinions are valued, a facilitator can guide a group toward more inclusive discussions. This not only shifts perceptions but also paves the way for more effective collaboration, ultimately leading to superior outcomes, such as the creation of exceptional software.

5.3   *Skill set of a facilitator*

The relationship between a facilitator's core competencies and their broader skill set is closely connected, as we've previously discussed. The trio of core competencies form the foundation for effectively using a wider range of facilitative skills. This relationship isn't one-directional; the additional skills you develop also help to strengthen and enhance your core competencies. For instance, the interaction between Holding Space and Compassion, shown in figure 5.4, demonstrates this point: while holding space is based on compassion, truly embracing compassion involves a deep understanding of the art of holding space.

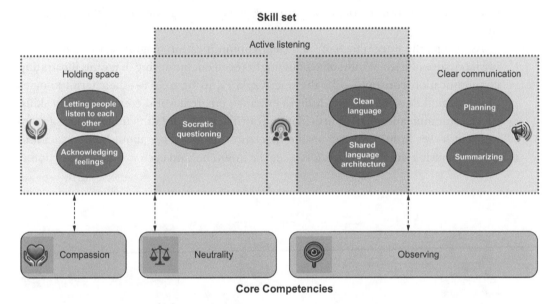

Figure 5.4   The relationship between a facilitator's core competencies and their wider skill set. Each skill set is tailored to refine your facilitation within that area. View these skill sets as a solid starting point for actionable techniques that you can use in your next collaborative modeling session.

In this section, we'll examine each of the following skill sets in more detail: clear communication, active listening, and holding space. We'll look at how these skills are not only important on their own but also how they support and reinforce the core competencies. For each skill set, we'll present specific techniques that you can apply immediately in your facilitation work. Keep in mind that the skills we discuss here aren't the only skills available. We're providing a snapshot of what we believe to be the most important fundamental skills at this moment. There are many practical skills that you can develop in each skill set, which will continue to evolve over time. View these skill sets as a solid starting point for actionable techniques that you can use in your next collaborative modeling session. In addition, be prepared to explore and develop your skills further in the ever-evolving field of facilitation.

5.3.1   *Clear communication*

During our childhood, there was a memorable activity. Participants were paired up; one person was blindfolded while the other provided verbal instructions to navigate a route filled with obstacles. Some called it a "game of trust" due to the blindfold. However, for us, it was more aptly a "game of clear communication." The challenge lay in articulating directions so explicitly that your blindfolded partner could follow them to a tee, even without the benefit of sight. For instance, you might say, "Take 5 steps forward." As your friend took their steps—one, two, three—suddenly, BAM! They'd crash into an obstacle, realizing it was really only three steps, not five. This highlighted that clear communication is tough but integral, making the game both challenging and fun.

As we age, the importance of such clear communication magnifies, though mastering it remains elusive. While some of us might recall encountering diagrams illustrating communication concepts—like the one displayed in figure 5.5—their terminologies often seemed detached, doing little to enhance our real-world communication skills. Clear communication means articulating your thoughts and directions in such a manner that leaves little room for misinterpretation or error. It's about being exact and direct, ensuring the receiver understands the intent behind each word or instruction.

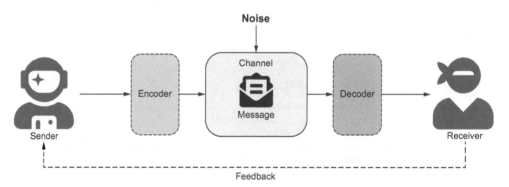

Figure 5.5   The communication lifecycle. A (not so helpful) diagram often used when teaching students about communication.

Communication is a dynamic, nonlinear process that involves the exchange of information, ideas, emotions, or intentions between individuals—not a linear process as depicted in figure 5.5. As a facilitator and a participant, you'll be communicating a lot, guiding the process of collaborative modeling or sharing your input. So, what can you do as a facilitator to communicate clearly? First, you need to develop your observing competence, which we discussed in the previous section. Second, clear communication flows out of good planning, shared language architecture, and summarizing. We'll dive a bit deeper into each one now.

PLANNING

Being well-prepared directly enhances how clearly you can communicate. Knowing the goal and objectives helps you understand what the group aims to achieve. When these goals are clear in your mind, you can express your thoughts with more clarity and confidence, answer questions effectively, and give important insights. In addition, when the purpose of the session is clear, you can communicate with more focus, keeping discussions on track.

That's why preparing for collaborative modeling sessions is so crucial. As a facilitator, you create a plan for the session. This preparation is all about organizing to ensure clear communication. You set a goal for the session that everyone gets, so they know that's the main point. You consider who should be there. You set up the meeting in advance and send out the agenda, so participants know what's coming and can get ready. Being prepared means you can also think ahead about possible questions or problems and be ready to respond clearly and effectively. This way of planning improves understanding and cuts down on confusion. Plus, it means you can adapt if things go in an unexpected direction during the session.

It's just as important for participants to come prepared, so letting them know what to expect is key for a successful session. We need to emphasize that some groups also need to do their homework before a session. These groups can handle a lot of information but need time to process it. We want to get all the useful information from everyone, and if these groups aren't ready for the session, they might not speak up, and we'll miss out on their knowledge and wisdom.

SHARED LANGUAGE ARCHITECTURE

Designing a shared language is a technique that helps people discover, understand, and develop their own language, symbols, and metaphors. Instead of forcing people to use the language that a facilitator is comfortable with, they will be helping the group and individuals understand their own language throughout the collaborative modeling. As a concrete example, for EventStorming, we're familiar with the word *policy* as a sticky note that indicates we need to react to a domain event, as mentioned in chapter 2. However, in an insurance company, the word *policy* is already a well-defined term, so using that as a concept might confuse people. We can architect a different word when doing EventStorming in that context. The same can happen for a business word, if we look at the following conversation from BigScreen:

> You: When you sell a ticket, do you always pay for a seat? When the business organizes a themed day, do they pay for a seat, or do they pay for entry?
>
> B: They pay for entry. We have multiple theater rooms that show movies; people don't select which one they will join beforehand.
>
> You: Okay, we haven't really modeled purchasing tickets for a themed day yet, let's do that now and see what is similar and what is different from purchasing a ticket for a movie.

After modeling the themed day purchase, the group realizes that not every ticket has a seat, so it would be confusing to keep saying that people pay for seats. They settled on calling the domain event Ticket Sold. A seat became optional, depending on what you're purchasing a ticket for. So shared language architecture in this context applies to two things: making sure everybody in the room understands each other (and themselves), and designing the ubiquitous language.

First, to make sure that everybody understands each other and themselves, you'll function as a translator. During collaborative modeling, people from different disciplines with different backgrounds will be joining the sessions. Each person has their own communication style and language that they use. At some points during a session, people are loudly agreeing with each other or silently disagreeing. As a facilitator, it's your responsibility to try and detect when this is happening and create clarity on this. You can create clarity by Socratic questioning, a technique we'll discuss a bit later in this section.

Second, you'll help to design a ubiquitous language, a pattern from Domain-Driven Design, which we discussed in chapter 2. The intent behind designing a ubiquitous language is to improve the clarity of communication. The domain language is something that grows organically over time. There are words that are overloaded or different words to point to the same concepts. Some examples of overloaded words are "customer," "client," and "product." These words mean very different things to different people. In software development, a product is the software system. In other contexts, a product is something physical. Customer and client often refer to the same concept. In figure 5.6, we show some examples specific for BigScreen. You'll help the group clean up these misconceptions, for example; "Seats paid" or "Ticket sold" could be referring to the same domain event. It's your job to dig a bit deeper into the language here, find out their meaning, and clean it up as needed.

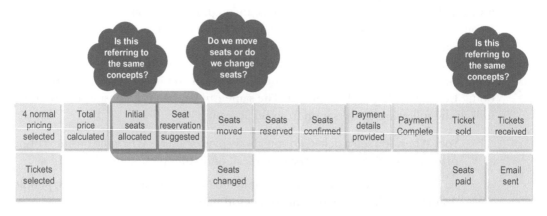

Figure 5.6   Domain language isn't always clean. When there are multiple words referring to the same concept, misconceptions arise because of the language. Make these terms explicit during a collaborative modeling session.

SUMMARIZING

Summarizing during collaborative modeling sessions is more than just a tool for recapping information; it's a navigational aid that steers the collective understanding and guides the trajectory of discussions. Before diving into the specifics, it's essential to recognize that summarization isn't merely a passive reiteration of events or dialogues. Instead, it's an active process that distills the essence of exchanges and insights, refocusing the group's attention and setting the stage for what's to come.

Throughout the session, your role transcends mere facilitation; you become the group's compass, providing real-time summaries that encapsulate decisions, reflect opinions, and, importantly, confirm or redirect the group's understanding. This continual synthesis serves a dual purpose: it ensures no one veers off the shared path due to confusion or misinterpretation, and it verifies your grasp of the information, which is crucial for maintaining the session's coherence and momentum.

Closing summaries, provided at the session's conclusion, aren't simply about action points or conclusions. They're strategic overviews that guide the group toward deciding what comes next. What problems warrant a deeper dive? What deserves immediate action? These summaries act as both a mirror, reflecting the session's accomplishments, and a window, projecting the next steps. Incorporating summarization as a fundamental component of your sessions acknowledges its power not just as a reflective tool, but as a proactive strategy for enhancing clarity, improving overall communication, and, crucially, providing a clear, shared direction for your diverse group.

5.3.2 *Active listening*

Active listening is a concept that finds its origin in clinical psychology. It emphasizes the importance of explicitly verifying whether you truly understood the message, verbally and nonverbally. One of the ways to do that was already discussed when talking about clear communication: cleaning language and summarizing. When you're cleaning the language, you're explicitly verifying the meaning of words and concepts, trying to understand what is being said.

In addition, active listening requires asking a lot of questions. We'll dig a bit deeper into Socratic questions and clean language here, but there are a lot of different categorizations to be found when googling.

SOCRATIC QUESTIONING

Throughout the previous chapters, we mentioned that the stakeholders need to have a deep, shared understanding of the business problems. We understand that it's easier said than done. Luckily, as a facilitator, you can help develop that deep and shared understanding by using Socratic questioning which we learned from Tony Bruce. *Socratic questioning* aims at creating a thoughtful dialogue to validate and improve the understanding of one's own thoughts, ideas, opinions, and beliefs.

Clarifying thoughts and beliefs	Challenge assumptions	Providing evidence
Why do you say this? Could you give me an example of x? How do you believe this solves x?	Are you assuming x? Why do you think that this is still true in this case? You say always; would it still happen in case of x?	Why do you say that? Is there a reason to assume that x is incorrect? How does that link back to our previous topic?

Discovering alternative viewpoints	Exploring consequences	Questioning questions
Does everyone agree? What is an argument against your point of view? Is there any way to model this differently?	How does x affect y? If x happened, what else would be the result? How does that link back to our previous topic?	Why do you ask this question? Why do you think I asked you this question? What is the importance of this question?

Figure 5.7   The six categories of Socratic questioning with generic example questions that you can adapt during a collaborative modeling session

In section 5.1, we briefly touched on the conflict between Rose and Jack from BigScreen. In the next paragraphs, we'll dig a bit deeper into the six categories (figure 5.7) of Socratic questioning by analyzing the interviews that we did with the two developers.

- *Clarifying thoughts and beliefs*—During the interviews, both developers mentioned that they believed the other person didn't want to understand their point of view. It's important to clarify what their opinion actually is. We dug a bit deeper by asking questions such as the following: "Why do you think your solution for the redesign is a good one?" You're trying to find the origin of their thinking to clarify it for you, and these questions often clarify things for them too.

- *Challenging assumptions*—People make unconscious assumptions. As a facilitator, it's our responsibility to find and question those assumptions. The two developers, Jack and Rose, made a lot of assumptions about the other person's intentions and saw this as "the truth." One of those assumptions was that the other person didn't want to understand them. We challenged that assumption: "Are you sure that Jack/Rose doesn't want to understand you?" Who is to say that the other person wasn't trying to understand their opinion? Conflicts often arise from built up assumptions over time. These assumptions aren't conscious. Neither Jack or Rose thought at some point "from now on, I am going to believe they don't *want* to understand me." This assumption of not wanting to understand became part of their view and then influenced their interpretation of the other person's actions and words.

By challenging this, we wanted to bring Jack and Rose back from their belief "my point of view is the truth," to an understanding of "this is how I experienced it." Once both parties understood that this was their experience, there was room for an open dialogue again between the two.

To shift their point of view on the conflict, we also challenged the content of the conflict (my solution is the best solution): "Under which conditions would your solution not be the best one to move forward with?" In a conflict, people start getting overly attached to their solutions, and we want them to see and accept other perceptions as well. We believe nobody holds the monopoly on the truth. We'll talk a bit more on how you can let people see other perceptions as well by staying in the holding space. In chapter 8, we'll explore conflict resolution deeper as well.

- *Providing evidence*—Once you clarify someone's thinking and beliefs, and challenge their assumptions, you ask for evidence to support these. We reminded them that there was a time they got along when challenging their assumptions about the conflict. Then, we asked for examples to solidify those new discoveries: "Can you give an example of a disagreement between you and Rose where she was trying to understand you?"

- *Discovering alternative viewpoints*—In this scenario, we already have alternative viewpoints that resulted in conflict, but it never hurts to look for more. The team was much larger than just Jack and Rose. Perhaps because of the conflict, other people's ideas were forgotten or not mentioned. We might ask, "Did everyone agree to pick your solution?" and "Was there someone who had another solution?"

- *Exploring consequences*—There are people who overvalue the benefits of their ideas and the downsides of other people's ideas. You don't want people to shoot an idea down, you want them to explore the consequences of this option and compare it to the other possible solutions. This can be done by asking questions such as the following: "How easy would it be to continue redesigning with Jack's approach?" and "If we picked your design, what would be difficult as a result of that?"

- *Questioning questions*—Questioning questions makes people better at asking questions themselves: "Why do you think I asked for an example of Rose listening to you?" and "Why was it important that we asked you about why Jack sees it another way?" This type of question helps people reflect on what happened and helps them learn from it. In the future, when Rose and Jack disagree again, they will remember our questions, as well as our questions about the questions, and ask them themselves. At least, we hope they do.

CLEAN LANGUAGE

Socratic questioning can be an effective tool for delving deeper into a domain or technical topic and examining its tradeoffs. However, it's important to consider the context and subject matter before using this method. In the case of Jack and Rose during the interviews, it was a helpful technique. However, when topics are emotionally charged or sensitive, it can come across as a critique of the speaker's experiences, causing them to feel unheard and unsafe.

In that case, we use *clean language*, which is a therapeutic technique to facilitate communication and exploration of thoughts and feelings. It involves asking questions that are simple, open-ended, and free of interpretation, allowing the speaker to articulate their thoughts and experiences in a clear and concise manner. The objective of clean language is to create a safe and nonjudgmental space for the speaker to access their internal resources, leading to increased self-awareness, personal growth, and problem-solving ability. The core principles of clean language include the following:

- Asking questions without including the questioner's assumptions or suggestions, thereby allowing individuals to explore their own ideas and experiences without external influence or bias
- Using the respondent's exact words or phrases to formulate questions, which shows respect for their model of the world and helps keep the conversation centered on their thoughts and feelings
- Avoiding metaphors or expressions that carry specific cultural or emotional baggage, which could influence or steer the conversation in a particular direction
- Encouraging self-exploration and self-discovery, rather than suggesting or leading toward any particular insight or conclusion

Avoiding metaphors or expressions

The reason for avoiding metaphors and expressions during active listening is rooted in their cultural specificity. Metaphors and expressions are often unique to a particular culture, which means their use can unintentionally exclude or confuse the person you're communicating with. Due to their cultural ties, they can be ambiguous and lead to misunderstandings.

To illustrate this, consider a humorous example involving the authors of this text, all of whom are Dutch speakers although they hail from two different countries: Belgium and the Netherlands. These countries share the Dutch expression *met een sisser aflopen*. In the Netherlands, this phrase implies something along the lines of "It could have been much worse." Contrastingly, in Belgium, it means something akin to "It ended quite disappointingly." Despite using the same language, this expression conveys opposite meanings in these two cultures. So, if you were to use this expression with the authors, depending on their cultural background, you would likely receive very different reactions.

In practice, clean language involves using a set of standard questions that are designed to be as free from assumption and direction as possible. These questions are often simple and are used iteratively, encouraging individuals to explore their thoughts and feelings more deeply.

For examples let's revisit the challenging assumption example from before. When Jack makes assumptions about Rose, we can ask the following clean language questions:

- What kind of understanding do you feel is missing from Rose?
- Is there a specific moment or instance that made you feel Rose doesn't want to understand you?
- (later as a follow-up) When you believe "they don't want to understand me," how does that affect your response or behavior toward Jack/Rose?

Through this method, the speaker is given space and autonomy to delve into their own psyche, construct meaning, and arrive at their own conclusions, promoting a deeper, more personal understanding of their experiences and thought processes. (For more insights, see the reading recommendation in section 5.8.)

5.3.3 Holding space

The third skill that a facilitator needs is holding space for people. *Holding space* means that the individuals in the group have the opportunity to voice their ideas, opinions, concerns, and so on about a topic in a way that makes them feel safe. This is why holding space is sometimes referred to as offering psychological safety for every individual in the group. People should feel comfortable expressing their ideas, opinions, problems, and emotions the way they want to.

For example, some people like to have a dialogue where it's okay to interrupt and talk through each other, while others like to fully tell their story before the other can start talking. Both are equally effective ways, and it depends on the person how they want to communicate. Another example is that some people just tell what is on their mind, while others need to grasp the full story before they will speak up. Some people are very passionate in sharing their emotions, while others will just use a few words. Regardless of how they communicate, they should not be scared of being punished or humiliated for asking questions, expressing concerns, or even for making mistakes.

When it comes to expressing their problems and emotions, they should be able to express those without getting unsolicited advice from you, the facilitator, or the group. It's very common to jump into solution mode and start offering people advice on how to deal with a problem they're facing and the emotions that come with that. Often, the person isn't even finished with explaining the problem when we already put on our solution hats. So, holding space also means holding off advice and intercepting when people in the group start offering it. Clean language and Socratic questioning as discussed previously are powerful techniques that you can employ here. Holding space during a collaborative modeling session can be done by clean language, which we just discussed, letting people listen to each other and acknowledging feelings.

LETTING PEOPLE LISTEN TO EACH OTHER

Are you a good listener? In general, nobody wants to answer no to this question. People want to be perceived as good listeners. Yet, people have this habit to listen so they can respond, not to understand. What does it mean when we say people listen to respond, not to understand? While someone is listening to an idea or opinion of another person, they are already formulating their counterarguments or their opinion on the topic. They are listening, but they aren't actively listening. People feel like they have to convince the other person that their idea or opinion is better during a discussion. They often get trapped in "Your opinion is wrong, and my opinion is right." Even as a facilitator, you can get caught in this right versus wrong trap.

Facilitators are actively listening to people during a collaborative modeling session. They are asking questions to understand, withholding their own opinion on the topic until they have reached a deep understanding. A good trick to hold space during a collaborative modeling session and to make sure people are actively listening to each other is to model the different ideas, which we also did at BigScreen, as shown in figure 5.8. We made people listen to other people by making sure everyone's opinions and ideas were presented and well understood by the entire group. This technique also shifts the focus from the person to the model. We challenge assumptions about the model; we don't challenge the person.

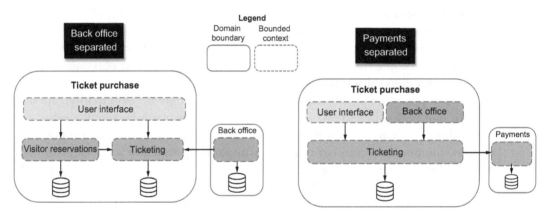

Figure 5.8   When people have a different vision or idea on something, model both ideas. Give the model a name so you can easily refer to it. Ask the group if anyone has the same opinion. If somebody has another opinion, model that one too.

ACKNOWLEDGING FEELINGS

As mentioned before, you can't ignore the emotional aspect of being a human during a collaborative modeling session. We're dealing with people, and people have emotions. To help people deal with their emotions, it's important to acknowledge them, including the positive feelings. In a previous company, we were asked to create a new design for the UI. After presenting it, we were disappointed when it became clear that the manager didn't like it. The manager dismissed the feeling of disappointment and responded by saying: "It's not because you put a lot of effort into it, that I have to like it." We felt hurt by their reaction to our disappointment, as it seemed unnecessary. When discussing this with the manager, they dismissed it again by saying we were "just easily offended." It wasn't the manager's intention to hurt our feelings when he didn't like the new design, but their actions had. Dismissing our feelings not once, but twice, had only made the situation worse, not better. "It's my impression you felt disappointed that I didn't like your proposal" would have been a much better start.

While we described a lot of skills in this chapter you may already have—or may be valuable to acquire—on how to explore and especially acknowledge people, human beings are neurodiverse and complex. Not everyone will react the same way on how you facilitate and how you employ these skills, and it can quickly become an unpleasant dynamic. In the upcoming chapters, we'll follow up more on when that happens and what you as facilitator can do about it.

5.4   *Facilitating sensemaking and collaborative styles*

As explained in chapter 4, section 4.3, sensemaking is a very effective way to open up conversations about things that live in a group's shadow, such as conflicts, negative emotions, and disturbed relationships. So why would you need a facilitator to guide you in these exercises? Why not just do it yourself? To answer that question, let's take one step back. As mentioned in the introduction of this chapter, the word facilitation comes from *faciliter* and means "to render easy." Facilitation can therefore be interpreted as the "act of making something easier." An important addition here is that it's about making *the flow* easier, not the experience. A facilitator should have no skin in the game. They have no interest in the content of the sensemaking exercise or its outcomes, but rather are focused on the process of getting to that outcome and guiding the conversation toward it.

As we saw in some of the examples in chapter 4, section 4.3, sensemaking is usually about delicate matters that can lead to uncomfortable, even painful situations. A facilitator can guide the group through these conversations, while creating a safe space for everyone to speak their minds. As explained in chapter 1, we see facilitators as catalysts. By using and choosing relevant heuristics, practices, principles, styles, and tools, the facilitator enables a group to reach its full potential. Mixing all the chemicals to create a safe space and use the full potential and wisdom of a group is a challenging role that requires the skills and capabilities we described in section 5.2 and 5.3.

In this section, we go into the need for a facilitator during sensemaking and collaborative styles. We dive into what the role of facilitators is during sensemaking exercises, including check-ins and check-outs; how you can prepare yourself optimally for these sensemaking exercises; and how we can switch styles effectively.

5.4.1   *Why do you need a facilitator?*

One of the misconceptions we sometimes run into is that facilitating is mainly about coordination and being a taskmaster. Facilitating isn't just about logistics and practicalities. The required skills we mentioned earlier in this chapter demonstrate that facilitation goes beyond that. Especially with delicate topics that usually get addressed during sensemaking, it's about creating a safe space and including the entire wisdom of the group. Turning on the flashlight to make the shadows visible for everyone is hard and difficult, especially when emotions get into the mix, which is often the case when doing sensemaking exercises.

Sensemaking is almost never about lightweight, neutral topics that aren't too important to people. They are usually around sensitive topics that live in the shadows and that we don't let out that often. It's where conflicts, disagreements, negative emotions, and polarities live. Remember the BigScreen example about physical proximity during a session from chapter 4, section 4.3.2? We never had to deal with this situation before, and some people felt judged because of their preferences. Another example is the EventStorming session BigScreen did where it came down to the question of whether they were building a standard product or customized solutions. It can feel really unsafe to speak your mind on topics like these. Your perspective might differ from the majority, or from management, in which case, it requires some vulnerability and strength to share your perspective. A facilitator can create that safe space where all perspectives can be on the table. As mentioned earlier in this chapter, facilitation requires skills on different levels. Observation, listening, asking questions, holding space, and so on are skills that need to be trained and require focus.

Facilitating sensemaking exercises when you're part of the group is very hard because you most likely have an interest. It matters to you what the outcomes look like and how the conversation afterward flows. You can't objectively facilitate those conversations. It wouldn't be allowed and/or appreciated by the group either, probably because it can smell like persuasion. Next to all these rational arguments, it would be very uncomfortable to facilitate such sensitive exercises on topics that go into emotions of the group. Even if you do manage to stay neutral during the facilitation of those conversations, you might be left feeling frustrated because you couldn't express your opinion.

That's why you need a facilitator that can act neutral, make sure everyone gets the chance to speak their minds, create a safe space, ask the right questions, and guide the conversation. A facilitator can make sure it won't turn into a conflict where no one listens to one another anymore, and instead create that safe space where people actually listen to each other. In the next sections, we'll dive into the role of a facilitator during sensemaking: What does it take to get up that mountain safely?

5.4.2   *The role of a facilitator during sensemaking*

To get to the essence of certain conflicts, everything needs to be on the table. The sensemaking exercise is a stepping stone to the conversation that is needed. Seeing all perspectives reflected in dots or people's physical position in a line during a sensemaking exercise creates awareness about the topic. Next up is creating mutual understanding and guiding fruitful conversations with more listening than talking. During that conversation, the facilitator listens, asks objective questions, and gives observations and summaries back to the group.

Doing that requires experience. There are lots of strong and weak signals flying around that a facilitator needs to look out for. Strong and weak signals are both pieces of information, activities, behaviors, or events that indicate changes that might affect a session, outcome, or result. Strong signals are obvious and easy to observe; weak signals are harder to detect. These signals tell you something about the dynamics, perspectives, and relations in a group. They can help you understand the shadows better.

Weak signals are harder to detect than strong signals. Weak signals might seem random and disconnected from the matter at hand, but can become important patterns when connecting it with other observations, signals and information.

Let's relate it to the BigScreen example of standard product versus customized solutions. A strong signal would be if someone very clearly stated they are building a standard product and have always done so, and that this whole conversation is nonsense. A pretty strong signal of dissatisfaction and frustration. A weak signal in this situation would be if someone makes a seemingly harmless joke about joining the Friday afternoon drinks of another team this week. This might seem harmless and random, but could indicate that this person is disagreeing and not happy with the outcome, which makes them think about leaving the team. For a facilitator, these weak signals are especially important. Remember that one occurrence doesn't make a pattern, so it's about observing patterns by picking up on the strong and weak signals while guiding the group through a conversation. Nobody said it would be easy.

Another aspect of creating a safe space is making sure no one is put on the spot. It's a common observation in many sessions—and sensemaking exercises—and you'll probably recognize it: there's a conversation (or discussion) going on about a certain topic and one (or a few) people stay very quiet. After a while, it starts to frustrate others because they might feel they are the only ones fighting for a perspective that they know is shared by the quieter people in the room. At that point, someone might put someone on the spot by directly addressing them and asking them to speak up because they've been quiet for a while. It might come across aggressive and result in a very uncomfortable situation. There's probably a good reason for that person to remain quiet. Putting someone on the spot never results in what you were aiming for. It usually leads to politically correct answers, siding with the majority, or shallow reactions that don't add any wisdom to the conversation. As a facilitator, this is where you intervene. Mitigating that spotlight and bringing the group back to a collective conversation. Even though you might feel that urge to put someone on the spot yourself while facilitating, we strongly advise you to never do that. It won't add anything to the conversation and will only raise the bar for that person—and others—to speak their minds later on.

This may feel like a lot to grasp, and, honestly, it is. To get you started, we've provided the steps we use when facilitating sensemaking exercises for inspiration. Every facilitator has their own style and techniques. Nevertheless, these steps might get you on your way:

- Identify potential topics for sensemaking up front (polarities, conflicts, frustrations, tensions, etc.).
- Prepare potential sensemaking exercise(s) based on what you discovered.
- Observe patterns by picking up on strong and weak signals (write them down!).
- When you feel it's the right time, stop the session, and gather the group.

- Show and explain the sensemaking exercise, and tell them what you expect from people (placing a dot on a sensemaking exercise, standing in a line, etc.).
- Let the group do the sensemaking exercise.
- Take a step back, and let everyone observe the output.
- Ask the group if anyone wants to react to the output.
- Ask the group if anyone wants to share something on why they placed their dot somewhere or why they are standing where they are.
- Ask the group if something stands out by looking at the output.
- Encourage people to listen before reacting.
- When a minority perspective is being shared, ask who partly agrees with that by showing hands.
- Guide the conversation, share your own neutral observations, and provide summaries.
- Never put someone on the spot, and intervene when others do that.
- Ask what the group needs to continue.
- Make agreements, and continue with the session.

5.4.3   *Facilitating check-ins and check-outs*

As we've mentioned, check-ins and check-outs are a form of sensemaking with a specific purpose and timing. Having someone facilitating the check-in and check-out is important. That means preparing the check-in and check-out by sensing important topics for the group and creating questions around it, being an active listener, summarizing what has been said so everyone feels heard, capturing essential signals that you can elaborate on during sessions, and capturing and incorporating feedback you get from check-ins and check-outs to optimize collaborative modeling sessions. As you can see, there's more to facilitating check-ins and check-outs than what you might guess at first.

Another important aspect of the role of the facilitator is showing vulnerability. By being vulnerable, you can lead by example and hopefully lower the bar for others to also be (more) vulnerable. This is also why a facilitator takes the first turn in the check-in/ check-out. You can set an example by answering the questions with some vulnerability. When you share something more personal with the group, others might also feel more comfortable and safer to share something personal, thereby building strong personal connections. From a practical perspective, this means you start your check-in and then stay quiet and wait for someone else to start sharing (following the popcorn style). Someone will always follow. It might take a while and feel uncomfortable at first to stay quiet, but it will be fine. Then, your job is to listen very actively and carefully. Making connections in your head (or on a piece of paper) between what people are sharing and clustering them. When you summarize what has been shared, make sure everyone feels heard by mentioning all the bigger clusters and some specific examples that stood out.

Afterward, you ask if you missed something and if there's anyone who wants to react to something. After that, you wrap up the check-in and move to the next agenda item.

A facilitator can also get a lot of information from a check-in and check-out that they can use to make a session better. You get a sense of the important topics and themes that exist within a group, and how the group feels about them. Do you observe a lot of sarcastic jokes when talking about a certain topic, for example? Then it's very likely that there is some resistance to that topic. When it's being mentioned multiple times that the follow-up of this session is extremely important and that it shouldn't be just talking (as usual), it's a clear signal for the facilitator. There might be some shadows lingering and waiting to be made explicit and talked about. Picking up on these signals—strong or weak—can help you as a facilitator guide the group toward better outcomes.

Similar to the steps we described regarding sensemaking in the previous section, we also use certain steps when it comes to check-ins and check-outs. Again, this is meant as inspiration, and we highly encourage you to gain experience and develop your own style and steps:

- Identify potential topics for the check-in or check-out up front (polarities, conflicts, frustrations, tensions, etc.).
- Decide on the questions for your check-in and check-out: Is there a balance between personal questions to get to know each other better and questions on the session itself (e.g., goals)?
- Decide if you want to send out some sort of pre-check-in where participants can already think about one or more questions, such as "What do you want to achieve in the upcoming session?"
- If you sent out a pre-check-in, discuss it somewhere during the actual check-in.
- Think about if and how you want to gather feedback during the check-out (e.g., the Wow/How about? method from chapter 4, section 4.4.4).
- Prepare the check-in and check-out either on paper or a digital whiteboard.
- When the session starts, explain what a check-in is and introduce the questions (use the characteristics we described in chapter 4, section 4.4.2).
- As a facilitator, you go first in answering the questions, so you can show vulnerability and set an example in what others can share and how long they can take.
- Give everyone the opportunity to share something.
- Intervene when people interrupt or start a conversation during someone's check-in (it's a monologue!).
- Summarize what you've heard during the check-in.
- Ask if you missed anything.
- Ask if someone wants to react to something that was said.
- Close the check-in or check-out and continue.

5.4.4   *Preparing to facilitate sensemaking*

Being fully prepared for anything that could happen before, during, or right after a sensemaking exercise is an illusion. You never know what might pop up during a session that could benefit from sensemaking and require you to come up with a relevant exercise on the spot. It could also be that one exercise has a ripple effect and flashlights even more shadows or parts of them, meaning follow-up exercises are needed, or you need to guide a conversation that follows from an exercise. There are some things, however, that you can do to prepare yourself when it comes to sensemaking. Having some preparation work as backup—that you can adjust as you go—can help you with smooth facilitation of a session. We also keep previous sensemaking exercises and their outcomes. In follow-up sessions, it might be valuable to reflect on them or make them part of a conversation. Apart from the steps we described in the previous section, we want to dive into a few things separately, to help you prepare your next session.

As a facilitator, you want to turn on the flashlights in the room so shadows become visible. Having an idea of what possibly lives in these shadows up front prevents surprises and helps you open conversations. We always try to get a feeling of what might be going on in the shadows of a group:

- Are there any conflicts or disagreements present in the group?
- Is there an ongoing debate about certain parts of a process, way of working, or decisions?
- Are there any potential polarities that we need to consider?
- Is there any tension between certain people?
- Looking at the invited participants, do we expect powerplay or hierarchy?
- Are there any potential hidden or second agendas in the group?

You won't get an answer to all of these questions, but by having a conversation with someone from the group up front, you'll have a hunch. When talking about the goal of the session, why they decided to have it at this moment in time, how excited people are, and if there is anything you should know up front, you'll get a better feeling about potential shadows.

When we were preparing for an EventStorming session with BigScreen, we discussed the session initially with Ralph, the product owner. One of the topics we talked about was the timing of the session: it had to happen now, because the development team really needed to show some progress and results. The management was already questioning the new campaign and strategy, and feature delivery didn't go as fast as they hoped it would. That's why Meera, the CTO, pretty much invited herself to the session to see what it would bring. For us as facilitators, there's a whole lot of information in this short talk: the development team is experiencing pressure and most likely frustrated, the product owner is under pressure to deliver and really wants to satisfy the management team, and the presence of Meera might cause fear or a feeling of unsafety for people. All of this lives in the shadows people brought to that EventStorming session. Based on the information we got, we could already prepare some sensemaking exercises to guide the session and conversation. Figure 5.9 shows an example of one of the exercises we used during that session. This triggered the conversation about feature delivery and expectations. This was also an opportunity for Meera to ask questions about this outcome and for her role and effect to be challenged.

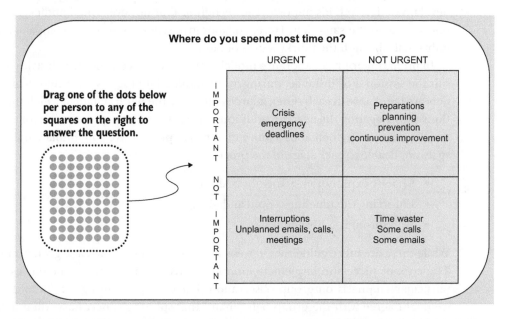

Figure 5.9 One of the sensemaking exercises we did during an EventStorming session. We wanted to trigger a conversation on feature delivery and expectation so we asked the participants to place a dot where in general they spend most of their time on.

Preparing sensemaking exercises also means preparing to be uncomfortable. Usually, emotions are involved, and conversations can get heated. If you expect this to happen, think about possible outcomes and what you as a facilitator could do to guide the group in its conversation; similar to the premortem thinking we discussed in section 4.3.6. As you gain experience in facilitating sensemaking, this whole process will become more intuitive to you. We encourage you to use this as inspiration and start experimenting with sensemaking exercises in your own team or organization.

To add to this already delicate and complex matter, we also have to deal with a mix of in-person, remote, and hybrid sessions. Facilitation of these different sessions requires different focus and things to look out for. In section 5.5, we'll dive into this.

5.4.5 *Facilitating collaborative styles*

Sensemaking is pivotal at every phase of a collaborative modeling session: beginning, during, and end. Preparation is key, as is understanding the versatility of collaborative modeling styles. Chapter 4, section 4.6, previously explored various collaborative styles, highlighting their significance in larger groups where achieving effective collaboration, deeper insights, and inclusivity becomes increasingly challenging. With our discussion on liminality, we've identified an additional application for these collaborative styles: assisting participants in navigating the inherent chaos and uncertainty. Liminality, defined by these very characteristics, offers a valuable opportunity for learning and growth, allowing us to leave behind outdated concepts and embrace new knowledge. Yet, it's important to recognize that not everyone handles chaos and uncertainty in the same way. Here, collaborative styles serve as our compass, guiding individuals through the murky waters of liminality.

In preparing for a collaborative modeling process, we consider which styles will best suit the session. For instance, during an Example Mapping session where team members are familiar with each other, anarchy might be the natural state in which the group flourishes, negating the need for additional styles. In contrast, preparation for a Big Picture EventStorming demands a more nuanced approach. We contemplate the specific styles applicable to each stage of the process:

- Chaotic exploration -> Together, Alone
- Enforcing the timeline -> Split and Merge
- Walkthrough -> Ensemble

While these are mere guidelines, it's essential to remember that each group is unique. The crux of successful implementation lies in using your core competencies, with a particular emphasis on group observation. For example, during a Split and Merge, we might agree with the group beforehand that splitting is necessary when membership exceeds a manageable size, perhaps seven or even five. Establishing this "contract" is crucial, ensuring the group's agreement with the discussed terms. Should we then notice the group's size ballooning without any splitting action, we can reflect their situation back to them: "I see your group has more than seven people." A well-structured contract set at the beginning often encourages the group to take the necessary action themselves. It's vital to remember that the group owns the outcome, and our role is to aid them in self-reflection and provide direction when they encounter obstacles. While this method was demonstrated for a Big Picture EventStorming, it's adaptable and applicable when using other tools. The imperative is always to establish a contract and secure the group's agreement prior to transitioning to a collaborative modeling style. We must avoid imposing collaboration methods on the group, as doing so would inadvertently rob them of their ownership of the outcome.

5.4.6   *What if you're not the facilitator?*

Earlier in this chapter, we emphasized the need for a facilitator's neutrality and detachment from having stakes in the game. But what happens when you, as a participant, find yourself in a position where you're not neutral and have a vested interest? So far, we've highlighted the importance of sensemaking, check-ins and check-outs, and adapting styles. But what if you're in a session where these needs aren't being met, either due to the absence of facilitation or because the appointed facilitator hasn't recognized the need?

This is precisely why we advocate for everyone, not just aspiring facilitators, to read this book. By understanding the nuances of what makes some sessions less effective, you're better equipped to intervene and help the session progress. The ultimate goal is for every software team to be conscious of these social dynamics, enabling them to more effectively navigate and enhance the flow of their sessions.

> **GUIDING HEURISTIC**   In scenarios where you're not the facilitator but have noticed a specific pattern within the group that could help in progressing the session, it's recommended to share your observation based on your own needs. This approach allows you to contribute constructively without overstepping the facilitator's role, offering insights that could be crucial for the group's advancement.

When you decide to step in, it's crucial to communicate from your personal perspective and observations. For example, if you notice the session began without a check-in and sense a general reluctance in the group, including your own, due to not knowing who's present and their expectations, you might express this by saying, "Hey, I feel a bit hesitant to start because I don't know who's who and what everyone's expectation is from today. Does anyone else feel similarly?" This method of sharing from your own perspective is key. As you're not the facilitator, you don't need to maintain neutrality; you can freely express your needs. This approach helps you contribute positively without overstepping the facilitator's responsibilities. Rather than directly proposing a check-in, you raise the problem and probe whether others share your sentiments. If others resonate with your observation, it opens up the opportunity to suggest a check-in might be beneficial. At this point, either the facilitator can step in to conduct the check-in, or you could offer to facilitate this part of the session before continuing.

5.5   *Dealing with remote facilitation*

Everything we discussed and described in this book so far applies to facilitating collaborative modeling sessions in general. The same goes for the skills a facilitator needs as described in this chapter. They all help in guiding a group and making shadows visible. A trend we've been seeing over the past years is that more and more collaborative modeling sessions take place online. We find ourselves facilitating both in-person and remote sessions, and the scale is pretty balanced. Whether you facilitate remotely or in person, the required skills remain the same. However, there are also differences in the nature of an in-person versus remote session, that you as a facilitator have to account for. The most obvious one is the lack of physical presence in remote sessions. You're not in the same room, and communication depends on cameras and microphones. As a facilitator, this means you potentially miss a lot of private and nonverbal communication that you would have observed in in-person sessions.

Hybrid collaborative modeling: A unique challenge

You may have noticed the absence of hybrid methods in our discussion on collaborative modeling. This is no oversight—we advocate for sessions to be conducted entirely in person or online. The intricate nature and potential conflicts within these sessions make the hybrid approach particularly challenging. Disparities in technology access, obstacles in effective communication, and inconsistent participation levels can all introduce complications. Proper facilitation becomes exceedingly difficult, if not unfeasible, under these conditions.

As mentioned earlier, should you find yourself in a hybrid scenario, we recommend a simple workaround: have all in-person participants use headphones and sit at their individual desks. This approach effectively converts the session into a fully remote one, leveling the communication playing field for everyone involved.

Long story short, there are benefits and potential downsides to both options. As a facilitator, it's up to you to discover how you can make up for the lack of physical proximity and build connections in a digital manner. You'll have to come up with structured whiteboard templates for the collaborative modeling tools you want to use, and think about how to get the most out of the exercise. Whether in a remote or in-person session, you'll have to tailor your approach to the needs of the group. In this section, we'll dive into the differences between remote and in-person facilitation, including benefits and downsides. Note that this entire section is from the perspective of the facilitator, not the group. With that in mind, we'll also discuss how to prepare remote sessions and how you can observe nonverbal communication and weak signals in remote sessions.

5.5.1   *Benefits and potential downsides of the different forms*

Collaborating via sticky notes and markers on brown paper in an in-person session is quite different from working together on a digital whiteboard such as Miro in a remote session. And then in a remote session, when you finally get a break and can step away from your laptop for a while, you find yourself talking to your cat instead of relaxing and chatting with colleagues over coffee or tea. As facilitators, you don't get to observe what happens during the breaks in that context, which is usually very useful information that can tell you a lot about group dynamics and shadows. On the other hand, how wonderful is it to facilitate and participate in sessions in the comfort of your own home where your cat can lay down next to you, and you can enjoy some decent coffee or tea for a change? Not to mention that documenting outcomes after a remote session has never been easier for a facilitator because everything is already on the digital whiteboard. Table 5.1 provides our experiences and examples of benefits and potential downsides of facilitating in-person versus remote sessions.

Table 5.1 Benefits and potential downsides of facilitating in-person vs. remote sessions

	Benefits	Potential Downsides
In-person session	■ Natural social experience occurs that enables relationship building. ■ Spontaneous or organic conversations can take place during breaks. ■ Sessions receive focused attention and have fewer distractions. ■ Participants can be in a session and consume content for a whole day. ■ You can observe nonverbal communication (gazes, gestures, body language, positioning, group forming). ■ Creating a safe space is a bit easier to do. ■ Movement is an option, which keeps people more engaged and energized.	■ Documenting outcomes afterward is fairly time-consuming. ■ The presence of certain participants can be experienced as intimidating and lead people to stay more quiet. ■ It can be challenging to observe everything that's going on in the entire space. ■ Some parts of the workshop are only available for people who were actually there.
Remote session	■ Documentation afterward is easy through digital whiteboards. ■ Digital whiteboards can be used to work collaboratively. ■ There are potentially fewer ranking challenges because everyone appears in the meeting the same way and on the same frame size. ■ People might feel more comfortable in their own space and therefore open up more easily. ■ Recording (parts of) the session makes it easier to share knowledge with people who weren't in the session afterward.	■ More digital distractions are present. ■ We limit remote sessions to a maximum of 3 to 3.5 hours. ■ People might find it harder to stay focused and engaged, which is an extra challenge for a facilitator. ■ Observing nonverbal communication is more difficult. ■ It can be challenging to keep an eye on both participants on a small frame and the digital whiteboard at the same time. ■ Slowdowns occur due to technical problems or people who aren't comfortable with the tools at hand. ■ Natural conversation flow can be challenging. ■ More preparation and coordination from facilitators is required.

5.5.2 *Preparing a remote facilitation*

When it comes to preparing for remote facilitation, there are a few things you need to take into account. In chapter 4, section 4.2.2, we already explained a bit about how we prepare a space for remote facilitation. Chapter 4, section 4.3.5, elaborates on sensemaking in remote settings. In this section, we'll look into a few potential challenges that come with remote facilitation and share our perspective on how to deal with those.

PHYSICAL PROXIMITY

The most visible difference when it comes to remote sessions is the lack of physical presence, meaning you're depending on technology to make up for what you're missing as much as possible. We always discuss working agreements at the start of a collaborative modeling session, and this might be even more important in remote sessions. One of the working agreements we often use is "cameras are on as much as possible." Of course, it can happen that someone needs to step out for a bit and turn off the camera, but the working agreement is cameras on. When someone has a good reason for keeping a camera off, it can be discussed at the start of the session, which can avoid misunderstanding and even frustration later on. As a facilitator, make sure you can see the group at all times. When working on a digital whiteboard, it usually works best to have both the whiteboard and people on a (separate) screen.

OBSERVING NONVERBAL COMMUNICATION

Related to the lack of physical proximity is the diminished possibility to observe nonverbal communication. When you're in the same room, it's easier to observe body language, facial expressions, intonation, gaze, and group forming. Very often, weak signals (discussed in section 5.4.2) are communicated through nonverbal communication, which is why it's so important for a facilitator to be able to observe this. Think about a closed or defensive posture, which we can observe by someone standing with their arms crossed or an evasive gaze when it comes to a specific topic. As facilitators, we try to observe patterns. In a remote setting, this is harder to do both because you only see a small part of someone via a camera and because you see everyone in the same frame in a similar manner at the same time. There are still things you can observe, but you need to pay attention to different things. For example, is someone leaning forward or sitting back with their arms crossed? Where are people looking—a screen where the session is happening or a different screen? Do people seem distracted? Are you seeing people looking at their phone or different distractions? Are people smiling, nodding, or making hand gestures? If people can choose a breakout room, do you observe anything about the groups that are formed? It's different from being in the same room, but there's still a lot to observe when it comes to nonverbal communication.

UP-FRONT COMMUNICATION

We always send out some sort of communication to the participants before a collaborative modeling session. This is where we share the agenda, goal of the session, and some logistics. When it comes to remote sessions, we also share a link to a digital whiteboard that people can use to prepare themselves. In this introduction board, we add some guidance on how to use the tool so people can get familiar with it before the session, and we add some sensemaking exercises. Usually these revolve around the goal of the session: What do participants want to get out of the session, and what do they find most important? It's a way to get used to the tool and our way of working, as well as a way to gather input before the session starts. We try to send this out a week before the session happens.

TECHNOLOGY

During remote sessions, you depend on technology. You need a communication tool such as Zoom to talk to each other, a digital whiteboard to collaborate on, and a VPN connection (for some organizations). You can't mitigate this risk fully, but you can be clear about the different technologies that participants will need during the session and provide proper instructions up front. Prepare the digital whiteboard properly, provide instructions on an introduction board, and be available to answer questions. Provide the right links and passwords, and ask participants to check everything is working before the session. As a facilitator, it's important that all participants can properly hear and see you. Make sure that the room you're in isn't too dark or light, that there's no movement going on in the background and no background noises, and so on.

BREAKOUT GROUPS

We use breakout groups very regularly during collaborative modeling sessions. Sometimes, it's preferred to split up a group when doing exercises or when they are enforcing the timeline during an EventStorming session. It can be helpful to prepare these breakout groups up front. Open the meeting early and create the breakout rooms before the group gets in. That way, you only have to assign people to a room or let them choose when the exercise starts. Sometimes, it can be helpful to think about the groups before the session. If you know the participants already—because you're in a follow-up session, for example—and you know what kind of exercises you're going to do, you might want to get certain people together in a breakout group. Or, you might not. During EventStorming sessions, we also let people decide for themselves which breakout group they wanted to be in and let the group self-organize. All are possibilities, and as a facilitator, it helps to think all of them through ahead of time.

BREAKS

Breaks are always important, and in remote sessions even more so. It's harder to stay engaged and focused when you're behind a screen and alone than when you're in a room full of people walking around. Account for this in your planning. Take lots of breaks, and check in with the group regularly if they need a break or if they're good to continue. We usually plan for a break each hour, but regularly check with the group about what they need. When we co-facilitate, we try to have one facilitator stay present in the call with the camera on. In remote sessions, you miss the spontaneous social chitchat that would happen over coffee in in-person sessions. By staying in the call as a facilitator, it provides people the opportunity to stick around and chat for a bit. Co-facilitators can obviously rotate turns here.

5.6 Collaborative software design catalysts

- In your upcoming collaborative modeling session and/or meeting, make a conscious effort to incorporate the following Socratic question: "Could you provide further insight by offering an example of *X*?" Feel free to rephrase the question in a way that feels more natural to you. Examples clarify a lot of confusion when discussing a topic. With practice, it will become second nature to ask for clarifying examples.

- When someone in your next meeting expresses a heavy or negative emotion, give them your full attention. Be careful not to interrupt or offer solutions/personal opinions. Start simple by asking an open-ended empathetic question: "Can you tell me more about what you just shared?" At some point, summarize to show you've been actively listening to them: "Let me make sure I understand, you're saying . . . ." This is your first step toward holding space!

- Get ready to conduct a sensemaking exercise in your upcoming collaborative modeling session. Once everyone has finished, initiate a discussion with the following inquiry: "Which observation stands out among the results?" Allow the dialogue to flow by asking neutral questions such as these: "Who can somewhat relate to what's been said?" and "Who sees it differently?" Particularly when there's a moment of silence, practice the art of staying silent yourself.

5.7   *Chapter heuristics*

Guiding heuristics

- When words and music don't go together, they point to a missing element.
- When someone says "this is how we do it here," you know you've found a pattern of their specific culture.
- If you feel the urge to react to opinions being made, write these down, and reflect on them after the session.
- If you find yourself feeling drained or exhausted by the facilitation process, it might be an indicator that you're taking on too much responsibility or don't have enough skills yet to facilitate that specific session. Facilitation should not be overly taxing.
- If you find yourself feeling drained or exhausted by the facilitation process, it might be an indicator that you're taking on too much responsibility or don't have enough skills yet to facilitate that specific session. Facilitation should not be overly taxing.
- In scenarios where you're not the facilitator but have noticed a specific pattern within the group that could help in progressing the session, it's recommended to share your observation based on your own needs. This approach allows you to contribute constructively without overstepping the facilitator's role, offering insights that could be crucial for the group's advancement.

5.8   *Further reading*

- *Clean Language: Revealing Metaphors and Opening Minds* by Wendy Sullivan and Judy Rees (Crown House Publishing, 2008)
- *Coaching Agile Teams: A Companion for ScrumMasters, Agile Coaches, and Project Managers in Transition* by Lyssa Adkins (Addison-Wesley Professional, 2010)
- *Crucial Conversations* by Joseph Grenny, Kerry Patterson, Ron McMillan, Al Switzler, and Emily Gregory (McGraw-Hill, 2021)
- *Sitting in the Fire: Large Group Transformation Using Conflict and Diversity* by Arnold Mindell (Deep Democracy Exchange, 2014)
- *The Art of Holding Space: A Practice of Love, Liberation, and Leadership* by Heather Plett (Page Two, 2020)
- *The Definitive Book of Body Language* by Allan and Barbara Pease (Efinito, 2022)
- *The Thinker's Guide to The Art of Socratic Questioning* by Richard Paul and Linda Elder (Foundation for Critical Thinking, 2016)

Summary

- A facilitator makes the collaborative modeling process easier for the stakeholders and makes sure the group is responsible for the outcome of a collaborative modeling session.
- A facilitator is a role not a job title, and anyone from team lead, software architect, software engineer, to product owner, tester, and user researcher can perform the role.
- During the process, as a facilitator, you take on different stances such as an observer, a coordinator, a coach, an enabler, a counselor, and a task organizer.
- The three core competencies—neutrality, observing, and compassion—are vital skills as a facilitator and form the basis of all other facilitation skills.
- Core competencies are culturally and status dependent, as well as dependent on the people allowing you to use them.
- As a facilitator, you'll be communicating a lot, that's why we need to work on our communication skills.
- Active listening emphasizes the importance of explicitly verifying whether you truly understood the message, verbally and nonverbally.
- Facilitators need to work on holding space, which means that the individuals in the group have the opportunity to voice their ideas, opinions, concerns, and so on about a topic in a way that makes them feel safe.
- Turning on the flashlight to make the shadows visible for everyone is hard and difficult, especially when emotions get into the mix, which is often the case when doing sensemaking exercises.

- By being vulnerable, you can lead by example and hopefully lower the bar for others to also be (more) vulnerable.
- Not everyone thrives in chaos and uncertainty the same, so the collaborative styles will help us guide them through that liminality.
- Whether you facilitate remotely or in person, the required skills remain the same. However, there are also differences in the nature of an in-person versus remote session, that you as a facilitator have to account for.

The influence of ranking

6

This chapter covers

- Implicit and explicit ranking
- Symbolic violence and how it affects collaborative modeling
- How ranking affects the design and architecture
- Influencing ranking as a facilitator

In the previous chapter we talked about facilitating a collaborative modeling session. We also spoke about the responsibilities and the skills a facilitator requires, and how those help you facilitate. In this chapter, we'll dive into the meaning and function of ranking in collaborative modeling sessions. When we're talking about *ranking*, we mean a relative position in a social hierarchy. Social hierarchies come in many different forms, including collaborative modeling sessions. Where we position ourselves in a social hierarchy compared to others shapes how we think and behave. This means ranking is subjective.

Ever been in a situation where you felt like everyone else was much more knowledgeable than you, had much more experience than you, and had a more valuable perspective than yours? If you did, you've experienced ranking firsthand. You might have been impressed by that situation and thought twice before speaking your mind. Or maybe you waited for others to speak first before you gave your opinion. In collaborative modeling sessions, we observe some people speaking up easily, where others stay quiet and refrain from the group a bit. We observe some people taking the lead and making decisions, while others are waiting to see what will happen. All of these behaviors might have to do with ranking, and this affects the way we design software. So, it's essential as a facilitator to know the influence that ranking has on a collaborative modeling session and how you can help the group get unstuck from ranking hierarchies that constrain discovery.

6.1   *Ranking explained*

Ranking is highly related to power gradients, which might be a more familiar or recognizable concept in the organizational context. Your position in a social hierarchy is influencing decisions, behavior, and thoughts. We all have experienced situations like the one described earlier. Maybe you found yourself in an opposite situation as well: you were the most knowledgeable, experienced, and/or powerful person in the room, which meant a higher ranking in that social hierarchy. How we perceive ranking in a social hierarchy and whether it's hindering or helping us, depends on our personal rank in different situations (social hierarchies). In this section, we'll dive into ranking and what it means, why it's not a bad thing, and how it helps us in groups. We'll also talk about symbolic violence and the difference between explicit and implicit ranking.

6.1.1   *What is ranking?*

To explain what ranking is, we'll go into a little bit of theory and then give some practical examples. Ranking is something that can be observed in collaborative modeling sessions because it has a lot to do with social hierarchies and power gradients within a group. Understanding how this works in collaborative modeling and how it may affect outcomes can help you in facilitating sessions.

SOCIAL RANK THEORY EXPLAINED

Ranking is a relative position in a social hierarchy. As mentioned in the introduction, where we position ourselves in social hierarchy often shapes our thinking and behavior. This is also what makes ranking subjective and context-dependent. If we position ourselves in a higher rank, we'll probably show different behavior than when we position ourselves in a lower rank. Ranking is related to research that focuses on social classes. The social classes they refer to are working class and middle class. In "Social Class as Culture," the authors described that for working-class individuals, the "self" tends to be more tied to others, and there is an emphasis on strong social bonds. In contrast, middle-class individuals tend to define themselves as separate from others and are more focused on their own uniqueness.[1] These identities are being taught to children from a young age, and it influences thinking and behavior. This means that

---

[1]   Kraus, M. W., Callaghan, B., & Ondish, P. "Social Class as Culture." In D. Cohen & S. Kitayama (Eds.), *Handbook of Cultural Psychology* (2019, pp. 721–747). New York: The Guilford Press.

social classes also affect how we perceive our own abilities. People from higher social classes tend to have more favorable views of themselves compared to people from relatively low social classes. They might show higher self-esteem that may even lean toward overconfidence.[2]

In *Sitting in the Fire,*[3] Arnold Mindell provides tangible guidance on ranking in groups and how to deal with it. According to Mindell, a *rank* is a conscious or unconscious social or personal ability or power arising from culture, community support, personal psychology, and/or spiritual power. In other words, a person's rank is the sum of their privileges. Within the context of collaborative modeling, it's important to know that ranking has to do with (in)formal power and how we position ourselves compared to others in the group. Ranks can differ per social hierarchy (group). It lives mostly in people's shadows and can heavily affect the flow of a session.

In short, we're conditioned by society and the social hierarchies we live in to position ourselves and everyone around us in a certain rank. To be clear, this isn't a bad thing. Doing this helps us make sense of the world and all the information that we need to process. It helps us to make sense of the group we're in and position ourselves and others quickly. That, in turn, will help us determine how to behave in a certain situation. Note that (luckily) we're not doing this consciously most of the time. Because we have experience and are conditioned, we're able to do this quickly, which helps us to move on fast.

RANKING IN PRACTICE

Imagine you'd have to do this positioning consciously every time you enter a group—there wouldn't be any time left to do collaborative modeling, that's for sure. So, this ranking phenomenon actually helps us—most of the time. It can also hinder flow during a session or prevent the group from adding the full wisdom and potential. As a facilitator, ranking is something you need to be aware of. You need to be able to observe it in a group and make it explicit if desired or necessary. In section 6.3, we'll dive more into how to facilitate ranking.

Now that we know some more about some of the scientific theory behind ranking, we want to explain how it works in practice. More specifically, we need to know how it affects collaborative modeling sessions. In a lot of those sessions, you see certain behavior that occurs regularly and might have something to do with ranking. For example, some people stay very quiet and take quite a long time to take part in a conversation. Some people are hesitant to share their opinion or formulate it in a question. Some people are very comfortable taking the lead and impose solutions and decisions on the group. Subgroups that emerge when working on the timeline or people standing in front of the group or more to the back are behaviors that might seem meaningless, but very often they have something to do with where people position themselves in

[2] Belmi, P., Neale, M. A., Reiff, D., & Ulfe, R. "The Social Advantage of Miscalibrated Individuals: The Relationship between Social Class and Overconfidence and Its Implications for Class-Based Inequality," 2019. *Journal of Personality and Social Psychology,* 118(2):254.

[3] Mindell, A. *Sitting in the Fire: Large Group Transformation Using Conflict and Diversity,* 1995. Portland, OR: Lao Tse Press.

comparison to the rest of the group, that is, how they rank themselves within a group and adjust their behavior to that rank.

Becoming conscious of ranking gives you a choice on how to use it, feel it, or be aware of it in different instances. This is where it gets even more interesting. When overusing your rank, you create a sense of power and control over others. In some situations, this can be useful. In most collaborative modeling sessions, it can prevent the entire wisdom of the group from being added to the outcome. For example, you derive a sense of power from being a CTO, which means your ideas, solutions, and suggestions can become more important and valuable to others in the room. This may cause them to conform with the CTO's ideas and thereby not share other perspectives. That's not necessarily what you want to achieve in a collaborative modeling session where you're focusing on gaining all perspectives and wisdom from a group. In a different situation, where the CTO needs to make a decision on their own and where only their opinion is decisive, they can actually benefit from their rank. Not everything needs to be a democratic decision—thankfully. In chapter 9, we'll go into various decision-making styles and their advantages.

This does mean that the people higher in rank should be aware of this and adjust their behavior to this knowledge. For example, when they want to include the wisdom of the group, they postpone giving their opinions, it is better to avoid taking the spotlight, and they do ask questions instead of providing solutions. In section 6.3, we'll explain why it's important to own, play, and share your rank within a group.

As mentioned earlier, a facilitator plays a big role here. Ranking can be a sensitive subject when it's made explicit and can cause uncomfortableness within a group. In the context of collaborative modeling sessions, facilitators tend to be relatively high in rank given their experience and role within the group, and that comes with a responsibility in terms of facilitating ranking.

WHAT DOES RANKING LOOK LIKE?

Let's illustrate ranking in practice with an example from one of the collaborative modeling sessions we facilitated. One of the greatest things about collaborative modeling (at least we think so), is that when it is facilitated correctly, it's so inclusive. We need all relevant stakeholders and their perspectives and knowledge. That also means there's a lot of potential difference in ranking. This was the case for this particular session. Participants ranged from CTOs to middle management to product owner to developer to marketing and HR, so there was lots of wisdom in the group. While ranking can affect the group, it can also affect facilitation. We, the facilitators, were one woman with a light technical background but heavy background in social sciences, and one man with a heavy technical background and more years of experience. As facilitators, we absolutely love this balance because we complement each other. At one point, we found ourselves in a conversation with one of the male participants about pivotal events. Following is a part of that conversation:

> Male participant: So, *<Male Facilitator>*, I'm not sure if I fully grasp the concept of pivotal events. Could you explain again what exactly classifies as a pivotal event?

Male facilitator: Sure, let's go over that again. As <*Female Facilitator*> just explained, a pivotal event is a key event to start sorting and structuring the domain events. These are events that are very important to the group and mark a key point in the flow: only when this happens, other events can happen.

Female facilitator: And the reason we introduce them here is to start structuring the timeline. We can place stickies to the left or right of those pivotal events. In that way, we can split the group and merge after a while.

Male participant: Ah, yes, I see. So <*Male Facilitator*>, can they appear anywhere in this timeline? If we need to structure the timeline, we might need some direction.

Male facilitator: Correct. As <*Female Facilitator*> just explained, we use this to split up the group so we can speed up.

Male participant: Right, and what would you, <*Male Facilitator*> pick as a pivotal event in this timeline?

Male facilitator: That's up to the group. But <*Female Facilitator*> did provide some suggestions to the group when she was explaining the concept of pivotal events. I suggest <*Female Facilitator*> goes over them again.

Male participant: I don't fully recall which suggestions were made. Maybe you can go over them again.

Female facilitator: [Stunned.]

This example is a perfect illustration of how ranking works. It's pretty clear how the male participant positions the facilitators and himself in this social hierarchy. Note that there is no judgment here. This is a consequence of how we're conditioned and that affects our behavior. There were absolutely no bad intentions or deliberate ignorance at play here. In this social hierarchy, the male facilitator was placed in a higher rank because of how we're conditioned. Being a man, having experience, and having a technical background suggests a higher rank in this context. Based on that, the male participant asked his questions to the male facilitator. In section 6.1.2, we'll dive further into characteristics that determine ranking.

What helped in this situation was the male facilitator being very much aware of ranking and what it can do, and anticipating that. By saying things such as "as <*Female Facilitator*> explained" and "I suggest <*Female Facilitator*> goes over them again," the male facilitator made sure the rank of the female facilitator remained high. He could have done the opposite by taking all the questions and credit, thereby overruling the female facilitator. By not doing that, he tried to keep their ranking equal.

(Fast forward: later in this collaborative session, the concept of ranking was explained to this group. The male participant wasn't aware of the concept and how it affected his thinking and behavior. Reflecting on the example above with the group made the concept of ranking tangible and explicit. No feelings were hurt in this example.)

Exercise 6.1

Think about your own experience: When did you encounter a situation where you felt hindered or empowered by your personal rank? How did it affect your own behavior? Write down your thoughts, and, if you like, discuss it with others to share experiences and perspectives.

6.1.2   *Implicit versus explicit ranking*

When talking about ranking, we make a distinction between explicit ranking and implicit ranking. *Explicit ranking* refers to the relative powers that come with a specific position someone has in a certain situation, for example, your position in the organizational chart, your formal level of power, your job title, and so on. These are things that are related to formal levels of power that were developed within a social hierarchy. *Implicit ranking* refers to relative powers that are usually unearned and are supported by social norms. It's about things such as gender, skin color, age, ethnicity, nationality, education, knowledge, experience, and so on. Implicit ranking is also about relative powers beyond the formal power structures; for example, implicit leaders are people who have a natural form of charisma and people want to follow them, despite their position in the organizational chart.

Ranking isn't a fixed concept. It depends heavily on the context and social hierarchy you're in, which makes it subjective. Implicit ranking is a more sensitive subject and harder to observe and interpret. It also greatly depends on the social context (group) you're part of whether you score high or low on these items. In a board meeting with only men of 50+ years of age, a 32-year-old woman might be the lowest in rank, but that same 32-year-old woman could be highest in rank in the context of a training on facilitation where she is the trainer. Ranking is heavily dependent on the social context we're in. This also makes it hard to be constantly aware of our own rank and anticipate it. During our workshops and training, we sometimes use an exercise to assess the ranking within a group.

We did the same exercise with BigScreen. Because ranking can be a delicate subject, we always take time to do this and start with explaining to the group what ranking is and how it can affect a group. Especially within the context of collaborative modeling, we discuss how ranking can affect behavior and what you can observe. We share some of our own experiences with ranking and open up to the group, inviting them to share their own experiences if they want to.

The conversation described in section 6.1.1 is an example of what we would share with a group when it comes to our experiences. After that, we want to make the ranking within the group explicit by using a ranking assessment tool. Figure 6.1 shows the questions we use to make ranking explicit. On the right, there are a couple of questions related to both explicit and implicit ranking. We ask people to score themselves individually on these questions in the following way: How do you position yourself compared to others in that specific group? If you feel you score lower on a certain question than others in the group, you get 1 point; if you feel neutral, you get 2 points; and if you feel you score higher than others in the group, you get 3 points. All of these points add up to a total number. Those are represented in the stickies in figure 6.1. This is subjective and can differ per the group you're a part of, which is also what makes it delicate and sometimes sensitive.

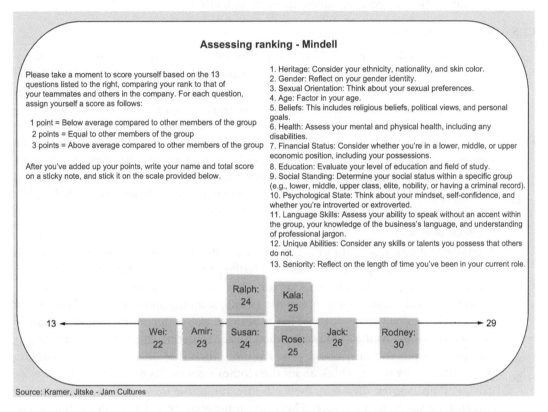

Assessing ranking - Mindell

Please take a moment to score yourself based on the 13 questions listed to the right, comparing your rank to that of your teammates and others in the company. For each question, assign yourself a score as follows:

1 point = Below average compared to other members of the group
2 points = Equal to other members of the group
3 points = Above average compared to other members of the group

After you've added up your points, write your name and total score on a sticky note, and stick it on the scale provided below.

1. Heritage: Consider your ethnicity, nationality, and skin color.
2. Gender: Reflect on your gender identity.
3. Sexual Orientation: Think about your sexual preferences.
4. Age: Factor in your age.
5. Beliefs: This includes religious beliefs, political views, and personal goals.
6. Health: Assess your mental and physical health, including any disabilities.
7. Financial Status: Consider whether you're in a lower, middle, or upper economic position, including your possessions.
8. Education: Evaluate your level of education and field of study.
9. Social Standing: Determine your social status within a specific group (e.g., lower, middle, upper class, elite, nobility, or having a criminal record).
10. Psychological State: Think about your mindset, self-confidence, and whether you're introverted or extroverted.
11. Language Skills: Assess your ability to speak without an accent within the group, your knowledge of the business's language, and understanding of professional jargon.
12. Unique Abilities: Consider any skills or talents you possess that others do not.
13. Seniority: Reflect on the length of time you've been in your current role.

13 ← Wei: 22 | Amir: 23 | Susan: 24 | Ralph: 24 | Rose: 25 | Kala: 25 | Jack: 26 | Rodney: 30 → 29

Source: Kramer, Jitske - Jam Cultures

Figure 6.1   Outcome of a ranking sensemaking exercise at BigScreen. The assessment is from Mindell (Source: *Jam Cultures* by Jitske Kramer [Management Impact, 2021]). It guides individuals to score themselves on factors such as heritage, gender, health, and education. Participants rank themselves relative to their peers and place their total score on a scale. From here, we can create subgroups from both sides of the scale and better understand the effect ranking has on the group.

The next step is discussing these outcomes—not with us as facilitators, but within the group. What we usually do is pair up the highest number, the lowest number, and someone from the middle. We ask the duo to talk about their scores and how they got there by looking at differences and similarities, and sharing some personal experiences around ranking. When were you hindered by your rank? When did you benefit from it? Are there any situations that, in hindsight, were affected by your rank or the rank of others? We always ask afterward if someone would like to share something, but we never push people. We do this exercise to let the group become more aware of their ranking and how it affects the group. In our experience, very valuable conversations take place in this part of a session.

Understanding the nature of ranking, along with the distinctions between explicit and implicit ranking, can enhance awareness of group dynamics. Before we explain how to become aware of ranking, we need to first discuss two critical concepts closely intertwined with ranking theory—symbolic violence and epistemic injustice—that significantly influence collaborative software design efforts.

6.1.3   Symbolic violence

Symbolic violence describes how behavior is affected in situations or groups where there is a power differential. It's about a type of nonphysical violence that is a result of ranking and power dynamics. To understand this concept, we have to dive into sociology for a bit, and more specifically, into the work of sociologist Pierre Bourdieu on symbolic violence. Symbolic violence is strongly related to what we described earlier in this chapter about ranking and social hierarchies. Bourdieu uses the concept of symbolic violence to explain how social hierarchies and inequalities are maintained less by physical force than by forms of symbolic domination. Next, we'll dive into the symbolic and violence part of this concept to understand how it affects collaborative modeling. For the record, no physical violence is involved whatsoever.

SYMBOLIC POWER

Symbolic violence has to do with *symbolic power*. Bourdieu defines symbolic power as power based on recognition: "renown, prestige, honor, glory, authority."[4] Although this concept might sound vague, everyone has an idea of what this symbolic power looks like. To illustrate: when we see two people standing next to each other, we can usually tell who has more power. That is because we're all conditioned to recognize characteristics (or symbols) of power when we see someone. We often associate power with physical power, but symbolic power is more than that—it's about understanding power in broader terms. Think about the clothes someone is wearing, the car they're driving, their gender, their age, their job title, the music they listen to, the food they eat, and the sports they practice. There's an infinite list of traits (symbols) that tell us something about the relative amount of power someone has. It's important to note again that this is subjective. The amount of power we describe to someone depends on the situation, culture, and the person ascribing the power.

Note the relation between the symbols of power and implicit and explicit ranking. Symbols such as a job title are related to explicit ranking, where gender, ethnicity, and age are more related to implicit ranking. Symbolic power is about all of these traits. Again, this is a subjective concept. You might yield more power to someone based on symbols of violence, but that doesn't mean that person actually has more power.

Based on those symbols, we all develop a symbolic ideal—or mental image—of what we see as dominant/strong and dominated/weak. This symbolic ideal changes over time and differs per social hierarchy and culture. It's very context dependent. For example, there was a time when being overweight was a sign of wealth and power.

---

[4]   Bourdieu, P. *Distinction: A Social Critique of the Judgment of Taste*, 1984. London: Routledge & Kegan Paul.

This symbolic ideal changed over time for certain cultures. New norms and social and cultural ideals also change the symbolic ideals of people. The more traits (symbols of power) someone possesses from that list within a specific context, the more symbolic power we'll yield to them. Based on this, we'll establish social structures and levels of power in a group. According to Bourdieu, we accept and internalize these power structures and hierarchies in a social group into our mental structures (*habitus*, as Bourdieau calls it). In other words, we very often unconsciously accept a social hierarchy based on this symbolic power.

EXAMPLES OF SYMBOLIC POWER

Let's clarify symbolic power with an example. For quite some time, it was (or in some industries it is) culturally accepted that boardrooms were dominated by men. This follows the theory on symbolic power, which goes way back in this case. For a long time, it was socially accepted that men were the better gender to do this kind of work. Women were lower in rank when it came to the context of boardrooms. Men possessed more traits of that list and thereby more symbolic power than women. Think about the level of education, gender, working experience, social position in society, accessories worn, and so on. So, in that sense, it made sense that boardrooms were dominated by men. Society accepted that. Things have changed over the past few years. Organizations actively steer toward adjusting the symbolic ideal and yielding more symbolic power to women when it comes to boardroom positions. The reason this has been so hard has to do with the way we're conditioned with that symbolic ideal. It takes time to change that within a society.

Here's another example: within a collaborative modeling session, there is symbolic power flying around as well. It's often part of the shadows of people, but people can sense it in a way. A CTO usually has more symbolic power than a developer. That might mean that the group is more likely to accept suggestions and solutions from the CTO than from a developer. In most collaborative modeling sessions, this power structure is accepted and internalized, and it takes active effort to counter the power structure when desired. The CTO needs to be aware of their symbolic power and rank and adjust their behavior to what they want to achieve with that session. If they want to achieve completeness, which means everyone needs to add their wisdom to the group, it might be effective for the CTO not to talk first all the time, not to talk in terms of solutions, and to ask questions more often and provide answers less. The symbolic ideal and power are always there, but we can choose how we act upon it. As facilitators, it's very important to be able to observe and anticipate this symbolic power.

For Bourdieu, this all means that every individual is constantly classifying themselves and others as alike or different. Based on the symbols of power, we symbolize social similarity and social difference from one another, which helps us define power structures.[5] In other words, we're continuously making sense of these symbols that are flying around when we're in social hierarchy, and we use those symbols to determine the

---

[5] Weininger, E. B. "Pierre Bourdieu on Social Class and Symbolic Violence," 2003. *Alternative Foundations of Class Analysis*, 4, 83.

position of ourselves and others. When doing collaborative modeling, it's useful to be aware of this because it will determine how people behave in terms of who will act more dominant and who will act more submissive. Note that there is nothing wrong with this concept and its effects on groups and collaborative modeling. It's how we're wired as societies and how we make sense of the world around us. All we're saying is that it helps to understand these concepts, symbols of power, and dynamics to be better able to facilitate groups.

THE VIOLENCE IN SYMBOLIC VIOLENCE

So where does the violence come in, you might ask. The good news is that there is no physical violence involved in this theory. The point here is that symbolic violence is something we do to ourselves. Following Bourdieu's theory, we could state that when you're in a room with someone that has more symbolic power than you, you're basically conditioned to be more submissive to that person—to a certain extent, of course. Because we very often (unconsciously) internalize power structures, we show certain behavior that makes sense within that context and power structure. If we feel we have less power than others, we're more likely to follow suggestions of the more powerful, we're more hesitant to challenge their input, and we let them speak first, for example. When we have more symbolic power than others, we (unconsciously) might speak more, interrupt others easier, suggest solutions, and provide answers, for example. That's the violence part. We can suffer from these internalized power structures, experiencing violence. We can also exert this violence by using it to our advantage when we have more symbolic power. Violence can go both ways, and in both ways, the amount of symbolic power determines our behavior. By doing this, we create and maintain a certain hierarchy or power structure.

According to Bourdieu (as described earlier in this section), we absorb the structures and hierarchies of the social settings in which we exist into our mental structures, almost becoming part of our subconscious mind. The power structures and the submissiveness or dominance become more or less natural and so does our behavior in these social settings. Again, this symbolic violence is something we do to ourselves. We're conditioned to have these symbolic ideals, and we rank ourselves given the information at hand. We decide for ourselves whether we have more or less symbolic power than others. Remember the ranking assessment tool we described in section 6.1.2? We score ourselves on these items. It's not a rational scale where everyone would get to the same number for each person.

Although the structures and hierarchies that became part of our mental structures are often unconscious and not explicit, we can feel the effects of symbolic violence. In black and white terms, there is someone suffering from symbolic violence, and there is someone benefiting from it. The person who is "suffering" from symbolic violence takes the lesser part of the deal here. Being lower in rank might cause you to feel inferior. Imposter syndrome will be very present, so you might feel like you should educate yourself more before you give your opinion or maybe you feel like people might not take you seriously. All of this could result in more submissive behavior. The person benefiting from this symbolic violence—the one with the most symbolic power—very often isn't aware of this violence taking place. This person will be higher in rank than the other person(s), and there are lots of benefits related to that: they will probably not get interrupted, people will listen to them and accept their suggestions and solutions more easily, they won't be challenged a lot, and they are likely to get what they want.

EXAMPLES OF THE VIOLENCE PART

Let's step back to our examples from earlier: the boardroom filled with men and the collaborative modeling session where the CTO participates. We established the symbolic part of these situations: in the boardroom, men usually have more symbolic power than women, and in the collaborative modeling session, the CTO has more symbolic power than others. So, what does the violence part look like in these situations?

Let's say there is one woman in that men-dominated boardroom. She might position herself in a lower rank than the men in the room and adjust her behavior to that internalized power structure. She's a woman, younger than the others, has fewer years of experience, and is less senior, but she does possess some magical powers—people are willing to listen to her, follow her, ask for advice, and trust her more than all the board members. Because of how she positions herself compared to others in the room, she might be quieter during board meetings. She might go last in question rounds, adding her agenda points last, and ask what others think of her ideas. This doesn't mean the people higher in rank are consciously exerting their symbolic power or have bad intentions—not at all! This is the symbolic violence we do to ourselves. If there was a facilitator in that board meeting, they could make that ranking and symbolic violence explicit to help the group overcome it where desired by sharing what they observe in terms of behavior, explaining how ranking and symbolic violence works, and making the ranks in the group explicit.

The collaborative modeling situation is similar. Others in the room will be more likely to go with what the CTO suggests, ask the CTO for advice, and let that CTO speak first when they position themselves lower in rank than that CTO. They might think, "The CTO will probably know better due to all their experience, knowledge, and education, so I will shut up." The same can happen during pair programming sessions, for example. Sometimes, juniors get paired up with seniors so they can learn from them, which, in theory, is a good idea with even better intentions. In reality, the symbolic power of the senior can cause the junior to not speak their mind, not challenge anything the senior says, and learn absolutely nothing.

6.1.4 *Epistemic injustice*

The intertwined relationship between ranking theory and epistemic injustice is important in collaborative modeling. Miranda Fricker introduced the term *epistemic injustice* in her book *Epistemic Injustice: Power & the Ethics of Knowing* (Oxford University Press, 2007) to describe the harm done to someone in their role as a knower. In collaborative software design—or, if you ask us, in all facets of software development—the focus is on learning and knowing. It's the driver for what to build. Understanding the effect of this dynamic during collaborative modeling is essential.

Symbolic violence involves attributing power through symbols, leading individuals to downplay their contributions if they feel they rank lower. Epistemic injustice occurs when someone's credibility as a source of knowledge is unfairly diminished due to biases linked to their identity, such as gender, race, or social class. A clear example is the often ignored or overlooked contributions from women and marginalized groups in IT, which becomes even more shocking when similar suggestions from others are readily accepted. Fricker refers to this as *testimonial injustice*, emphasizing the importance of embracing diverse perspectives in collaborative software design for crafting effective, adaptable software.

Additionally, the advent of AI has shed light on another aspect of epistemic injustice. The higher misidentification rates of people of color and women by AI-based facial recognition systems point to biases originating from nondiverse training datasets. Fricker names this *hermeneutical injustice*, which highlights interpretative gaps that obscure the experiences of certain social groups. For software design, this means that without comprehensive research or representation of diverse customer groups, products may fall short or exclude specific demographics, potentially harming the brand. The most concerning problem arises when groups not represented in AI datasets are inadvertently marginalized even further.

NOTE Abeba Birhane, a cognitive scientist specializing in human behavior, social systems, and ethical AI, offers an extensive collection of resources on this topic of automated systems and bias at https://abebabirhane.wordpress.com/2017/09/20/1162/.

Within software development, a similarity can be seen with epistemic injustice when developers, although not being a marginalized group as Fricker writes about, aren't given access or input to domain knowledge, which is often justified as making things simpler or protecting them from the complexities. Such exclusion overlooks the valuable insights developers can offer in addressing domain challenges and promotes a perception of IT departments as mere "factories" tasked with executing solutions devised by architects, analysts, and product managers. While collaborative modeling seeks to involve developers more inclusively, especially developers from marginalized groups, it falls short if the problems of symbolic violence and epistemic injustice aren't tackled among stakeholders and within development teams.

In our collaborative modeling sessions, we strive to grasp the interplay of symbolic power, epistemic injustice, and group ranking. We can foresee some of these dynamics through explicit rankings, but others emerge and need to be addressed in the sessions, especially with individuals in leadership roles, focusing on how to distribute their influence more equitably. This approach prepares us to delve deeper into the role of ranking in collaborative modeling and its effects on software systems, design, and architecture, which will be the focus of section 6.3.

6.2   Becoming aware of ranking during collaboration and software design

In section 6.1.1, we already gave an example of ranking during a collaborative modeling session: a participant addressing all of their questions to the male facilitator even
though the female facilitator was teaching the concepts. In this section, we'll talk a bit
more about patterns that we've observed over the years when it comes to ranking and
how those patterns influence the design, architecture, and software system itself. We're
not the only ones who noticed these patterns, and some of them were given a name.
We're using those names, despite the negative connotation they often have, to make
it easier for you to link back to your already-existing mental models around ranking.
Please understand, we don't always like these names.

6.2.1   Group ranking

Although each individual has a rank, a specific group inside the company also has a
social status and a rank associated with that status. By being part of that group, the
explicit or implicit rank of a person is influenced because they are part of this group.

INTERNAL VS. EXTERNAL PRODUCT TEAMS

Parts of a software system in a company can be internally or externally facing. For
the sake of simplicity, let's take some liberty with the word *product* and call these the
internal and external products of a company. When a company has both internal and
external products, as is the case with BigScreen, the external products are perceived as
contributing to the revenue streams, and the internal ones are seen as a necessary cost.
These associations carried an implicit rank that has an effect on the budgets assigned
to the teams. Internal teams get less budget because they are seen as less important.
Money creates status, so because those teams have less money, they are seen as less
important. This is called a *reinforcing loop*.

When there is more budget, a team can hire more developers or hire for specific
roles, such as architect or product owner, which other teams can't do. After a while, the
teams working on the internal products can't keep up with the requests from the business. They start taking shortcuts, such as skipping tests or collaborating on the design.
Certain design qualities go down, or the bug count in those products goes up. The
decline in delivered quality also affects or confirms the implicit lower ranking of those
teams.

CORE DOMAIN TEAMS

Similar patterns can be detected between teams in the same "group," depending on
the type of subdomains they are working on. In Domain-Driven Design, there's a distinction between three different types of subdomains:

- *Core domain*—This domain contains the business logic that is most important to
  the company and often is what sets the company apart on the market. It's the reason you're writing a customer software system.

- *Supporting subdomains*—These domains still have business logic inside of them, but it's not the market differentiator.
- *Generic subdomains*—These domains are necessary to have a functioning company, but there is no specific business logic in there.

We notice in companies that the people who don't work on the core domain have a lower ranking than the people who work on the core domain. The idea is that because they don't work on the most important parts of the software system, their "unique abilities" (refer to figure 6.1) must be a lot less. There are a few consequences because of that. The first one is that their opinions or ideas get dismissed during collaborative modeling. The second one is that the supporting and generic subdomains are deemed as unimportant, which isn't true, and their struggles get less attention during a collaborative modeling session. Yet, to have a good system design, you need to investigate those subdomains too. If you don't, this will have a negative effect on the product. For example, even though the Payments bounded context from BigScreen is a generic subdomain, customers can't finish purchasing a ticket if this part of the system isn't functioning well, leading to more customers contacting the customer help desk and putting pressure and stress on that department.

LOW-RANKING TEAMS

One of the less obvious examples of ranking in collaborative modeling is the absence of a representative for a group of people during a session. Good examples of this are the customer help desk or the system administrator (sysadmin). These roles are often associated with a lower implicit ranking and therefore overlooked when setting up a collaborative modeling session, even though they have insights into customers and infrastructure. It's harder to detect this implicit ranking because the people associated with these roles aren't present during a session.

6.2.2 People

Ranking resides on an individual level of which group status is just a small part of the equation. Different people can also assign a different implicit rank to someone. On top of that, those rankings from different people can contradict the explicit ranking that somebody has. Let's look at a few examples of patterns associated with people instead of groups.

THE GENIUS

When there is a developer that has been around for a very long time and therefore has a deep knowledge on the current system or who is seen as a *genius developer*, their implicit ranking is high. The rest of the team looks at that person during collaborative modeling to lead them because of their deep knowledge of the current system. This great knowledge, which has helped out the team on many occasions and is seen as something amazing, also makes them struggle to talk to the business because they have a hard time letting go of the way the system already works. You'll often hear sentences like these:

- You want us to also add a unique constraint for the email column in the user table? That will be hard because we'll have to do some data cleanup because we didn't have that constraint before.

- That will be difficult because of how the system works right now. See, the way it works right now is that we send a request to the server, and so on.

This leads to very restricted modeling sessions that are often too focused on the technical details of the current system, causing the domain experts not to see the value of collaborative modeling. So, the implicit high ranking of genius developers has a negative effect on the collaborative modeling sessions and leads to even less collaboration with the domain experts.

> **NOTE** Take a moment to reflect on the different traits (for example gender, background, culture and so on) you initially attributed to this genius. What assumptions did you make, and what do they reveal about your own biases? Don't be too hard on yourself or view these thoughts as inherently wrong–they simply are, shaped by your experiences and surroundings. This reflection offers a valuable opportunity for growth and adjustment, should you feel it's necessary.

The other team members also look to the genius developer to come up with good software design and models that fit the business. The solutions that they propose are based on the knowledge they already have and are less effective in dealing with changes coming from the business.

Sometimes, the genius goes by a different name, the dungeon master. The *dungeon master* was first mentioned by Alberto Brandolini in his "Rise and Fall of the Dungeon Master" blog post (https://mng.bz/oex2) as "deeply entrenched with the software, in fact they know the software better than anyone else. Even if they are no longer software developers, they are still at close distance from its creation." A dungeon master is a genius but with one big difference: it's not viewed as positive, so a dungeon master has a low implicit ranking. A person can be a genius to a higher manager (high implicit ranking) but be considered a dungeon master by their team members (low implicit ranking).

A good example of a dungeon master/genius is the programming CTO. When a company is just starting, the CTO has a very good knowledge of how the system was designed and functions because they helped build it. After a while, the company becomes bigger, and the CTO has to dedicate less time to keeping their knowledge of the system up-to-date and starts focusing on other things. This is a normal evolution of a company. They don't understand or have difficulty admitting that they lost track of all the changes that happened in the system, but they want to believe they still have the correct knowledge to advise. Because the CTO is explicitly ranked higher, a lot of people on the development teams find it difficult to go against their opinion, even though they realize that the CTO's advice is based on outdated system knowledge. So, they implement the CTO's advice or models, leading to more accidental complexity or bad models.

ROCKSTAR DEVELOPER

We've seen many job applications asking for a rockstar developer. Companies think this is a cool way to advertise for a software developer position. The truth is, none of these companies would actually want a rockstar developer on their team. Let us explain what we mean. There is a paradox called *the preventable problem*, coined by product management consultant Shreyas Doshi: "Any complex organization will over time tend to incentivize problem creation more than problem prevention." With *problem creation*, they don't mean consciously creating problems when working at a company. It means it's more beneficial for an employee to let problems arise and fix them, than to prevent them.

Rockstar developers get their high implicit, and sometimes explicit rank because they fall in the first category of this. Urgent user requests piling up? Rockstars are the first to make a real dent in it! (Code quality be damned.) Bug in the system? You know who is the first to fix! (Maybe we should pay more attention to that code quality.) Server down at night? They are the first ones behind their computer! (Why is that server running out of memory so often anyway?) Management knows them and loves them. Who wouldn't? They are rockstars, after all! You can't blame rockstar developers for how they operate because the company rewards this type of behavior. We want to be appreciated, we want to be seen as extremely good at our jobs, we want that pay raise that goes with that, and problem prevention doesn't really accomplish that. Nobody at work ever talks about that time that you did such a good job, the microservice just worked. So no, a company doesn't really want a rockstar developer. Problem prevention is far more beneficial for the software system and the company in the long run.

TESTERS

Testers are another group of people that are often seen as lower in ranking. Testers are very good at finding bugs and flaws in the software system, but their input is often used in a reactive way instead of a proactive one. When you use the full potential of a tester in a proactive way, they are part of the development lifecycle and can prevent a flawed design from being implemented and pushed to production.

SILENT PERSON

Another example is the silent person in the room, which is the opposite of the genius status from the first section. Some people have difficulty expressing their views or concerns to the group, so they have an implicit lower ranking. Because they are perceived as lower in ranking, the group doesn't take the time to understand the person's concerns, or their ideas are easily dismissed, as a result, certain problems with the chosen design only become apparent when the solution is already implemented and pushed to production.

THE NEW ONE

Ever hired a new developer who immediately started to suggest that you change the way the team works because that is what they did at their old company and it worked really well? They suggest it so often, it even comes a bit annoying? Yes, so have we. One of the reasons they do that is because they want to prove themselves. They want to feel like they have a good rank in the team or confirm their explicit rank ("yes, I am really senior").

Take software architects, for example, who are often perceived as higher in ranking. When they join a company, they want to make a good impression and "improve" the architecture. Every architect has their own preferences or definition of what a good architecture is, so they push for their definition. For example, the new architect believes that microservices should be bigger than the last architect did. Even though the team is still working toward the architecture that the previous architect designed, the new architect decides it's time to start merging microservices again. This change of direction is well intended, but not beneficial for your software system. Halfway through a redesign, swapping directions again will cause the overall design and architecture to become messy. It's also not beneficial for team morale and will affect the implicit ranking of the architect in a negative way. Instead of proving that their explicit high rank is correct, they just lowered their implicit rank. This will make it more difficult for them to do their job and affect the system architecture even more negatively, even if their ideas are good.

PETER PRINCIPLE

The last pattern we want to discuss here is called *the Peter principle*. It's a pattern within management that was developed by Canadian educator Laurence J. Peter. This principle states that eventually somebody will be promoted into a position where they become incompetent. A good example from the software world is a developer. They start as a junior developer, and they get promoted to medior and senior. The next step in the promotion ladder is Team Lead, Technical Lead, or Engineering Manager. These developers are excellent developers, which is why they get promoted, but being a team lead requires a vastly different set of skills than being a developer. Higher management won't promote them further because this person isn't competent at their new job and demoting them isn't something management can just do. So now they are stuck in that position. Although their explicit ranking is high, it's different from their implicit ranking, which is a lot lower. Due to the implicit ranking, the team dismisses their input and ideas quickly without real consideration. Imagine this person tries to introduce collaborative modeling to the team. The impression they have of this person would be projected upon the idea that they are trying to introduce. The team would not give this a fair try because it's very hard for people to separate the person from the message.

Exercise 6.2

Have a conversation with your own team about ranking within teams: Do you experience an effect of ranking when it comes to collaboration? You could start this conversation in a team meeting by asking open-ended questions. You could consider the following questions:

- Have you ever felt like the most or least knowledgeable person in the room? Anyone want to share their example?

(continued)
- Have you ever withheld opinions or ideas because you thought they weren't good enough? Anyone want to share their example?
- Have you ever experienced or felt a power play during group sessions? If so, how did you notice?
- Do you experience any effect of power in our/this team? If so, can you provide an example?

If you'd like, also discuss the different "roles" that were mentioned in section 6.2.2. Ask if they perceive them in your own team and organization.

6.3 *Facilitating ranking*

You might be able to imagine now that ranking plays a crucial role in collaborative modeling, and, as facilitators, we can influence it. Let's now dive in and explore a Big Picture EventStorming that took place at BigScreen with 30 participants from different parts of the organization collaborating on one model. In our experience facilitating these sessions, people from these different parts of the organization have never met before. In these situations, people tend to unconsciously assess their rank compared to others, causing uncertainty and lowering psychological safety. Have you ever been in that situation, walking in on a session without knowing everyone in the room? What did that do to you, and how did you behave?

We most certainly have experienced that. We have a saying in Dutch of "looking the cat out of the tree," meaning we're cautious and first watch what happens. We feel uncertain about what we can and can't say and what we should or shouldn't do in such a group. That uncertainty, in turn, restricts the flow of information, lowers collaboration, and makes the outcome of the session not include the full wisdom of the group. Even if the group is familiar with each other, higher-ranking individuals may suffer from dominance blindness, where they fail to recognize or acknowledge the privileges and advantages they have and fail to understand the daily effect it has on someone with lower ranking. While those lower in rank are more susceptible to symbolic violence. To better understand the effect of ranking, we'll reflect first on past sessions where we weren't fully aware of its effects, and then we'll explore ways to see how we could have led more effectively as facilitators.

6.3.1 *Analyzing the group rank*

One of the first times we facilitated a Big Picture EventStorming, it didn't go fully as we expected. We made sure to include the correct people—26 in total of one department of a company. Everyone mostly knew each other, and they held quarterly planning sessions together. Not everyone would work together on a weekly basis, but at least they would do so during those planning sessions. We actually attended one of these sessions before we organized the Big Picture EventStorming, so we knew who to involve. We had the full support of the head of engineering, and he believed the session would help him align the domain model to one overview. Back then, these collaborative modeling sessions, such as Big Picture EventStorming, were hard to plan with most organizations. You really had to persuade certain people. So, we were thrilled that we got support from someone high up with explicit ranking this time.

> **GUIDING HEURISTIC** Let someone with a high explicit ranking introduce you to the group you will facilitate.

We thoroughly planned the Big Picture EventStorming as outlined in chapter 4. The head of engineering, who was fully supportive of the session, communicated the goal and agenda in one of their weekly updates and sent out the invitation to the necessary participants. We also prepared a check-in question and some sensemaking exercises to enhance the session. With everyone on board and fully engaged, we were confident that the Big Picture EventStorming would be a success, and we got right to it.

During the session, we divided the large group into two smaller groups for a check-in exercise. We asked the participants about what was working well and what needed improvement in the current process. The explicitly higher-ranking individuals didn't dominate the conversation, and the responses from each group were quite similar. So, we didn't have the feeling from the check-in that people were afraid to speak up.

We then began the chaotic exploration step in Big Picture EventStorming. We asked the participants to write down all of their domain events as they happen currently. However, some of the group got stuck and were talking among themselves. When we asked what was holding them back, someone mentioned not knowing the level of granularity to write the events at. That question is asked a lot during a Big Picture EventStorming, and we always explain that the goal was to get a complete overview of the business process, not to be overly concerned with accuracy. We want to get everyone's model out and get an entire overview of the business processes and how they group them together in smaller processes. We emphasized that we were using sticky notes, and any inaccuracies in the granularity of the domain events could be adjusted later.

Our answer took away that person's concern, and the moment they wrote down and put their stickies up, we noticed other people started doing the same thing. We took note, but didn't see it as a huge concern at the time thanks to something called cognitive bias, but we'll talk more on that in the next chapter. So, we continued and ended up with a huge 20-meter wall with roughly 500 domain events sorted in a timeline, as shown in figure 6.2.

After writing down roughly 500 domain events, the group is tasked with merging them into a single, consistent timeline in the enforcing the timeline step of EventStorming. This is where the collaboration, communication, and learning process truly begins. However, in this particular instance, the group quickly diverged into a discussion about the way some individuals wrote their domain events. Despite being instructed to model the current state, some members wrote down events they wished to see in the future, causing conflict within the group. (We'll talk more about resolving conflicts in chapter 8.) One person seemed to lead that discussion against the head of engineering and had some other people in the group that agreed with their point of view. This was the second time an individual who seemed not to be explicitly high in rank was able to lead and influence the session because we had not been aware of the symbols of power in the culture of the organization.

Figure 6.2   An example of the outcome of the Big Picture EventStorming step 1: chaotic exploration. Some people might already group domain events together, and some people might make their own timeline for themselves.

PARTICIPATORY OBSERVATION

Leading collaborative modeling sessions and effectively facilitating a group requires that one is given the power to do so. However, simply having explicit power isn't enough. It's also important to be aware of implicit power dynamics within the group, as these individuals may also hold influence over the rest of the group. To identify those with implicit power, it's recommended to observe the symbols of the culture of an organization. Shared symbols make social interaction possible and usually create reactions and emotions. To observe these symbols, we can learn from anthropologists.

Participatory observation is a method used by anthropologists to observe a culture from inside. This is known as the *emic perspective* and represents the lived experience of an individual within the culture. In the context of a Big Picture EventStorming session, for instance, a person might experience fear of writing down the wrong events, so they wait until someone else puts up an example event. By collecting and analyzing these stories, we can give our own conclusion or judgment as to why that has happened. Anthropologists call this the *etic perspective*, and it's how an outsider experiences that same culture. Participatory observation helps us understand the culture's emic perspective and make more informed judgments about the power dynamics at play. For us it's important to look at an organization through an anthropologist view to understand the implicit ranking and how participatory observation can help with that.

NOTE If you want to learn more about the work that anthropologists do, we recommend Danielle Braun and Jitske Kramer's book, *The Corporate Tribe: Organizational Lessons from Anthropology* (Routledge, 2019).

At the start of our engagement with BigScreen, we took time to familiarize ourselves with the organization's practices and routines. This involved attending team sessions such as dailies, refinements, retrospectives, and other operational meetings the teams have. But we also went to the coffee corner, had lunch, and especially liked playing table tennis or Mario Kart after lunch. According to Braun and Kramer, entry is crucial in any new environment. Before you can truly observe the emic perspective, you need to build trust. That's why we introduced ourselves clearly, explaining our role as support for the development team in successfully delivering the project, with the goal of understanding their needs and addressing any pain points.

GUIDING HEURISTIC Entry is everything, so make sure the first time you join a new group, team, or organization, you have a good introduction. Be humble and open to retain your neutrality.

We were careful not to present ourselves as the "fixers" of the project, as this can lead to resistance and suspicion from the team. Perhaps you've been on a team where they "flew" in a consultant to fix the problem you didn't know you had. What did you notice happening to you? We've been in that situation and felt resistant and suspicious of sharing our information, did you? Instead, we approached the situation with humbleness and openness. By doing so, we were able to build a connection with all the teams and they started to share information with us during their meetings.

Another important aspect when entering a new environment is to make sure you're not perceived as being "of a person or group." When people perceive you as being of a person or a group it can affect your neutrality and implicit ranking. Yes, in our situation, our engagement was to support the development team, but that doesn't mean we can't hang out with other teams such as marketing, business administration, and the back office-supporters. Go have lunch with them, ask to sit for a couple of hours next to the customer supporters, and see what type of work they do. You'll be amazed what stories you can capture from that.

NOTE What about user research, UX and UI designers? If you're familiar with user research, UX and UI design, you'll recognize the approach we're taking. We believe that user research can bring significant value to software teams and that UX designers and developers can benefit from working together more often. After all, both groups have the same ultimate goal: to solve the problems faced by our users in the best way possible. This doesn't mean that we think developers should take over the role of user research, UX and UI designers, but rather that the two communities should collaborate more frequently to achieve this shared goal.

At BigScreen, we observed a lot of stories surrounding the development team. For instance, the marketing team asked how it's possible that it takes so much time to change a simple form that will make their work a lot easier. They also mentioned that every time developers release a new feature, it's not what they want, even though they clearly told Ralph, the product owner, their requirements. Capturing these types of anecdotes can tell us the emic perspective and make a model of the implicit ranking of an organization.

To better understand these experiences, we like to capture them in a map, similar to an organizational diagram or stakeholder mapping, as shown in figure 6.3. This allows us to see the emic perspective, that is, the implicit ranking of the organization. We include anecdotes shared with us, as well as observations of the office culture, such as seating arrangements and work styles. Interestingly, we saw some teams have a fixed seating arrangement, while others have a more flexible setup. However, there were flyers at the coffee corner promoting a flexible and hybrid way of working, which didn't seem to reflect how all teams are working. Jack and Rose from the development team were always at the office, while others worked more flexibly.

Because there is only so much you can observe by participating in these sessions, we also started planning interviews to grasp more information about the culture.

CONDUCTING INTERVIEWS

During our engagements, the first interviews we conduct with individuals will always be unstructured. We have a plan based on the observations we already gathered through participatory observation, and informal interviews in between sessions. However, our aim is to capture as much information as possible by allowing the conversation to naturally flow and using our active listening skills to follow the direction the person being interviewed wants to go in. It's important to start by stressing the confidentiality of the interview and assuring the person that the information gathered won't be directly linked to them. To start, we ask a question to gauge their expectations or perception of the engagement, such as "What are your expectations from our engagement?" or "How do you see our engagement being done?"

Here is the hardest part of the interview process. The interview requires a delicate balance of active listening and capturing as much information as possible. To make this easier, we usually conduct interviews with two people—one to write and the other for active listening and conducting the interview. We use an online whiteboard to capture notes, which is instantly shared with others, as we did for the map in figure 6.3. What we're looking for are shared symbols we spoke about earlier, such as the one we observed in a conversation among developers who were focused on finishing their user stories on time to meet their promised estimations. That might not sound weird to anyone who has worked in agile organizations, but we can observe a symbol we called "promising to deliver." During the interviews, we avoid jumping to conclusions, but through participatory observations and interviews, we identify symbols of power, such as delivering on time, resulting in implicit ranking. Delivering on time might not sound like a symbol at first, but more like an ability that is related to skills. Although that is true, the power

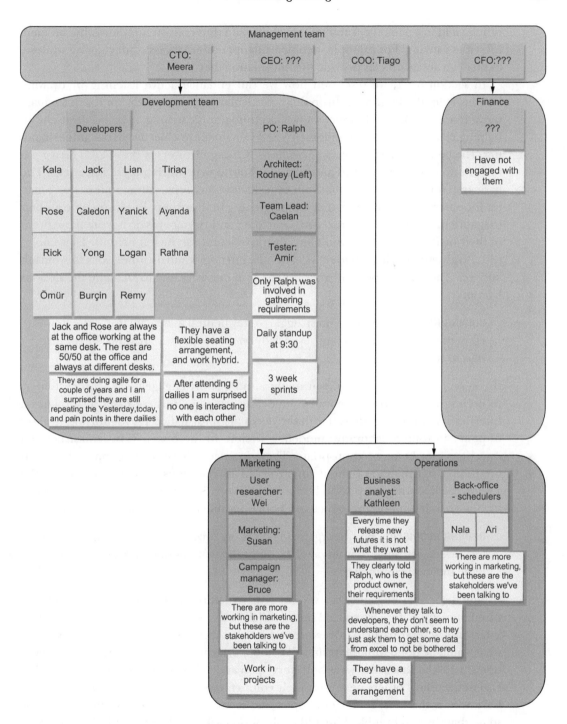

Figure 6.3   An example map of how to model the organization and capture symbols, anecdotes, and our own thoughts. In reality, this would be a lot bigger, so we like to use online tools where we can easily enlarge the area and collaborate on capturing our observations.

others yield to a person because of that ability and thus consistently delivering on time, increases ranking. For example, people from operations always contact Jack and Rose, as they can always quickly provide the information they need.

In section 5.2.1, we discussed how we can enhance active listening by drawing insights from the field of anthropology, particularly through their approach to qualitative research. One technique, known as ethnographic writing, is especially useful in helping us set aside our own judgments and remain more objective in our understanding. The book *Writing Ethnographic Fieldnotes* (Chicago University Press, 2011) is a good read for that. It gives you tips and tricks on how to write during these interviews. The basic trap you can fall into is that your own shadows and especially emotions don't matter for observing the patterns that are happening in the group. But if you try your best to ignore them, they will distract you. One thing anthropologists do is write those down in their field notes, so they won't be a distraction and can be left behind. These notes will also give you the insight to reflect after the interviews and do inner work for yourself later on. These field notes will greatly help us in our work and to facilitate the sessions later on.

> **GUIDING HEURISTIC** When you struggle to stay neutral as a facilitator, write down ethnographic field notes, and especially write down your shadows so you can start to reflect on these.

If you're a consultant like us, you might also do short engagements with customers to do just a couple of collaborative modeling sessions. In these cases, unstructured interviews may not provide you with the necessary information for identifying symbols of power in your collaborative modeling session. In these scenarios, semi-structured interviews may be more appropriate. These interviews have specific topics that focus on the goal of collaborative modeling. You can ask questions related to the goal of the session, such as what the person hopes to achieve or if they see any obstacles in reaching the goal. It's important to focus on both opposing aspects of the goal of a session.

> **GUIDING HEURISTIC** Before organizing cross-organizational collaborative modeling, do semi-structured interviews to collect the symbols of power that can determine the implicit ranking.

In our BigScreen engagement, we did semi-structured interviews after the unstructured one, just before we started doing collaborative modeling sessions. During these interviews, several participants expressed interest in the sessions but also questioned what would be done with the results. We noted a particular conflict between two developers, Jack and Rose, who were both very open and talkative during the interviews. We also noticed how others perceived their conflict, especially during our interview with Kala, who is the most senior developer. She seems to come over as someone who is somewhat shy and humble. She told us she wasn't asked to be involved in the previous decision to move forward. She also worked hard to implement the previous code and used a lot of design patterns that, in her mind, were what they decided. She was very annoyed that she was kept out of the loop and felt embarrassed reporting back to stake-holders that they needed to refactor a lot. These interviews made us assume we would see another symbol of power—being outspoken and direct—instead of shy, reserved, and humble being a symbol of power. There were several observations that gave us that assumption, but the most outspoken example is that Kala, with her experience, wasn't involved during decision-making. Again, being outspoken and direct might seem like characteristics instead of symbols of power at first glance. It's the power others yield to these traits that increases ranking. Note that this is highly context dependent. In other contexts, being outspoken and direct might decrease ranking.

It's important to note that conducting interviews prior to collaborative modeling sessions can help you establish yourself as a facilitator and gain implicit ranking. During these semi-structured interviews, focus on the needs of the individual, what they expect from the session, and how it can help them. Ask them what they need during the session and be clear about what you can and can't provide. Don't sell empty promises that give people expectations you can't fulfill because that will lower your ranking in the group that wants you to lead and facilitate them. These interviews provide context for the group you're facilitating, which can help make the session more collaborative and safer. If you already have enough information about the group, you may not need to conduct interviews. The goal is to understand the current symbols of power and ranking, which can help you gain ranking to create a safe space for collaboration from the start of the session.

After we gained a clear understanding, we were confident in organizing the Big Picture EventStorming at BigScreen. Together with Meera, the CTO, we used the preparation template as discussed in chapter 4, which you can see in figure 6.4. With this template, Meera could plan and invite the right people for the session, emphasizing her importance for the success of the project. During the interviews, most people expressed their concern about the campaign, mentioning that they were worried about the effect it will have on their work. They also mentioned that they felt those concerns weren't being taken seriously because those concerns might delay the deadlines Ralph has.

To address this, we incorporated their concerns into the phrasing of the session's goal. Meera explained the goal in her invitation email, emphasizing the needs of the participants we extracted from the interviews. By connecting with their needs, we eliminated confusion and created a need and motivation for them to attend. We don't want to force people to attend these sessions, but show them that the session will help them and meet the organization's concerns. We also sought feedback on the email to ensure its clarity. We aim to close the feedback loop and continuously observe, allowing us to make adjustments to how we facilitate the session where necessary.

6.3.2 *Own, play, and share your rank*

On the day of the Big Picture EventStorming, we arrived early to set up the room, ensuring we had at least an hour to prepare. We put up the paper roll; wrote the agenda, goal, and session explanation on the flip chart; and, most importantly, welcomed each participant personally. When you put people across silos from an organization into one

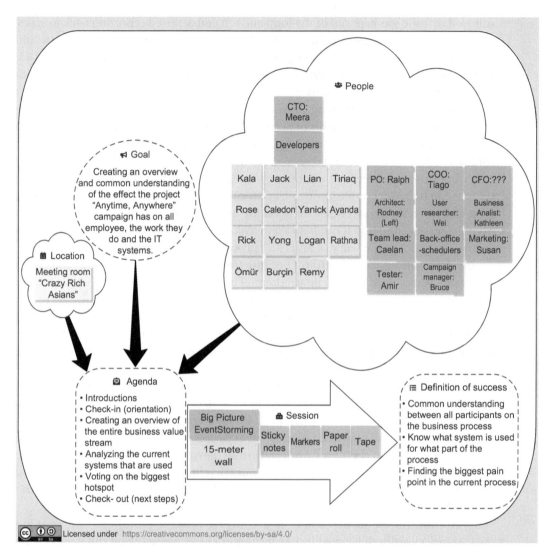

Figure 6.4   Filled-in preparation template for the Big Picture EventStorming we did together with Meera, the CTO at BigScreen. We connected the goal of the session with the shared need we extracted from the interviews.

room for a Big Picture EventStorming, you want people to feel comfortable from the start. You might be able to relate by thinking about how you feel when entering a room with people you either hardly know or never met, and you start to rank yourself against others. We need enough safety to know who can do or say what and, especially, what is my place here. So, the first moments a group gets together, it's important to make it just clear enough for people to start feeling comfortable.

Remember in section 4.4 we said we start our training with an exercise where we introduce EventStorming to a group of strangers and begin within the first 5 minutes. The atmosphere can become tense and uncomfortable for both attendees and facilitators.

The reason for this is that the participants don't yet know each other's positions and rankings, leading to awkward silence. As a facilitator, it's crucial to establish a sense of safety for the participants by taking the lead. Before the session even begins, you need to establish yourself as a leader so that the attendees feel comfortable and know who to turn to if they feel uneasy. When people are in unfamiliar situations, they naturally look for someone to follow, so it's essential to provide them with a leader they can trust. That leader should own up to that rank, make sure they keep the rank by playing it, and then share it with the people.

OWNING YOUR RANK

As facilitators, we get explicit ranking to organize and start a collaborative modeling session, which is usually granted to us by people who have that power in the organization. Owning up to that rank is important for us as facilitators because it establishes our authority and sets clear expectations for our role in the group. Owning our rank can help establish a sense of safety and comfort for participants, as they know who to turn to for guidance or support during the session. Without owning our rank, there may be confusion or ambiguity about who is leading the session, which can lead to a lack of direction or disagreements among participants. Participants may not feel comfortable sharing their ideas or asking questions, leading to a lack of engagement and a missed opportunity for collaboration and innovation. The session might end in chaos.

Not owning your rank can also be condescending and disrespectful to the participants. We might not own our rank because we want to be equal to others, which we think is a good value to have. But if we're honest, we're not equal to the participants, just as a CTO isn't equal to the employees. We've been given certain power to lead the session, to facilitate it, to actually decide on the process the participants can't. Not owning your rank can then signal that you're not taking responsibility for your role and the success of the session. It can undermine the trust that the group has in you as a facilitator. If they sense that you're not willing to take the lead and guide them through the process, they may start to question your expertise and credibility. Owning your rank and taking responsibility to lead the session doesn't mean you should treat people disrespectfully or unequally differently.

> **GUIDING HEURISTIC** When you're high in rank as a facilitator, welcome everyone personally to the session and let them feel welcomed and comfortable.

To have a successful session, it's important to establish yourself as the leader and facilitator from the beginning. Start by introducing yourself as the person leading the session when participants join the meeting room. When the session starts, let the person who invited everyone kick it off. If that's us, we introduce ourselves. With the Big Picture EventStorming at BigScreen, we had Meera kick off the session and explain its importance, after which, she made it clear that we would be facilitating the session. When we took over, we made sure to properly introduce ourselves and explain what participants could expect from us. We discussed the agenda, roles, and safety rules of the session. It's important that all participants agree on the safety rules. We start with adding the "nobody holds the monopoly to the truth" safety rule from the Lewis Deep Democracy methodology[6] to promote an open discussion. If the session is online, we also add the "disable all unnecessary notifications and communications programs" safety rule. We ensure that everyone is on the same page, and we have the group explicitly agree to the rules by raising their hands. Now participants can also add safety rules themselves. During the session, safety rules can be changed or added as long as the entire group agrees. If there is a disagreement, it's important to address it before moving forward. We'll talk more about managing conflict in chapter 8.

> **GUIDING HEURISTIC**   When you're in a session where working agreements aren't explicit, set up safety rules that the group collaboratively agrees with. That way, you can always refer back to them if those safety rules are broken.

PLAYING YOUR RANK

Now that we've established ourselves and are owning our rank, it's equally or more important to play your rank. It's crucial to understand the distinction between leaders with *explicit* ranking, such as those in an organization's hierarchy, and leaders with *implicit* ranking, those chosen by the group based on social power. Because of the social power, our rank is in constant flux and depends on the culture's symbols of power. That makes it a very interesting topic but also a hard one to grasp as a facilitator because if we want to keep our rank, we should actively play our rank. Changes to our nonverbal behavior or our communication style can influence that rank so we can then share it with the group, giving people in the group power to express themselves. That's why it helps to know and understand the symbols of power of a group before the session.

> **NOTE**   There's a growing movement to create software teams that are self-steering, autonomous, and don't require direct management. While we think this is a great idea and support the notion of teams that can steer themselves, it's important to remember that we still need leaders. Without a clear hierarchy, people might start to wonder who's making decisions. If we don't establish and collaboratively design an alternative hierarchy that's inclusive and fair, things could quickly become chaotic and unsafe for everyone involved. In these situations, the strongest and most influential people tend to rise to the top, which can be detrimental to creating a safe, equal, and inclusive work environment.

During the Big Picture EventStorming at BigScreen, we focused on being outspoken and the importance to deliver symbols of power we analyzed. We gave the participants 20 minutes to write down their first set of events during the chaotic exploration phase, and we provided time updates at the 5-minute and 2-minute mark. It's crucial to ensure everyone has enough time to express themselves, so we also asked if anyone needed more time. We were mindful that there may be people in the group who don't

---

[6]   Kramer, J. *Deep Democracy–De wijsheid van de minderheid* ("The Wisdom of the Minority"), 2019. OH: Management Impact Publishing.

align with the traditional symbols of power, so we made sure to provide enough space for them to contribute. It's important to play our rank as facilitators without losing the trust of those who may be in the minority. Building this trust is crucial when trying to gain implicit ranking and share it with others.

> **GUIDING HEURISTIC** As facilitator, favor more passive participation at the start of a collaborative session, and then transition into more active participation.

During the Big Picture EventStorming, we made sure to actively participate in the group discussions by asking questions or giving comments on the events that were put up. This was a change in our usual approach of being more observant at the beginning, but we knew the importance of playing our rank as facilitators. However, playing your rank can be tiring, especially if the cultural symbols of power are different from your own. If you're a shy, reserved, and humble person, you may struggle to assert your rank. Sometimes, you can't even play the rank because the person you are is by default lower in rank. For example, in cultures where being a tall white male is a symbol of power, anyone else will struggle. In such cases, it may be necessary to have another facilitator who can represent that part of the group. In our Big Picture EventStormings, we always have at least two facilitators, one who can actively play the rank and another who can observe more passively. This way, we build trust with different people from the group, and the majority and minority are represented.

> **GUIDING HEURISTIC** Facilitate Big Picture EventStorming with two people who can represent different power symbols of the group.

SHARING YOUR RANK

Owning and playing your rank can help you gain enough influence within the group to share that influence with all participants. This helps to make the collaborative modeling process easier for everyone involved. During our Big Picture EventStorming session at BigScreen, we knew that shy, introverted, and humble individuals may have a harder time being heard by the group. By using our rank, we can make it safe for them to speak up and ensure that those who are dominating the conversation give others a chance to share their opinions. When someone with lower rank speaks up, we can help to amplify their voice and give them a platform to express themselves in the group. Because we have explicit and implicit rank, people are more likely to accept behavior from us that they might not accept from others in their culture. By sharing our rank, we can allow leadership to emerge from the group as a collective responsibility, rather than being the responsibility of a single individual. Ultimately, we want the group to take collective responsibility, and sharing rank with everyone in the group is an important part of achieving that goal.

> **NOTE** The concepts of owning, playing, and sharing your rank come from Danielle Braun and Jitske Kramer. They talk about the importance of these concepts in their books, so we've included two of them in the further reading list at the end of the chapter.

6.3.3   *Making the group aware of their rank*

Groups and cultures can become coagulated, and get stuck in their behaviors because these behaviors provide a sense of meaning and safety within the group. We like to be safe, and any change in the group can be seen as a threat and be rejected. Ranking is a crucial factor, as those in higher positions often decide what is acceptable within the culture and tend to promote people who are similar to them. This can lead to a lack of adaptability and resistance to change and will end up in what we call *groupthink*. Group-think results in an irrational or dysfunctional decision-making outcome in a team, and thus also in collaborative software design. As facilitators, it's our responsibility to help the group move past groupthink, and learn to include new ideas. One thing that will help the group become aware of groupthink is the use of sensemaking.

Sensemaking (as explained in chapter 5) can get a group to change the current rank and even let them become aware of their rank. As mentioned earlier in the chapter, we can use tools such as the Mindell test we showed in figure 6.1 to create an understanding of people higher and lower in the group. At the Big Picture EventStorming at BigScreen, we added a sensemaking exercise right after the check-in. Here, we can use the information again that was gathered from the interviews. As mentioned, the concern was the effect this campaign would have on their work. Right after the check-in, we did a sensemaking exercise asking them from low to high how much they think the campaign would affect their work. We did this in the room, and let people stand in a line. But if we would have done it online, it would look like figure 6.5.

> **GUIDING HEURISTIC**   After the check-in, use a sensemaking exercise to confirm if everyone is on board with the session's goal.

We then invited people from both sides to speak up about why they placed themselves on that specific part. Doing a sensemaking exercise at the start makes sure to validate that we're tackling the right problem of the group. It also connects the participants with the challenge before we start tackling it, enabling them to fully engage.

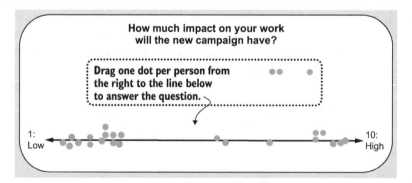

Figure 6.5   An outcome of a sensemaking exercise diving into the pain points of the group to clearly see the disconnect between the participants.

During the Big Picture EventStorming, we kept doing this sensemaking focused on getting more understanding between the groups and helping people in higher ranks to become aware of their own rank. We also asked the participants at some point about how important the deadline is. We again formed a line from not important to important, and this time made them discuss their position in groups of three to four. These groups are formed by someone from the left side, someone from the right, and someone from the middle. That way, people got to understand each side of that symbol of power, and people became aware of why it is or isn't important to deliver. After 10–15 minutes, we let each breakout group explain what they discussed and bring it back to the group. Those conversations created space for the people lower in rank to express their need and gave an opportunity for change for the people in higher rank to accept and start supporting the entire group.

GUIDING HEURISTIC   After a sensemaking exercise on ranking, split up the group to smaller breakouts with people from the left, right, and middle of the line.

It's important to always focus sensemaking on the session at hand, blending it within the session, and not overdoing it. Find the natural moments in the session you can do these; they usually show themselves in the form of polarities (we'll talk more on polarities in chapter 9).

6.4   *Collaborative software design catalysts*

- Write down symbols of power that you see in a group you're currently working with. This could be your team, people you're working with in your organization, or a group of people who are doing collaborative modeling.
- Before your next meeting, check who is invited, and determine which individuals you consider powerful and which less powerful. Why did you make those choices? How could that affect the meeting and outcomes? Try to write down specific behaviors or traits.
- In the next session you're facilitating, let someone with a high explicit ranking introduce you to the group you will facilitate.
- When you expect power gradients or rankings to have an effect on an upcoming session, discuss your thoughts with highly ranked participants. Discuss what the goals of the session are, and strategize for it in terms of ranking. If your goal is to be complete and let everyone speak their thoughts, then make sure people higher in rank don't share their thoughts first.
- Reflect with your team on how ranking affects your collaboration.
- Consider using a sensemaking technique to start a conversation about ranking. For example, place a dot on a line for the following question: "Do you experience an effect of ranking on this team?" Let them go from "not at all" to "absolutely."

6.5   *Chapter heuristics*

Guiding heuristics

- Let someone with a high explicit ranking introduce you to the group you will facilitate.

- Entry is everything, so make sure the first time you join a new group, team, or organization, you have a good introduction. Be humble and open to retain your neutrality.

- Write ethnographic field notes, especially your shadows, so you can start to reflect on these. That insight can help you stay more neutral as a facilitator.

- Before organizing cross-organizational collaborative modeling, do semi-structured interviews to collect the symbols of power that can determine the implicit ranking.

- When you're high in rank as a facilitator, welcome everyone personally to the session and let them feel welcomed and comfortable.

- When you're in a session where working agreements aren't explicit, set up safety rules that the group collaboratively agrees with. That way, you can always refer back to them if those safety rules are broken.

- As facilitator, favor more passive participation at the start of a collaborative session, and then transition into more active participation.

- Facilitate Big Picture EventStorming with two people who can represent different power symbols of the group.

- After the check-in, use a sensemaking exercise to confirm if everyone is on board with the session's goal.

- After a sensemaking exercise on ranking, split up the group to smaller breakouts with people from the left, right, and middle of the line.

6.6   *Further reading*

- *Epistemic Injustice: Power & the Ethics of Knowing"* by Miranda Fricker (Oxford University Press, 2007)

- *Jam Cultures: About Inclusion; Joining in the Action, Conversation and Decisions* by Jitske Kramer (Management Impact Publishing, 2021)

- *The Corporate Tribe: Organizational Lessons from Anthropology* by Danielle Braun and Jitske Kramer (Routledge, 2018)

- *Writing Ethnographic Fieldnotes* by Rachel I. Fretz, Robert M. Emerson, and Linda L. Shaw (Chicago University Press, 2011)

Summary

- Ranking is a position in a social hierarchy that shapes our thinking and behavior.
- Explicit rankings are the related powers that one is perceived to have because of their position in the visible hierarchy like an organization chart.
- Implicit rankings are the related powers that one is perceived to have because of other characteristics, such as status, gender, education, skin color, age, knowledge, experience, and so on.
- Symbolic violence describes nonphysical violence between two people or two groups of people with different ranking.
- It can be a highly vulnerable experience to acknowledge or establish ranks in a group. Be mindful of this sensitivity and facilitate this properly.
- Highly ranked people (explicit or implicit ranking) often take up a lot of space during collaborative modeling, while people who have a lower ranking during collaborative modeling have a harder time being heard.
- Ranking during collaborative modeling can lead to overly complex designs, shallow models, and messy software architecture.
- Teams lower in ranking will be under a lot more pressure because they often don't get the resources required to implement new features, maintain their part of the system, and still deliver on time.
- As a facilitator, you need to make your explicit rank as leader clear during a collaborative modeling session.
- Before a collaborative modeling session, try to understand the power dynamic in the company and between the stakeholders you're inviting.
- During a collaborative modeling session, make people aware of each other's implicit rank. Additionally, create sensemaking exercises to show the division on difficult topics.

7
The effect and opportunities of cognitive bias

This chapter covers

- Defining, recognizing, and embracing cognitive bias
- Understanding how cognitive bias affects collaboration and software design
- Altering behavior through nudges
- Becoming a choice architect

The previous chapter explained ranking and its effect on collaborative modeling sessions. Similar to ranking, *cognitive bias* affects group dynamics and outcomes. Cognitive bias is a systematic pattern of deviation from a norm that affects decision-making and judgment, that is, mental shortcuts that help us make sense of the world. Isn't it strange that when you're thinking about buying a car from a specific brand, you seem to see that car way more often than before? It's like everyone is driving that car now. Spoiler alert: this has to do with cognitive bias.

Sticking with the car example, have you ever driven on a highway and all of a sudden realize you've driven quite some miles without consciously registering everything that happened around you? Did you pass a car on the right? Were there any traffic signs? Did anything noticeable happen? Realizing you were driving that car sounds a bit dangerous now, right? Driving a car requires you to make many decisions on the spot: you have to react to other drivers by tapping the gas, possibly changing gears, slowing down or speeding up, staying in your lane, avoiding obstacles, and so on. It doesn't sound like an activity best done partly unconsciously, and yet, we end up a few miles farther than we remember. This, too, has to do with our brains using mental shortcuts to make decisions quickly and effectively.

Just like in the preceding example, this happens regularly during collaborative modeling sessions. In some situations, it's beneficial because decisions can be made quickly and effectively. In other situations, the mental shortcuts can be a hindrance, and we need to find a way to properly manage them. In this chapter, we'll dive into cognitive bias and how they can affect collaborative modeling sessions. We'll discuss some of the examples we see regularly and how you can recognize them. As facilitators, observing cognitive bias can help you unblock groups and nudge them toward rethinking solutions and withholding judgment when necessary. This chapter will provide you with guidance and heuristics on how to observe, benefit, embrace, and overcome cognitive bias when desired.

7.1 Cognitive bias explained

This section will dive into the meaning and effect of cognitive bias in collaborative modeling sessions. As mentioned in the introduction, cognitive bias is a systematic pattern of deviation from a norm that affects decision-making and judgment. The "systematic" part in this definition is important. Because it's systematic, it becomes predictable. This is why we can observe, anticipate, and we see similar biases occurring in almost every collaborative modeling session. As facilitators, this gives you an advantage because you can share your observations with the group and decide where these biases help and where they hinder the group and its progress.

As you can imagine, a lot of (unconscious) decisions are being made during collaborative modeling: Which pivotal events do we choose? How do we split the group? Where do you place your stickies on the timeline? How much detail do you add to the board? Where do you start in the process? When do you move on from a discussion? That's just a few of the possibilities. A lot of these decisions partly rely on cognitive bias, which means cognitive bias can trigger behavior too. Understanding and recognizing biases therefore is a useful skill when doing collaborative modeling.

For the record, we're fans of cognitive bias. It sometimes has a negative connotation, but without these biases our lives would be so much more complex and much less fun. In the coming sections, we'll explain this further and provide lots of examples. We'll start with explaining cognitive bias using some theory and research. Equally important are the misconceptions we'll discuss because there are many of them.

7.1.1 What is cognitive bias?

In our daily lives, a lot of information is coming our way almost continuously. We have to make sense of all those chunks of information by processing them and giving meaning to them. It sounds easy, but it's actually a ton of work. Imagine having to consciously, deliberately process every tiny bit of information you encounter. For example, can you describe and explain every single decision you had to make this (or yesterday) morning to get from your house to work? These decisions range from turning off your alarm clock, to taking a shower, making breakfast, checking your email, leaving the house, driving your car, parking your car (or going to the train station, taking a train), entering the office, and so on.

Our human brains are brilliant and powerful, but they are also limited in the amount of information they can structurally process simultaneously. The brain simply can't register, identify, process, analyze, and understand every single chunk of information that's thrown at it in a rational way—there are limitations. So, what our brilliant brain then tries to do is simplify this information processing. Cognitive biases can be a result of our brain's attempt to simplify information processing. You could consider them mental shortcuts, or rules of thumb, that help you make sense of the world, process information quickly based on previous experience and knowledge, and help you make a decision with relative speed. For example, our brain may take only the information it needs to make a decision, which can be convenient during collaborative modeling sessions. If we had to process everything consciously, we wouldn't have a lot of time left to do the actual modeling part.

7.1.2   *What does cognitive bias look like?*

Now that we know a little bit more about what cognitive biases are, we need to know how they operate in our daily lives. More specifically, given the context of this book, it's valuable to know how they operate in collaborative modeling sessions. Section 7.2 will go into this topic in more detail, but we'll provide two brief examples here to further explain the concept of cognitive bias.

During EventStorming, the group needs to decide on pivotal events at one point. What we often see happening is that someone, usually relatively high in rank, points at one domain event as a pivotal event: "In my opinion, this event should be a pivotal event." The rest of the group goes along with that suggestion or sometimes suggests alternative pivotal events that are close to the first suggestion on the timeline. This is the *anchoring effect*—a cognitive bias—in full swing. The first suggestion made here serves as an anchor that the rest of the group will move to. They may adjust it a bit, but the group will move toward that anchor, which means that whoever drops this anchor, strongly influences group decisions. The anchoring effect can be reinforced by ranking, as we saw in the example situation. If the person who drops the first anchor is relatively high in rank, people will tend to follow their suggestion and might be hesitant to share their initial thoughts and perspective. This particular example illustrates how several social dynamics (in this case, anchoring effect and ranking) can influence and reinforce each other, which is exactly why it's so important to deal with them properly.

Another example where we see cognitive bias in collaborative modeling is when people work together in subgroups on a solution, model, or proposal. In our training, we deliberately do this to demonstrate cognitive bias. Let's take Example Mapping as our example. Different subgroups are asked to come up with rules and examples for a specific challenge. We let the groups work on it, and after some time, we ask them to walk around and see what the other groups came up with. After that, we ask them to do the sensemaking exercise shown in figure 7.1.

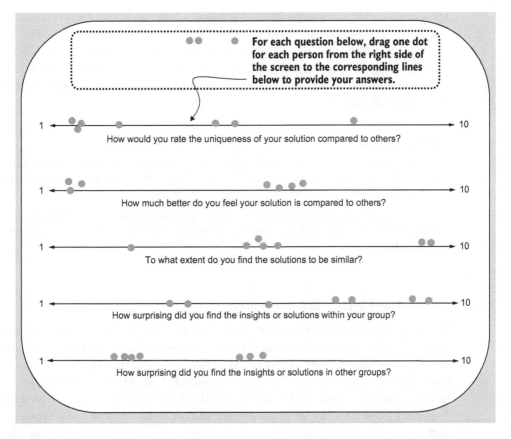

Figure 7.1 Sensemaking exercise to demonstrate cognitive bias during collaborative modeling

We usually see very similar outcomes and examples in the different groups. Apart from the anchoring effect just described, various cognitive biases are involved here:

- *Availability bias*—A mental shortcut that heavily relies on examples that come to mind quickly and easily. This is based on the notion that if something comes to mind so quickly, it must be important. More or less, the same information likely comes to mind for all individuals, creating similarity in their models or solutions.

- *Functional fixedness*—A cognitive bias that affects creativity. This is about getting stuck in what we know, which hinders us from taking on new perspectives to solve problems. We all have the same mental image of what a cinema looks like, for example. That often limits our creativity when thinking about solutions.

- *Bandwagon effect*—A cognitive bias that describes the tendency of people to adopt certain behavior or decisions just because others are doing it. When the whole group agrees on an example or takes on a certain strategy to come to those examples, it's easy to follow the majority and jump on that bandwagon.

To take this a bit further, we have to explain a little bit about what is called *System 1 and System 2*. Described in detail in Daniel Kahneman's book *Thinking, Fast and Slow* (Macmillan, 2013), System 1 thinking is an almost instantaneous process—our automatic pilot that's intuitive and requires little effort. System 2 thinking is slower, more conscious, and rational, requiring more effort. Our System 1 thinking heavily benefits from cognitive bias.

Exercise 7.1

Think about your recent meetings or collaborative modeling sessions; did you observe (in hindsight) the anchoring effect, availability bias, functional fixedness, or the bandwagon effect? If so, how did it affect the outcomes of the session?

Hint: If you can't think of any examples, that might be your System 1 thinking being predominant. Try to talk to others about the session to see if they can indicate some examples of bias.

7.1.3   *System 1 and System 2: A crash course*

Psychologists and philosophers have been busy with the distinction between instinctive thinking and conscious reasoning for many centuries. As mentioned earlier, in *Thinking, Fast and Slow*, Kahneman managed to get the distinction between automatic and conscious thought processes into mainstream thinking. More specifically, he popularized the concepts of System 1 and System 2 thinking[1] to describe the two processes.

System 1 operates almost automatically and quickly, with little to no effort. This system is about intuition and drawing conclusions. It's a very valuable system that helps you function in and navigate through a fast-paced world that throws information at you continuously. System 1 helps you deal with things such as driving for a long time on an empty road, solving 1 + 1, and detecting emotions in voices and facial expressions. After enough repetition, more complex tasks can become routine decisions that can eventually be taken care of by System 1. An example is driving a car in general. When you first get your driver's license, you have to actively and consciously think about every decision you make while driving. After a few years, this becomes more of a routine that can be handled by System 1. System 1 relies on mental shortcuts based on experience and repetition. This is also where cognitive biases come in.

System 2 thinking is slower than System 1. It's more rational and refers to consciously making decisions. We use System 2 mainly for more complex mental activities such as solving 37 × 17, deciding between two potential new houses or jobs, or writing a book. System 2 is also very useful for challenging System 1's conclusions when necessary.

It might seem that these are two separate systems that we can use as we please in specific situations: for routine work, we use System 1, and for complex activities, we ping

---

[1]   Stanovich, K. E., & West, R. F. "Individual Difference in Reasoning: Implications for the Rationality Debate?," 2000. *Behavioral and Brain Sciences*, 23(5): 645–726.

System 2. When System 1 draws conclusions (too fast), we ask System 2 to challenge them. Sounds almost too good to be true right? It is. There needs to be some nuance added to this story. Some of this nuance and depth got lost when the concepts of System 1 and System 2 became more mainstream and popular. As Kahneman explains in his book, this dual-system approach combines both forms of reasoning because (almost) all information processing is based on a mix of the two systems. We may rely a bit more on System 2 in mentally complex situations, but both systems work together, which is actually the beauty of it all. Together, these systems enable us to enhance our overall decision-making and make effective decisions.

Note that this is just another model to think about and deal with—in this case—cognitive bias. Like we mentioned earlier, we consider all models to be wrong, but some models can be helpful. The model of System 1 and System 2 isn't the holy grail. There are downsides and criticisms of course, as with every model. Keep this in mind when deciding which models are useful to you.

7.1.4 *Embracing cognitive bias*

System 1 is sensitive to cognitive bias. We rely on System 1 a lot, but that doesn't mean most of our decisions rely on biases. Luckily, the dual-system approach helps us make effective decisions. We can spend a lot of time actively questioning System 1, but this would be a waste of time. Instead, we should embrace both systems and learn to recognize situations in which potential mistakes are very costly and cognitive bias might influence the outcome of our decisions. Recognizing these situations and cognitive bias isn't enough, of course. It's about balance. If you recognize them, what's your next step? Do you need to challenge bias or not? There's no good or bad here—it's all context dependent. We'll give some examples on how to apply this balance in sections 7.2 and 7.3.

An important reason to embrace cognitive bias—apart from the huge help in our decision-making—is that it influences behavior. Human behavior is extremely complex and context- and person-sensitive. The same bias could influence behavior of different people in different ways. So, during collaborative modeling, you need to be aware of this. If you feel like challenging certain biases, be aware that they affect behavior in different ways. Section 7.3 will elaborate on how to facilitate this during collaborative modeling.

Finally, cognitive biases often have a negative connotation, which we feel needs to be removed because biases help us. Sure, in some cases, they lead to poor judgment and decision-making. However, in most cases, these biases don't make us irrational but rather effective and efficient, which is exactly what we need in collaborative modeling. As long as we can bring balance and facilitate properly, we can stop referring to biases as synonyms to irrationality and poor decision-making. Instead, we can embrace them and benefit from their effect on collaborative modeling.

Now that we've explained cognitive bias and its effect on group dynamics, it's time to dive into collaborative modeling specifically. How do you recognize biases, when do they pop up, and how can you anticipate them when facilitating? Sections 7.2 and 7.3 will go into these topics.

7.2   *Cognitive bias during collaboration and software design*

You may have heard someone say, "This blog post says it's a good choice to go for boring technologies, so we were right to use background processes with library X, instead of using message queues!" while not realizing some libraries that enable you to do message queueing have been around a lot longer than the library that they picked out to schedule background processes. Or maybe this sounds more familiar: "I listened to a talk by Eric Evans, and he used approach X in his project and said it was an excellent choice too." These are examples of decisions made on software design and architecture driven by cognitive biases. Some of these decisions will affect the software system for years to come, and making decisions like this won't have a positive effect on the system. In this section, we'll dive into a few biases that you should become aware of in others and most importantly in yourself, and we'll walk you through the effect they have during collaborative modeling and on your software design.

7.2.1   *Confirmation bias*

The first example in the introduction illustrated *confirmation bias*, in which people search or interpret information in a way that confirms an already held belief. We see this one happen a lot in software development teams when designing their architecture. The same bias can happen when you try to introduce collaborative modeling in your organization. During one of our sessions at BigScreen, Caelan (team lead and invited to participate) was skeptical about the technique. While we were modeling, he looked for reasons to confirm that this wasn't going to work. At one point, one of the other participants asked a question about how to deal with the absence of the customer in these sessions. We explained that being able to invite customers directly would be more beneficial to examine the customer journeys, but that we could compensate by making some informed assumptions and then implement a monitoring system to validate those assumptions. Caelan immediately responded with this: "So, what you're saying is that collaborative modeling isn't optimal for BigScreen because we can't invite our customers to this session?" This had a huge effect on the collaborative modeling sessions Caelan participated in. The other people in the session became very guarded and reluctant to speak. Even we, the consultants, started weighing our words because we knew we would have to spend time countering Caelan's arguments on why collaborative modeling wasn't going to work for BigScreen.

7.2.2   *The law of triviality*

The *law of triviality*, also known as "bike-shedding," is probably the best-known cognitive bias in the software industry. The law of triviality states that people within an organization spend more time discussing trivial problems than important ones. When we were designing the bounded contexts at BigScreen, we spent a lot of time discussing what the name should be of the bounded context that would be used by both systems instead of discussing what this bounded context would be responsible for, how we would design the public interface to serve both systems, or how to extract this from the current system. Making those design decisions required difficult discussions, and even though the problem had been settled, the team still remembered the conflict between the developers and architect whenever the architecture was discussed. Finding the perfect name, which was a "trivial" decision compared to the other decisions we had to make, got a lot of attention from the team. We were definitely bike-shedding!

The origin of bike-shedding

When C. Northcote Parkinson, a British naval historian best known for his law on bureaucracy, wrote about the law of triviality, he offered the example of an executives meeting in which three budgets needed to be approved. The first one was approving the budget (£10.000.000) for an atomic reactor; the second budget was the new bike shed that was going to be built at the office, which would cost £350; and the last one was the annual budget for refreshments during meetings, which was £21. He stated that the time spent on approving a budget would be disproportionate to the amount needed to be approved. Because the executives in the meeting would have limited or no knowledge of atomic reactors, this item would be discussed the least, even though it had the biggest budget. The bike shed and the coffee, however, would be discussed at length because each executive felt they could contribute to those topics.

When retelling the story, as often happens with stories, people didn't mention the budgets and the coffee, and spoke about time spent approving an atomic reactor and a bike shed. It resonated with a few people in the software industry because discussing details of a specific topic, such as the color or the position of a button on a page, is often given more time than the important decisions that need to be made (What does this feature have to do?). As it gained traction, the law became known as bike-shedding.

7.2.3 *False-consensus effect*

Confirmation bias and bike-shedding are cognitive biases that pop up during a collaboration session, so you have to be aware of and manage them. Other cognitive biases have a greater effect on the design and solutions. One of the most common cognitive biases that will not only harm your collaboration but also your solutions is the *false-consensus effect*, the assumption that your personal qualities, characteristics, beliefs, and actions are widespread through the general population. Put differently, people assume everybody is just like them. For collaborative modeling, this translates into assuming that everyone using your software system is just like the people in the session. During one of the sessions at BigScreen, we were digging a bit deeper into the Seat Allocation bounded context. This bounded context is responsible for suggesting and reserving seats when people purchase a ticket to a movie. We decided to do some Example Mapping to come up with specific examples of how Seat Allocations should work. After a while, we noticed that none of the groups had an example of how this should work when somebody in a wheelchair was purchasing a ticket. This is the false-consensus effect bias at work—the assumption that the people we have to allocate seats to are just like everybody in the room.

7.2.4   *Availability bias*

During collaborative modeling, we want to generate different designs so we can evaluate them and pick the best aspects of each of those as a basis to create the architecture. This isn't always easy because of the aforementioned availability bias: when we're trying to make decisions or assess information, we add more value to information that can be recalled easily, or at least find it more important than alternative solutions not as readily recalled.[2] When it comes to collaborative modeling, this bias often makes participants favor the first design they came up with because they substitute "good" for "easy."

During a modeling session at BigScreen where we were designing the Movie Scheduling bounded context, we tried to create a good model for the concept: a movie is shown at a specific time in a specific hall of a theater at a specific date. We did a first iteration and came up with a "movie" (figure 7.2, left), which had a name, a duration, and a playtime. In this proposed solution, we would have movies that together represented the schedule. We started iterating on this and eventually came up with a "movie showing" (figure 7.2, right). When we asked which one is better, Caelan responded, "Well, the left one." When we asked him why that was the better model, he said, "Because we spent less time on creating it. We struggled a lot to come up with the second one, so it has to be less fitting." That is the availability bias at play here. Caelan confused the quality of the model (the left model is better than the right model) with the suitability of the model (the left model was easy to come up with, and the right one wasn't).

Part of designing a good architecture is designing your models in different ways to gain knowledge of what would be the best way to represent a concept in your system. You need to dig deeper than the first thing you can come up with!

7.2.5   *Loss aversion*

Once we have our models in production for a while, it also becomes hard to think about a better solution. We become emotionally attached to our solution, and we have a hard time letting go of it. One of the biases at play here is *loss aversion*, the tendency to avoid losses over gaining wins. This is because we have a stronger emotional response to a loss than to a gain.

Flexibility in our software design is something we want to achieve as good software developers. We want software to be able to change easily, but at the same time, loss aversion prevents us from letting go of what we've already designed. That is also a reason we start model fitting. *Model fitting* in the context of software design is deforming, that is, adding or leaving out elements from the problem domain to force it into an already existing model, metaphor, or abstraction.

---

[2]   Schwarz, N., Bless, H., Strack, F., Klumpp, G., Rittenauer-Schatka, H., & Simons, A. "Ease of Retrieval as Information: Another Look at the Availability Heuristic," 1991. *Journal of Personality and Social Psychology*, 61 (2): 195–202.

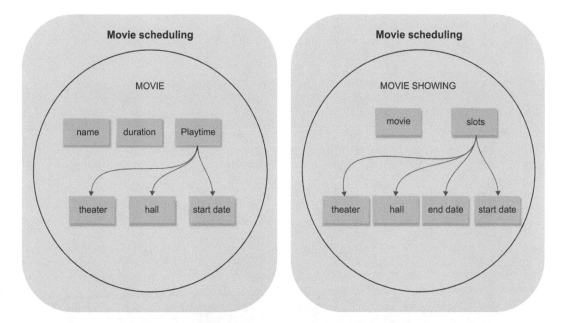

Figure 7.2   On the left, we see the first model we came up with, Movie, to represent the concepts of "a movie is shown at a specific time in a specific hall of a theater at a specific date" On the right, you can see the model we came up with when digging deeper into this concept. We realized that a better model to represent this concept would be Movie Showing, where we linked a movie to specific slots.

Let's have a look at a model fitting example from BigScreen. The Movie Showing model has two concepts: slot and movie. A slot is a moment where a movie can be played. It has a specific theater and hall, and a start and end date. So, a Movie Showing captures which movie is being played for specific slots. This model was designed in one of our early sessions and put into production. It worked really well. BigScreen also has private movie showings in which a company can book a company event at BigScreen. They can pick a movie from a list and select the type of reception they want. BigScreen has a reception room in each theater where the reception takes place.

When this concept was explained to the software developers, they were afraid to lose two things. First, they were afraid to lose the current model, which was working very well for the purpose it was designed. Second, they were afraid to lose face in front of the business because the current model could not deal with a private movie showing and they would have to redesign the Movie Scheduling bounded context to implement this.

To prevent this, they said, "Oh, private movie showings are just movie showings with two slots: one for the reception, and one for the movie." The software developers adapted the already existing movie showing and added a property `IsPrivate` to the Movie Showing model to indicate whether or not this is a private showing. They also added the property `IsReception` to a slot, so they could check whether or not the hall should be filled in. When the slot is a reception, it will have no hall assigned to it (see figure 7.3). Due to their loss aversion, they fell into the trap of model fitting.

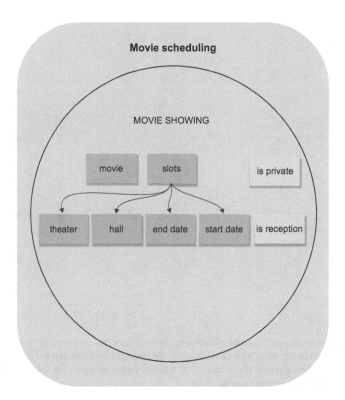

Figure 7.3   A visualization of model fitting at BigScreen. The concept of a private movie showing was fitted into an already existing model, Movie Showing, by adding IsPrivate to the model. A slot is now being used to not just represent the playtime of a movie but also a reception that only happens when a company books a private movie showing.

7.2.6   *Additive bias*

Many biases are interconnected, each influencing the other. For example, the software developers who were afraid to lose face engaged in model fitting and the addition of properties to the model due to loss aversion. This aversion is closely tied to our default strategy of introducing new elements rather than removing existing ones, known as the additive bias. Though distinct, this behavior shares roots with loss aversion and presents challenges in developing software that is secure, maintainable, protects data privacy, and is decoupled. At BigScreen, the goal was to break down the existing big ball of mud (BBoM) architecture for a system that is maintainable and loosely coupled, enabling the team to deliver a sustainable fast flow of business value and allowing the company to swiftly adapt to changing user demands.

Ignoring this bias and adding extra properties means that developers working within a specific bounded context will need to know more concepts that are relevant to solving the business problem at hand, increasing cognitive load and the risk of making mistakes. This situation can also lead to a type of coupling known as *connascence of name*, where multiple bounded contexts need to agree on the naming of an entity. If these properties are added across various bounded contexts and later need to be updated simultaneously, coordinating among different teams managing these contexts could slow down the delivery of business value and extend time to market. Overlooking the additive bias might inadvertently lead BigScreen back toward creating a BBoM. Like many biases, this tendency often goes unnoticed, with people typically unaware of how their emotions influence their decisions and actions. Now that we've introduced several examples of cognitive biases and their potential effects on architecture and software systems, we'll explore in greater detail how these biases can be addressed.

> **Exercise 7.2**
>
> Prepare for possible cognitive biases in your next collaborative modeling session: Which of the mentioned biases could potentially affect your next session and in what way? Then, when you observe them in the session, make them explicit by discussing what you observe and how it can affect the outcomes of the session. Discuss this with the rest of the group.

7.3 *Facilitating cognitive bias*

Now, you might be thinking that cognitive bias sounds like a big problem for collaborative modeling and group decision-making. And you'd be right—cognitive bias can definitely get in the way of achieving a common goal. But here's the cool part: with the right approach to facilitation, cognitive bias can actually be a useful tool to help groups work together more effectively.

That's exactly what we did in one of the follow-up sessions with BigScreen where we used Example Mapping. In that session, we facilitated the group to be aware of the effect of cognitive bias they had while Example Mapping. By shining a light on these biases and using some helpful heuristics, we were able to show them how to use cognitive bias to their advantage. Suddenly, the team was able to explore new possibilities and gain a deeper understanding of the problem at hand.

Of course, it's not always easy to identify and work with cognitive bias in a group setting. In fact, we've all probably experienced situations where it felt like our ideas were getting lost in the shuffle. So, before we dive into our work with BigScreen, let's take a closer look at how cognitive bias can affect group decision-making when it's not properly addressed.

7.3.1 *Self-fulfilling prophecy*

Before our engagement at BigScreen, we were tasked at another organization with determining the optimal time to lock agendas in a team planning software, considering the different factors that could affect the timeline. As the participants walked into the conference room, we introduced them to the agenda of the day and collaborative modeling. Before starting the session, we did a check-in with the participants to get a sense of what they hoped to get out of the session and what might hold them back from achieving the desired outcome. The participants answered that they hoped to get new ideas to tackle the problem of the user story we were discussing in refinement. Up until now, they experienced a lot of bugs in production because of a misunderstanding of the rules and use cases. They also said they tried a lot of different ways to make these refinements better and were worried they would get the same outcome as before. For us, it was nothing out of the ordinary—this is what we usually hear.

Now as facilitators, we must recognize that we aren't immune to biases. In this case, we were affected by two biases: the false-consensus effect as discussed previously and the *overconfidence bias*. The overconfidence bias refers to the tendency for individuals to have more confidence in their own abilities or judgments than is objectively justified. In our case, we had done these refinements before, and we heard nothing out of the ordinary. We expected the session to overcome what was said in the check-in—I mean that's why they hired us! But it made us not really listen to what had been said. This led us to overlook the biases that the group was facing, such as confirmation bias and the *status quo bias*, which affected the session's effectiveness. The status quo bias is the tendency to prefer the current state of affairs over changing to a new one, even if the new option may be better.

As we continued with the session, we introduced the participants to the collaborative modeling tool called Example Mapping, as explained in chapter 2, and you can see how such a session might look in figure 7.4. The challenge was to determine when to lock the agenda, considering the different factors that could affect the timeline. However, we soon noticed that the group was struggling to write down new examples.

That was because the group was facing the status quo bias, which is closely related to the availability bias and the anchoring effect. The user story we tackled with Example Mapping was rather complicated, with many things that can happen during a specific time period. Now we had already EventStormed that timeline, and Example Mapping would help them move forward by running through several use cases from that Event-Storming. Because we didn't have a predefined template with several use cases, the group stopped writing down their examples because they required the visualization of a timeline. We thought the EventStorm itself was enough to write those examples. Unfortunately, the participants went back to discussing things among themselves without visualizing, which meant that they were sticking to their traditional methods and not using the new tool. We realized that we needed to provide more structure to the process and nudge them to use the tools effectively. We're aware of other factors that can be at play here, such as unfamiliarity with tools that might lead to uncomfortableness or simply not knowing how. While many factors can influence the preference for specific tools, cognitive bias is very often one of them. If we're not careful of the effect of biases, collaborative modeling can become a self-fulfilling prophecy.

From this experience, we learned that collaborative modeling tools such as Example Mapping can be powerful assets in decision-making processes, but they require careful consideration of cognitive biases and appropriate facilitation. Our experience showed us that we can't assume that we understand the needs and biases of a group, and that it's important to be mindful of our own biases as facilitators. By providing structure,

Figure 7.4   An example of how an Example Mapping looked at BigScreen. The groups are divided and are using index cards on the table to collaboratively model and discover new scenarios and acceptance criteria.

guidance, and support, we can help groups overcome their biases and make the most of these tools.

We learned from our mistakes when we started engaging with BigScreen. With the lessons we learned from our previous experience, we were able to anticipate and address potential biases from the beginning. Let's look at how we facilitated that exactly by using nudges during an Example Mapping session we did at BigScreen in one of the follow-up sessions.

7.3.2   Altering behavior through nudges

In the follow-up session, we were tasked with finding a solution for a tricky problem: How should seat allocations work? It may seem like a simple question, but when you consider the complexity of cinema layouts, seating arrangements, and customer preferences, finding a satisfactory answer can be challenging.

Because we learned from our previous experience, we together with the software engineering team prepared specific templates to visualize what a cinema looks like. We already showed you how we did Example Mapping in chapter 2, where we used a specific template to visualize what a cinema looks like. The templates, shown in figure 7.5, helped us to establish a common understanding of what different types of cinema seating arrangements there are in BigScreen. From there, we could dive into specific scenarios and discuss what to do in each situation. We would have definitely wanted to collaboratively create those templates together with the stakeholders, but sometimes they don't have enough time to do so.

GUIDING HEURISTIC   When doing Example Mapping in complex or complicated scenarios, spend some time up front to design a template in which you can discuss these scenarios so that you don't spend too much time on visualizing the examples.

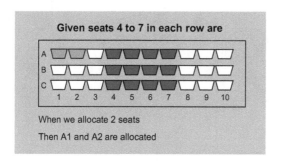

Figure 7.5   An example of the template we created together with the engineering team for use in an Example Mapping session. Although this is a very basic version of a cinema seating arrangement, it can be easily adapted to, for instance, add in a corridor in the middle. Sometimes, a good first example is enough.

When we as facilitators asked the team to create templates together up front and bring them to the session, we were using a nudge. A *nudge* is a way to alter people's behavior of making decisions in a predictable way. For example, you can nudge employees to have healthier lunches by putting healthy food on display that is easy to grab and keeping the unhealthy food more out of sight. The idea of a nudge was popularized by Richard Thaler and Cass Sunstein in their book *Nudge: Improving Decisions About Health, Wealth, and Happiness* (Penguin Books, 2009). One key aspect of a nudge is that it should always be optional, meaning a nudge always retains freedom of choice. Changes in behavior aren't forced in any way, just triggered. The nudge should be easily avoidable by the group, and they shouldn't be made to feel like they don't have a choice to act on the nudge or that they are being manipulated. For example, in our sessions, we presented the templates to the group and explicitly asked for their agreement before using them as a foundation for our discussion.

We're using the template as a nudge here because talking about complex scenarios can overwhelm our brains and make us susceptible to cognitive biases such as the availability bias, anchoring effect, and confirmation bias. This is one of the main reasons visualization is so important in collaborative modeling—it reduces the effect of these biases and allows us to make more informed decisions. And the template makes it easy for the group to visualize their conversation.

Not all nudges require explicit agreement as we asked for during our BigScreen Example Mapping session. As a facilitator, you can also lead by example and start drawing a visualization of what the group is discussing. This can encourage others to do the same and start visualizing their ideas. Remember, the group should always be able to decide not to use the nudge if they prefer and keep having a conversation without visualizing. It's not up to us as facilitators to decide if a cognitive bias is affecting them. Our responsibility is to make it easy for the group to do collaborative modeling. If they don't see they are affected by a bias, they can decide not to do anything about it.

> **GUIDING HEURISTIC** When a conversation isn't being visualized, lead by example as the facilitator and visualize the conversation.

When we use nudges, we either trigger cognitive biases or work around them to reduce their effect. In the case of Example Mapping, we wanted the group to be affected by the functional fixedness bias we talked about earlier to achieve our goal of focusing on allocating seats in a cinema room. When we think of a cinema, we picture the traditional setting—rows of red chairs, a big screen up front, and no windows. This preconceived image we hold in our minds can stifle our creativity when it comes to designing new ideas. The session's goal was to focus on the rules that were in place for allocating seats in a cinema room. And everyone had preconceived knowledge and a model in mind of what a cinema room looked like, as well as how to allocate seats for it. Now a competing heuristic here can be to not take any templates with you initially to an Example Mapping session if you want to avoid the functional fixedness bias.

> **GUIDING HEURISTIC** When doing Example Mapping in complex or complicated scenarios, use a little structure up front to avoid the effect that functional fixedness might have on the session.

As an example, when the COVID-19 outbreak happened after our engagement at BigScreen, the team was asked to design a way to reopen within a 1.5-meter distance between reservations. The template affected their creativity to think outside what they already knew. When you run the same session with the templates, people came up with two seats in between reservations, one row in between reservations, or maybe even thinking diagonally. But perhaps we can solve it in a different way and be more creative, which requires us to go around the functional fixedness bias. We say to go around the bias, because you can't cancel out or fight the bias. In his book *Thinking, Fast and Slow*, Kahneman explains that even if you're aware of the bias, it doesn't necessarily help you overcome the possible down sides the bias gives you. Because the team used the template we created a lot with stakeholders, not using a template during Example Mapping didn't lower the effect of functional fixedness. So, the team needed to design nudges to go around it, and one of our favorite ones to use for functional fixedness is to model it wrong.

> **GUIDING HEURISTIC** Model it wrong. Think about how you don't want the model to be and see how that gives you insights to improve your current model and go around functional fixedness.

Model it wrong means think about models, rules, and scenarios that you don't want. Let the participants get creative and experiment with different scenarios, such as seating vaccinated people on one side and unvaccinated people on the other. You could even get really wild and make people sit in plastic bubbles or remove the chairs altogether and have them stand vertically to fit more people in the room.

Now this can be perceived as all fun and games, but we can learn from it. In the session we had with BigScreen, the example that sparked creativity was the idea of returning to a system where tickets are distributed per screening, allowing people to self-organize and find their own seats upon entering the room, rather than having the able to pick seating in advance. They wondered how many people would still come per reservation and what was allowed. Currently, there was a rule that you could have eight tickets per reservation max, and the attendees needed to sit together in a row. But the COVID-19 rules only allowed for a maximum of two people to sit together from more than one household. So, the question was, what would most reservations look like, and can our cinema room be optimized for that? So, they took a different approach where they wouldn't allow people to pick from all the seats, but instead, they could choose from predefined seats that conformed to the COVID-19 rules.

7.3.3   *The different dimensions of nudges*

Now that you've been given a short introduction on how nudges can affect decision-making and collaborative modeling, let's talk about what we find are the most important dimensions we can categorize nudges in, type 1 and type 2, transparency of the nudge, and the changes or additions to the decision-making environment.

TYPE 1 AND TYPE 2

The most crucial dimensions for us are type 1 and type 2. These dimensions are related to the System 1 and System 2 model discussed earlier. It's essential to differentiate between these dimensions because, as Pelle Guldborg Hansen and Andreas Maaløe Jespersen point out, "while nudging always affects automatic modes of thinking, it doesn't necessarily involve reflective thinking."[3] Type 2 nudges are important as they influence attention and thinking actively and enable people to reflect on the nudge. These types of nudges are essential to reduce the influence of cognitive bias. Merely being aware of a bias that is affecting you doesn't necessarily decrease its effect. Therefore, it's necessary to let people decide for themselves how to reduce the effect of the bias.

Let's consider one of our sessions at BigScreen, where Caelan was skeptical about the technique. As mentioned earlier, he was influenced by confirmation bias and sought out information that supported his existing beliefs. This made the rest of the group more guarded and hesitant to speak, and the session veered toward discussing whether collaborative modeling would be beneficial for BigScreen. As facilitators, we used a type 2 nudge in this scenario and asked Caelan what evidence could change his mind. This triggered his system 2, leading him to reflect. Now two things can happen: he could start opening up the dialogue, and we can have a group discussion about the pros and cons of the session. Alternatively, he could close down and say nothing could change his mind, leading to a conflict that we'll discuss in more detail in the next chapter.

---

[3] Hansen, P. G., & Jespersen, A. M., "Nudge and the Manipulation of Choice: A Framework for the Responsible Use of the Nudge Approach to Behaviour Change in Public Policy," 2013. *European Journal of Risk Regulation* (1): 3–28.

In some cases, only one person may be affected by confirmation bias, but it could also affect the entire group. In the next chapter, we'll explain how to allow the group to deal with conflict themselves.

> **GUIDING HEURISTIC**   When you feel someone is affected by confirmation bias, ask what evidence can change their mind.

While type 2 nudges are used to allow people to reflect and minimize the effect of cognitive bias, type 1 nudges take advantage of the opportunities that cognitive bias presents. For instance, during our Example Mapping session, we used functional fixedness by introducing templates. We were up front and transparent about using these templates to uncover existing rules. However, there are times when we want to be less transparent about our use of these templates because it could affect the nudge's effectiveness. This leads us to the second essential dimension—the level of transparency.

LEVEL OF TRANSPARENCY

Transparency is a crucial aspect of nudging, as a nudge that lacks transparency can be manipulative and reduce awareness of choice. Consider the example of the anchoring effect discussed earlier in this chapter. As facilitators, if we have a stake in the game, we may set the anchor of a pivotal event where we want it, potentially influencing or even manipulating the decision-making process. As a facilitator, it's essential to ensure that our nudges are as neutral as possible, meaning that the nudge itself should be neutral even though the decision to design and use the nudge is not.

Let's explore how we can design nudges with different levels of transparency using an example from a BigScreen session, which was affected by the availability bias when designing bounded contexts together. This bias is one of *the* biases that affect designing more effective models for our problems with stakeholders. We often use familiar language and models because they come quickly to mind, but this can hold us back in finding better models to solve our problems. While designing bounded contexts with BigScreen, they were consistently using the word "reservation" because that was what the old system called it, and it kept popping up during several sessions.

To combat this, we used our favorite nudge, which is to give counterexamples to the words being used. For instance, when consistently hearing the word "reservation," we used alternative terms such as "allocating seats," "assigning tickets to seats," or "making a placement to a seat" to broaden the group's thinking.

> **GUIDING HEURISTIC**   When a specific word is used a lot during collaborative modeling sessions, try to change the word to see if that can change the model.

The "Use different word for a domain concept" nudge is a nontransparent nudge, where we didn't make it clear that we were using a nudge and aiming to reduce bias. This is different from the transparent nudge we applied when introducing the Example Mapping templates talked about earlier in this chapter, where we openly asked for the group's consent before using them to guide our discussion. The main difference is that transparent nudges involve openly sharing your intention and method, unlike nontransparent nudges, where we don't. For example, we chose to use a different term than the usual one without informing the group or explaining why. Our goal was to encourage them to reflect on the language we used, placing this strategy in the Type 2, Nontransparent category, as shown in figure 7.6.

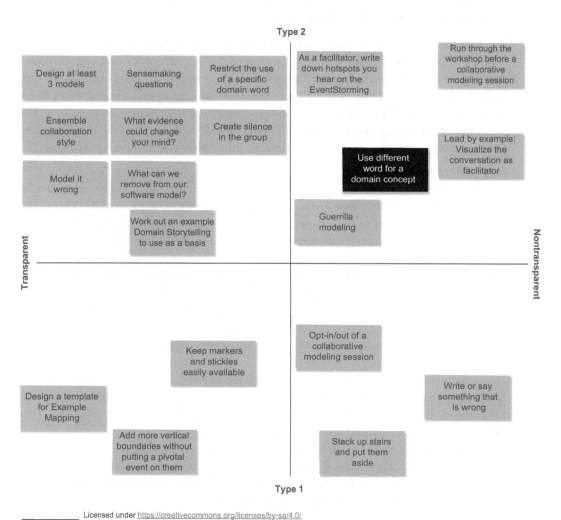

Licensed under https://creativecommons.org/licenses/by-sa/4.0/
Based on: Hansen, P.G., Jespersen, M. (2013), Nudge and the manipulation of choice (a frame work for the responsible use of the nudge approach to behavior change in public policy).
European Journal of Risk Regulation, no.1, p.3-28.

Figure 7.6 Nudges are organized based on their type and level of transparency. The figure highlights the significance of visually categorizing nudges into quadrants before application. For transparent type II nudges, individuals are informed and provided time to consider whether they wish to respond to the nudge. On the other hand, nudges that fall into the Type I, Nontransparent category are characterized by a lower awareness among people that nudges are being applied. These can potentially manipulate individuals, and the lower they are placed within this quadrant, the more unethical their use becomes. This framework serves as a guide for ethically applying nudges by understanding their effect on awareness and choice.

Even though the group continued to use "reservation" in our discussions, they started to think more about the words we used. This change was partly due to insights from domain experts, who pointed out the clear difference between issuing tickets and reserving seats, a distinction we covered in chapter 3. As a result, they divided the concepts into "ticketing" and "reservations," which was helpful. However, "reservation" began to be used in the context of ticketing, creating confusion about the two concepts. It turned out that what they meant by "reservation" wasn't really about reservations at all. The nudge we initially used didn't succeed in making them reconsider the term "reservation."

To help them think in more explicit smaller bounded contexts for a specific problem, we restricted the use of the word "reservation" during one of the follow-up Event-Storming sessions. We encouraged them to come up with counterexamples of using that word. They quickly realized that "reservation" was an ambiguous word that could have a lot of different meanings and was holding them back from making deeper insights.

As a result, they renamed the Reservation context to the Seat Allocation context. Although sometimes naming a context is trivial, in this case, it triggered cognitive biases such as availability and functional fixedness, which restricted their thinking about the model. It may take multiple sessions to fully transition to the new model, but the group is now reinforcing the use of these two new concepts by themselves.

> **GUIDING HEURISTIC**　When a certain word can be ambiguous or overused, try to run a collaborative modeling session and restrict the use of the word to find out if that changes your models.

Now you can imagine restricting people to use a certain word changes the environment they can make decisions in, which brings us to our last important nudge dimension.

CHANGES OR ADDITIONS TO THE DECISION-MAKING ENVIRONMENT

Nudges can change the decision-making environment in different ways. Some, like restricting the words we use, change the decision-making environment directly. Others can add to the decision-making environment. For example, when deciding on pivotal events, we let people discover them on their own, but sometimes they get stuck in discussion mode without making decisions.

To address this problem, we added more vertical boundaries without putting a pivotal event on them. This was a nudge that didn't change the decision-making environment directly. We found that it's easier to add to the decision-making environment than to make changes, and too many changes can lead to resistance to the nudge. In the next chapter, we'll explain why this is the case in more detail. But, for now, it's important to remember this heuristic.

> **GUIDING HEURISTIC**　Favor additions of nudges to your decision-making environment to change the decision-making environment.

Whether a nudge is considered an addition or a change to the decision-making environment depends on the context. For example, the nudge we discussed earlier, where we lead by example and visualize conversations when they're not already being visualized, can change the decision-making environment if people aren't used to visualization. However, if people are already used to visualizing but stopped doing so for a specific reason, then using the nudge is an addition.

This distinction is important because people in the first context may be more reluctant to follow your lead, while in the second context, they may gladly start visualizing again. In the first context, using the nudge may make people dependent on you to visualize, which can be a problem if you're organizing several sessions. You want people to own the flow and outcome, and nudges that change the environment can make people dependent on you, which isn't ideal. While using the nudge for a single session to achieve the desired outcome might not be a problem, it's important to be mindful of this in the long run.

To combat the problem of people sitting back and not actively participating in collaborative modeling, we can make use of the bandwagon effect. We can demonstrate how to do it and then ask others to continue while we step back. When at least one person joins in, others will eventually follow. We also try to get someone in the group to support us and let others join the bandwagon.

> **GUIDING HEURISTIC**   If you want to let people take ownership of the collaborative modeling session, show them an example of what is to be done and then step back.

> **GUIDING HEURISTIC**   If you expect a lot of people to remain idle during a collaborative modeling session, see if you can run through the session beforehand with two people who might nudge the rest of the group to come along.

This same approach can also be used to get people on board with doing collaborative modeling. We are often asked how to get people on board, and the easiest way to be successful is to start using Guerilla modeling during a meeting that should have been visualized and intentionally make mistakes. Someone will likely correct you, and, from there, you might get others to join in. Of course, the most successful approach is to make collaborative modeling the default. This means facilitating sessions in meeting rooms and providing whiteboards and sticky notes as tools. We've supported making collaborative modeling the default by ensuring that each meeting room has a whiteboard and a box of sticky notes.

> **GUIDING HEURISTIC**   If you want people to do more collaborative modeling, make it easy to start doing these sessions during meetings. They should have all the tools available to easily start visualizing.

7.3.4 *Becoming a choice architect*

When designing nudges, it's essential to remember that they're culturally dependent. Research on cognitive biases can be biased itself because humans are complex, and different cultures can be affected differently by their environments. Research often involves people from the same cultural group, age, and other factors, which means that copying and pasting nudges might not work in your situation. Our heuristics can be a helpful starting point to become a better facilitator and a *choice architect*, as referred to in Richard Thaler and Cass Sunstein's book, *Nudge: Improving Decisions About Health, Wealth, and Happiness* (Penguin, 2009). A choice architect is someone who designs and structures decision-making environments in a way that encourages people to make better choices. However, these nudges are never silver bullets, so we encourage you to start designing and using your own and then share them with the world.

There are already many books explaining heuristics and nudges, and our training approach follows the work of Sharon L Bowman's book *Training from the Back of the Room! 65 Ways to Step Aside and Let Them Learn* (Pfeiffer, 2008). Some of her training techniques can also help you become better at facilitating collaborative modeling. She talks about how "different trumps the same" when people are learning during training. We try to change the way we do collaborative modeling sessions within a company by avoiding using the same structure and session for retrospectives since they can become boring. Instead, we aim to make each session different and engaging.

7.4 Collaborative software design catalysts

- Write down behavioral patterns from people during a meeting or a collaborative modeling session. See if you can link the patterns to the biases described in this chapter. What are the effects of this bias for the process, outcome, and group dynamics? If you're comfortable, share your insights with the group during or after the meeting/session.

- In your next meeting where knowledge is shared, make sure there is room for individual contribution before the group conversation to avoid the anchoring effect. You can do this, for example, by having everyone write down their individual ideas on a sticky note before sharing it with the group.

- Be the first one to start visualizing a flow when only conversations happen between people without visualizing the flow. Observe the effects.

- Prepare nudges you could use in your next session or meeting, such as a template you designed up front, you starting to visualize options or conversations, or using specific words and concepts. Define the nudge and what you want to achieve with it.

7.5 Chapter heuristics

Guiding heuristics

- When doing Example Mapping in complex or complicated scenarios, spend some time up front to design a template in which you can discuss these scenarios so that you don't spend too much time on visualizing the examples.

- When a conversation isn't being visualized, lead by example as the facilitator and visualize the conversation.
- When doing Example Mapping in complex or complicated scenarios, use as little structure up front to avoid the effect that functional fixedness might have on the session.
- Model it wrong. Think about how you don't want the model to be and see how that gives you insights to improve your current model and go around functional fixedness.
- When you feel someone is affected by confirmation bias, ask what evidence can change their mind.
- When a specific word is used a lot during collaborative modeling sessions, try to change the word to see if that can change the model.
- When a certain word can be ambiguous or overused, try to run a collaborative modeling session and restrict the use of the word to find out if that changes your models.
- Favor additions of nudges to your decision-making environment to change the decision-making environment.
- If you want to let people take ownership of the collaborative modeling session, show them an example of what is to be done and then step back.
- If you expect a lot of people to remain idle during a collaborative modeling session, see if you can run through the session beforehand with two people who might nudge the rest of the group to come along.
- If you want people to do more collaborative modeling, make it easy to start doing these sessions during meetings. They should have all the tools available to easily start visualizing.

7.6   *Further reading*

- Choiceology, an original podcast from Charles Schwab by Katy Milkman
- Cognitive Bias Codex (https://mng.bz/x2z7. Licensed by John Manoogian III under a Creative Commons Attribution-ShareAlike 4.0 license)
- "How the Bias toward Additive Can Lead Us to a Suboptimal and Costly Software Design" by Kenny Baas-Schwegler (https://mng.bz/rVEj)
- *Noise: A Flaw in Judgment* by Daniel Kahneman (Little, Brown Spark, 2021)
- *Nudge: Improving Decisions About Health, Wealth, and Happiness* by Richard H. Thaler and Cass R. Sunstein (Penguin, 2009)
- "Nudge and the Manipulation of Choice: A Framework for the Responsible Use of the Nudge Approach to Behaviour Change in Public Policy" by Pelle Guldborg Hansen and Andreas Maaløe Jespersen (*European Journal of Risk Regulation*, 2013)
- *Predictably Irrational: The Hidden Forces That Shape Our Decisions* by Dan Ariely (Harper Perennial, 2010)

- *Thinking, Fast and Slow* by Daniel Kahneman (Farrar, Straus and Giroux, 2013)
- *Training From the BACK of the Room! 65 Ways to Step Aside and Let Them Learn* by Sharon L. Bowman (Pfeiffer, 2008)

Summary

- Cognitive biases can be a result of our brain's attempt to simplify information processing. You can consider them mental shortcuts, or rules of thumb, that help you make sense of the world.
- Cognitive bias is a systematic pattern of deviation from a norm that affects decision-making and judgment.
- System 1 and system 2 distinguish between automatic and conscious thought processes. The automatic process is affected by cognitive biases.
- Cognitive biases help us but can also affect our decision-making and behavior.
- Confirmation bias, bike-shedding, false-consensus effect, availability bias, loss aversion, and additive bias are all examples of cognitive biases that can affect our collaboration.
- A nudge is a way to change people's behavior of making decisions in a predictable way, and they should be easily avoidable by the group.
- A nudge can come in different dimensions: type 1 and type 2, transparency of the nudge, and the changes or additions to the decision-making environment. It's important to know where to categorize the nudge.
- One important aspect in designing nudges is that they are always culturally dependent. You should design the nudges and create your own set of heuristics.

Resistance and conflict resolution

8

This chapter covers

- Conflict and resistance, and why they occur
- Conflict and resistance in collaborative modeling
- The effect of resistance and conflict on software design
- Resolving and facilitating conflict and resistance

In the previous two chapters, we discussed ranking and cognitive biases and the effect they have on your software design and architecture. The following social-related topic that we'll cover that has a major influence on your software design and architecture is conflict and resistance.

First, we'll walk you through what conflict and resistance are exactly and what type of behaviors you might observe. Next, we'll discuss how conflict and resistance show up during collaborative modeling and the effect they both have on your software design and architecture. Lastly, we'll teach you a few techniques you can use while facilitating collaborative modeling.

234

8.1 Why people show resistance and have conflicts

In general, conflict has a very negative connotation and is seen as something that should be avoided. This is partly due to people's definition of conflict. Whenever the word *conflict* pops up, we imagine people getting angry, yelling at each other, and slamming doors. *Resistance* on the other hand, can also be seen in a more positive light. We associate it with movies like *Star Wars*, where brave people fight against an evil institution that has taken over the universe. Unfortunately, neither one of those are accurate depictions of what conflict and resistance actually are. In this section, we'll dive a bit deeper into the meaning of these two terms.

8.1.1 What conflict is all about

Let's start with conflict. The heavy clashing between two people is just one form of conflict—an extreme one. Before people reached this level of conflict, it was simmering underneath the surface for a while. There was a conflict, we just didn't consider it one. In its most basic form, a *conflict* is a difference of opinion between two or more people. There is nothing inherently negative about it. Conflict is natural. Most of the conflicts we encounter in our lives aren't memorable. We disagree with another person, have a discussion about it, and come up with a satisfying resolution. We move on and don't even consider it a conflict.

We want to emphasize the distinction between functional or task-based conflict and dysfunctional or relationship conflict.[1] *Functional conflict* occurs in the form of healthy and constructive disagreements. These functional conflicts are mainly focused on content and tasks, and they can drive progress, innovation, and growth. This is the type of conflict you don't want to avoid because it will help you grow. The other type of conflict—*dysfunctional conflict*—is often more revolved around emotions and individuals. These conflicts can be unhealthy, hinder the group from progressing, and can reinforce power dynamics, for instance the negative effect on ranking can become larger. Dysfunctional conflicts harm relationships and can increase psychological unsafety within a group.

> **GUIDING HEURISTIC** Whenever you encounter a conflict, determine if it's a functional, task-based, or dysfunctional relationship conflict. Do this by figuring out if it's task related or emotion related, and if it's helping or hindering progress and outcome.

Dismissing ideas or opinions without fully understanding them isn't uncommon in a company. That is when problems start arising. Yet, investigating all opinions or alternatives is what leads to more sustainable decisions. When we don't dig into the different perspectives, people might start to feel that their opinions aren't being valued enough. They also have difficulties expressing that their opinions are not valued enough, so it's not always obvious to detect. The conflict retreats into the shadows.

---

[1] Grant, A. *Think Again: The Power of Knowing What You Don't Know*, 2021. New York: Viking (p. 84).

The odd one out

In every company there is a "Harry." Harry[2] stands for the person in the room whose ideas always sound crazy or unachievable. Their opinions on the topic are being dismissed or not taken seriously. People make jokes or comments about this person, often in front of them. When a new person joins the group, they get informed not to take Harry too seriously: "Yeah, that's Harry, always having crazy opinions, don't mind them too much!"

This behavior of everyone toward this person is causing conflict, which people aren't aware of. Harry is also the person that will laugh with you when the group is mocking them. Yet, investigating Harry's ideas could trigger other ideas or realizations you otherwise wouldn't have. So don't dismiss Harry that easily, and be a Harry once in a while yourself. You might be surprised at what you come up with because you're examining crazy solutions.

The behavior of dysfunctional conflict does follow a certain path[3] when it comes to how conflicts develop and escalate. Nobody follows this path to the letter, and it's possible for people to skip stages or show behavior from multiple stages at once. These stages help us in observing the behavior of people to find out if there is a dysfunctional conflict happening or brewing and how much it has escalated.

TENSION AND TABOO

Whenever a certain topic is brought up, the atmosphere starts to get tense. Sometimes the tension gets so high that the topic can't be discussed anymore. It becomes taboo to talk about it.

DOUBLE MESSAGES

In chapter 5 we discussed Gerald Weinberg's "The incongruence insight," which are double messages. These double messages refer to when you're saying one thing, but behaving or meaning something else. Because the topic is taboo or you don't want to deal with the tension anymore whenever the topic comes around, you start communicating as if the conflict isn't there: "No, I am okay moving forward with this design." Shortly after, you turn off your camera or have to go to the bathroom all of a sudden.

ARGUING WITH YOURSELF

At this point, we know the dysfunctional so well that we believe we can argue both sides all by ourselves—and we do. We play variations of the discussions we had before over and over in our head. We get ourselves worked up over a conflict that isn't "active" at the moment because the person we're having the conflict with isn't there.

GOSSIP

We try to reassure ourselves by gossiping with others that we're on the right side. We're looking for people that agree with us or trying to persuade people to join our side. This is our confirmation bias from chapter 6 at work. Gossiping can also be about creating

---

[2]   Kramer, J. *Jam Cultures*, 2021. Ashland, OH: Management Impact Publishing.
[3]   Lewis, M., & Woodhull, J. *Inside the NO: Five Steps to Decisions That Last*, 2018. Deep Democracy.

the sides in a dysfunctional conflict. This can be a way to seek support from others, which is normal human behavior that is needed in cultures.

COMMUNICATION BREAKS DOWN

Sometimes, we stop talking directly to the person altogether and start to ignore them. We solicit other people to do the work for us: "Maybe you can try talking to them and get the message through that they are wrong!"

WHAT WAS THE PROBLEM AGAIN?

Sometimes, dysfunctional conflicts last so long that nobody remembers what it was about originally. The dysfunctional conflicts lost all context, and most discussions aren't about the original conflict anymore, which could have started as a functional conflict, but now everything about the other person is wrong.

-ISMS

In society, we have polarization and stereotyping, such as ageism, sexism, racism, and so on. We start seeing the other party in the conflict through those stereotypes: "They are just an ivory tower architect!"

WAR OR SEPARATION

Participation and collaboration have totally stopped, and everyone is exhausted. Other areas are starting to get affected by the dysfunctional conflict. There is only one solution, which is to go your own way. You quit your job, you get a divorce, you ask for a transfer to another department, or you stop being friends. But there is also some light in this phase: the original conflict is no longer taboo, and you can communicate openly about it again. It's over anyway.

These stages all sounds pretty bad, although we said conflict didn't have to be negative. That is still true: as long as a conflict is visible, you don't have too much to worry about. It might cause some tension and make people feel uncomfortable, but as long as it's dealt with it eventually will resolve itself. Problems arise when a conflict is being suppressed or ignored. Two things are possible here. When people are avoiding a conflict, and start oppressing the emotions connected to that conflict, they will start showing edge behavior. When a conflict continues to go unresolved, they will start showing resistance. We'll dig a bit deeper into edge behavior first.

Exercise 8.1

Reflect on one of your personal recent conflicts. Remember, a conflict in its most basic form is a difference of opinion between two or more people. Which of the just-mentioned behaviors did you observe in others and within yourself?

8.1.2   Edge behavior

Conflict makes people really uncomfortable, so they try to avoid it. In psychology, this is referred to as *conflict avoidance*. When a person goes into conflict avoidant mode, they start showing edge behavior. *Edge behavior* means showing behavior that at first glance seems illogical and contradictory, just like the incongruence insight. A person exhibiting edge behavior wants to avoid a conflict because they don't feel comfortable addressing it yet. Edge behavior lives on the border between consciousness and unconsciousness of an individual or group, which contradicts what is happening in the consciousness, as shown in figure 8.1.

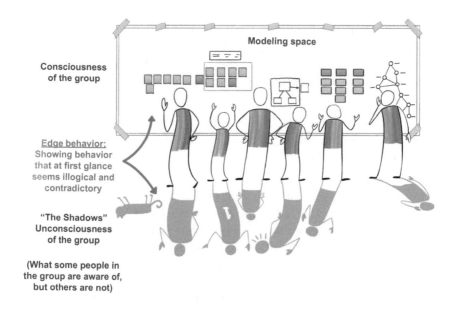

Figure 8.1   Edge behavior happens when someone tries to oppress their inner shadows, but we can observe it because the unconscious behavior contradicts what we observe in the conscious behavior. As mentioned in chapter 5, when words and music don't go together, they point to a missing element.

To illustrate, edge behavior is also very visible with our furry cat friends. Maybe you recognize this: whenever cats are about to enter a fight, one of them might suddenly start grooming themselves. This is also an example of edge behavior. It's important to not judge this behavior. It's very hard to sit in your own discomfort—trust us. We've been practicing for many years, but still go into edge behavior sometimes.

When people are on the edge, you'll notice confusing communication and mixed signals. They will say one thing ("Everything is fine" or "I'm okay with the decision"), but exhibit contradicting behavior (not show up for a meeting). Confusing communication is a common behavioral pattern we observe during collaborative modeling. Part of the goal when modeling collaboratively is to get rid of ambiguity and confusing communication. This is why recognizing patterns of confusing communication is a useful skill. We'll discuss a few of the most common communication patterns when people are on the edge. Note that these confusing communication patterns could happen in both remote and physical collaboration, and this list isn't complete nor finite.

ABSENCE

Physically, people are present—they nod, they smile—but mentally they are absent. Their mind is somewhere else altogether, and they aren't actively participating anymore in the discussions. They've checked out.

INTERRUPTION

People start interrupting each other more and more. They don't allow for the other people in the room to finish sharing their thoughts or opinions. They aren't really open to other perspectives. When observing, it's interesting to see how and when the interruptions happen:

- Is it one person interrupting one other person in particular?
- Is it happening on a specific topic?
- Is it happening when someone expresses a minority opinion?

These observations will help you when addressing this behavior in the group because you can be more specific when bringing it up.

MULTIPLE MONOLOGUES

Instead of having a dialogue, people are having monologues with each other. They just share their own opinion and aren't actively listening to what other people have to say anymore. What they are saying isn't an extension of what somebody already said or a question to get some clarification—they are just talking next to each other.

GOING OFF-TOPIC

Another conflict avoidance communication pattern is to go off-topic completely. Often, the person in question is conscious that they are going off-topic and informs the group of it: "I know this isn't related to what we're talking about, but Mark's question just made me think of this: Do we know *<insert different topic here>*." In some cases, it's not a problem if a group diverts or goes off-topic, but it's important to notice when this happens as an avoidance mechanism.

QUESTIONS THAT AREN'T QUESTIONS

Another way people show edge behavior through communication is by asking questions that aren't questions. When somebody doesn't feel comfortable outright stating their own opinion, they express it in the form of a question. There's also judgment, assumptions, and direction hidden inside the question. Let's clarify with an example from collaborative modeling. Imagine a group is doing EventStorming and trying to reach consensus on pivotal events. They are discussing which domain events could be good candidates. The follow conversation happens:

> P1: The event "Price was calculated" is a pivotal event for sure!

> P2: Do you think it won't cause a problem to take this domain event as a pivotal event?

> P1: No, I don't. I think it makes sense that this is a pivotal event.

> P2: Are you sure it won't be a problem?

P2 is asking a question that isn't a question; instead, they are expressing their own opinion. They are seeing some problems with "Price was calculated" being a pivotal event, but they don't feel comfortable stating that. It's a disagreement hidden as a question: "I think it's a problem to take this domain event as one of the pivotal events." This person is asking these questions because they hope others agree with them and will come forward.

Note that asking questions that aren't questions has more of an effect when it's being done by someone with a higher ranking. Others will be more inclined to agree with the person asking because they are afraid to go against the hidden opinion in the question.

INDIRECTNESS

Another way to express your own opinion without openly expressing it is indirectness. *Indirectness* during conversation can happen in three forms:

- Speaking in the third person when expressing your own opinion
- Replacing a person or group with a more general term
- The "guardian angel" bringing up a topic to be helpful to others

People express their opinion in the third person when they don't feel comfortable openly stating their opinion. They will say things like "There are people here who don't think this new architecture is the right way forward" instead of "I don't think this new architecture is the right way forward." Speaking in the third person gives them a safe feeling. If needed, they can still go back into avoidance and claim they aren't part of that group of people.

The second form, replacing a person or group with a more general term, happens when people don't feel comfortable putting a specific person or group on the spot, for example, "Someone made a mistake when filling in the meeting topics" or "A department requested more time, so now we're running behind schedule." This can easily backfire because the person or group being referred to in a general way knows this statement is about them. So, a person's attempt to avoid conflict can actually trigger a bigger one.

The last form of indirect communication is the guardian angel. A person brings up a topic to be helpful: "I don't have a problem with the new schedule, but some people might struggle with this." It sounds like they are trying to be helpful, but it often has the opposite effect. If the people that are struggling with the new schedule due to the delays aren't willing to speak up, you're not helping them with trying to be their guardian angel. This form of indirectness isn't easily distinguishable from the third person indirectness. It could be that this person is expressing their opinion in an indirect way, or they genuinely don't have a problem with it and are trying to be helpful. The ambiguity created by indirectness reduces psychological safety within the group, as people grow anxious about who the conversation is about and how it might affect them.

FALLACIOUS ARGUMENTS

Fallacious arguments are logically unsound arguments, also known as fallacies. They are part of the cognitive biases and are specifically about faulty reasoning. From our experience, fallacies usually pop up when someone wants to achieve a certain goal, and the quality of reasoning is subordinate to this goal. Let's look at a few examples to illustrate this better.

Ad hominem (or *to the person*) is a fallacy that attacks a person's characteristics instead of attacking their argument. Relevance is key here; ad hominem happens when the argument is irrelevant to the discussion in which it's used. For example, when discussing bounded contexts during collaborative modeling, the new team member makes a suggestion, and another team member responds as follows: "It's almost impossible for you to determine bounded contexts because you've never worked in an environment like this." Never having worked in a similar environment is irrelevant to being able to come up with good suggestions on bounded contexts.

A *straw man fallacy* means you take an argument of someone else, tailor and/or exaggerate it, and then argue against that distorted argument. Imagine this conversation at the end of a long EventStorming session:

> Rodney: I'm getting the feeling we're really getting somewhere with this, but I'm not sure we picked the right boundaries. I think we should try to redraw them.
>
> Kala: I don't want to redo the whole exercise; that is a waste of everyone's time! We should iterate on the boundaries that we already found.
>
> Jack: Oh hell no, I completely agree with Kala; we shouldn't redo the whole exercises. We should iterate on the boundaries.
>
> Rodney: That is not what I said AT ALL!

Kala is arguing against "I want to redo the whole exercise," not Rodney's original statement: "I want to redraw the boundaries." Because she is arguing against a distorted version, it's starting to cause a conflict. Other ways somebody can make a straw man argument is oversimplifying a complex problem, arguing against a black-and-white version of your argument or taking your argument out of context.

Most people don't consciously choose one of these confusing communication patterns. They don't think "let me just ask a question that will derail the current conversation" or "let me use the third person in this question because I don't want to have a direct conversation right now." They are at the edge of the line between the conscious and unconscious. These are simply things that people do or say when they want to avoid a conflict.

8.1.3 What is resistance?

When people don't feel listened to or feel that their opinion isn't being taken into account, they will start showing *resistance* as a form of conflict that happens when someone doesn't feel heard. Examples of resistance include someone starting to stare out the window whenever a specific topic is brought up during a meeting, or, in a remote setting, someone turning off their camera. This specific type of resistance is called *poor communication/breakdown*. There are other types of resistance. The Lewis Deep

Democracy methodology[4] refers to the types of resistance somebody can exhibit as *the terrorist line*. In later works based on that of Myrna Lewis, this is called the *resistance line*.[5]

The resistance line (figure 8.2) shows the most common stages of resistance that people go through when they feel they aren't being heard or their opinion isn't being valued when making group decisions. This might be seen as immature or childish, but nothing is further from the truth. Resistance is a normal behavior; everyone does it—yes, you too! People can either resist as a group, which is most of the time the minority group in Deep Democracy, or as an individual. As facilitators, our goal is to observe and identify coherent patterns along the line of resistance—whether they relate to the session itself or broader tensions within the company. A sarcastic joke, for instance, doesn't necessarily disrupt the group's dynamics.

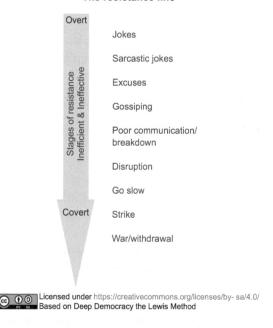

The resistance line

Overt

Jokes

Sarcastic jokes

Excuses

Gossiping

Poor communication/breakdown

Disruption

Go slow

Covert   Strike

War/withdrawal

Stages of resistance
Inefficient & Ineffective

Licensed under https://creativecommons.org/licenses/by- sa/4.0/
Based on Deep Democracy the Lewis Method

Figure 8.2   The resistance line. The further down the line the minority group goes, the less efficient the group will be able to function.

SARCASTIC JOKES

Jokes or sarcasm is one of the most common ways to express resistance. At first glance, they may seem very innocent but they interrupt and can make a group lose track of the conversation. Detecting whether the jokes and the sarcasm are expressing resistance

---

[4]   Lewis, *Inside the NO.*
[5]   Kramer, J. *Deep Democracy: De wijsheid van de minderheid,* https://deepdemocracy.nl/de-boeken/.

isn't always easy. This heavily depends on the cultural circumstances, which a facilitator should be aware of.

EXCUSES

Everyone has heard the following at some point in their life: "I didn't do that yet. I was about to do it, but then something more important came up, so I had to do it first." The "just about to do it" excuse is one of the most common. Making excuses for why you're not following the decision that has been made is another form of resistance. Excuses are difficult to deal with because there often is a piece of truth in them. It could very well be that something more urgent came up for that person. If excuses keep popping up, that can cause a problem.

GOSSIPING

Another form of resistance is to start gossiping about a decision that has been made. The interesting thing about this form of resistance is that the person is expressing their opinion openly at this time. So, gossip also can be a good way to detect how people really feel about a decision that has been made.

POOR COMMUNICATION/BREAKDOWN

Stopping or limiting communication is the next type of resistance: "If they don't want to listen to me, then I'm not going to talk!" This can be dangerous because without proper communication, a group will start functioning more inefficiently.

DISRUPTION

Once communication starts to go poorly, the resistance toward the decision or the decision makers starts to be more open. People start talking among themselves during meetings, or put up obvious roadblocks, such as having to make an official request with the department head to be able to move forward.

GO SLOW

Slowing down creates an even bigger inefficiency in a team or department. In this context, slowing down means slowing down the execution of a decision. Agenda items being pushed to the next meeting, requesting extra information, and so on are examples of slowing down as a form of resistance.

STRIKE

When people still don't feel heard, they will stop participating completely. This can be individually, such as not taking part in team building days or office parties, or as a group when the entire department decides to put down their work.

WAR/WITHDRAWAL

War or withdrawal is the last stage of the resistance line. The minority group resists by withdrawing from the majority group. This can be either physical or mental withdrawal. Another option in the last stage is war, where the minority group decides to go to battle against the majority. War can also take either a mental form or a physical form in the same cases. This might seem far-fetched, but it isn't. We've all seen strikes on television that turned violent, erupting into a physical attack because the crowd became so angry.

Exercise 8.2

Think back on a few moments where you showed resistance toward a decision that had been made. What type of behavior(s) did you exhibit during those moments? Add them to the resistance line, as shown in figure 8.3. If you'd like, you could also think of the behaviors of others that you observed when you noticed resistance toward a decision. Do you see patterns there?

The further down the line we get, the more inefficient a group will become due to this behavior. Making a joke or even responding sarcastically is still a very subtle way to show resistance. It might make a few people uncomfortable, but it doesn't bring the efficiency of a group that much down. Once you go into disruption or war, a group can't function effectively anymore.

As a facilitator, it's important to observe the group to detect this type of behavior and bring the conflicts that are causing it out of the shadows and into the group where they can be discussed and resolved. In the next sections, we'll give you examples of edge behavior and resistance, show the consequences they have on your software design, and teach you some techniques for dealing with these types of behavior.

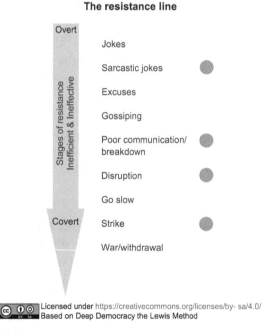

Licensed under https://creativecommons.org/licenses/by- sa/4.0/
Based on Deep Democracy the Lewis Method

Figure 8.3   An example of exercise 8.2. The authors added their favorite go-to behavior when showing resistance.

8.2   *Resistance and conflict during collaboration*

Collaborative modeling is a great place for resistance and conflict. We put people together in a room, and we hope they will collaborate, create a shared (mental) model, and agree on the best possible solution. This isn't always the case. People will disagree about the bounded contexts that are proposed, pivotal events that are chosen, the value of proposed solutions and parts of the model, social hierarchy, and speed of progression—just to name a few. To make it even more difficult, there will be a multitude of mental models flying around during collaborative modeling. We want to bring these together and create a shared, unambiguous model, but this is way harder than you might expect.

As stated in section 8.1, resistance and conflict are often considered negative concepts that should be avoided whenever possible. The truth is, resistance and conflict can tell us a lot about a group and its social dynamics. They can point us to the topics that are at the root cause of any hindrance we might encounter. Because resistance is inevitable, we need to learn to expect it, make it a part of the flow, and normalize it. As a facilitator, this is one of your key responsibilities during collaborative modeling.

Earlier in this book, we talked about other social dynamics, including cognitive bias and ranking. Resistance and conflict are related to these concepts, and they can strengthen and/or reinforce each other. For example, when a person with a high rank drops an anchor on a pivotal event or bounded context, this might lead to conflict. Due to ranking, the concerns or counterarguments might not be made explicit, resulting in people completely zoning out as a form of resistance. This might affect your software design because you're missing out on possible relevant input and perspectives.

Note that the concepts of resistance and conflict are extremely complex and are often used as container concepts. We very often see groups trying to oversimplify these concepts of resistance and conflict by using them as one big umbrella to categorize a lot of behavior, interpretations, and assumptions. For example, we might interpret someone who's not moving a lot of stickies around as disengaged or in resistant mode. However, this person might be creating a mental model by absorbing everything around them and taking some time to organize all those observations before speaking up and moving stickies around.

In this section, we'll dive into what resistance and conflict could look like in collaborative modeling, nuancing the two concepts so you can properly recognize them and approach them as learning opportunities. We'll also cover the effect of resistance and conflict on your software design.

8.2.1   *Recognizing resistance and conflict in collaborative modeling*

Collaborative modeling is a place where resistance and any sort of conflict are bound to happen. As mentioned earlier, these two concepts can be used as umbrella or container concepts. You should be careful with using these container concepts like resistance and conflict. Try to avoid assumptions and interpretations. Just observe behavior and patterns. In the following subsections, we'll describe some examples of behavioral and communication patterns that could indicate resistance and/or conflict during collaborative modeling.

During collaborative modeling, there are different behavioral patterns that could indicate the presence of conflict and/or resistance. For the record, *behavior* for us means someone doing something or saying something that we can observe. We consider behavior to be a pattern when we can observe it three times in an objective manner. Remember how we talked about core competencies of a facilitator in chapter 5? Neutrality and observation competencies are very useful when trying to recognize (hidden) conflict or resistance.

RECOGNIZING EDGE BEHAVIOR DURING COLLABORATIVE MODELING

At BigScreen, there had been many discussions on the new software design between stakeholders. We can only support that because, in most cases, it leads to better solutions. In one discussion though, we observed edge behavior from one developer (Jack) in particular. In a discussion with Rose about the design, we noticed how he checked out after a while. He was still nodding and humming along with the conversation, but he wasn't actively contributing anymore by suggesting ideas and options. Before this checking out happened, we observed Jack interrupting Rose a lot and only focusing on his own ideas and suggestions. Almost every time Rose suggested something, Jack interrupted her and asked questions like, "Wouldn't it be better if we . . . ," "Do you believe that . . . ?" We identified this as edge behavior: Jack was interrupting, asking questions that weren't questions (see section 8.1.2), and eventually became absent.

With the developments over the past few years, we've been working together online more and more. As we discussed in chapter 5, remote facilitation makes certain things more difficult, including observing behavioral patterns. You have to observe through a small camera window, which makes it easier to miss subtle behavior. In some cases, though, edge behavior in remote collaboration is rather obvious.

At BigScreen, we had a combination of in-person and remote sessions. During one of those remote sessions, we were going over some design decisions with the development team. A couple of these decisions were leading up to heated discussions, and we could already observe some edge behavior: developers interrupting each other all the time, the team lead going off-topic, and ongoing monologues. At one point, we as facilitators started to notice that whenever the discussion focused on one design decision in particular, the architect, Rodney, turned off his camera. It happened once, it happened twice, and when it happened the third time, we felt the need to deal with it. This was clear edge behavior, specifically absence, by literally becoming invisible when a certain topic popped up. We noticed the rest of the group getting frustrated with Rodney's behavior and starting to show some resistance by making sarcastic jokes and causing disruptions.

RECOGNIZING THE STAGES OF A CONFLICT

A conflict is a great learning point and can be very fruitful. The longer a conflict is ignored, the harder it is to fix it, and requires us to return through all the stages of conflict we've been in. In the beginning of our careers, we found a company that advertised Domain-Driven Design, collaborative modeling, and the whole shebang.

Obviously, we submitted our resumes and we were overjoyed when we heard we got the job. Unfortunately, we started working in an IT department that was in a highly dysfunctional conflict. During lunch, during coffee breaks, and after meetings, the same thing was always discussed: how bad the product owner was, how they just didn't get it, and how they lost touch with modern technology. Everything they did was wrong, and the development team was right.

> **GUIDING HEURISTIC** You know when a conflict turns dysfunctional when dialogues or discussions move toward the notion of right or wrong. As a facilitator, this is your cue to start resolving the conflict.

That person just could not do anything good anymore. The original conflict that started it all was long forgotten. This was a clear case of "What was the problem again?" Back then, we didn't have the skills yet that we have now. We tried to talk to the product owner, but because the conflict had reached a stage where it became invisible, they just thought we were the ones with the problem. There was no one there who could help fix what was broken between the product owner and the team. It was a toxic environment to work in, and eventually we decided to find a new job—we were ready to withdraw. Sometimes a conflict is beyond repair. It's important to try and get a grasp of where a conflict is, who it is between, and how far along it is. Don't bang your head against a wall trying to fix something that has been going on for too long to find a good resolution. Trust us, it hurts.

RECOGNIZING RESISTANCE IN COLLABORATIVE MODELING

A few clients back, we were contacted to organize an EventStorming session. As external facilitators, we don't always know what happened before we arrived. This was one of those times where the important information didn't come up during our interviews, but smacked us in the face 2 hours into our first session. One of our participants started yelling at the organizer:

> *This is the fifth session we're talking about this nonsense, and nothing EVER comes from it! This is going to be more of the same, and I am sick and tired of it. It's your fault, you just don't listen and want us to blindly approve your solution. You say no to every suggestion I make without giving an explanation as to why it's not a good solution. You're just completely ignoring me, and I have had it!*

After that, they turned around and stormed out of the room. It was very clear to us that this person had just gone on a strike, which didn't change the fact that we lost control of the session.

This is just another way to say that no matter how much experience you have at collaborative modeling or dealing with the social dynamics of a group, once in a while, it just goes wrong. A lot of people come to us thinking collaborative modeling is the answer to their problem and that it's a tool to realize breakthroughs and get consensus. It's true, you can have amazing breakthroughs with collaborative modeling that lead to better design decisions, but that can only happen if we manage and start resolving the conflicts. If we ignore conflicts, this will lead to even worse designs.

8.2.2   *The effect of resistance and conflict on software design*

Because we're focusing on software design decisions in this book, it might be worthwhile to zoom in a bit on how conflict and resistance affect that specifically. Conflict and resistance that aren't managed properly won't lead to the best model for your business problems. To get to the best models and solutions, we need a shared mental model instead of multiple, different mental models built into the same software. With collaborative modeling, we aim to create this shared mental model that will be the foundation for the software design. If conflict gets in the way and holds people back from sharing information, listening to each other, and accepting other suggestions and solutions, we'll get to less contextual solutions with probably a lot of language ambiguity.

Talking about language, poor communication can also have a serious negative effect on your software design. Imagine our BigScreen architect Rodney in a collaborative modeling session talking in an indirect way all the time:

- "So, we can all agree these are the most logical boundaries, right?"
- "The group seems to agree on the bounded context."
- "Everyone here understands what we mean with customers."

The session ends, and Rodney is optimistic and assumes everyone is on the same page. No bad intentions whatsoever. Fast-forward to implementation, and then conflict starts to arise. Developers going against design decisions, not agreeing with boundaries, and a lot of language ambiguity. Rodney's first reaction is, "But I thought everyone was on board with this." The conflict that started during implementation is a consequence of the poor communication during the collaborative modeling. The assumptions made there are now part of the software design, and they didn't make it better. If this had been resolved during the session itself by making assumptions explicit and asking the right (counter)questions, it would not have led to conflict during implementation.

Another possible consequence of this confusing communication is people not taking ownership. We know this is an abstract and broad concept, but we focus on people feeling responsible for the solution in this part. When indirectness is being used, or people talk in the third person, it might lead to feeling less responsible for the eventual solution. This, in turn, is related to the *not invented here syndrome*, which means that people tend to feel more certain about the usefulness and importance of something when they created it themself, than similar ideas, suggestions, or solutions that others came up with. This syndrome also leads to the tendency to avoid using solutions, ideas, models, or knowledge from external origins. People seem to have a strong bias against ideas from others or the outside. This also means we're less likely to accept or adopt an idea or solution that comes from somewhere that feels like "the outside." Let's take it back to the collaborative modeling session example: if there is a lot of indirectness, talking in the third person, and not being able to personally get acquainted with the model or solution, people will be less likely to feel responsible for it. That will affect your software design in a negative manner.

With the risk of repeating ourselves, conflict and resistance aren't necessarily bad things. A difference of opinion can be classified as a task-based or functional conflict, and the same goes for a language ambiguity discussion. Yes, if they aren't being managed properly, they will heavily affect your software design in a negative way, which is why having someone observing and facilitating them is crucial. Now, let's dive into some practical guidance on how to do this in the next section.

8.2.3 *Resistance and conflict as learning opportunities*

How we deal with and resolve resistance and conflict are what determines their effect. We can learn from conflict and resistance because they tell us something about the group, their shadows, and their potential demons. Knowing this and making them explicit so we can resolve them can prevent disasters from happening. So, instead of seeing conflict and resistance as something we need to avoid, let's see where the learning opportunities are. From our experience, we'll describe a few learning opportunities we think are highly valuable.

First, conflict and resistance behavior is an opportunity to create mutual understanding. We can observe behavior that might be classified as resistant or conflict-causing. We often ask ourselves this question: "Why is someone doing that or saying that?" Usually, people show behavior because there is a positive consequence related to that behavior for them. So, apparently, by showing resistant behavior or arguing, a positive consequence is following for the person showing the behavior. Finding out what that is can be very helpful. For example: you observe a lot of gossiping going on during lunch breaks. The same people seem to be involved, and the topics are recurring as well. By gossiping about certain things, processes, or people, this person might get a form of attention they strive for. Maybe it gives them the feeling of being heard and being able to get on "a stage" and spread their own ideas. Or maybe it provides them with a higher informal rank because more and more people are going along with the gossiping behavior. Whatever it is, the behavior is yielding positive consequences for the person showing that behavior. A facilitator can help figure out what those consequences are and thereby interpret the resistant behavior. This is a huge learning opportunity for the group, and it can result in having better outcomes by flash-lighting the shadows and making them smaller.

Second, conflicts make different perspectives and opposing sides visible and explicit. This might not sound like a learning opportunity right away, but by making those explicit, a group gets the chance to counter functional fixedness for example. To illustrate, if one part of the group feels things need to speed up, and another part feels things need to slow down, it might feel like a highly challenging problem. What are you going to do as a facilitator: slow down or speed up? In fact, this is what we call a *polarity*: two sides of the same coin that affect and need each other. You don't solve this polarity by choosing A or B, but you manage it by going back and forth. Chances are, you encounter a lot of these polarities that are often mistaken for conflicts. In chapter 10, we'll dive into these polarities and how to manage them.

Note that facilitators have a great effect on and role in seizing these learning opportunities. Section 8.3 will dive further into this and provide you with tools and techniques to manage conflict and resistance.

8.3   Facilitating toward a resolution

Let's dive into how we can resolve resistance and conflicts with a software design EventStorming session we facilitated at BigScreen. Let's first reflect and remember the importance of the observer role as a facilitator. The goal of facilitation is to make it easier for people to collaborate and participate in their own way.

One crucial skill for resolving resistance and conflict is having good observation skills. We recommend practicing observing patterns in groups. When you do, think about how you felt when someone didn't speak much during a session and when they spoke up again later. Consider what you experienced when someone raised their voice and dominated the conversation, causing the room to fall silent. These are all important observations to make as a facilitator. Because of your inner conflict, those emotions as shadows can heavily influence the social dynamics of the group.

8.3.1   Resistance and conflict in practice

Have you ever found yourself assuming something about a situation or person, only to later realize that your assumptions were influenced by your own biases? As we explain in the previous chapter, it's a natural tendency, but failing to recognize these biases in ourselves while noticing them in others is what we call the *bias blind spot*. And if we're not aware of these blind spots, they may lead to conflicts which can turn into shadows and demons that entangle themselves with the group that we're supposed to facilitate, as depicted in figure 8.4.

Figure 8.4   An example of how our bias blind spot can lead to shadows and demons getting entangled with the group in a software design EventStorming session at BigScreen. Not being aware of how your own bias interplays with that of the group might lower your effectiveness as a facilitator.

As humans, we all have different perspectives and opinions. This is a good thing—it opens up opportunities for learning and growth. But sometimes, holding a strong opinion on a particular topic can become a problem, especially when we're facilitating discussions. For instance, we strongly believe that Kubernetes isn't useful in most situations. That can result in quickly labeling others' opinions as wrong and our own as right. And it's a short step to falling into a confirmation bias by finding the cons. This can be problematic when someone is expressing a different viewpoint, as it can cause us to lose sight of our role as facilitators and the need to create an open and respectful dialogue or debate.

> **GUIDING HEURISTIC**   Frame discussions or disagreements as a dialogue or debate. People have a mental model of what a dialogue or debate is compared to a discussion or disagreement, and it will focus on ideas instead of personal conflict.[6]

In fact, labeling things as "right" or "wrong" can reinforce that confirmation bias. This can cause us to become even more entrenched in our own opinions, while the other person may do the same. The problem isn't about labeling something as right or wrong—it's about being aware of our biases and avoiding falling into this pattern of biased thinking. By staying mindful of our own biases and remaining open to different perspectives, we can create a more collaborative and productive environment for everyone involved.

UNDERSTANDING YOUR INNER CONFLICTS AND HOW THEY MIGHT AFFECT YOUR FACILITATION

Getting caught up in a conflict or tension because of someone else's opinion is a common experience that can turn into inner conflicts which creates shadows. It will distract us from our goal of supporting the group effectively. When our inner conflicts and judgments come into play, we may act out in negative ways. Maybe we start with making some sarcastic jokes about Kubernetes, or start lobbying against it during the break. Or maybe we've interrupted or shut down someone who was expressing a different viewpoint. That's not very helpful behavior as a facilitator, right? But it's all too normal to do if you're holding strong opinions, which, if we're fair, most of us have in IT.

As facilitators, it's important to be aware of our own behavior and how it can affect the group. When we're not behaving in a neutral way, our biases and negative emotions can hinder our ability to create a productive and respectful environment. We might show resistance or use confusing communication to get our point across, further breaking down communication and creating more dysfunctional conflict. Even worse, we might go slow and start using confusing communication and asking questions that aren't really questions, such as "Are you sure that it's a good idea?" Think about it for a second, did you do those in the past? We certainly did! It's easy to get caught up in conflict or even start one as a facilitator. But change can only happen if we acknowledge and address our own behavior. It can all start by acknowledging the behavior of the resistance line and the conflict stages in yourself.

---

[6]   Tsai, M-H., & Bendersky, C. "The Pursuit of Information Sharing: Expressing Task Conflicts as Debates vs. Disagreements Increases Perceived Receptivity to Dissenting Opinions in Groups," 2016. *Organization Science*, 27(1): 141–156.

GUIDING HEURISTIC   Investigate and reflect on the strong opinions you're hold-ing. What you think is wrong to do might make you lose your neutrality and keep you from facilitating the group the best way possible.

We created more resistance and tension in the group by showing edge behavior, which also causes conflict, as mentioned earlier. This has lowered our own rank in the group, and it's difficult to regain it. This is why it's important to do inner reflective work and be aware of our behavior and the shadows within us. We know that distancing yourself from certain viewpoints is very hard to do, especially in a leadership role such as an architect, tech lead, consultant, or product owner. Having both the role of facilitator and a leadership role can cause a paradox. On one side, you want to stay neutral as a facilitator, guiding the group to make a decision. On the other side, people expect you to also make decisions. Expressing opinions and taking autocratic decisions may cause resistance and conflict, and that creates a tension that leads to conflict and even-tually can end up triggering the resistance line. That is one of the hardest parts of facilitation—managing that paradox. Again, you can resolve that paradox by reflecting on your own resistant and conflict behavior, the shadows that are inside, you and the biases you have. Don't turn a blind eye to those!

Exercise 8.3

Write down the three strongest opinions you're holding. Reflect on each of them:

- What happened to make this such a strong opinion?
- How do you feel when someone has an opposite opinion?
- What emotion/behavior does it trigger after someone challenges that opinion?

These exercises help you prepare for your next facilitation to stay neutral.

UNDERSTANDING THE GROUP CONFLICTS

We mentioned before how important our observation skills are that we introduced in chapter 5. They are especially useful if we want to understand the group conflicts to help resolve them. In one of the exercises, we asked you to write down some pat-terns you observed during your meetings. These can include observed behavior you see people repeating or certain words people kept repeating. Some of these patterns can create tension, for instance, patterns that are on the resistance line and confusing communication patterns. Although not all patterns need to lead to escalation of a con-flict, we need to be mindful of those that do, that is, the ones that show edge behavior. These are shadows in the group wanting to come out in the open, and people always have the tendency to move away and to suppress the shadows. If we're not facilitating the group to deal with the shadows of the group, they will turn into demons and show themselves. To help the group deal with these shadows, we must first become aware of the shadows in the group. But sometimes, a conflict has already gone too far, so before intervening in a conflict, it's important to understand the stage it's at. Let's see how that works in action!

In section 8.2, we explained what can happen if we don't understand the group conflicts. When we engaged with BigScreen we decided to do things differently. In our preliminary conversation with Meera, the CTO, we already noticed that there were a lot of dysfunctional conflicts going on. When she started walking us through their problems, she told us about their agile transformation and that the architect left. When we asked her about why she didn't hire another one for a couple of years, she told us about the misconception of no up-front design in agile and how that led to a conflict between two of the developers, Rose and Jack. This conflict prevented her from hiring another architect for a while because she was under the assumption the team would manage architecture.

That information led us to the decision we wrote about in chapter 6 to start joining the team sessions, including dailies, refinements, retrospectives, and other operational meetings the teams had at the start of the engagement, and to observe. We saw a lot of communication breakdowns. Jack and Rose almost never interacted in these sessions; they never had a dialogue, as in listening to each other and reacting to what the other said. Although they were listening, it wasn't to understand one another but to be able to dispute the other's argument. A lot of fallacious arguments were going back and forth about the person, not about the topic itself. It's important to notice that we didn't intervene or facilitate the sessions here because we could lose trust with any of the parties. Another important observation is that the rest of the group mostly stayed silent and did what was asked.

What we also observed was that Jack and Rose used a lot of stereotyped words, such as ivory-tower architect, and used absolutes in sentences like "She always does . . . ." But we got a different vibe from the other developers on the team. In the team sessions we joined, they were mostly quiet, but in the interviews, most of them started to open up. That gave us a lot of information about the shadows in the group. Almost every time there's a conflict between two people, others are inevitably affected. A conflict is never isolated; it's always part of the group dynamic. That's why we aim to probe neutrally, using active listening to understand how others feel about the situation. The topic of the conflict was the software design, how that was decided, and the reason for the architect leaving. It was a topic that came back in every consecutive interview. In those interviews, we could probe more and see what information was in the group conscious and unconscious. And we could hypothesize about which information is important to bring up during our collaborative modeling sessions. These patterns we observed and then reflected on drove the design of the check-ins and sensemaking.

Doing consecutive interviews also helped to start resolving the conflict. Just using active listening and letting someone be heard already begins resolving the conflict. They probably never felt understood or safe to express how they felt. Most of the time, people jump to conclusions by trying to fix someone. Telling them they are making assumptions and perhaps they are wrong. But in these interviews, we like to focus on what they have to say and that it's allowed to be said. That already takes a lot of pressure off the conflict. In our case, it did, and the conflict didn't escalate too far for us to save it from separation. We saw small changes happening, especially with Jack and Rose. They didn't collaborate yet with each other, but the language they were using was already toned down.

> **GUIDING HEURISTIC**   Use an interview to understand a conflict. During interviews, check the behavior people show, and plot these on the conflict stages to get a grasp of what kind of intervention is necessary.

For the kickoff session, we didn't need to solve the conflict straight away, as those sessions are focused on getting an understanding of the current situation. Of course, if they would stand in the way of progress, we would need to deal with some of it. But because we weren't designing and coming with solutions in the kickoff, we also didn't need to dive into the conflict yet. But we already nudged the group in those kickoff sessions toward starting to resolve the conflict, as we focused on letting everyone be heard, as explained in chapter 6. Getting all these different perceptions in the group conscious already helped Jack and Rose understand other people's perspectives. But once we went into the software design EventStorming in one of the follow-up sessions, we needed to start resolving the group conflict.

8.3.2   Kissing the group over the edge

Because the previous kickoff and follow-up sessions created positive vibes in collaboration with the team, we decided not to do what we call a *hot check-in*. A hot check-in instantly dives into the conflict, for instance, asking the group what the quality of the current design or architecture is or how valuable they think an architect would be for the team. That could put the group straight back into a pressure cooker and might push the conflict back to the *-isms through polarization* or, even worse, to the *war or separation* conflict stage. What we did instead is focus on what everyone's need was as we observed it from previous sessions. When there is a polarization happening, it's best not to put extra fuel on each side, but to find what the people in the middle, or as Bart Bransdma calls "the silent,"[7] want. He calls these people the silent because they are stuck in the middle, not being heard in the polarizing conflict, and eventually are forced to choose a side. In our case, we focused on better understanding the business problems, so we kept it light and did an impromptu networking with three rounds as a check-in, as introduced in chapter 4. We told people to interact with each other using the following prompts as nudges:

1 Tell the other person an anecdote of a reservation you made in your personal life that is funny or weird.
2 What part of the reservation flow are you involved in?
3 What are some funny, good, or bad events that you saw happening in the current flow?

---

[7]   Brandsma, B. *Polarisation: Understanding the Dynamics of Us versus Them*, 2017. Amsterdam: BB in Media.

As always with a check-in, we introduced how the impromptu works, and we shared an anecdote on the first question as an example. Then, we asked them to preferably do the impromptu with someone they knew the least. Essentially, we told them at the end, we'll ask people what they heard from someone else, instead of what they have to say.

Explaining what you hear from someone else makes people more focused on listening to understand instead of reacting. That is an important job for us as facilitators, to nudge people to start understanding instead of reacting, and an impromptu can help start that off and change that behavior unconsciously. Another thing an impromptu does is that people can find someone safe enough to engage with. When there is tension in the group, it can be unsafe for people to speak up in the group. With an impromptu, they can find someone in the group they feel safe with to start engaging with the topic. It also gives us some time to observe, see who will talk with whom and especially who avoids whom. There are always people who feel safe enough to start a conversation with a person they don't know yet.

Another effect is that people need to start moving around the room, which gets them activated. One thing to understand is that if groups and people are stuck in conflict or resistant to change, you often see this reflected in their body movements as well. They will literally stand still and not move. If you want to make the conversation flow, it can help to also let the people move physically. After the impromptu, we invite people to share what they heard from others.

GUIDING HEURISTIC   When groups are stuck in a conversation, let the group move physically in an exercise. Movement trumps sitting, and it can help to unblock the flow of the conversation.

We could now start the modeling with tools stage with software design EventStorming. Because the group had a total of 18 people, we decided to split it into two groups. We let people divide themselves with one rule, that the team is equally divided among domain knowledge. We had two reasons for doing it this way. First, smaller modeling groups go faster. Because there are fewer people with divergent models, everyone gets enough air time in the group to get the opportunity to be involved. Second, that gives people the opportunity to join a group they feel safest to share in. The only danger here is that we must be careful that the groups aren't focusing and putting extra fire on the polarization, instead of focusing on equally sharing the models in that group.

That is why at the start of the session, we always discuss some safety rules, or agreements. One we use all the time comes from the Lewis Deep Democracy methodology: no one holds the monopoly on the truth. We ask the participants if they agree and understand that before we start the session. That agreement can help us later on, when the group shows a pattern of not complying with those rules. We were with two people to facilitate the session, so we divided ourselves between the groups.

Now we need to stay in contact with ourselves, reflect on our own tensions and edge behavior and our inner shadows, and continuously work on our neutrality. Not losing your neutrality is inescapable because judgments and assumptions are so easily made (and also really fulfilling sometimes, we know!). Through staying in contact with ourselves, we can observe the patterns that are happening in the group, spot resistance, and sense where the *hotspots* are. In Arnold Mindell's *Sitting in the Fire* book, he described hotspots as emotionally charged situations, problems, or moments during a conflict in a group setting. These hotspots are seen as opportunities rather than problems because they indicate where we should focus our attention. Diving into these hotspots is an opportunity to lower the waterline, and they often lead to profound understanding and resolution for the group.

From here we can let the group become aware of the edge, that is, pull the edge to the conscious part of the group by "kissing the group over the edge," as Myrna Lewis says. This is a metaphor for our desire to guide the group gently beyond their comfort zone to confront and work through their difficult problems, conflicts, or tensions. Throwing a group over the edge and pressuring the group beyond their comfort zone, isn't a good idea. It can cause stress and anxiety, as well as damage relationships. This tactic can even lead to a burnout or cause a group to fracture beyond repair. Pushing the group usually is the effective with people of lower rank. One of our favorite facilitation techniques for kissing groups over the edge is called a climate report.

CLIMATE REPORTS

A *climate report* is a series of steps that you take as a facilitator to gently confront the group with a hotspot, as follows:

- Make neutral, factual observations.
- Offer these observations as feedback to the group. Use their words, not your own, to do this. Be aware that presenting a climate report is a judgment on your part as facilitator, as you believe the observed pattern may hinder the group's progress or obstruct the session's information flow.
- Stay quiet and let the group address your feedback. It's crucial to understand that, as facilitators, we don't decide whether something is dysfunctional; that responsibility lies with the group.

We applied this technique after we split the group into two teams of nine. Both teams began in the typical fashion, with each team generating domain events individually before progressing to the timeline enforcement phase. Some teams might begin enforcing the timeline during the chaotic exploration stage, which is acceptable as long as the remainder of the team can still contribute. It's crucial to ensure that higher-ranking individuals don't dominate the conversation, leaving little room for those in lower ranks to participate. This is precisely what occurred in both teams by Jack and Rose, along with Susan, Bruce, Hadiza, and Dmytro. We observed the following: before the rest of the group could finish writing down their domain events, they had already started enforcing the timeline, engaging in active discussions about their domain events and their sequence. While enthusiasm isn't inherently negative, it was apparent that some members were still working on their domain events, and others appeared somewhat confused about the situation and their next steps.

We had explicitly instructed the group to allow everyone the opportunity to write down all events they could think of and place them on the paper roll before proceeding to the timeline enforcement phase, so it was understandable that confusion arose. This pattern isn't unique to our BigScreen context, as it occurs in almost every EventStorming session we conduct. Multiple people looking up and ceasing their writing can be perceived as edge behavior, indicating that tension is building. It's essential to address this tension early, but we must exercise caution in our approach, as it can significantly affect our neutrality and standing within the group.

We opted to use the climate report as a gentle nudge for the group to assess whether they can identify with our observations. Determining when to introduce a climate report is a bit tricky. If they aren't ready for it, we risk losing our neutrality and, consequently, our ranking within the group. We want to be sure the group is ready to recognize the problem as an impediment and that they are prepared to accept it. However, if we delay too much, the shadows beneath the edge may transform into a demon, resulting in more significant conflict and necessitating additional time for conflict resolution. Fun, isn't it, to be dealing with that uncertainty? We've been on both sides and learned it the hard way as well!

In the situation involving Jack, Rose, Susan, Bruce, Hadiza, and Dmytro, who began enforcing the timeline before the others had finished, we provided the following climate report to the group: "I notice some of you have already started enforcing the timeline, while others in the group are still in the process of writing." As you can see, everything mentioned is factual, allowing the group to reflect and decide on their next course of action. It's crucial to present a climate report addressing a pattern relevant to the entire group, rather than one or two individuals. Directing a climate report on specific individuals puts them in the spotlight, potentially making them feel unsafe. Feeling unsafe can lead to decreased participation or withdrawal from the group by those individuals. While some individuals may thrive in the spotlight, they typically already assume that position. The objective is to extract knowledge and wisdom from the entire group, and we want to avoid alienating individual members.

GUIDING HEURISTIC Address feedback and concerns to the entire group; avoid putting a spotlight on one or two individuals, especially when they are low in ranking.

In many sessions, individuals with higher rank tend to dominate the conversation, often overshadowing others. We refer to this as the *karaoke player pattern*, where someone takes charge and dictates the group's direction. At this point, we have two options, depending on our own rank. If we have the ranking to address the problem, we should do so. Because karaoke speakers have already placed themselves in the spotlight, it's acceptable, for the group's benefit, to comment on their behavior or encourage input from other group members. This may result in a conflict between you and the karaoke speaker, but it's part of the job and allows for conflict resolution. We can play our rank to share our rank with the rest of the group, as discussed in chapter 6.

However, there may be instances where the karaoke speaker is the one who hired you, possibly without you realizing the specific purpose. They might simply require you to facilitate the group in understanding and adopting their perspective. In situations like these, it can be challenging to address the problem during the session, as you may be overruled. Instead, discuss the matter with the individual afterward, ensuring the session remains safe and constructive for all participants as much as possible.

> **NOTE**   Addressing the group, not the individual is a core principle in our facilitation approach. Our goal is to create a safe space where everyone can collaborate in the most effective manner for them. This is why we don't assign turns during check-ins, as we want participants to feel at ease and freely express their thoughts. If we spotlight someone who isn't prepared, they may only share what is socially acceptable or considered safe within the group, rather than their genuine thoughts and beliefs, which require courage and a safe environment. When facilitating a workshop or providing training, consider the type of feedback or information you seek from the group. If your goal is to uncover participants' true thoughts, allow them the room to express themselves when they feel comfortable doing so. Facilitators play a vital role in fostering this environment.

When presenting a climate report, it's crucial to capture the full attention of the group to facilitate reflection on the information being shared. After speaking, we remain silent and observe the group's reaction. Instead of drawing conclusions ourselves, we patiently wait for a group member to break the silence. Before proceeding, we must confirm that the group can relate to and accept the climate report. If the group remains silent for an extended period, we can seek confirmation by asking, "Does what I just said resonate with you?" We should refrain from proposing a solution until the group's feedback indicates acceptance.

In most instances, the group will find a solution to the problem on their own, as occurred in this scenario. The members who had already begun enforcing the timeline opted to fetch drinks for everyone while waiting for the others to finish. This allowed them to discuss the events without ignoring their enthusiasm and without disrupting the rest of the group. Everyone concurred, and our sole responsibility was to assist them in discovering their solution. We also suggested taking an additional 5-minute break for those who were still writing once everyone had finished. With everyone in agreement, we continued with the session.

Exercise 8.4

Think about a situation where you could have presented a climate report to the group or a situation in which another facilitator could have done this. Describe the situation, and create the climate report that could have been presented to the group.

ADDRESSING THE CONFLICT

You might be thinking that conflict was an easy one to solve, and you're right. Let's now explore a situation where the group struggles with longer unresolved conflicts, resulting in edge behavior. During our session, we observed that Rose and Jack joined separate groups, which wasn't unexpected. The problem emerged after 40 minutes of enforcing the timeline when both groups reached the portion of the EventStorming that dealt with the central disagreement between Jack and Rose. They both began to push their agendas within their respective groups, attempting to persuade others to support their side.

Unintentionally using their rank, Jack and Rose started dominating the conversation, leaving less speaking time for other developers and leading to a breakdown in communication. Both Jack and Rose displayed a considerable amount of confirmation bias, which is common in conflicts that revolve around determining right and wrong. As a consequence, the remaining developers, feeling unheard in their own group, started eavesdropping on the other group's conversations. This edge behavior emerged in both groups.

We provided both groups with the following climate report: "We've observed that some individuals are speaking more than others in each group, and we also noticed people from one group eavesdropping on the other group's discussions." After presenting the climate report, we remained silent and observed the group's reactions, looking for signs of acknowledgment or acceptance. When approximately 1 minute had passed without any response, we broke the silence and used our active listening skills by asking if anyone could relate to our observations or had a different perspective.

Jack took the initiative to defend himself, rejecting the feedback and arguing that he contributed more because the other developers weren't engaging. This response not only worsened the conflict but also shifted it from being between Jack and Rose to Jack and the group. This behavior, known as the *scapegoating fallacy*, involves shifting blame onto others. Addressing such confusing communication with a climate report alone is insufficient. To improve communication and comprehension within the group, it's essential to practice active listening, create space, and pose unbiased questions.

The effectiveness of these techniques depends on the response of an individual or group to a climate report. In her book *Jam Cultures*, Jitske Kramer delineates each response and how to address it. For example, they might initiate an attack, which often results in aggression, anger, and tears. Others might deny the climate report, make sarcastic jokes, change the topic, or talk over it. They could also begin to isolate themselves, form small groups, or adapt to the situation by becoming silent and waiting. They can also do like Jack did, be defensive or resistant, with many "Yeah, buts" emerging. People may not listen, or, if they do, they only listen to react and confirm their biases. In these situations, acknowledging emotions and reflecting on what you hear is crucial. In any scenario, active listening and demonstrating empathy for the individual or group are essential for reopening dialogue.

Let's examine how this played out when Jack felt targeted by the climate report and exhibited the scapegoating fallacy. We asked him, "Why do you think the group isn't engaging?" The question evidently troubled Jack, who responded with agitation, "How should I know? They hardly ever speak up!" To this, we replied, "I can imagine it's difficult to understand others when they don't speak up." It's important to recognize that we didn't want to direct the conversation. Although we have our own opinions and assumptions based on our observations and understanding of rank, asking questions that are steering the conversation such as "Why do you think people don't speak up?" wouldn't lead to a breakthrough and could potentially make the situation worse. Our objective was to allow Jack to navigate his own way toward a breakthrough while we facilitated his journey. If Jack is unsure about the next step, he can ask for assistance, and then we would have an agreement with him to offer advice and pose questions. As a facilitator, it's vital to establish this contract with the group or individual to preserve your neutrality and rank. Asking steering questions can be risky, as it might be dismissed and negatively affect your role as an impartial facilitator.

GUIDING HEURISTIC   Only give the group or an individual advice when you've created a verbal contract with them in which they agreed to you giving them advice.

8.3.3   *Creating role fluidity*

Sometimes, the conversation gets stuck by active listening and holding space, and leads to a dead end. From our experience using climate reports, active listening and holding space solves most of the sessions we've been in, but the conflict at BigScreen was brewing for a while, and, as you can see, you won't solve that in one session. The conversation with Jack reached an impasse. When the heat of the conflict is this high, people are afraid to lose face to others. So, it's hard for Jack to take responsibility and change his viewpoint. He already built alliances with other people, and the group is polarized. Polarized groups are stuck because they stopped understanding the other's viewpoint and stopped relating others' viewpoints within themselves. We call this cognitive dissonance because the other's viewpoint can't exist with their own. So, we need to make these viewpoints fluid again, and the way Deep Democracy looks at these views is with role theory.

ROLE THEORY

In the context of the Lewis Deep Democracy methodology, *role theory* refers to the idea that individuals and groups have distinct roles and responsibilities in a democratic system. These roles are shaped by the interplay of personal characteristics, social and cultural norms, and power structures, and they help to define the relationships between individuals and groups. A role can be anything someone can take a viewpoint in. It can have social roles such as a mother, daughter, or father, or they can be functional roles such as leader, researcher, supporter, architect, or engineer. They can also be personal roles such as extravert, pusher, analytic, or connecter. And don't forget emotions such as anger, happiness, and sadness. In addition, thoughts, themes, ideas, opinions, behaviors, illnesses, dreams, and archetypes can also be roles. As Myrna Lewis says, "A role can be bloody anything!" These roles can live both in the conscious and unconscious part of the group, as shown in figure 8.5.

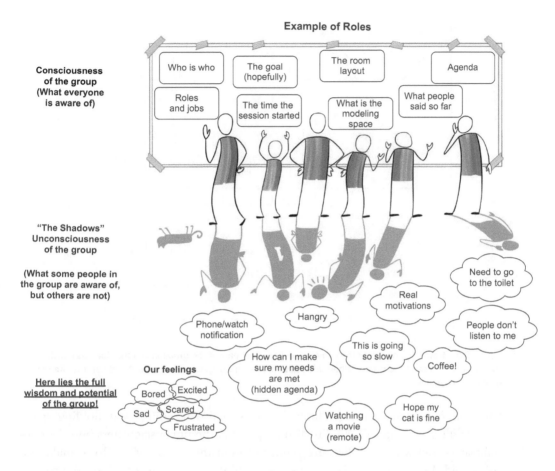

Example of Roles

Consciousness of the group (What everyone is aware of)

"The Shadows" Unconsciousness of the group

(What some people in the group are aware of, but others are not)

Here lies the full wisdom and potential of the group!

Who is who | The goal (hopefully) | The room layout | Agenda

Roles and jobs | The time the session started | What is the modeling space | What people said so far

Need to go to the toilet

Real motivations

Phone/watch notification | Hangry | People don't listen to me

This is going so slow

How can I make sure my needs are met (hidden agenda) | Coffee!

Our feelings

Bored | Excited | Sad | Scared | Frustrated

Watching a movie (remote) | Hope my cat is fine

Figure 8.5   The conscious and unconscious part of the group and an example of what roles there might be in both

Now we can identify with these roles and make them active in the consciousness of the group, as shown in figure 8.6. As an example, I can show that I'm happy, sad, or angry. Now that the group is aware that I'm happy, they can also be happy (for different reasons). So, a role is more than an individual. And, if I am happy, I can also be sad at the same time, or angry or hangry, or want to be with my cat and smother them. Therefore, an individual is more than a role. As long as people can identify with different roles in the unconsciousness and consciousness of the group, everything will be fine, and the session will flow smoothly. People will exchange and recognize themselves, for different reasons. It becomes problematic when we start identifying a person with a role. Like the Harry role we mentioned earlier, Harry is always weird. What happens after a while is that we can't see Harry differently anymore. We projected Harry up, as they say, to be weird, and that stops the flow of the conversation. So, we want to create *role fluidity* and make sure people can keep identifying with all roles that show up. When we can recognize ourselves in others, we have different conversations. We start to understand each other, conflict will be resolved, and peace can be made for this specific conflict.

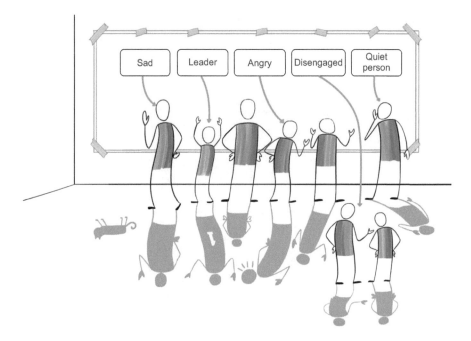

Figure 8.6   How roles can get stuck to certain people or part of the group in isolated icebergs within the consciousness of the group. When this happens, the group gets into a conflict and can't relate to the other role anymore.

Check-in/outs, sensemaking, climate reports, active listening, and holding space already start creating role fluidity. You help to get the unconsciousness into the consciousness. But when conflicts are high, not even these tools will help to make the roles fluid. In our session, Jack was stuck in thinking the others took on the role of disengaged. He can't see the role of being afraid to speak up, introvert, oppressed, or many other roles that the others could take on. When these tools aren't sufficient, we can try to find alternatives in the group. You can ask the group who sees it differently than Jack. Now again, wait and see if you get an answer from the group. Eventually, Kala opened up and said, "I don't speak up because I don't know what problem your solutions usually solve." Kala now identifies with a role of unknowing. Now it's essential to spread that role actively in the group. Ask the group, "Who can somewhat relate to not knowing what the solutions solve?" Raise your hand to signal other people to do the same. You want to have a visual recognition from the group that they can relate to the role. It's important to note that we add "somewhat" to our question about relating because while it's hard to fully relate to the others for many different reasons, people are more likely to sort of relate to the others. Try to use your own wording, and integrate these two sentences in your own facilitation to create better role fluidity.

>   **GUIDING HEURISTIC**   When someone expresses a need or opinion, ask if someone
>   sees it differently to make other opinions conscious in the group.

What happened next was that other developers raised their hands, and the conversation started to flow again. We didn't solve the entire conflict in that session because that takes multiple sessions and coaching people one-on-one. But what we did succeed in at that meeting was bringing some shadows out of the unconsciousness of the group before they turned into demons by getting people to start listening to each other. The dominant symbol and pattern of the group here was that people in the team jumped to solutions fast, which didn't give other people a chance to understand the problem as well. So, people didn't feel part of the conversation anymore because they had the feeling they didn't understand the problem correctly. That gave Rose and Jack an insight they never had, and, in the end, they agreed to be coached by us on how to make sure others are on the same page as them. It's very hard to get agreements on solutions, but it's easier to agree on the same need or problem. If we first start to understand and relate to each other's needs, decision-making will be a lot easier. We'll talk more about that in the next chapter.

8.4 Collaborative software design catalysts

- Track behavioral patterns during collaborative modeling (or a meeting if you don't do collaborative modeling yet). Write down your colleagues' behavior, and mark how many times they show this specific behavior. Don't bring this up during the meeting/session as we're not trying to be a guardian angel here; we're simply learning to observe behavior.

- Examine the behavior that you wrote down. Try to determine how neutral you were when you were observing. Is there any judgment, assumption, or interpretation there? (Spoiler alert, there will be.) And see what you can do different next time in your behavior.

- Schedule a one-on-one meeting with one of your colleagues to start a conversation. Try to use the steps of the climate report during this conversation. Be careful not to offer unsolicited advice. Remember, the goal is for people to feel heard so the conflict can de-escalate, not for you to solve this for them. If you want to help people feel safer, share not only the facts but also how they affected you—what emotions you experienced and ask them how they see it. For more on resolving one-on-one conflicts, refer to *Crucial Conversations* in the further reading section.

- If you think there is a conflict going on between yourself and a colleague, you can apply the same steps. Be cautious though because it's tricky to do this when you're the one involved in the conflict; staying neutral is a lot harder. Focus on the other person feeling heard by you—the person they have a conflict with.

8.5 Chapter heuristics

Guiding heuristics

- Whenever you encounter a conflict, determine if it's a functional, task-based, or dysfunctional relationship conflict. Do this by figuring out if it's task related or emotion related, and if it's helping or hindering progress and outcome.

- You know when a conflict turns dysfunctional when dialogues or discussions move toward the notion of right or wrong. As a facilitator, this is your cue to start resolving the conflict.

- Frame discussions or disagreements as a dialogue or debate. People have a mental model of what a dialogue or debate is compared to a discussion or disagreement, and it will focus on ideas instead of personal conflict.

- Investigate and reflect on the strong opinions you're holding. What you think is wrong to do might make you lose your neutrality and keep you from facilitating the group the best way possible.

- Use an interview to understand a conflict. During interviews, check the behavior people show, and plot these on the conflict stages to get a grasp of what kind of intervention is necessary.

- When groups are stuck in a conversation, let the group move physically in an exercise. Movement trumps sitting, and it can help to unblock the flow of the conversation.

- Address feedback and concerns to the entire group; avoid putting a spotlight on one or two individuals, especially when they are low in ranking.

- Only give the group or an individual advice when you've created a verbal contract with them in which they agreed to you giving them advice.

- When someone expresses a need or opinion, ask if someone sees it differently to make other opinions conscious in the group.

8.6   *Further reading*

- *Inside The NO: Five Steps to Decisions That Last* by Myrna Lewis with Jennifer Woodhull (Deep Democracy, 2018)
- *Polarisation: Understanding the Dynamics of Us versus Them* by Bart Brandsma (BB in Media, 2017)
- "The Good Fight: With Guests Adam Grant & Tom Crouch" by Katy Milkman (Choiceology podcast)
- "The Pursuit of Information Sharing: Expressing Task Conflicts as Debates vs. Disagreements Increases Perceived Receptivity to Dissenting Opinions in Groups" by Ming-Hong Tsai and Corinne Bendersky (*Organization Science*, 27, 2016)
- *Think Again: The Power of Knowing What You Don't Know* by Adam Grant (Viking, 2021)
- *Writing Ethnographic Fieldnotes*, 2nd ed., by Rachel I. Fretz, Robert M. Emerson, and Linda L. Shaw (University of Chicago Press, 2011)

- *Crucial Conversations*, revised edition, by Joseph Grenny, Kerry Patterson, Ron McMillan, Al Switzler, and Emily Gregory (Atlas Contact, Uitgeverij, 2022)

Summary

- Conflict and resistance have negative connotations, but, in reality, conflict is a difference of opinion between two or more people and is natural.
- Suppressed or ignored conflicts can lead to resistance and edge behavior.
- Edge behavior is a result of conflict avoidance and is shown by a person who wants to avoid conflict but doesn't feel comfortable addressing it yet.
- It's important not to judge edge behavior, as it's hard to sit in one's discomfort.
- Resistance and conflict aren't necessarily negative and can indicate important topics at the root cause of hindrances.
- Facilitation is crucial in resolving resistance and conflict in collaborative modeling.
- Resistance and conflict are related to other social dynamics such as cognitive bias and ranking.
- Observing behavior and communication patterns can indicate resistance and conflict in collaborative modeling.
- Confusing communication patterns include indirectness, interrupting, questions that aren't questions, and fallacious arguments.
- Making assumptions can result in bias blind spot, and inner conflicts and biases can turn into negative behavior, leading to resistance and tension in the group and preventing effective facilitation
- Writing down and reflecting on patterns observed during meetings helps you categorize patterns over time.
- A conflict has many different stages that require different approaches for dealing with them.
- A climate report provides neutral feedback to the group about their behavior and the observations that were made using the group's own words that they can relate to. It can help the group deal with a conflict themselves
- A facilitator must maintain their neutral rank by not giving unsolicited advice, but instead offering assistance through a contract with the group or individual.
- Role theory in Deep Democracy and the Lewis Deep Democracy method refers to the concept that individuals and groups have specific roles and responsibilities in a democratic system.
- A role can be anything that someone can take a viewpoint in, including social roles, personal roles, emotions, thoughts, behaviors, and so on, and these roles can exist both in the conscious and unconscious part of a group.
- The goal is to create role fluidity, where individuals can identify with different roles and the group can recognize themselves in each other.

Making sustainable design decisions

This chapter covers

- Sustainable decisions and what you need to make one
- Decision-making styles and the levels of buy-in
- Facilitating sustainable decisions

What is the most difficult decision you've had to make in your life? The answer to that question will be different for everyone. How did you approach this decision? That question might yield more similar answers. "I weighed my options," "I asked for advice," "I went with my gut feeling," and so on. Making a decision clearly involves comparing things with each other, but what else does it entail?

We've spoken about ranking, cognitive bias, and conflict. All of these things happen when you're trying to design your software solution in a collaborative setting. What is software design if not making decisions? We haven't really spoken about what decisions are, so we're going to do that in this chapter. We'll dive a bit deeper into what a decision is, giving you a framework to reason about decisions in general. We'll discuss software design–related decisions and how to improve the sustainability of those decisions by using Deep Democracy as a facilitator.

9.1 *Decisions, decisions, decisions*

Decisions are everywhere. They take up a lot of our time. We lose sleep over them: "Did I make the right decision quitting my job?" We judge ourselves because of them: "What the hell was I thinking buying that car?" We judge other people because of them: "I honestly don't understand why they bought that house; I wouldn't have done that." We have to live with the consequences of our decisions, or other people will have to live with them. Yet, most of us were never taught how to make decisions. We aren't even taught what exactly a decision is.

9.1.1 *What is a decision anyway?*

A *decision* is a conscious choice between two or more alternatives that involves an irrevocable allocation of resources.[1] There is a lot to unpack there. Let's start with "a conscious choice."

A CONSCIOUS CHOICE

A choice is the act of choosing between two or more possibilities. "The act of choosing" tells us that a decision isn't a thing, but a process you have to go through and not just going through the motions, but consciously. This is sometimes referred to as *actional thought.* If you don't think and act, there is no decision.

The opposite of a conscious choice is a habit. The whole point of a habit is that you don't have to decide what you're going to do, but simply execute a set of actions. Introducing habits can take away a lot of mental bandwidth because making decisions takes up a lot of time. Of course, it pays off to examine your habits once in a while and decide which ones to keep and which ones are no longer useful.

ALTERNATIVES

If we know that a choice means the act of choosing between two or more possibilities, why do we explicitly say this again in the definition? Well because a possibility and an alternative aren't exactly the same thing. *Alternatives* are a set of plans that you need to choose from. A *plan* is a set of intended actions you'll take to reach the desired outcome of the decision. We'll discuss alternatives a bit more in section 9.1.3.

IRREVOCABLE ALLOCATION OF RESOURCES

The definition also mentions "irrevocable allocation of resources." *Resources* can be time, money, or energy. To have made a decision, you need to put time, money, or energy into it. Even more, the resources you put into the decision can't be undone—they're irrevocable. This means that there is a cost in being wrong. Undoing your decision will cost you time, money, or energy. This is important to determine whether or not a decision was made. If changing your decision costs you nothing, you didn't make a decision. Think back on all those New Year's resolutions—all those people stating that they decided this is the year they will go to the gym, start swimming, and so on. Most of those people don't even get started with their New Year's resolutions. Declaring that

---

[1] Abbas, A. E., & Howard, R. A. *Foundations of Decision Analysis,* Global Edition, E-Book, 2023. London: Pearson (p. 30).

you've made a decision is cheap; actually making one requires you to put your money, uh, resource, where your mouth is!

This also means that you can quantify the importance of a decision by the resources you need to allocate. How much do I stand to lose when I pick the wrong alternative? The more you stand to lose, the more up-front analysis you should do when making a decision. So, when you're deciding on your software architecture, the design decisions that are hard to change in the future, you want to invest more time analyzing the decision. Yet, we've noticed that those decisions are often based on shiny new trends, familiarity, the loudest voice in the room, the highest paid person's opinion (aka HIPPO), or the "run hard in the opposite direction" attitude.

9.1.2   Decision vs. outcome

When we make a decision, we have a goal or objective in mind. The *outcome* of a decision is what actually happened and can be different from what we expected. When we're executing our course of action, unforeseen consequences or events can happen that influence the outcome. The outcome can be better or worse than we expected; in other words, the quality of the decision is different from the quality of the outcome.

Let's take a look at two common architectural patterns: monolithic and microservices.[2] The decision to go with one or the other is often because of the run hard in the other direction attitude we mentioned earlier: the development team tried microservices and had a bad outcome, so they now go for a monolith, or vice versa. Imagine that you're the architect on that team, and you have to decide between a monolithic or microservices approach. You decide to go for a monolithic approach. Two years down the road the monolith has turned into a big ball of mud (BBoM), and you need to put a lot of effort into restructuring it.

People might argue that you should have gone for microservices, that your decision was bad. Is that true? It's hard to answer that question because we don't have enough context right now to understand it. What we do know is that people have a tendency to think about the quality of a decision in terms of the quality of the outcome. They will call something a bad decision, when it's actually the result that's bad, and vice versa. In the poker world, there is even a word for this: resulting. *Resulting* is the tendency to equate the quality of the decision with the quality of the outcome.

It's not uncommon that people don't separate the quality of the decision from the quality of the outcome. "Of course, your monolith turned into a big ball of mud, they always do. They should have seen this coming and gone for microservices instead!" Reactions like this show the hindsight bias in action. The *hindsight bias* allows us to believe that past events were more predictable than they actually were. The person reacting like this forgets that microservices can also end up like that; we call these Distributed BBoM.

Whether to go for microservices or a monolithic approach depends on the context. This is why it's important to not just document the alternative you picked when making

---

2   Richardson, C. *Microservices Patterns: With Examples in Java*, 2018. Shelter Island, NY: Manning.

the decision, but the entire decision and analysis. We'll dig a bit deeper in how to do this in chapter 11.

Exercise 9.1

Try to find an example from your personal or professional life, where you were confusing the quality of the decision with the quality of the outcome, that is, resulting. Do this for a decision where you had a bad outcome as well as one when there was a good outcome.

9.1.3 *What you need to make a decision*

You want to make good decisions because you want to avoid paying the cost of being wrong. To make good decisions, you need to understand the elements that need to be present when making a decision. There are three main components needed when making a decision (see figure 9.1):

- *Alternatives*—What we can do
- *Information*—What we know
- *Preference*—What we want

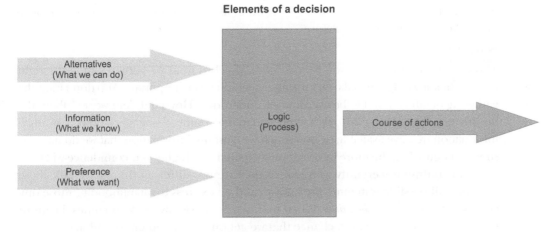

Figure 9.1 The key elements that are needed to make good decisions

Those three components are the input for making the decision. Every decision has a decision-maker. What comes out of a decision is the plan we're going to execute. To take those components and turn them into a course of action, we need some logic to guide us. Let's dig a bit deeper into all these elements, starting with the decision-maker.

A DECISION-MAKER

The *decision-maker* is the person that has the authority and the permission to allocate the resources when an alternative has been chosen. The person has the authority when they have the explicit rank that allows them to allocate the resources. The more resources that need to be allocated, the higher the explicit rank of the decision-maker. By *permission*, we mean that everyone involved in the decision is in agreement that this is the decision that has to be made.

It's possible that the decision-maker isn't involved in the decision analysis itself, but relies on a team of experts to analyze the decision for them. The experts report their findings to the decision-maker, including the best course of action according to their analysis. It's still within the decision-maker's power to pick a different course of action though. Another option you have as a decision-maker is to place the decision with the group that has to live with the consequences of the decision, but we'll talk more about that in section 9.2.

ALTERNATIVES

We already explained in the previous section what an alternative is, but we haven't dug too deep into it. Let's do that now. First, the decision-maker has to believe that the alternatives available will lead to a different future. If all your alternatives have the same desired outcome, it doesn't matter which one you pick. When it doesn't matter which one you pick, you don't have a decision to make.

Second, the definition explicitly states that you need to choose between two or more alternatives. But what if there isn't more than one alternative? Well, keeping things as they are is always an option, although under most circumstances, it isn't the one we want. Still, there is a lot of value in making "keeping things as they are" a visible alternative. You can now compare this with the other alternative and make a conscious decision to keep things the way they are.

INFORMATION

The second input of a decision is *information*, which is what we know. Getting the right amount of knowledge to make an informed decision is very important. You don't want the gathering of information to be overdone or underdone. How confident we feel about the information that is available to us is expressed in uncertainty. *Uncertainty* shows how much information we have available or how much we trust the information that we do have. As shown in figure 9.2, the more information we gather, the higher our confidence will be.

Don't confuse uncertainty with risk, as they are two different things. We talk about *risk* when all possible outcomes are known, and we express the likelihood of those outcomes to happen in *probabilities*. When we flip a coin, we have two outcomes: heads or tails. We know there is a 50% chance that we get one or the other. Not all decisions we have to make have known outcomes because we don't have all the information available at the point of making the decision.

This is also why we try to postpone certain design decisions until a later moment during our design activities and simply express our uncertainty by adding hotspots during the collaborative modeling. The more information we have, the better we'll be able to evaluate all the alternatives available to us. During collaboration, you can also see if you're digging into the right hotspots. If the confidence level of participants isn't changing, or only changing slightly with the information you're gaining, you're digging into the wrong place (see figure 9.3).

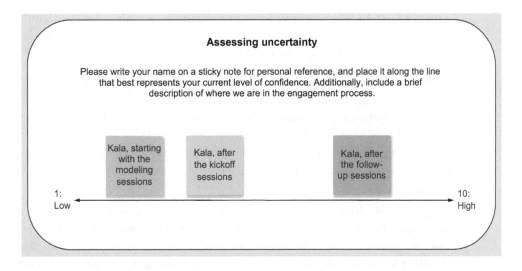

Figure 9.2 Tracking the confidence of participants during collaborative modeling is a great way to know if the information they are getting out of the sessions is valuable. In this example, we show the confidence of Kala, one of the participants. The more she discovered about the domain, the higher her confidence was.

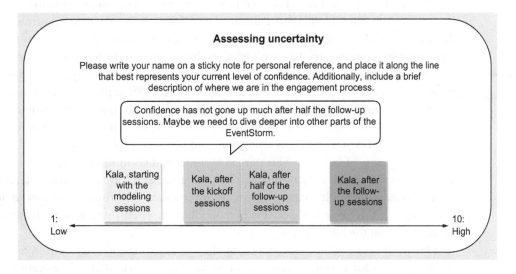

Figure 9.3 If the confidence level of participants during collaborative modeling isn't going up, try diving deeper into a different part of the EventStorm by picking a different hotspot.

Uncertainty and the difficulty of a decision are intertwined with one another. To make a decision easier, you need to gain more information or get the right information. That way, the uncertainty goes down, and the decision is easier to make than it was before. A good heuristic to know which information you need to find is the following:

GUIDING HEURISTIC   Imagine you were talking to a clairvoyant and could ask them a single piece of information about the decision you're trying to make. What piece of information would it be?

What makes a decision easy or hard is how well informed you feel about the decision you have to make. Picking your ice cream flavor can be labeled as an easy decision. Whether or not you want to invest money in a start-up is already a lot harder. Why is that? The knowledge readily available for those two decisions is different. I don't have any knowledge that will help me assess whether or not a start-up is worth investing in, and most people don't have that either. There is a lot of uncertainty involved here.

PREFERENCE

The people involved in making the decision will have a preference on the available alternatives. *Preferences* (what we want) are the criteria or values by which they will compare one alternative with another one. Basically, what consequences are acceptable according to our values? Do we care more about how much money it will cost or how much time we have to spend on executing the plan? Or do we care more about the eco-friendly alternatives? Preference means that certain alternatives are more desirable because the outcome of those are more desirable. If nobody cares about the consequences, and any future will do, there is no decision to be made.

Making these preferences for each person involved in the decision visible is a good way to avoid conflict. We all have a different set of values we evaluate alternatives against. If we know by which values the people around us are evaluating the alternatives, we create better understanding. This isn't an easy thing to do because a lot of people don't fully understand their own preferences, which makes it difficult to communicate those to somebody else. As we mentioned in chapter 5, you can apply active listening: "I am scared that going for this design will create too many single points of failure in the system." With Socratic questioning, you can try to find the preferences and challenge their assumptions: "Do you think any communication between different parts of the system are single points of failure?" This person believes that communication between different parts of the system creates single points of failure that have a possible risk attached to it. We can mitigate that risk, however, by finding more information on how to do this and seeing if the preference of this person changes when there is more information available about the alternatives.

Our preference will be influenced by the way information is presented to us, and we'll present information in a more positive or negative light depending on our preference. If we emphasize the gains of a certain alternative more than our losses (or leave out the losses completely), we'll prefer that alternative because it seems better. This is referred to as the *framing effect* in social sciences. So be careful how you share information and tradeoffs during the decision analysis!

LOGIC

The last element of a decision is logic. *Logic* is a process to derive which course of action we should take from what we can do (alternatives), what we want to do (preferences), and what we know (information). The process will lead us to a conclusion of the decision analysis. There are two possible paths you can take as a process:

- Perform a decision analysis.
- Use heuristics.

Which one you pick depends on the effect of the decision. If you have to make a decision that involves millions of dollars and years to execute, you'll do a deep decision analysis. The type of decisions you have to make when designing your software system aren't the right fit for a decision analysis. That is why we use heuristics when designing software. During collaborative modeling, we use heuristics in two ways: design heuristics help us to generate alternatives, and guiding heuristics help us to move forward in the process.

PROBLEM STATEMENT

Now that we know all the key elements that need to be present when making a decision, we want to talk about what needs to happen before we start to analyze the decision. Before starting the analysis, it's important to answer this question: What problem are we trying to solve? This is the *problem statement*. It doesn't matter how well you analyze the decision if you're solving the wrong problem.

A problem statement that we often hear in software teams is "Our system is too coupled, we need to decouple the system." When digging a bit further into it, we notice that it's a communication problem, not a software problem. The system has loose coupling, and it doesn't send out a lot of unnecessary messages to other services either. However, the teams communicate with each other through documentation only, and often that documentation is outdated. Even if you have a loosely coupled system, you'll still need to communicate with other teams.

Another common mistake is stating the problem in terms of the solution. "Should we use EventSourcing?" isn't a good problem statement. Whether or not to use EventSourcing isn't the problem that we're trying to solve, but a possible solution.

To come up with a good problem statement, it's important to select the proper frame. The *frame* is the boundary we draw around the problem:

- What are the constraints we have to live with?
- What decisions do we need to make to solve the problem?
- What decisions are out of scope for now?

Whenever we're invited to consult with a company, we always check the frame. How much freedom do we have? Can we redesign the whole system? Are you willing to reorganize your teams? Are there any important feature deliveries you can't miss? Who can we invite? Depending on those constraints, we know which decisions are in scope and which are out of scope right now. We try to find the correct frame. To have the correct frame, you need to do the following:

- Identify the correct problem.
- Clarify the problem, so everyone understands it.

- Look at the problem from different perspectives.
- Assess the business situation in regard to the problem.
- Create the appropriate alternatives/options.

Identifying the correct problem isn't easy. That's why it's important when designing software to first understand the problem you're trying to solve, before you try to come up with alternative solutions for it. Domain-Driven Design tries to help with solving the right problem. If we think back on the principles mentioned in chapter 2, we can see there is much overlap with what you need to do to find the right frame. By using the concepts of problem and solution space, we explicitly focus first on finding the right frame, before we start designing toward a good architectural solution for our software system.

9.1.4   Reactive vs. proactive decisions

When you have to make a decision, there are two ways you could have reached this point. Something happened, and now you have to make a decision. This is called a *reactive decision* because you're reacting to an event. Here are a couple of examples:

- You got fired, and now you need a new job.
- Your house stops being for rent, and now you need a new place to live.

The second is a *proactive decision*. You want something to change, so you take charge and try to change it by making a decision. Here are two examples:

- You're starting to lose interest at work, so you want a new job.
- Your rent is getting too high, so you want a new living space.

It might not seem important to know what kind of decision you're making, but it is. Think about our first reactive example. Getting fired is something that will trigger other emotions than when you start to dislike your job and want to get a new one. The way you look at all the alternatives available to you will be influenced, consciously or unconsciously, by these emotions, so your preferences will be different. The time you can spend to make the decision will also be different. Even though it might not seem important, it has a big effect on the decision and its process.

A lot of development teams that we encounter are in a reactive decision-making mindset. The business makes a decision that affects the software system, and then the development teams have to react to that decision. Collaborative modeling helps software teams go from reactive decision-making to proactive decision-making. During collaborative modeling, you can discover business opportunities that would not be possible without software and pitch those to the domain experts. You can explore and design those opportunities together with the business.

9.1.5   Sustainability in software design

You might be thinking that this is all great and interesting, but my job is to solve problems. You're correct in that—our end goal is to come up with a good software solution.

But what makes a software solution good? Is it how well it fits the user needs? Or how easy it can be maintained? Maybe it's about how well the software developers understand the code? Or how well teams can be structured around it? For us, it's all of these and more. We refer to that as sustainability. To have sustainable software solutions, you need to make sustainable design decisions. *Sustainable design decisions* consider the sociotechnical effect of the alternatives. After designing and analyzing the alternatives, you pick the one that gives you the best sociotechnical tradeoff with the information available. You create a feedback loop in your design process to improve it along the way. Over time, you'll find yourself making decisions in a similar way. This is when your decisions become sustainable.

It's important to understand that designing software isn't a single decision that you have to make. It's a series of smaller decisions that push your design in a certain direction, which becomes the solution. Decision-making is a subpart of the bigger problem-solving process. When you're generating alternative designs, you're solving the problem. Once you have a few alternatives, you analyze them and pick the one with the best tradeoff, which is decision-making. You need decision-making to make sustainable design decisions. This means you have to set up a decision-making process, and this process requires refinement:

- How are we making decisions, autocratic or democratic?
- What do we need to look out for?
- How are we creating buy-in?
- What are the relevant factors for us to base our decision-making style on?
- Who can make decisions?
- What do we do when not everyone is on board?

All of these are relevant questions that need to be addressed in your decision-making process. We'll now dig a bit deeper into those questions.

9.2 *Decision-making styles and levels of buy-in*

The decision-making process heavily affects the outcomes and the software design. Are we making decisions in isolation or together with a bigger group? How much space is there to provide input, feedback, and alternative suggestions to proposed decisions? These are complex questions to answer, and doing that consciously is crucial for sustainable design decisions that consider the sociotechnical effect of the alternatives. Decision-making style and levels of buy-in are aspects of the decision-making process that should be considered early on. This section will elaborate on two main decision-making styles, autocratic and democratic, and the levels of buy-in that are related to these styles.

9.2.1 *Autocracy vs. democracy*

Decisions are crucial, and so is the style of decision-making. Both affect software design, and it's important to understand how they do so. There are many different decision-making styles, but in this section, we'll zoom in on two of them: *autocratic* (one person decides) and *democratic* (the entire group decides).

As mentioned in section 9.1, every decision involves a decision-maker, which is the person that has the authority and permission to allocate the resources when an alternative has been chosen. This means that both in democratic and autocratic decision-making, there is one decision-maker who has the "decision rights." When it comes to these two different decision-making styles, the important difference is that with democratic decision-making, the decision-maker defers this right to a group of people, which doesn't happen in autocratic decision-making.

Both styles are effective in different contexts, and they can help you think about communication strategies as you dive into a situation. When you make an autocratic decision, you'll communicate differently than when you want to make a democratic decision—or hopefully you will. When a decision-making style matches the communication style, it helps group members understand their role and the influence they have on a decision, which reduces conflict and resistance. This also goes the other way, of course: when the decision-making style doesn't match the communication style, it will lead to confusion, frustration, and potential conflict. In this section, we'll dive into examples of both situations. Before we go there, let's explore a little further on the difference between democratic decisions and autocratic decisions.

AUTOCRATIC DECISION-MAKING

Autocratic decision-making involves one person being in control and responsible for a decision. This means that there is no larger group involved or consulted in the decision-making, or, if there is, it's to a very minimal extent. There is a very strong top-down approach in this decision-making style. An example here is an architect making all architectural design decisions and then handing those over to the development team who is responsible for implementation. None of the team members were involved with or consulted about the architectural choices, and their input isn't included in the final decisions.

This autocratic decision-making style has both advantages and disadvantages, and its effectiveness depends on context. Following are some of the main advantages of autocratic decision-making we see are:

- *Autocratic decision-making is fast decision-making.* When there is no bigger group involved and/or consulted, it takes less time to come to a decision. Decisions are made based on personal knowledge, experience, and perceptions of that particular situation. There is no time spent on discussing and defending the decision before it's made, which saves a lot of time and potential money.

- *Autocratic decision-making increases clarity around expectations.* When done right, the person making the final decisions will communicate clear expectations around what needs to be done, which means little to no confusion. The decision is based on personal knowledge, vision, and experience, which makes it less of a compromise and more straightforward. There is more clarity on who should be doing what, and people understand better what is expected of them.

- *Autocratic decision-making lowers ambiguity.* The less people are involved in a decision, the less room there is for ambiguity, interpretation, and compromising. There is an obvious chain of command, and structure and direction are clear.

Following are the main disadvantages of solely autocratic decision-making:

- *Autocratic decision-making neglects the wisdom of the group.* The bigger group holds a lot of wisdom and knowledge that would be valuable to make a decision. This combined wisdom can account for a higher quality decision. When making decisions in an autocratic way, that wisdom isn't included, which means you're potentially not making the best decision.

- *Autocratic decision-making will most likely not lead to sustainable decisions.* Because not everyone is included in the decision, this can lead to resistance, meaning it can also trigger the resistance line discussed in chapter 8. If you aren't managing the resistance line, it will increase resistant behavior and decrease buy-in even more. In addition, autocratic decisions often lack feedback loops, which can fuel the resistance line.

- *Autocratic decision-making can decrease creativity.* Not being involved in a decision and getting clear instructions and expectations may vanish all forms of creativity. People might feel there is no room for them to think about alternative solutions, so they might not even try. Killing this creativity won't lead to the desired outcome because you're missing out on a lot of valuable input.

- *Autocratic decision-making can negatively affect morale.* It can lead to distrust, resistance, and inefficiency, especially when people aren't on board with the decision. People might feel like their input isn't valuable, and they will start doing only the bare minimum to get the job done. This won't bring you high-quality results.

DEMOCRATIC DECISION-MAKING

In contrast to autocratic decision-making, democratic decision-making is more about shared responsibility and decision-making. As mentioned, there is still one person who has the decision right, but here, it's deferred to a group of people. An example of democratic decision-making is an architect working together with all stakeholders on models, designs, and implementations of architectural decisions. Everyone involved needs to be on board with the decisions and be able to provide input, feedback, and perspectives to the decisions.

Just like autocratic decision-making, democratic decision-making has both advantages and disadvantages, and effectiveness depends on context. Following are some of the main advantages of democratic decision-making:

- *Democratic decision-making leads to commitment, participation, and engagement of group members.* Because everyone affected by the decision was included in the decision, people will feel more valued and willing to support the decision. People will have a stake in the success of the decision because they feel part of that decision. In other words, democratic decision-making will most likely lead to sustainable decisions because everyone was included and is on board with that decision.

- *Democratic decision-making provides an opportunity to include the wisdom of the entire group.* This will create a shared sense of ownership and responsibility for the decision and making it into a reality.

- *Democratic decision-making can positively affect morale.* Autonomy, creativity, commitment, and engagement as a result of being included in the decision can lead to higher satisfaction within groups. This can help people go an extra mile instead of doing the bare minimum for what's needed.

Following are the main disadvantages of solely democratic decision-making:

- *Democratic decision-making can be a slow, time-consuming process.* Including everyone in a decision means you have to allocate time to consult every relevant stakeholder and domain expert. Properly creating a shared understanding about the decision at hand, what is asked from group members, how their input will be included, and the wisdom of the group members themselves can take a lot of time.

- *Involving the right stakeholders can be challenging.* Who needs to be involved in which decision? Who decides which people get to be involved? Who decides which people have the right skills, expertise, and input to contribute to a decision? This can be very challenging when there is no full clarity on roles and/or context. When you don't include the right people, you're missing out on valuable wisdom after all, which is exactly what you want to avoid with this decision-making style.

- *Democratic decision-making can increase ambiguity.* The more people are involved in a decision, the more mental models, assumptions, and interpretations are involved in that decision. This can increase ambiguity when it comes to language, meaning, and understanding. Managing and facilitating this ambiguity is complex and time-consuming.

AUTOCRATIC OR DEMOCRATIC, THAT'S THE QUESTION

With this elaboration on the two styles, you might wonder which decision-making style is better. When it comes to making effective decisions, should you use autocratic or democratic decision-making? Our opinion—which might not be a surprise—is that it depends. We believe this isn't an either/or situation but a both/and situation. Depending on the context, you have to decide which decision-making style is most suitable. It may even mean you have to go back and forth between the styles depending on the context and decisions that need to be made.

Which style is best suitable in a certain situation depends on factors such as time, money, effect, deadlines, and pressure. If deadlines are approaching fast, and a project is already heavily over budget, autocratic decision-making might be more effective. At the same time, autocratic decisions can kick-start the resistance line, depending on how that autocratic decision was framed and made.

When you're in a situation where decisions will have a big effect on a large group, and everyone agrees they need to spend significant time and money gathering input and commitment, go with democratic decision-making. In that last case, be sure to get a facilitator that can lead conversations and the decision-making process.

Let's illustrate this with an example we've encountered multiple times: deciding which technology to use. This decision has quite an effect and depends on several factors. Following the company strategy, the development team of this company needed to grow. They were aiming to hire a significant number of new employees to realize the technological goals the company envisioned. This also meant that the existing team was facing some changes in structure, way of working, and preferred technologies. After all, if you want to attract and recruit a lot of new people, you have to match market trends when it comes to technologies. Using a rare technology will make recruitment extremely challenging. In other words, it's not about choosing the best technology from a technical point of view, but about choosing what's best for the team and company. A classic sociotechnical decision needs to be made.

So, the architect was left with a decision to make: given the goals and strategy we set out, which technology are we going to use? Factors such as effect, pressure, and deadlines were considered, and eventually it turned out to be a partly democratic and partly autocratic decision. Let us explain how that works.

The architect could have made a fully autocratic decision here: "This is the technology we're going to use." However, this might lead to resistance within the team and might not be the best technology for the team. On the other hand, the pressure was on, and deadlines were approaching fast. The architect decided to create a proposal for the team with a list of two choices. The alternatives were based on the growth ambitions of the company, market trends, and recruitment opportunities, as well as existing knowledge within the current team. These alternatives were discussed with the team, and the architect clearly explained how the presented alternatives were arrived at. It was now up to the team to decide which of these alternatives was the best fit with the team. The architect gave autocratic boundaries by providing alternatives to choose from, and the team was able to make a democratic decision within these boundaries about what would be best for the team.

This is a good example of how you can consider several factors when choosing a decision-making style. Note that it doesn't have to be an either/or choice. You can mix autocratic and democratic when that suits the needs of the group. What went well here was the transparency around the decision-making process by setting clear boundaries and being straightforward about where the group could influence the decision.

To summarize, when a decision or decisions need to be made, analyze the situation based on relevant factors such as time and effect, and then choose your decision-making style. The important thing is to be clear about what you ended up choosing. It's very frustrating when it seems like decisions are being made in a democratic way, but, in reality, there is one person making all final decisions in an autocratic way. People need to know and have clarity about their role and the level of influence they have on decisions. We'll dive into this further in the next section.

9.2.2   *Creating buy-in on decisions*

All stakeholders need to actively support and participate in implementing the course of action following a decision. We call this creating *buy-in*. If you don't put effort into creating this buy-in, you can stumble upon resistance in the process. You want this buy-in to make sure people are on board and willing and able to do what's required of them in the actions following a decision. If people aren't given any buy-in, they might start to slow down by asking a lot of questions and questioning the decision in general, for example. Other forms of resistance could be people refraining from actions that need to be taken, making regular sarcastic jokes, and gossiping about the decision and potentially about stakeholders.

LEVELS OF BUY-IN

One of the main reasons people start resisting is related to the way the buy-in is being framed. Often, decision-makers feel uncomfortable putting a decision in the right level. If these levels are applied in a right and consistent manner, it will help make sustainable decisions. In the Lewis Deep Democracy method,[3] there are four levels of buy-in that you can create when making a decision:

- *Idea*—You have an idea, but nothing has been done yet. If the idea is ill received, you're more than happy to let it go. It's an open question, and everyone is allowed to influence it. You're looking for a group of people who want to help you generate and analyze options.
- *Suggestion*—You have clear intentions, you've investigated options, and you have a preference on one of the options, but other insights are welcome.
- *Proposal*—You have a concrete worked-out plan for an option, and only serious objections can influence the decision.
- *Command*—You have made the decision and want to inform others of the decision and their responsibilities.

It's important to make clear to the stakeholders which level of buy-in they have. Nothing is more frustrating for people than when you frame the decision in a different buy-in than it actually is. The most common misframing happens around commands; the person in charge of the decision doesn't always feel comfortable to frame a command as it is. Commands can have a negative association and lead to resistance as people may feel they have nothing to say or add to a decision.

Let's illustrate this misframing with an example. A few companies back for one of the coauthors, the team lead wanted to introduce more homogeneity in the codebase by introducing a code formatter. They made a suggestion: "We'll start using tool *xyz* under the default settings; what do you think? I would love to hear your thoughts on code formatting and what you think is the best way to do it." Everyone was very interested of course, including the coauthor. They created their optimal settings and scheduled

---

[3]   Kramer, J. *Deep Democracy-De wijsheid van de minderheid* ("The Wisdom of the Minority"), 2019. Ashland, OH: Management Impact Publishing.

a meeting with the team lead. During the meeting, it became very clear that the decision to use the tool under default settings had been made, and nothing would change their mind. The coauthor in question became annoyed and frustrated toward the team lead. The coauthor understood and agreed with the team lead's decision when listening to their arguments, but, at the same time, they felt resentment toward the team lead because they had wasted the coauthor's time by pretending that this was anything other than a command. So, the coauthor didn't use the new formatter, and they weren't the only one with a similar reaction.

Imagine the team lead had said this: "I want to improve the homogeneity in the codebase. We'll start using the formatter xyz. I want to avoid endless discussions on what the best settings are, so we'll use the default settings. It will take some time getting used to the new code style, so in nine months, we'll evaluate if the default settings aren't causing readability problems for the team. Is there anything you need to go along with this decision?" Framing it this way, the majority of people would probably have agreed with it, and used that tool for nine months under default settings. By that time, they would have adapted to the new style of the code and been able to evaluate the readability. But because the team lead had presented this as a suggestion, they had created resentment that resulted in resistance (not using the tool) and were unable to achieve their goal of improving homogeneity.

LEVELS OF BUY-IN AND DECISION-MAKING STYLE

These four levels of buy-in relate to autocratic and democratic decision-making styles we discussed in section 9.2.1. There isn't a one-to-one relationship between the styles and the levels, but they do correlate with each other. Autocratic decision-making creates little buy-in, where democratic decision-making creates lots of buy-in. Autocratic implies more commands because decisions have been made by one person and it's more about informing others about that decision than including their feedback and/ or input. Democratic implies mainly ideas because it's about open questions, and everyone is allowed to provide input before decisions are made. Figure 9.4 visualizes the levels of buy-in related to the decision-making style.

It's usually best to define the decision-making style first: Does this decision require autocratic or democratic decision-making, and why? Consider relevant factors, and decide what best fits the situation at hand. This will guide you in the levels of buy-in. Whatever you decide, always be clear about that level. Making it explicit in terms of what people can expect and what you expect of others will remove ambiguity and prevent frustration and resistance.

Another concept that we need to take into consideration when talking about democratic decision-making and creating buy-in is *giving consent.* Giving consent means that a smaller group of people is given consent to make a decision. This foundational step is crucial for setting clear expectations and boundaries in decision-making. The entire group decides collectively that a subgroup of people can make the decision. This is especially helpful from an efficiency perspective. Some design decisions can be picked up by a subgroup after being given consent, and they can bring that decision back to the group. Doing this still creates relatively high buy-in, as it's a form of democratic decision-making.

Lower buy-in

Autocratic decision-making

Command — Decision made
Mainly about informing

Proposal — Only serious objections

Suggestion — Intentions are clear
Insights are welcome

Idea — Fully open question
Group of people who helps generate
and analyze options

Democratic decision-making

Higher buy-in

Licensed under https://creativecommons.org/licenses/by- sa/4.0/
Based on Deep Democracy the Lewis Method

Figure 9.4   Levels of buy-in plotted on the spectrum of democratic and autocratic decision-making styles

9.2.3   *Buy-in on software design decisions*

Software design decisions can also require buy-in from stakeholders. One way to create that buy-in is collaborative modeling. All relevant stakeholders can work on a shared model that includes all input and perspectives that are needed to make the best decisions possible. Using collaborative modeling won't automatically create buy-in for the stakeholders. With collaborative modeling, you visualize the proposed solutions of the stakeholders. Because all the stakeholders that need buy-in are in the room, you make it easier to evaluate those solutions and gather feedback on them.

At the end of a session, you can still pick a solution that not everyone is on board with. This is why it's important to ask what the stakeholder needs to go along with the solution that they didn't decide on and see what you can add to the decision. Again, clarity is crucial here.

> **GUIDING HEURISTIC**   After a decision is made, always ask the following: "We're going with this decision, so what do you need to go along with it?" And decide what can be added in the decision to get these people to go along with it.

This is a very powerful question that is hardly ever being asked. From our experience, this question can lead to increased buy-in because it provides an opportunity for people to be heard and express concerns. It won't change the course of the decision, but it will clarify what individuals need to go along with that decision. Often, we find these needs aren't huge and impossible, but rather practical and realistic needs that can be added to the decision rather easily. For example, a need to create a clear storyline and communication that can be shared with other stakeholders within the organization, a need to have regular check-in moments to stay aligned and focused, or a need to get a one-on-one meeting with the architects to ask clarifying questions and better understand the decision.

We like to weave in the Lewis Deep Democracy method[4] in our facilitation to come to consensus-driven, sustainable decisions. Our biggest motivation for doing so is that after the decision is made, there will be less resistance and hassle because all relevant stakeholders were involved in that decision. When we have plenty of time and can make fully democratic decisions, we include all the steps. If time is short or we lack buy-in from the decision maker, we might only incorporate step 4. Remember, we prefer to weave this method into our flow, adapting it to our facilitation style without always explicitly mentioning Deep Democracy. It's not about strictly following the steps but about the outcome of reaching sustainable design decisions. The Lewis Deep Democracy method describes five steps for sustainable decision-making:

1 *Gain all points of view.* The first step is to make sure that everyone has the opportunity to express their opinion on the decision that needs to be made. It's up to you as a facilitator to create the space to make this possible.

2 *Find the unspoken alternative point of view.* Have you ever been in a meeting where everyone just agrees? Yeah, so have we. At least we thought everyone agreed at the time. However, more often than not, the disagreement just surfaces much later. That is normal because not everyone feels comfortable speaking up. It's better though for disagreement to surface as fast as possible, so go hunting for it.

3 *Spread the alternative point of view.* When somebody is brave enough to speak up when they disagree (and even when they have no problem disagreeing), it's important that they don't feel alone in their disagreement. That is what step 3 is all about: spreading the disagreement from a single person to more by making their point of view relatable.

After going through several rounds of steps 1 to 3, it's time to vote and see how the group is divided. We only do this if we believe one option will likely have a majority or if we sense that taking a stance might surface more unspoken perspectives. Clearly present all alternatives and remind everyone that they can only vote for one. Also, let them know that an option needs more than half the votes to gain a majority. If no majority is reached, we return to steps 1 to 3, repeating this process up to three times before moving on to step 5.

4 *Add the perspective of the minority group to gain a unanimous vote.* Excellent, we have a majority vote, and the decision has been made. Wrong! It's now time to focus on the minority. Ignoring the minority is a good way to create resistance or push

---

4 Kramer, *Deep Democracy.*

a conflict into the shadows until it comes out as demons. If 40% disagrees with what was chosen, we have a majority *and* a problem. Even if just a single person disagrees, it's better to understand where they are coming from and resolve the disagreement before it causes conflict down the line. Ask them what it will take to come along with the chosen option. Incorporate the minority needs into the decision, and then vote on each one until you reach unanimous agreement on the improved decision that now includes the needs of the minority.

5 *No unanimous vote? Go Fishing!* The last step is optional. When you can't reach a unanimous vote, it's a sign that there are still things left to be said before everyone can agree. It's time to start fishing for those unspoken alternative points of view again.

In section 9.3, we'll elaborate on how weaved in these steps in our facilitation by describing one of the sessions we had at BigScreen.

9.3   *Facilitating sustainable design decisions*

In this section, we'll return to the end of the design EventStorming we talked about in chapter 8. Then, we'll go into the domain message flow modeling session conducted after the design EventStorming discussed in the previous chapter and briefly mentioned in chapter 3. From that design EventStorming, we developed three potential bounded context design alternatives. Although we facilitated conflict resolution within the group during the design EventStorming session, resolving the dysfunctional conflict between Jack and Rose, they still could not reach a consensus on the optimal approach for the bounded context design. The conflict had become functional, enabling Jack and Rose to listen to each other. Nevertheless, if we don't carefully facilitate the group's decision-making process, we could quickly reenter the -isms conflict stage.

9.3.1   *Moving toward a majority vote*

In chapter 8, we already demonstrated how we weaved in the first three steps of the Lewis Deep Democracy method. However, we didn't label them as such. Now that you know what these steps are, we want to show you what those steps look like during collaborative modeling. But first, let's review a session from a two-day workshop at another company to illustrate what can happen when minority needs aren't included in the decision-making process.

FACILITATING THE FIRST 3 STEPS OF THE METHOD

The workshop was with a variety of stakeholders and two software teams to break down their current BBoM system. Our approach involved using EventStorming and domain message flow modeling. We consistently improved our alternative design options for possible bounded contexts throughout the session until we had a few distinct designs. By using this method, we were able to gather the necessary information needed to make a well-informed design decision.

EventStorming and other collaboration tools are great because they prompt you to weave in step 1 to 3 almost unconsciously. The points of view you're looking for are the mental models of the participants they wrote down on stickies at the start. Then by asking questions such as the following about events that are contradictory, you dig deeper for alternative points of view: "You said you always pick all the items first before assembling them, but the night shift mentioned partial assembly due to stock shortage. Can you think of a situation in which the day shift partially assembled something?"

To discover which of the designs of the session was the best option for stakeholders and teams, we gathered everyone's opinions and wrote them down per design. We used the lilac-colored sticky notes for all the cons and green for the pros, and added the tradeoffs for both designs. This is again the first three steps of the Deep Democracy method.

When we were altering a design, we tried to spread the alternative point view by asking questions on the adaptation:

- Why do you want to change this design?
- Who agrees this is an important need for the design?
- Is there anyone who thinks there is a similar need not present in the design right now?

That is what step 3 means: making someone's opinion relatable. When someone is expressing a less popular opinion, they often feel uncomfortable or alone in their point of view. This triggers the resistance line that we want to avoid.

As you may have noticed, this is an iterative process. When you're designing, you can't think: "Okay, so now first step 1, then step 2, and so on." Designing your software system is iterative, so we have to adapt the method. As a facilitator, we have to make sure that steps 1–3 all get enough attention and are included in your collaborative modeling session.

At some point, it was time to pick one of the designs. That is when we vote. We asked the group how comfortable they were in picking one of the designs, and everyone felt confident enough to vote. Out of the 14 participants, a majority of 9 voted for one of the designs, and we all agreed that this was the best option for the teams.

We were excited to move forward with it—or so we thought. When the team started to implement the design in code, we noticed a lot of merge requests with comments popping up such as "This isn't what we decided" and "This is the better route to go, let's stay agile and adapt." It was clear to us from the resistance behavior we observed that not everyone was on the same page when it came to the design decision we had made. So, even if you analyze the decision correctly, find alternatives, gain all the information we need for the decision, and determine all preferences to the group, you can have a minority who are stuck with a decision they didn't make. For them, that feels similar to an autocratic decision, and that will definitely trigger the resistance line.

GUIDING HEURISTIC   Ask people who didn't vote for the majority alternative what it takes for them to go along with the decision.

We forgot to ask the five people who didn't vote for that design what it would take for them to go along with the decision. We forgot step 4, getting to a unanimous vote! This is something that happens a lot in companies. The majority wins, and the minority is simply neglected. That is a recipe for conflict. As mentioned, it's important to ask the group that voted against the design why they disagreed and what they need to do to go along with the majority. We want to include those needs into the decision and vote again. That vote has to be unanimous because we want everyone to go along with the decision.

FACILITATING ROLE FLUIDITY

Now let's go back to the design EventStorming session from the previous chapter and see how we did better at BigScreen. From the design EventStorming, we ended up with two alternative bounded context designs: Back-Office Separated (as the left decision) and Payments Separated (as the right decision) (figure 9.5).

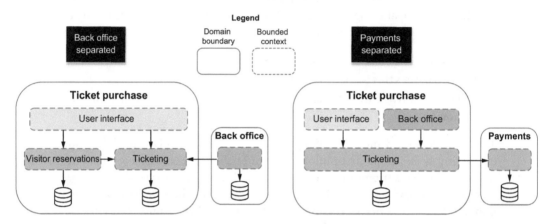

Figure 9.5   The bounded context designs after the design EventStorming. Both designs started to evolve and include wisdom from the group. The left design, Back-Office Separated, started to split Visitor Reservations from Ticketing to choreograph a reservation from a paid ticket. Payments Separated, on the right, started to move toward more orchestration where Ticketing goes to Payments to finalize a ticket.

Next, we used an adaptation of the Small Group Diverge and Converge collaboration style (chapter 4) to analyze the two designs in figure 9.5. We did this to create understanding between the two camps of what a person feels they need that pushes their preference to one of those two designs. We paired up participants so they could interview each other on the problems their preferred design solved. To form pairs, we asked participants to choose their preferred design and then partner with someone who favored the opposing design. We wanted to create relatability and move away from two sides of the conflict.

The interviewer's task was to extract the underlying design heuristic from the conversation. They documented the design heuristics on index cards, following Rebecca Wirfs-Brock's Question-Heuristic-Answer (QHE) format (https://wirfs-brock.com/blog/2019/04/13/writing/). The problem the interviewee mentioned was turned into a question on the index card, and the heuristic was extracted from the way the design solved that problem. Exercises like these are beneficial for two reasons:

- They help to make design decisions more tangible by extracting key heuristics.
- They promote role fluidity by encouraging active listening and understanding of each other's needs.

After two rounds, we asked everyone to group the QHE card by the design it was extracted from. We then let everyone read all the cards and asked them what was something that surprised them or that they didn't expect. On both sides, there was the following question: "How can we split up our teams?" As you might have noticed before, the current development team consists of 15 people, and they are getting in each other's way when they code.

> **GUIDING HEURISTIC** Begin by establishing a shared understanding of the problem or need that requires solving before moving on to discussing potential solutions.

Both teams had the same question using the same design as mentioned, but they used them in different ways. As depicted in figure 9.5, the left design isolated the planning and scheduling, while the right design singled out the payments. Once it was clear that everyone shared similar requirements, this facilitated stronger connections among the group members. Consequently, a new kind of discussion emerged, focusing on each design's bounded context.

FACILITATION TO A UNANIMOUS VOTE

This discussion began with a question to Jack's group about their rationale for setting payments as an independent domain. Jack explained that his work often involved conversations with colleagues from operations and finance to determine the most effective way to manage payments, making these departments key stakeholders in the payment domain. He further clarified that these discussions were typically initiated in response to problems raised by the operations teams regarding customer complaints about payment failures.

> **DESIGN HEURISTIC** Align bounded context around parts of the domain where different domain expertise is present. With domain expertise, we don't mean specific people but different knowledge and skills.

In many instan ces, these problems were mainly bugs caused by modifications in the rules for seat allocation, as requested by the finance team for optimizing revenue. For a while, finance wanted to change the way they calculated ticket prices, and the easiest way to experiment with that was making changes to the price calculation for seat allocations. These changes could lead to unexpected responses from the system. As a result, payment processes might fail due to these bugs. By setting Payments as a separate boundary, the rules for seat allocation could be disassociated from executing the payments.

During a discussion following Jack's presentation, Caledon from the left design team suggested breaking the payment function into two parts: seat allocation and payment processing, as shown in figure 9.6. He reasoned that this division would make more sense, as in paying and pricing are two distinct business problems, needing both their own bounded context to solve those in. He came up with the idea because of the term he had heard Jack use, payments and pricing constraints. Thus, Caledon suggested, also shown in figure 9.6, to rename the Payments domain to Pricing and Payments. Jack expressed his reservations, unsure if a more detailed division might complicate things.

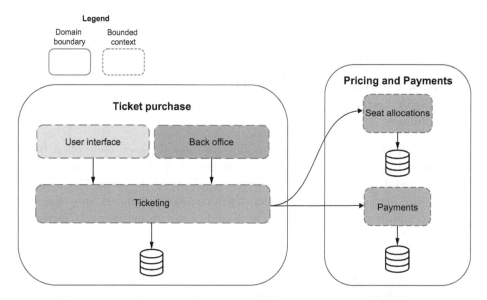

Figure 9.6   Caledon's suggestion to further split up the Payments bounded context into two and renaming the Payments domain to Pricing and Payments

The team agreed to vote on the matter. The team was faced with two options: maintain the current design or adopt Caledon's proposed alteration to the design. Everyone was allowed to vote once, and majority rule was to be implemented. The team understood and proceeded with the vote. First, we asked who was in favor of option 1, maintaining the current design. Three participants, including Jack, raised their hands in agreement. Next, those in favor of the second option, further division, were asked to vote. Fifteen participants voted for this choice.

As a result, the team chose to further divide the domain Payments as Caledon had suggested. We asked the essential question—What would it take for them to go along?—to those who hadn't voted for this decision. Jack was the first to respond. While not against the choice, Jack felt that if they were considering further divisions, it was only fair to examine the Back-Office Separated design for potential divisions too.

This example highlights that individuals might not opt for something they prefer due to some underlying problem. In Jack's case, it was the fact that his design had been improved, but Rose's design hadn't been given the same exploration. It had nothing to do with the improvement itself. It's good to remember that these underlying problems may not be evident at the time of decision-making, only surfacing after a choice has been made. Collaborative modeling sessions often favor the extroverted, quick decision-makers, leaving the more analytical thinkers to catch up during voting or even after the session. This is a broad generalization, but it illustrates why individuals may cling to the status quo.

By asking people what would convince them to go along with a decision, we can glean more information and better understand their preferences. This is a valuable trick for making more inclusive and informed choices.

SWITCHING COLLABORATIVE MODELING TOOLS TO GAIN MORE INSIGHTS

Rose, who had initially proposed the design, also disagreed with the decision. We asked her what it would take for her to go along with the decision, and she hesitated. As facilitators, we must be cautious not to make hasty assumptions and instead use our active listening skills to create a supportive environment. It's vital to exercise situational awareness, especially when contentious topics arise. We risk falling back into conflict and encountering resistant behavior, particularly from Rose, if we don't approach the situation delicately.

After a brief pause, Rose confessed she was a bit unsure if there is anything that she needs to go along. We could have easily brushed this off and moved forward, but we felt a tension—which could mean more shadows and that we hadn't provided a safe space for her to genuinely express her needs. When we reflected on that tension we remembered that the entire session she was very vocal about her design and about what was going wrong, and now she is quiet. We might have observed edge behavior, and it's up to us to help her at this point express what she needs to say. So, we respond with, "You are a bit unsure?" and let the silence sink in again.

Rose then answered that she feared that further dividing the bounded context would require a significant increase in communication. When asked why she saw this as a problem, she explained that more communication could overcomplicate things. She and the team were used to a single-model approach that facilitated consistent transactions and simplified changes due to its singular codebase. Splitting into separate bounded contexts, she argued, could make it difficult to adapt to unforeseen changes, necessitating alterations in both boundaries and their intercommunication. And not having the experience to write code in that way makes it even more difficult and a risk for the project.

You might ask yourself now, why are we putting so much effort into the dialogue with Rose despite having already reached a decision. This dialogue was valuable to the group as it provided additional insights into the group's dynamics and preferences. We turned on the flashlight and let shadows out in the consciousness of the group. Understanding Rose's perspective might influence our current decision and is far more cost-effective at this stage than during implementation. Moreover, this dialogue reassured Rose that her views were acknowledged and valued. This attentiveness to individual needs is integral to sustainable decision-making.

Continuing the dialogue, Rose expressed concerns about increased complexity due to further splitting. In our role as software designers, this problem presented a design challenge we needed to address. Designing bounded contexts requires us to consider essential complexity, which we can't reduce, only manage. Smaller bounded contexts are easier to manage because they contain less of this essential domain complexity, but the essential complexity increases between bounded contexts. To fully understand the effect of the size of our designed bounded context, we can use domain message flow modeling. This is why we repeatedly emphasize the need for using multiple collaborative modeling tools; each offers a unique perspective on the problem at hand.

Our initial plan for the next session was to use Example Mapping on one of the bounded contexts, with domain message flow modeling later in the process. However, we felt we needed to address Rose's concerns first, mostly because if Rose has this concern, role theory (chapter 8) teaches us that others will have that concern as well. So, when we asked the group who else had the worry that the communication between bounded contexts can become too complex, most raised their hands. With the group's approval, we proposed conducting domain message flow modeling in the next session, postponing Example Mapping to a later date. We would model both options for the right group's design and do the same for the left design as if similar concerns arose.

Here, you can see us use a more autocratic decision-making style. We did a proposal in this case to address Rose's worries and tried to make it more comfortable for her to get along with the decision. It's important to notice that we tried to include everyone's needs that we knew so far. That is why we used a proposal, so if something might be in the unconscious of the group that we don't know of, we can adjust if needed. Autocratic decision-making isn't bad, as long as you include the wisdom of the group and connect it to their needs!

When we asked if anyone disagreed with our proposal or if they needed anything else to support it, no one in the group disagreed or needed anything further. We then moved on to the left design, which was also divided into two options. That division on the left side also improved the option Caledon gave for the right design, as shown in Figure 9.7.

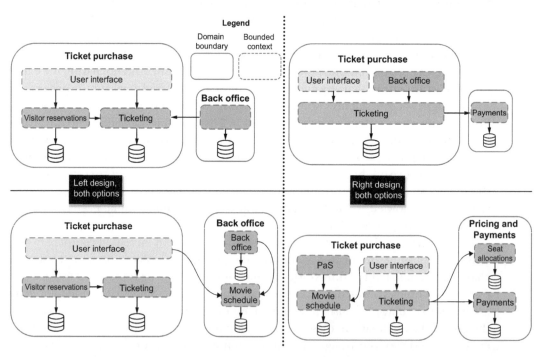

Figure 9.7   All bounded context design that we ended up with at the end of our design EventStorming session. The left and the right design both offer another alternative that further split up the bounded context from the domain split.

9.3.2 Go fishing!

So far, we've managed to achieve unanimous agreement on the choices or decisions we need to make. But what if that's not possible? What if there are more than two options without one having the majority? Or what happens when we don't get a unanimous vote for the needs we added from the minority? We encountered that exact scenario in the follow-up session we did with domain message flow modeling.

During that session we split up into three groups, each doing a domain message flow modeling on one of the designs from figure 9.7 with the same use case scenario: purchasing tickets when they are available. We only did three teams because both left designs will look similar doing that use case. You can see the first outcome of the domain message flow in figure 9.8.

We asked each group to extract their design heuristics, and one competing heuristics between the designs emerged: orchestration versus choreography (https://mng .bz/VxDx), which are two ways you could implement the business process of ticket purchasing.

The left design employed choreography. Here, the visitor reservations system broadcasts an event that the ticketing system recognizes, prompting it to create tickets and send an email to the customer. In this setup, the Visitor Reservations bounded context has no knowledge of the Ticketing bounded context, leading to a loosely coupled architecture. However, this design doesn't have centralized management for the ticket purchase process. The process is distributed between the two bounded contexts, which would necessitate some form of monitoring or another bounded context to keep track of the status for each ticket purchase.

On the other hand, the right design used orchestration in the ticket purchasing process. The Ticketing bounded context manages the entire process. This is easier to maintain, but when the Ticketing bounded context is offline, the whole process halts. It also results in more interdependence between each bounded context because the ticketing system needs to be aware of the other context.

As the group engaged in a discussion about the designs, two main topics were addressed. The first topic was about the differences in splitting the business process into subprocesses and placing them in separate boundaries. The majority of the group felt the left design was more cohesive because the key business process of purchasing a ticket was confined to specific subprocesses and, thus, teams, and it didn't cross boundaries.

The second topic revolved around the debate between choreography and orchestration. Most group members seemed to prefer orchestration over choreography. They appreciated the reactivity of choreography, but given the team's lack of experience with reactive programming and their existing monolith's heavy reliance on synchronous calls, the preference leaned toward orchestration. From this discussion, someone suggested revising the left design to use orchestration rather than choreography, as shown in figure 9.9.

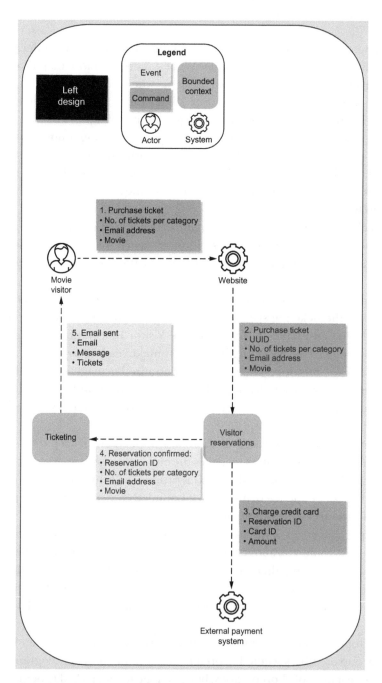

Figure 9.8   The outcomes from each group for a domain message flow modeling with the use case purchasing a ticket when available. We chose the same use case because it gives us insights to compare each design. Generally, you would model multiple different scenarios to show what actually would happen for that design in each scenario.

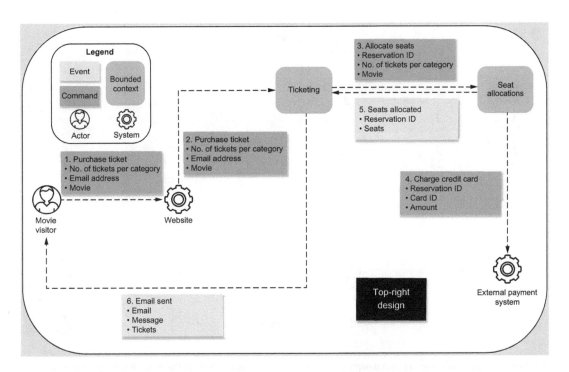

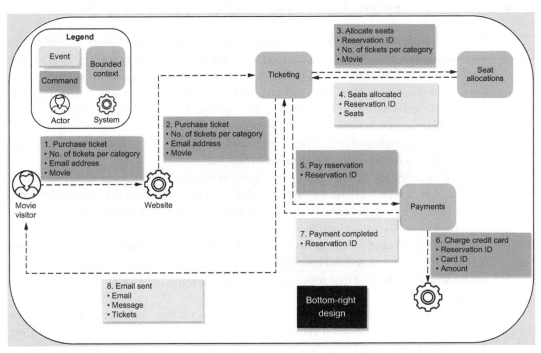

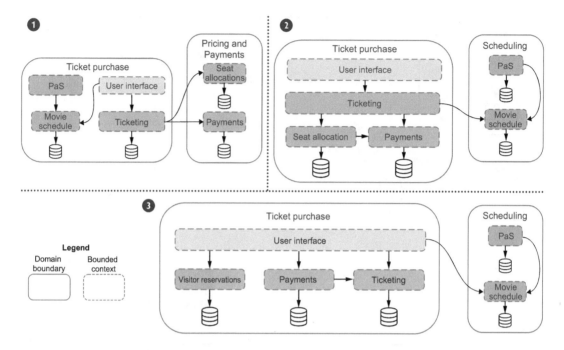

Figure 9.9   A third bounded context design emerged after modeling out several flows and distilling their heuristics. Spreading the needs that the heuristics solve throughout the modeling is key in finding new insights.

We like to have more than two designs because it also means the binary nature of two alternatives can greatly influence us versus them when deciding on a design. Using multiple collaborative modeling tools, extracting design heuristics, and spreading the needs that those heuristics solve will give you better dialogue because it creates a better shared understanding, more design alternatives to choose from, and less us versus them between two designs, which if you remember, we started with when we came into the company. It switched from being Rose and Jack and their designs to multiple designs that included all the wisdom the group had.

Next, we asked the group's confidence level in making a decision, and everyone indicated a 7+ on a scale of 1–10, signaling readiness to vote. Just as in the previous session, we initiated a voting process. With 18 participants, a majority design decision would require at least 10 votes to be selected.

In the initial round of voting, none of the designs secured a majority. The first design received six votes, the second had five votes, and the third got seven votes. This lack of a clear winner indicated that more discussion was needed for a well-informed decision to be made.

We then invited the group members to explain their votes, sparking further dialogue. As facilitators, we used active listening in the ensuing conversation, spreading the roles further within the group for them to be ready for the next voting round.

In the subsequent round, there was still no clear majority, but there was a shift in the vote distribution. The first design's votes dropped to three, while the second and third designs received seven and eight votes, respectively. Although a majority had yet to be achieved, there was a clear signal of progress toward a consensus. So now we asked the group to really try and persuade the others until the group was ready for another vote, which ended up in a tie between design 2 and design 3, meaning the group already decided to split the domain between ticket purchasing and scheduling. But the one thing they could not agree on was orchestration versus choreography. The group was divided in two camps again!

In situations where a decision isn't easily reached, it could be beneficial to delve deeper into the debate at hand—in this case, the choice between orchestration and choreography. As they suggest in the Lewis Deep Democracy method, it's time to "go fishing!"

There are two primary strategies for this. The simpler one is to let the entire group highlight the advantages of both sides. The second, which necessitates a more sophisticated understanding of conflict management and goes beyond the scope of this book, is to stimulate the group to critique both sides. If you're curious about the latter method, known as "throwing arrows," we recommend further reading or attending a training on Lewis Deep Democracy (www.lewisdeepdemocracy.com). It's important to note, however, that we seldom resort to the latter approach. The first strategy usually facilitates the decision-making process enough, and when that isn't the case, you might be better off with someone with a professional background in conflict facilitation.

The simpler strategy involves asking everyone in the group, even those who didn't vote for choreography, to either talk or write down stickies about all its potential benefits. Once the discussion dwindles, we switch to the orchestration side. We then repeat the process, as the second option can sometimes spark new insights for the first. We end with a final exploration of the benefits of orchestration.

Next, we prompt the group to reflect on the discussion and identify any standout points or triggers that resonated with them, or to put it different, what hit home? After a period of reflection, we ask everyone to share their thoughts, without interruptions from the group, similar to a check-in process. Jack spoke up first and told the group that he really wanted the company to work on the newest technologies, but what hit home for him was someone saying learning and failing in smaller steps, instead of making big jumps. He then follows up that he finds it hard to accept because he doesn't want to stay behind in his experience as a developer compared to the outside world. But he thinks it's better to first take a small leap toward that goal, and he will put his ego aside for the company and see if he can experiment himself at home more on those technologies.

This part of go fishing makes sure to lower the waterline further, allowing individuals to display vulnerability, which can inspire others to do the same. By sharing his feelings, Jack made it safer for others to also share their feelings. Though not everyone fully participated by sharing deeper emotions, it was enough that a few did, putting on the flashlight and letting shadows come out. Once everyone who wanted to had spoken, we returned to voting. Interestingly, the third design won the majority of votes, 16 to 2. The two minority voters suggested revisiting the debate once the team gained more experience with choreography. This was agreed upon, and we proceeded with the third design.

The design heuristics applied here addressed solvable problems. But occasionally, a group might encounter unsolvable challenges, such as when to start coding or when to continue collaborative modeling. These ongoing dilemmas, known as polarities, can hinder collaborative modeling. In the next chapter, we'll delve deeper into strategies for managing such polarities.

9.4   Collaborative software design catalysts

- Try to find the decision-maker for each decision that needs to be made during team meetings. Who has the veto power here? Who needs to approve the budget?
- When making a decision, regardless of the context you're in, try to see if this is a reactive or a proactive decision.
- When there is only one option (agree/disagree decision), see what other options you can come up with, and share them with the group. Even if you don't like the options you come up with, sometimes the usefulness of an option is that it might inspire other people to come up with their own.
- When you're in a meeting and someone is expressing a minority point of view, try to relate to that person. Is there a similar need that you could mention so this person doesn't feel alone in their opinion anymore?
- If you don't find a similar need, ask the question out loud: "Is there anyone who has a similar need? Is there anyone who can relate to what person X just said?"
- When making a democratic decision during a meeting, try to get a unanimous vote. You don't even have to make it explicit that this is what you're trying to do. Just ask the following: "Why do you disagree with this option?" or "What would it take for you to go along with it?"

9.5   Chapter heuristics

Guiding heuristics

- Imagine you were talking to a clairvoyant and could ask them a single piece of information about the decision you're trying to make. What piece of information would it be?
- After a decision is made, always ask the following: "We're going with this decision, so what do you need to go along with it?" And decide what can be added in the decision to get these people to go along with it.
- Ask people who didn't vote for the majority alternative what it takes for them to go along with the decision.
- Begin by establishing a shared understanding of the problem or need that requires solving before moving on to discussing potential solutions.

Design heuristic

- Align bounded context around parts of the domain where there different domain expertise is present. With domain expertise, we don't mean specific people but different knowledge and skills.

9.6   *Further reading*

- *Foundations of Decision Analysis* by Ronald Howard and Ali Abbas (Pearson, 2015)
- *Microservices Patterns: With Examples in Java* by C. Richardson (Manning, 2018)
- *Fundamentals of Software Architecture* by Mark Richards and Neal Ford (O'Reilly Media, 2020)

Summary

- A decision is a conscious, actional process involving a choice from a set of plans (alternatives), differentiating it from the automatic nature of habits.
- Decision-making requires an irrevocable allocation of resources (time, money, or energy), representing its cost and importance, which can be quantified by potential losses from incorrect choices.
- Resulting is a common bias where decision quality is erroneously equated with outcome quality; instead, decision quality should be evaluated based on the context and thoroughness of initial analysis rather than just the eventual result.
- Good decision-making involves the components of information, preferences, and alternatives, managed by a designated decision-maker with the authority to allocate resources.
- Alternatives should lead to distinct outcomes, with information gathering being crucial to influence the level of uncertainty and confidence in a decision.
- The decision-making process evaluates preferences against available alternatives, but these preferences can be influenced by how information is presented (framing effect).
- The decision-making process uses logic to derive a course of action, with the depth of analysis depending on the decision's complexity, and it begins with a clear problem statement that outlines the problem to be addressed.
- Decision-making can be reactive (responding to an event) or proactive (initiating change), with each type influencing emotional responses, preferences, and decision time frames. Collaborative modeling helps shift teams from reactive to proactive decision-making.
- To create sustainable software solutions, a series of smaller decisions considering sociotechnical effects must be made, which requires setting up and refining a decision-making process addressing factors such as decision-making style, buy-in creation, and conflict resolution.

- Decision-making styles, autocratic and democratic, greatly affect software design. Both styles have advantages and disadvantages, and the choice depends on the context, potentially even involving a mix of both.
- The choice of decision-making style should consider relevant factors such as time and effect, and the decision process must be communicated clearly to avoid confusion and potential conflict.
- Buy-in levels range from idea to command, and miscommunication of these levels can cause resistance, as seen in an example involving a software tool introduction.
- Autocratic and democratic decision-making styles correlate with buy-in levels; Lewis Deep Democracy method supports sustainable, consensus-driven decisions, particularly in software design.

Managing unsolvable problems

10

This chapter covers

- Managing polarities, instead of trying to solve them
- Using polarity mapping to manage a polarity
- Managing a polarity for the group

Have you ever faced a problem that felt extremely hard to solve because there seemed to be no clear solution, but rather something that needed to be balanced over time? If so, you were probably facing a polarity instead of a problem. Sometimes problems have one solution: we're either going left or right. We're either going to hire person A or person B for this job. But some problems seem less straightforward: Are we focusing on the short or long term? Are we working on this project individually or collectively as a team? It might be tempting to go with either one of the alternatives because who doesn't like simple clarity? But the latter examples are actually not problems that have an either/or solution. They are polarities that need to be managed in a both/and manner.

This chapter will define polarities and how you can spot them in the wild (more specifically, during collaborative modeling sessions). We'll also explain and teach you how to address polarities with a group by visualizing them in a map. Based on

299

common polarities during collaborative modeling, we'll explain how to manage them using BigScreen examples.

10.1 Polarities: Some problems can't be solved

Imagine you're working hard on a project for a while that will continue for a few more months. After a long day, you're tired and just want to lay down and close your eyes or kick back with a nice book to give your mind some rest. However, you also know that a nice workout will help you release stress, clear your head, and provide some energy. With the prospect of this stressful project running for at least another few months, what will it be: Rest or activity? Work out or relax to make it to the finish line in a sane way?

Although this might seem like a problem with an either/or outcome, it's actually a *polarity*: an ongoing problem or challenge that has no clear solution in terms of picking one of two sides. It's a problem that can't be solved because you're not dealing with either/or, but rather both/and. So, when you feel like the problem you're facing is something that you'll need to balance over a period of time—such as focusing on the long term or short term—you're dealing with a polarity. In a specific moment, you can choose one alternative over the other, but the challenge will come back sooner or later. Rest and activity form an interdependent pair that needs each other over time. You need the benefits of both sides (activity and rest) to function in an optimal way and get through this project without burning out. You want to maximize the benefits of both sides and minimize the downsides of both.

This is an example of a polarity you could experience in your daily life. There are actually many more polarities that we tend to treat as either/or problems (we can only pick one), where we should treat them as both/and polarities that we can manage. In this section, we'll elaborate on what polarities are and how you can spot them.

10.1.1 What are polarities?

Start coding or continue modeling? Centralized decision-making or decentralized decision-making? Planning or action? Stability or change? All of these are examples of polarities that need to be managed instead of problems that can be solved. With polarities, it seems or feels you have to pick one of the two: you're either going to start coding or continue to model for a while. We're either going to strive for stability in this project or we're embracing change and the wobbliness that might come with it. In fact, you need to manage this polarity by knowing when to strive for stability and when to let go to embrace change to stimulate new ideas, get unstuck, and boost creativity.

Polarities are ongoing problems or challenges that have no clear solution in terms of picking one of two sides. We often see groups trying to solve polarities with problem-solving skills that are aimed at choosing one over the other. Trying to solve polarities that way might even make things worse because polarities are interdependent pairs that need each other over time. In other words, you can't choose one over the other permanently. You have to know how to manage the polarity so you can maximize the benefits of both sides.

10.1.2 *Recognizing polarities*

Distinguishing problems to solve from polarities to manage can be really hard. Ever been in a situation where you were focused on and racing to produce short-term deliverables to make sure outside pressure didn't increase, while long-term goals went unaddressed because of it? Or your team wants to invest in interpersonal relationships because that's highly valued, but the team also wants to deliver products, which already takes up almost all of their time? You know you want and need both, but it sometimes feels like you have to pick a side. If you experience this feeling, that's how you know you're dealing with a polarity that requires both/and thinking, instead of a problem that has an either/or solution. To clarify the distinction between a problem and a polarity, consider the following:

- A *problem* has a solution. There is a right, or at least best, answer to the problem you're facing.
- A *polarity* is an ongoing problem or challenge that needs to be managed. It contains seemingly opposing ideas that are actually complementary and interdependent.

GUIDING HEURISTIC When you encounter a difficult dilemma, ask yourself whether this a problem we need to solve or a polarity that we need to manage.

Unmanaged polarities within a group can lead to recurring conflict. As we mentioned earlier in this book: conflict isn't a bad thing, as long as it's functional. The moment it gets dysfunctional—which can happen with unmanaged polarities—you're in trouble. This is why it's crucial to recognize polarities and determine whether you're dealing with a problem that needs to be solved or a polarity that needs to be managed. There are two helpful questions we ask ourselves when we try to figure out which of the two we're dealing with:

1 *Is the difficulty ongoing?* Are you facing a problem or challenge that has a clear endpoint and right—or at least best—answer? Then, you're dealing with a problem you could solve. For example, "Are we going to restaurant A or restaurant B for dinner?" is a clear either/or problem. If you're facing an ongoing challenge that requires balancing seemingly opposite ideas, you're dealing with a polarity. For example, "Should we race to deliver short-term results to keep shareholders off our back, or should we work on our long-term goals that will increase quality?" isn't an either/or decision, but rather a both/and challenge. You want to do both. It's just difficult to know when to move from one side to another and balance both sides.

2 *Are there two poles that are interdependent?* First determine whether or not you're dealing with two poles that are seemingly opposing. Individual versus team focus, working remote or working on-site, and innovation versus efficiency are all examples of seemingly opposing poles. The two poles in these examples are

complementary and interdependent—they need each other over time. Going back and forth between the poles is what will help us manage the polarity. When it comes to problems, there is no interdependency between possible solutions. The solutions can stand alone to be effective. We're either going to restaurant A or restaurant B. One doesn't need the other to be effective.

Table 10.1 summarizes the differences between problems and polarities that we just discussed. Use it to ask yourself which one you're dealing with.

Table 10.1   Distinction between problems and polarities

Problems to Solve	Polarities to Manage
■ Are not ongoing	■ Are ongoing
■ Have a right (or best) answer	■ Are unsolvable
■ Have a clear endpoint	■ No clear endpoint
■ Alternative solutions are independent.	■ Both sides are interdependent and complementary.
Alternative solutions are opposites: ■ Should we go to restaurant A or B? ■ Should we invest thousands of euros into this technology? ■ Should we add an architect to the team? ■ Are we going to buy a new coffee machine?	Sides are seemingly opposite, but aren't: ■ Short term AND Long term ■ Individual AND Team ■ Innovation AND Efficiency ■ Stability AND Change

Once you've established that you're dealing with a polarity, managing it properly is your next step. As a facilitator, there are several things you can do. Section 10.2 provides insights into a technique that helps you visualize the polarity in a polarity map. In any case, it's important to recognize the polarity and distinguish it from a problem. To manage polarities effectively, you must be able to see both perspectives at the same time to be complete in your perspective. Section 10.3 dives into this more. First, however, let's consider some common polarities you'll run across in collaborative modeling.

10.1.3 Common polarities in collaborative modeling

Collaborative modeling is a sociotechnical activity, as you probably realize by now. We put people together in a room and expect them to come up with some sort of an outcome, whether it's a model, a solution, a design, or a plan. All kinds of problems pop up during collaborative modeling sessions: Did we dive into enough detail to decide on boundaries here? Should we just start coding now and then see if we need to go back to modeling? Should we continue talking about the tasks at hand or focus on relationships and discuss how we feel about where we're going? Should we deep dive into individual challenges or only focus on the collective? And as a facilitator, are you maintaining control of the process, or are you empowering others to take the lead?

Polarities are present within the group, within individuals, and within (or between) the facilitator(s). As a facilitator, you have to be able to spot potential polarities and determine what you're going to do with them. Not all polarities need to be addressed during a session. Although they might be relevant, addressing and visualizing them right there and then might not bring any added value. Spotting polarities, validating them with the group, and then letting the group decide if it's worth addressing them (via visualization) on the spot is our usual approach.

GUIDING HEURISTIC   When you, as a facilitator, spot a polarity, validate it with the group, and then ask the group, "Would it add value to dive into this polarity right now (by visualizing it)?"

We've seen a polarity or two when facilitating collaborative modeling sessions. Table 10.2 shows some of the most common ones we've encountered. Let them be pointers for you when you're spotting polarities in the wild.

Table 10.2   Common polarities in collaborative modeling

One Side of the Polarity	The Other Side of the Polarity
Planning (collaborative modeling)	Action (coding)
Individual responsibility	Organizational responsibility
Stability	Change
Thinking fast	Thinking slow
Autocratic decision-making	Democratic decision-making
Centralized	Decentralized
Discussion	Dialogue
Toughness	Empathy
Part (e.g., individual)	Whole (e.g., team)
Task oriented	Relationship oriented
Innovation	Efficiency
Solo programming	Pair programming/ensemble
Short term	Long term
Bottom-up	Top-down

10.1.4 Crusaders and tradition bearers

As mentioned, it's crucial to be able to see both sides of the polarity if you want to manage it effectively. That's where it often goes wrong. We humans have this tendency to be right. And—whenever possible—explain to others why we're right and others are wrong. With polarities, however, there is no right and wrong because it's not either/or, it's both/and.

If we don't put in the effort to see both sides of the polarity, we'll never be complete, which is exactly what we're aiming for with collaborative modeling: creating a complete and shared sense of reality among all involved. This means everyone needs to see both sides of a polarity when it pops up during a collaborative modeling session. As soon as we become solely focused on being right and convincing each other, we'll never be complete.

Before we dive into common polarities in collaborative modeling and show you how to fill in the polarity map, we want to explain the role of crusaders and tradition bearers in polarities. In some cases, discussions on polarities can become very heated. People may have very strong opposite opinions that might lead to conflict. In Barry Johnson's *Polarity Management: Identifying and Managing Unsolvable Problems* (HRD Press, 2014), he talks about how crusader and tradition-bearing forces push for a shift from one side of the polarity to the other. In a polarity, there are *crusaders* and *tradition bearers*:

- *Crusaders*—Those who focus on what needs to change and want things to be different from what they are now, pushing things to the other pole. It's time to move to the other side because we're getting too much of the negative effects of the current side.
- *Tradition bearers*—Those who focus on the power of what is working the way it is right now in the current pole. They aren't in favor of moving to the other side because it might bring all the negatives of that side. Their motto is "If it's not broken, don't fix it."

You can imagine they are on opposite sides in a polarity. They focus on the positives of the side they are on and fear the negative aspects of the opposite side of the polarity. So, both fail to see the positives of the other pole because they experienced the negatives of the opposite side. This is problematic because the goal of managing a polarity is to stay as much as possible in the positives of both sides of the polarity.

When things are heated, both crusaders and tradition bearers might refuse to look at the polarity from the other side because they aren't willing to see the complete picture and understand the opposite perspective. This is a problem because a polarity needs both sides to exist, and we need to find a proper balance between the two sides.

10.2 *Visualizing a polarity*

As consultants, we come across polarities all the time. We actively look for them because we know managing them properly can help a group. Polarities hiding as conflicts can negatively affect collaboration and decision-making. Let's illustrate this with an example: coding versus modeling. After spending quite some time on collaborative modeling, there's often a part of the group that feels it's time to start coding. There are a lot of reasons why they feel this way: some feel that's where the real work happens, they feel stuck in their EventStorm, or they just like the coding part better than the modeling part. The other part of the group doesn't agree with this and wants to continue modeling. They think that continuing will reduce the risk of making costly decisions or mistakes, they want to fine-tune the language further, or they like the collaboration with all the domain experts.

Either way, the group gets torn, and it might turn into conflict. People are trying to convince others of why they are right, coming up with lots of arguments all aimed to get others to their side. They are disagreeing on what to do and wasting valuable energy on this misdiagnosed polarity. Meanwhile, there's not a lot of progress being made on the EventStorm or coding part. So, very often, the group looks at us as the "experts" and asks us what to do.

We know this isn't an either/or problem where we pick one of two options. We classify this as a polarity and introduce polarity management to deal with it. Mapping out the polarity at hand together with the group provides insight into the upsides and downsides of both sides, and it helps us recognize when we should move from one side to another. More specifically, it helps us see when we need to move from modeling to coding and the other way around. This is what we mean by managing the polarity. Done properly, the visualization exercise can do the following:

- Provide a complete picture of both sides.
- Visualize diversity and encourage you to look at something from different perspectives.
- Bring people closer together instead of alienating groups that focus on the differences in the perceived conflict.
- Provide predictability on how to move between the different poles based on shared agreements.

You can visualize a polarity with a polarity map. A *polarity map* (as described in *Polarity Management: Identifying and Managing Unsolvable Problems*, mentioned previously) is a simple visualization tool that will help you manage a polarity, as shown in figure 10.1. In this section, we'll walk through a polarity map, using the "Deep versus Wide" question we often get when modeling with a group of people.

When managing polarities, there are two main things you want to do:

- Create a shared understanding of the polarity.
- Visualize how the group will manage it.

10.2.1 Creating a shared understanding of a polarity

The first thing you need to do when managing a polarity is get a clear picture of the polarity. On the map shown in figure 10.1, we have four quadrants: two on the left (L) to represent one pole, and two on the right (R) to represent the other pole. Each pole has positive and negative effects, which are shown on the map with a plus and minus sign, respectively. If we combine those two, we get four quadrants: L+, L–, R+, and R– (figure 10.2).

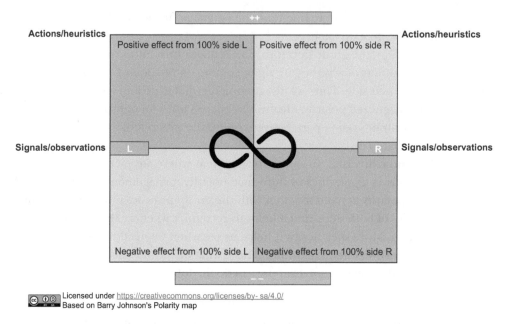

Licensed under https://creativecommons.org/licenses/by- sa/4.0/
Based on Barry Johnson's Polarity map

Figure 10.1   Empty polarity map

When you're stuck in a pole for too long, you forget there are benefits to the other pole. When you don't want to change poles, you can only see the downside that the other pole will bring. With both sides come positive and negative effects, and we want to bring back a shared understanding of the polarity and its effects. That is why we fill in the four quadrants on the polarity map first. In our example of the Deep versus Wide polarity, we placed Deep on the left side, which means the following:

- L+, the upside of Deep, represents all the positive effects we get from modeling in detail.
- L−, the downside of Deep, are all the negative effects we get from only modeling in detail.

On the right side, we have Wide:

- R+, the upside of Wide, represents all the positive effects we get from modeling something end to end.
- R−, the downside of Wide, are all the negative effects we get from only modeling something end to end.

Placing Deep on the left and Wide on the right was an arbitrary choice, it doesn't matter which polarity goes on which side. Furthermore, the Upside of Wide is connected to the Downside of Deep, and vice versa because the negative effects of one pole will be part of the positive effects of the other pole. One of the negative effects of modeling

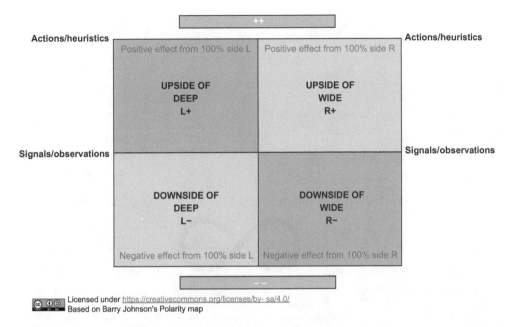

Licensed under https://creativecommons.org/licenses/by- sa/4.0/
Based on Barry Johnson's Polarity map

Figure 10.2 The four quadrants of a polarity map, representing the positive and negative effects of each pole. An alternative way to talk about positive and negative effects of a pole are the upside and downside of that pole.

something end to end is that you have a lot of questions and assumptions because you're at a very high level. Modeling in detail will give you answers to the questions and assumptions.

When you fill in the positive and negative sides of each pole, as we did for the Event-Storm Deep versus Wide polarity in figure 10.3, you need to think in extremes: What happens if we only model in detail/end to end?

A balanced polarity brings us the positive effects of both poles. We called these positive effects Solution-Oriented Modeling, and we called the negative effects Concealed Modeling, as shown in figure 10.3. Giving the positive and negative effects of a name makes it easier to talk about: "We want solution-oriented modeling and want to avoid concealed modeling." What we mean by this is that we want to experience as much of the positive effects of modeling deep *and* wide, and we want to avoid the negative effects of modeling deep *or* wide for too long.

INFINITY SYMBOL

In the middle of the four quadrants, there is a big lemniscate, or infinity symbol, touching all the quadrants (refer to figure 10.3). The lemniscate is a reminder of the never-ending balance you need to find when managing a polarity.

There are actions that you'll need to take when you start experiencing too much of the downside of one pole. Those actions will move you to the opposite quadrant, the upside of the other pole. We'll discuss this further in section 10.2.2.

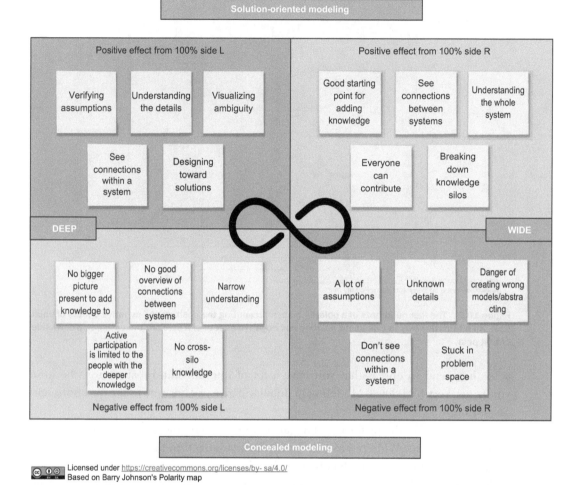

Solution-oriented modeling

Positive effect from 100% side L

Verifying assumptions | Understanding the details | Visualizing ambiguity

See connections within a system | Designing toward solutions

Positive effect from 100% side R

Good starting point for adding knowledge | See connections between systems | Understanding the whole system

Everyone can contribute | Breaking down knowledge silos

DEEP   **WIDE**

No bigger picture present to add knowledge to | No good overview of connections between systems | Narrow understanding

Active participation is limited to the people with the deeper knowledge | No cross-silo knowledge

A lot of assumptions | Unknown details | Danger of creating wrong models/abstracting

Don't see connections within a system | Stuck in problem space

Negative effect from 100% side L   Negative effect from 100% side R

Concealed modeling

Licensed under https://creativecommons.org/licenses/by-sa/4.0/
Based on Barry Johnson's Polarity map

Figure 10.3   The filled-in quadrants of the polarity map. After filling this in, we have a better understanding of the positive and negative effects of the Deep versus Wide polarity.

FILLING IN THE QUADRANTS

You can fill in the four quadrants any way you like, but we want to give you three helpful ways to do this: easiest, minority first, and hardest. The easiest way to fill in the quadrants is very straightforward. You start in the down left quadrant (L–), followed by R–. After that you fill in L+ and R+, respectively. This is shown in figure 10.4. This is the easiest way because it's a lot easier for people to think of negative effects. The positive effects can then be deducted from the negative ones of the other pole.

As we mentioned in the previous chapter, it's important to get the minority on board too. If there is a clear division between crusaders and tradition bearers, you can start by examining the viewpoint of the minority. This means that you start with the negative effects of the opposite pole that holds the minority. It sounds confusing, we know, so let's clarify with an example. In our Deep versus Wide polarity, modeling the domain Deep holds the minority. We put this on the left side of the map. We want to get the minority viewpoint first, so we start with the negative effects that Wide will give us. After that, you just follow the infinity loop again, which would give you R–, L+, R+, L–, as shown in figure 10.5.

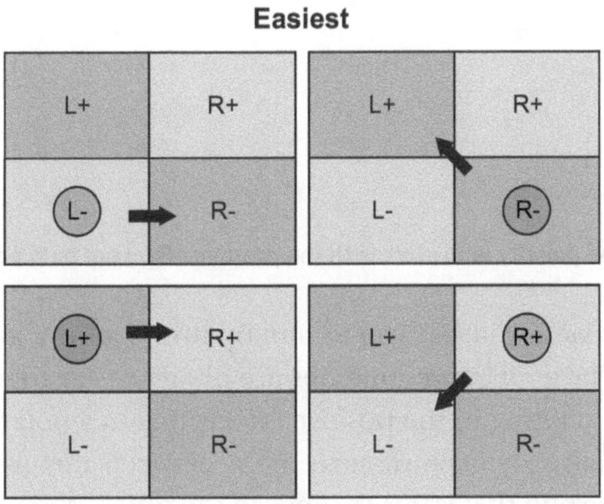

Easiest

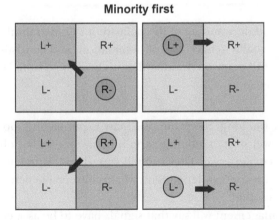

Figure 10.4   If you want to pick the easiest way to fill in the quadrants, start with L– and fill in the negative effects of both poles first with the group.

Minority first

Figure 10.5   The minority first way of filling in the quadrants. In this example, the pole of the minority was placed on the right side of the map, which is why we start with R–.

The hardest way to fill in a polarity map is to start with the positive sides of both poles (figure 10.6). The reason this is the hardest way is that it's a lot easier for people to come up with downsides than it is to come up with upsides of something.

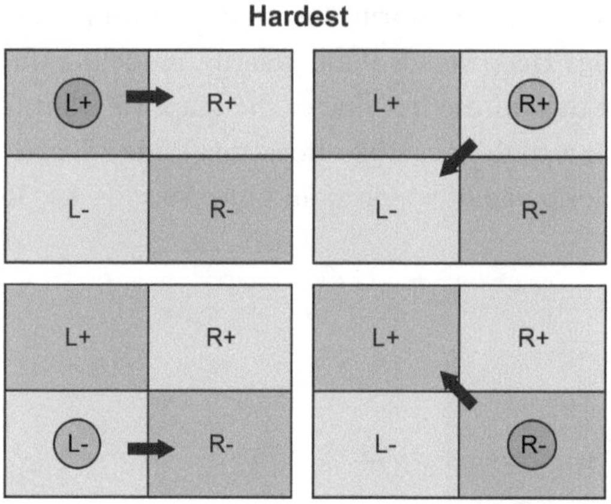

Hardest

Figure 10.6   The hardest way to fill in the polarity is to start with the positive effects of both poles.

Just think about all those job interviews that ask you to sum up three positive and three negative things about yourself. Those negative qualities are always easier to come up with. Yet there are a few benefits to filling in the positive effects first in a polarity map. Often, but not always, there has already been disagreement between the group that wants to stay in one pole and the group that wants to move to the other. When expressing this disagreement, a lot of the negative effects are mentioned. If you want to get people back into a positive mindset, remind them that *both* poles are needed to find a balance, and adding the positive effects will achieve that.

10.2.2 *Managing the polarity*

Now that we've created a shared understanding of the polarity, it's time to think about managing it with the group. The goal is to have a set of observations and heuristics that you can use when modeling that will help you decide when it's time to go from Deep to Wide and vice versa.

SIGNALS

If you get stuck in one pole for too long, the group will start experiencing too many downsides of that pole. People will start exhibiting certain behavior—called observations or signals—because of this experience. They will tell you when it's time to move to the other pole. These signals are context-dependent: what is observable behavior in one group, won't be present in another.

Some sources on polarity management will say that signals have to be as specific as possible. For example, a signal would be "Checking your watch three times" instead of "Checking your watch." We prefer to stay focused on managing the polarity instead of reaching thresholds. If you, as the facilitator, noticed that in the last 2 minutes, 4 people in a group of 10 checked their watches, it might be time to move to the other pole. You could also give a climate report, as we described in chapter 8. It's very important to stay neutral, as we mentioned in chapter 5, so add no interpretation to the observed behavior. We recommend giving signals a threshold when you start using the polarity map and then slowly move away from that.

ACTIONS

Now that we know what to look for, it's time to think about moving between the two poles. To get unstuck, you need to take steps to move to the other pole. These are called actions or heuristics. Signals and actions are connected; an action can be specific for a single signal (one-to-one) or work for many (one-to-many).

In our Deep versus Wide example (figure 10.7) we identified a few one-to-many actions. You can move away from confused participants by brainstorming what is still missing or modeling another scenario.

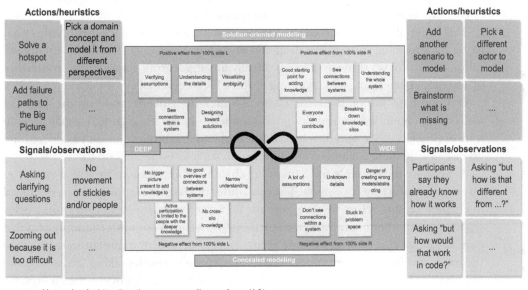

Licensed under https://creativecommons.org/licenses/by-sa/4.0/
Based on Barry Johnson's Polarity map

Figure 10.7 Complete polarity map of Deep versus Wide

Exercise 10.1

Fill in the polarity map for the Collaborative Modeling versus Coding polarity. Start with filling in the quadrants for both poles. Then, fill in the signals that you notice in your team, and try to find good actions for every signal.

10.3 *Managing polarities during collaborative modeling*

Now, let's delve into how we can adeptly manage polarities during collaborative modeling. To illustrate this concept, we'll present an example from a value chain mapping session we conducted. *Value chain mapping* is the initial phase of Wardley Mapping, focusing on the vertical axis. Conceived by Simon Wardley, *Wardley Mapping* is a strategic mapping tool that offers organizations a lens to perceive their competitive landscape. By delineating the evolution of components in their value chain, companies can harness actionable insights, guiding them toward sound strategic decisions. You'll learn more about Wardley Mapping in chapter 12.

This initial phase of Wardley Mapping that includes Team boundaries, has been referred to as "user needs mapping" by Rich Allen and Matthew Skelton of Team Topologies ("Exploring Team and Service Boundaries with User Needs Mapping," https://mng.bz/x2P6), emphasizing user needs because that usually is forgotten in organizations. Their approach uses the map to explore team and service boundaries with Team Topologies. Our exploration will take a similar approach to look for a series of interconnected capabilities in our value chain that teams could take ownership of.

This series of interconnected capabilities that a team can take ownership of is what we term a streamlet. A *streamlet* is designed to support a sequence of activities an organization uses to deliver those user needs. Ideally, an engineering team can take ownership of a streamlet, operating and changing it with a high degree of autonomy.

Our emphasis was on the value chain of a user, their needs, and how they interact with our new bounded context design, subsequently integrating it into our existing software architecture. We opted to bypass the horizontal axis of evolution to concentrate on discovering these streamlets and how teams can take ownership on them.

As we share the example from the value chain mapping session, we'll also guide you on how to conduct such a session. The remainder of Wardley Mapping will be discussed in chapter 12. But before we dive into our BigScreen narrative, let's reflect on a prior session with another organization where there was a gap in our understanding of polarities. In that specific setting, we came across a frequent polarity in the software industry: the tug-of-war between centralized and decentralized decision-making. So, grab some popcorn; it's time to delve deep into a pressing topic in the tech world—the emergence of autonomous teams!

10.3.1 *Getting stuck in a polarity*

The company that sought our consulting services was in a similar situation to BigScreen's: grappling with a massive, complicated monolithic application that looked like a big ball of mud (BBoM). Furthermore, four different teams were working on this application simultaneously. The concept of microservices architecture was trending at the time, being hailed as the ideal solution for teams striving for more autonomy in software development. The company requested our guidance to transition from their monolithic system to a microservices architecture.

To tackle this, we adopted a method similar to what we described in our book. We arranged collaborative modeling sessions that included all developer teams and key stakeholders. While modeling out the current state, we found that the monolith wasn't completely a BBoM, because it did have some bounded contexts. All the teams had ownership of their own bounded contexts, but those bounded contexts were coupled through what we in Domain-Driven Design (DDD) call a shared kernel pattern. In *Domain-Driven Design: Tackling Complexity in the Heart of Software* by Eric Evans, a "shared kernel" refers to a specific subset of the domain model with a clearly defined boundary that multiple teams have agreed to share. This kernel should be kept concise. Within this boundary, you should not only include this specific subset of the model, but also the relevant portion of code or the associated database design. Anything within this shared kernel holds special significance and shouldn't be altered without consulting the other team. This concept becomes crucial when you have separate models that all rely on a shared model, as shown in figure 10.8.

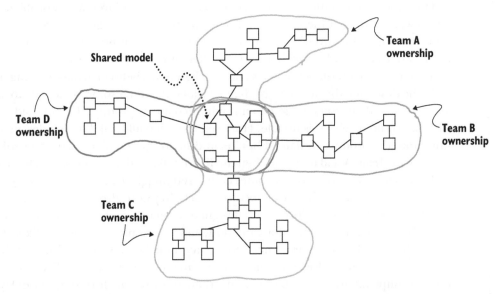

Figure 10.8 **A shared kernel pattern. Four teams each own their own bounded context, but they share a model. Every time that model is affected, they need to talk to the other teams to change it.**

A shared kernel requires frequent meetings to synchronize changes and ensure that all teams were aligned, which, while necessary, did decrease their autonomy and block there flow of development. In this context, *autonomy* refers to the ability of the teams to make decisions and progress independently without needing constant alignment or approval from others. When one team required the shared model to be changed, all the other teams had to be consulted and potentially needed to change parts of their model as well. That lowers the time to market, as the team is unable to release new features until the other teams have fixed those parts of their model. That additional coordination slows the time to market even more. Additionally, with the application being deployed as a monolith, all programming and library versions were shared. Upgrading these versions can be challenging, as it potentially affects code from another team, which requires more coordination on testing such upgrades. Therefore, the teams were eagerly anticipating the shift toward microservices, hoping for more autonomy, including the ability to manage version upgrades independently.

We guided them through this transition, ensuring that the teams could keep developing new features while moving the bounded context from the application to a microservices architecture. Over a year, most of the core software components were shifted to this new architecture, thereby reducing the frequency of changes to the shared kernel part of the system. We used a legacy as a service pattern on the shared kernel, which lowered the number of changes to the kernel. The weekly meetings at some point didn't have any agenda points anymore, so the teams decided to cancel those meetings and let the tech leads align once a change was actually to be made. Because there was a proper API now, changes within the team's own models would not affect the other teams much.

However, a few months later, we were called in again to address a new problem: most teams were finding it increasingly difficult to implement bigger feature requests on their backlogs. Our investigation revealed that each team now had full control over their own backlog and made their own architectural decisions. However, the increased autonomy led to interdependencies and misalignments between teams, causing delays.

While designing the new feature, Team A stated that their software needed to inform Team B once their users designed and published a new product. Team B had a REST API that could receive this update. However, the call could fail if it included new attributes that the product contained but Team B hadn't yet configured in their software. This meant Team A had to signal when the REST call failed and then send a Jira request to Team B to configure those attributes before retrying the call. Team A expressed their desire to use an event-driven architecture, which they were already using in their team. They proposed sending a "product is designed" domain event as a message to Team B. Team B can then handle that domain event, and if attributes are missing, fix it straight away. That way, Team A doesn't need to create Jira tickets anymore. However, Team B wasn't using an event-driven architecture or any messaging system. They were interested in implementing this, but it wasn't their priority, which resulted in delays and wasted time on alignment discussions.

The problem was that when we arrived, the organization was focused on a centralized decision-making approach. The pain of that focus on centralized decision-making led them to desire a transition to a more decentralized, autonomous decision-making process. However, at that time, neither we nor the organization were aware of the concept of polarities. As a result, the pendulum swung the other way—to decentralization—but without managing the polarity. Focusing too long on one polarity leads to experiencing the downsides of the other; in this case, the teams were waiting on each other. We initially thought we were resolving a problem related to team autonomy, but, in reality, we were dealing with a polarity. This was a valuable lesson that we learned and applied differently with BigScreen.

10.3.2 *Managing a polarity as facilitator*

From our experience, conflicts arise when both/and polarities are being treated like either/or problems. Start coding or continue to model? People can try to convince each other why they are right, and it should be one of the two sides. When you observe this as a facilitator, this is your cue to address and manage the polarity. We do this by making the polarity explicit first. For example, we use a sensemaking exercise by putting both polarities at opposite ends of a line and asking people where they stand. Or we give a climate report. Then, once the group collectively recognizes the polarity, we suggest to collectively fill in a polarity map to manage it properly, or we'll let the group decide to let us manage the polarity for them during that session.

During our value chain mapping at BigScreen, we noticed the Deep versus Wide polarity affecting the group, something that we had observed in earlier sessions. As facilitators, one is always weighing the decision: Should you intervene by subtly guiding the group, or should you enable them to navigate the polarity on their own? Each situation calls for its own unique approach. Giving the group the wisdom to handle the polarity is a gradual process. Initially, we tried to handle the polarity within the group, mirroring our approach from prior sessions.

> **GUIDING HEURISTIC**   Use the polarity that the group is affected by as polarized questions in your check-in or sensemaking.

After clarifying the outcome and reviewing the agenda, we prompted the group to outline the user journey for the "Anytime, Anywhere" campaign. This journey begins with the planning and scheduling of a movie screening and culminates with attendees receiving their tickets. Typically, our starting point in a value chain is the user and their core needs. While the core needs of a movie visitor are that they get a good seat and enjoy the movie, the act of paying for tickets and selecting seats isn't their primary need. However, given that the user journey had already been designed and guided by these core needs, we chose to leave them out of this specific value chain mapping and only model out the activity in the user journey.

By making this autocratic decision as facilitators, the first signs of the Deep versus Wide polarity began to emerge. There was a discussion among the participants about whether we needed to delve further into the core needs of the users on the map. We had clearly outlined that the goal was to find streamlets that teams could take ownership of, but some individuals wanted to delve deeper into the user's needs. This posed a challenge to our neutrality: on the one hand, we wanted the group to decide on the direction; on the other hand, as consultants, we had our own stake in coming up with a design.

USING PROPOSALS TO MOVE THE GROUP FORWARD

The first thing we did was revert to our role fluidity skills as mentioned in chapter 9 and question why we needed to delve deeper into the user needs. Why would it be necessary? The response was that the group wanted to verify whether UX had made the correct assumptions when designing the user journey. Some individuals, who weren't part of the initial decisions, found it challenging to grasp the details and see their connection to the user's needs. So, we asked who could somewhat relate to not seeing the connection. Some developers raised their hands. However, when we asked who sees it differently, quite a few people didn't see the value of delving deeper. They believed that it would overemphasize user research and cause us to lose time exploring the connections between the systems.

GUIDING HEURISTIC   Make a proposal autocratic decision for the team to manage a polarity when the polarity is affecting the goal of the session. You should connect all the needs in the proposal.

In this instance, we noticed that most people in the group aligned with the session's goal. Thus, we made a proposal to the group, explaining that we would continue and, after finishing this session, we could delve deeper into the user's needs or plan a follow-up session to do so. We asked if anyone had serious objections to this proposal, and what they need to go along. No one responded, and everyone seemed fine with the decision, allowing us to proceed and eventually ending up with what is shown in figure 10.9. We were prepared that the polarity of going deep into the user's needs versus going wide and finishing the map would arise. By employing role fluidity and using a proposal for decision-making, we could guide the group toward the goal, placing the responsibility of the session in their hands.

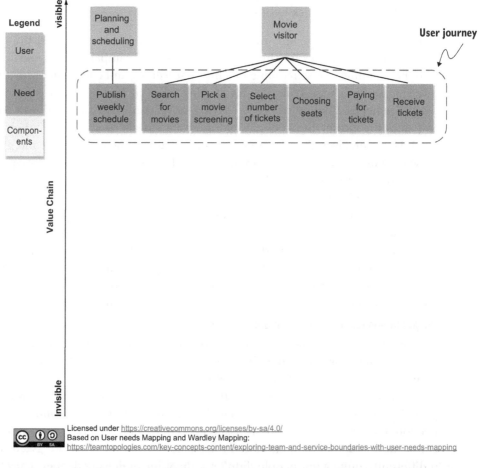

Licensed under https://creativecommons.org/licenses/by-sa/4.0/
Based on User needs Mapping and Wardley Mapping:
https://teamtopologies.com/key-concepts-content/exploring-team-and-service-boundaries-with-user-needs-mapping

Figure 10.9   The first step of mapping the landscape is a value chain. In this case, we didn't map the actual user needs, but kept it to the activities models as needs that were already designed to solve those actual needs in a user journey.

Note that we were fairly confident that the majority of the group wanted to proceed with the session and go wide, instead of going deep. We also clearly established the workshop's goal. We observed the downside behavior that happens when we stay in the Deep polarity, and we included a solution in our decision for those who wanted to go deeper on user research. Only by incorporating all of these aspects into our proposal could we make that autocratic decision without sacrificing neutrality. Unfortunately, this isn't always the case.

USING CLIMATE REPORTS TO LET THE GROUP DEAL WITH A POLARITY

After clarifying the users and the user journey, we adopted the Small Group Diverge and Converge collaboration style, which we mentioned in chapter 4. We formed groups of four to five participants, who then collectively mapped out the value chain for approximately 40 minutes. It's difficult to use a group of more than seven people for a value chain because the modeling space is limited. In addition, individuals who perceive themselves as lower-ranking often become silent and passive in larger groups. Therefore, our preference is for smaller groups, even though managing multiple groups can be challenging.

We tasked the groups with initially finishing the value chain by adding all the components of the software architecture that solves the user needs. In Wardley Mapping, these are known as *capabilities*, but because we solely focus on the software architecture, we rephrased them specifically for this session to *components* of the system. We closely observed the groups for any signs of drawbacks associated with a wide approach. Some of them started to debate after completing the map and going into greater detail. They began making assumptions due to unknown details in the current systems about the logic that is happening in the Movies component. Figure 10.10 shows what they were discussing.

The discussion revolved around how the back-office components Movies Pages, Movie Screening Page, and Seat Picker connected with the Movies component. Some group participants felt it was essential to understand these details as they believed it was critical to delve deep to be able to design toward a solution and visualize ambiguity. Others in the group didn't want to get overly detailed at this stage but preferred to stay wide and focus on the components in the current system to understand the whole system first.

At this point, we observed both deep and wide positive and negative effects emerging in the conversation. You can also recognize these effects from figure 10.6 earlier in this chapter. Previously, we had made a decision to keep the scope wide and avoid delving into user needs. Yet now, as polarities are, we often find ourselves confronted by both sides once again. Despite not fully developing the software architecture in line with user needs, we're unable to prescribe the best approach for the group. We couldn't facilitate decision-making to address their concerns, as they would likely face the same challenges in subsequent stages of the project. Our primary role was to pinpoint the existing polarity and devise strategies to help them navigate it.

About 25 minutes into the breakout session, we asked for the group's attention and provided a climate report (as explained in chapter 8). We informed them that all groups had completed the map, and some groups were now debating the level of detail

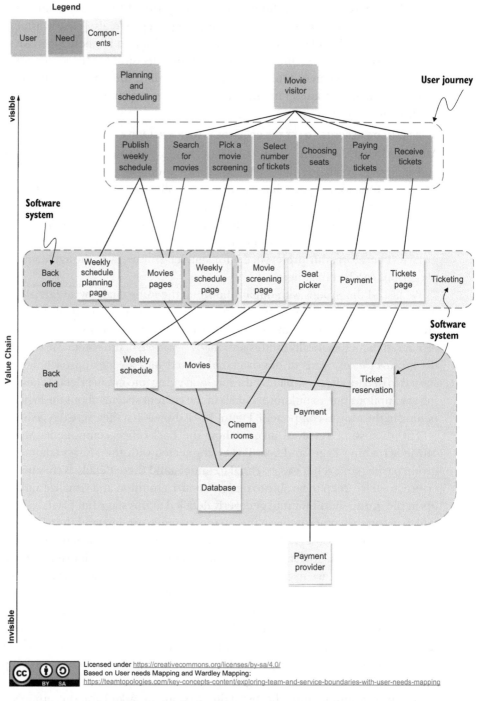

Licensed under https://creativecommons.org/licenses/by-sa/4.0/
Based on User needs Mapping and Wardley Mapping:
https://teamtopologies.com/key-concepts-content/exploring-team-and-service-boundaries-with-user-needs-mapping

Figure 10.10   The completed map is very simple, only showing a few components in the back office and backend. A lot of connections go to the movies part of the backend, and some believe they should further deep dive to better understand what is happening there.

necessary for the modeling. These discussions were preventing them from progressing on the map. We saw people acknowledging by nodding, so we told the group "I notice some members of the group nodding their heads." One person began to speak but was immediately interrupted by someone else, which is typical when dealing with a polarity.

> **GUIDING HEURISTIC**   Use a climate report to make the group aware that they are dealing with a polarity.

After letting the discussion go on for a few minutes, it was time for another climate report: "We observed a lot of back and forth conversation with frequent interruptions." The group became silent, and we allowed a pause for a minute. Someone then mentioned the frequent debates on how wide and deep they should go and how it often resulted in a heated discussion, impeding their progress. We proposed a short intermezzo to the session to collectively explore the deep vs width polarity, hoping it would help us move forward in the session. The group agreed, and we initiated a *conversation on four feet* from the Lewis Deep Democracy method (www.lewisdeepdemocracy.com). Let's dive into what a conversation on four feet is.

VISUALIZING THE POLARITY WITH A CONVERSATION ON FOUR FEET

A conversation on four feet is a useful exercise when groups get stuck in a polarity but aren't fully aware of it, or they can't quite grasp what the polarity is exactly. Our goal was to let the group explore and reflect on both sides and make the polarity evident. Many polarized groups tend to *listen to react* to get their point across instead of *listening to understand* the other person. They often focus more on arguing rather than having a dialogue. If this continues unchecked, decisions made will be heavily influenced by whichever polarity holds a majority in the group. This can lead to a binary either/or outcome. We aim for a both/and situation, so we need participants to understand both sides.

> **GUIDING HEURISTIC**   Use the conversation on four feet method to nudge people into listening to understand as opposed to listening to react.

In the conversation on four feet, enabling constraints are placed to ensure groups listen to understand. The setup involves a group standing with enough space to move around. It begins with someone presenting a statement to the group, followed by the facilitator standing next to that person and using active listening to clarify the statement if necessary. The facilitator then instructs the rest of the group to either stand behind the person if they agree with the statement or to find a place opposite that person if they disagree. The facilitator then approaches someone opposite the statement and asks them to speak up. Figure 10.11 gives a visual representation of the process.

By using the enabling constraint of not being able to reply directly, people need to first understand what has been said and then take a position in the group. It's important to state up front that if anyone doesn't want to speak up or take the spotlight, they can always move with the majority of the group, so we can make it safe for people who don't want to take a stand. As a facilitator, it's beneficial to keep a close watch on those who choose to do so, and perhaps converse with them privately after the session to under-stand their needs. Typically, the conversation lasts around 10–15 minutes before the group divides into two larger groups, and statements start to cycle back and forth. At this point, as a facilitator, you should halt the conversation and ask the group to share their observations.

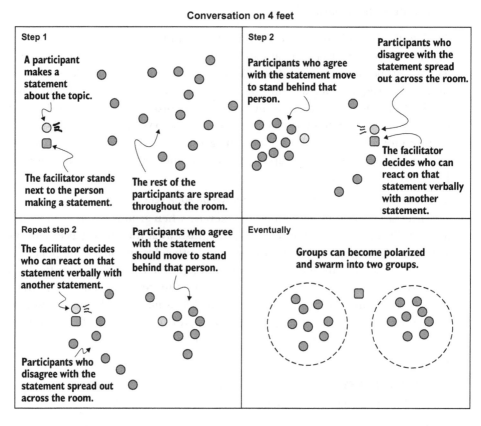

Conversation on 4 feet

Step 1

A participant makes a statement about the topic.

The facilitator stands next to the person making a statement.

The rest of the participants are spread throughout the room.

Step 2

Participants who agree with the statement move to stand behind that person.

Participants who disagree with the statement spread out across the room.

The facilitator decides who can react on that statement verbally with another statement.

Repeat step 2

The facilitator decides who can react on that statement verbally with another statement.

Participants who agree with the statement should move to stand behind that person.

Participants who disagree with the statement spread out across the room.

Eventually

Groups can become polarized and swarm into two groups.

Figure 10.11   Conversation on four feet starts with Step 1, in which one participant gives out a statement. Then, the group moves to Step 2, where either they agree and stand with the person giving the statement, or they disagree. At that point, the facilitator turns to someone disagreeing to give another statement. Eventually, you can see the group polarize.

Role mapping

Role mapping is another technique within the Lewis Deep Democracy method that also can be seen as a collaborative modeling tool by identifying the various roles within a given session. The initial step is to engage the group in brainstorming to uncover all the relevant roles; this, however, does require the group to have a basic understanding of what a role is. This understanding is crucial, as visualizing these roles not only aids in identification but also fosters a sense of fluidity and adaptability among participants.

Once identified, the group progresses to categorizing these roles, focusing on their inter-actions and how they align or contrast with each other. This step is instrumental in high-lighting the underlying tensions and identifying the dominant polarity facing the group. By categorizing roles in this manner, the group gains insights into the dynamics at play and can effectively group and categorize these in polarities. The map then clarifies the dominant polarity they are dealing with, so the team can use it as input on a polarity map.

After the observations were shared, we presented the group with two choices:

- *Polarity mapping*—We could guide them in managing this polarity through polar-ity mapping. This approach might divert our focus from the primary session's objectives, possibly requiring an additional session to accomplish our initial goals.
- *Facilitator-led polarity management*—Alternatively, we could consolidate the group's inputs into a single value chain map. As facilitators, we would manage the polar-ity and determine when to explore certain topics in-depth and when to adopt a broader perspective.

We asked if it was okay to put this to a vote, and no one in the group seemed to dis-agree. The vote ended with a majority favoring the merging of maps and letting us decide when to delve deeply and when to broaden the scope. For the minority, we added two things to the decision: to organize a polarity mapping session in the future, and to mark the parts that people wanted to delve into so that we could decide at the end of the session what to do with those areas. Everyone agreed, and so we continued the session.

We could now continue the session and finish the value chain map. You can see a simplified version in figure 10.12. The group gave us the authority to decide when to move on and when not to. We still needed to be careful not to lose that rank and avoid making a decision that would create too much resistance. Therefore, using the hotspots and continually observing the group behavior remained important. Even though the session ended the way we needed it to, we're not yet beyond that polarity. As we, the facilitators, are managing the polarity, the group is now dependent on us. As a result, any design session the group is doing will be affected by this polarity, and being depen-dent on the facilitator can serve as a bottleneck. I mean, even facilitators need to go on vacation sometimes. So, it's important before going to a check-out to address how we'll go forward with managing the polarity. Because we're responsible for managing that polarity, it's important to do a polarity mapping session with the participants.

10.3.3 Letting the group manage the polarity

We've already discussed in this chapter how we can use a polarity map to visualize a polarity. A polarity mapping session is also a collaborative modeling session, where we model how we want to manage the polarity. You can approach this session similarly to

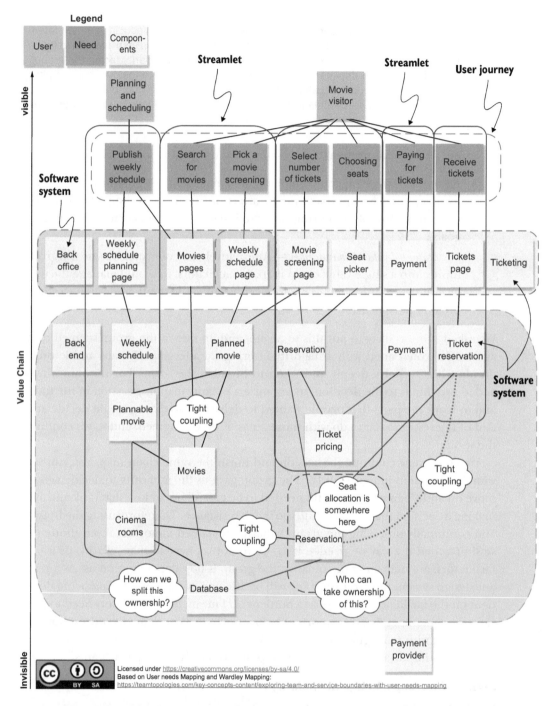

Figure 10.12   The simplified value chain map of the current situation. The text bubbles are hotspots where we can deep dive deeper if needed. Vertically rounded boxes that group together needs and components represent possible streamlets that can help split up the teams.

any other discussed in this book and use the six stages mentioned in chapter 4 to prepare for that session. You can incorporate the polarity in your check-in, during which we typically ask the group what happens when people delve too deep or spread too wide, and what they do to avoid it. This check-in can nudge the group to contemplate signals and actions for later on in the session.

In the case of BigScreen, we chose to divide the group into smaller groups, each having people from both polarities equally represented. During the conversation on 4 feet, we sensed that both sides were equally represented, so we initiated the session by asking each group to list all positive aspects of diving deep and spreading wide for about 7 minutes. After 7 minutes, we asked them to switch to the negatives. Then, we asked them to silently walk around and observe the other maps, and then return to their groups to further discuss any differences they saw in other groups. We also prompted them to think about their greatest fear of not managing the polarity and what they would like to achieve when managing it.

With a comprehensive overview of the polarity per group, we invited the group to take a break before delving into the signals/observations and actions/heuristics part of the map. While the first part of mapping the polarity doesn't require a lot of facilitation, the second part typically does. Some groups excel at describing the observations/signals, but others find it challenging. When groups get stuck, we often suggest that they first contemplate what situations would make them feel affected by the polarity. In the case of BigScreen, they noticed that it always occurs when software architecture decisions need to be made. Having that in mind, we ask them what they observe happening. You can see that outcome in the map we presented earlier in figure 10.7.

As stated previously in section 10.2, it's essential that our observations are concrete. For instance, confusion was identified as an observation in the figure. But how do we pinpoint this? What tangible behaviors or verbal cues indicate confusion? Maybe we observe no movement of people or stickies on the board, individuals asking a multitude of clarifying questions, or nonverbal cues such as frowning.

To ensure everyone is on the same page about when an observation such as confusion is taking place, it's imperative we establish clear criteria. In collaboration with the group, we've agreed that every time we assume there might be confusion to conduct a sensemaking exercise. If more than three people in the group express feeling confused, it signals that we need to take action. Crucially, these observational criteria and the subsequent actions must be accepted by the group. This collective agreement ensures that polarity is effectively managed by everyone involved.

Now that the observations and actions are accepted by the group, the group can start managing the polarity. Every time the group actively observes the signals discussed, they now know how to act based on the map. Over time, it will become the norm, and people will start to unconsciously show the behavior based on the signals without actively needing to observe the signals. Over time, the group will eventually encounter another polarity that will require active management, and that's why a polarity can't be solved but always needs to be managed.

10.4   Collaborative software design catalysts

- Write down some polarities you're observing or struggling with in your own context. Specify why these are polarities that need to be managed instead of problems that need to be solved.

- Identify one or two polarities that are significantly affecting (or hindering) you and the people you're working with. Bring them to the group as sensemaking or climate report to validate and discuss, and suggest visualizing the polarities.

- Find a moment to visualize the polarity together with the group. Use the polarity map from this chapter, including actions and signals. Discuss insights and outcomes afterward.

10.5   Chapter heuristics

Guiding heuristics

- When you encounter a difficult dilemma, ask yourself whether this a problem we need to solve or a polarity that we need to manage.

- When you, as a facilitator, spot a polarity, validate it with the group, and then ask the group, "Would it add value to dive into this polarity right now (by visualizing it)?"

- Use the polarity that the group is affected by as polarized questions in your check-in or sensemaking.

- Make a proposal autocratic decision for the team to manage a polarity when the polarity is affecting the goal of the session. You should connect all the needs in the proposal.

- Use a climate report to make the group aware that they are dealing with a polarity.

- Use the conversation on four feet method to nudge people into listening to understand as opposed to listening to react.

10.6   Further reading

- "Exploring Team and Service Boundaries with User Needs Mapping" by Rich Allen and Matthew Skelton (https://mng.bz/x2P6)

- *Polarity Management: Identifying and Managing Unsolvable Problems* by Barry Johnson (HRD Press, 2014)

Summary

- Polarities represent ongoing problems or challenges that can't be resolved by picking one side over the other; they are interdependent pairs that need to be managed over time to maximize the benefits of both sides.

- Proper polarity management can improve group collaboration and decision-making by providing insights into the advantages and disadvantages of each side, visualizing diversity, encouraging various perspectives, bringing people together, and creating predictability on transitioning between different poles based on shared agreements.

- As a facilitator, it's crucial to recognize potential polarities within a group or individual, validate them, and then allow the group to decide whether to address them.

- A polarity map is a visualization tool for managing polarities; it helps create a shared understanding of a polarity's positive and negative effects, encouraging thinking in extremes, balancing between poles, and facilitating easier communication about effects.

- When completing a polarity map, starting with the negative effects can often be easier due to human bias toward identifying downsides, and sometimes it's important to involve the minority viewpoint first to ensure all perspectives are accounted for.

- Managing a polarity involves recognizing context-dependent signals indicative of an imbalance and then taking appropriate actions or heuristics to move toward the other pole. Practicing this with a polarity map aids in identifying these signals and determining effective actions, ultimately ensuring a balanced approach to the polar problems at hand.

Communicating and documenting decisions

This chapter covers

- Formalizing decisions using Pros-Cons-and-Fixes lists and Architectural Decision Records
- Spreading knowledge through the company
- Approaching your modeling process as a whirlpool of feedback loops

In chapter 9, we touched on the decision process and creating sustainability in that process. What comes after is communicating and documenting those decisions. In this chapter, we'll talk about two documentation tools that will help you communicate decisions to your future team. We'll also discuss how to spread the decision through the company so that everybody is informed in the right way. Lastly, we mentioned that you can't make a decision and blindly follow the course of action that comes with it. The context in which you make decisions changes as you uncover information you didn't have while making the decisions, which is why you need to keep your design decisions alive.

11.1 Formalizing a decision

If you've ever tried to understand a previous decision made by someone else, you know how hard it can be to understand what others were thinking when they made it. An important part of any decision is formalizing it, so that our future selves have access to the decision. There are two things you need to do to formalize a decision:

- Find the consequences of the chosen alternative.
- Capture the decision on paper.

Let's start by looking at finding the consequences.

11.1.1 Finding the consequences

In chapter 9, we ended up with a majority of the votes for the third design. As you can see in figure 11.1, the final design, which we showed in chapter 1, and the design that got the most votes, are still different from one another. This is because we haven't yet looked at the consequences of the design on the left.

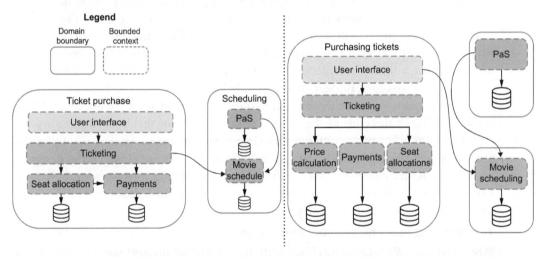

Figure 11.1 The design that received the most votes, 16 to 2, of the group (left) and the final design (right)

There is a Dutch saying "*Wie z'n billen brandt, moet op de blaren zitten*," which translates to "Who burns their bottom, must sit on blisters." In other words, when you do something, especially when it's stupid, you have to live with the consequences. Yet, we rarely take a moment to write down what the consequences are of an alternative. One important thing we realized is that visualized discussions are better at reaching a conclusion than simply talking about it. The technique also needs to be easy to use. One of those easy structures to visualize the consequences of an alternative you designed during a collaborative modeling session is the Pros-Cons-and-Fixes[1] list. We found it to be very

---

[1] Jones, M. D. *The Thinker's Toolkit: 14 Powerful Techniques for Problem Solving,* 1998. New York: Crown Currency (p. 97).

helpful when thinking about the benefits or drawbacks of an alternative. The *Pros-Cons-and-Fixes list* is an extension of the pro-con list. It helps you deal with the tendency to overfocus on the drawbacks of an alternative.

HOW TO USE THE PROS-CONS-AND-FIXES LIST

We start by writing down the advantages of the alternative, that is, all the things we'll gain if we pick this one. We know it's tempting to start with summing up the cons first because it's a lot easier to come up with those, but remember we're starting with the pros for a good reason. We don't want to end up in a conversation where we only talk about the negative. Think about biking to work for a second. You can likely come up with a lot more downsides than benefits from biking to work. For example, the cons might include it takes longer, you arrive sweaty, you get wet when it rains, and so on. Now think about the benefits: um, it's healthy to exercise? That's it, that's all we have, but let's get back to those cons. So, write down the pros first!

After that, you write down all the disadvantages of the design. This is where it gets interesting. After you write down a disadvantage, you think about the way you could "fix" it. Sounds simple (because it is), but it's very powerful. For example, one of the drawbacks of biking to work is that you get wet when it rains. There are a lot of ways to deal with that: put an extra pair of clothes in your office (that also works for being sweaty), buy water-repelling biking gear. Biking to work in the rain didn't become a joy all of a sudden, but these adaptations did neutralize one or two of the disadvantages.

That is what we did at BigScreen too; we filled in a Pros-Cons-and-Fixes list to visualize the consequences of the design that had the majority of votes (figure 11.2). When we were filling in the cons of the design, Kala pointed out that Seat Allocations also calculated the ticket price, which wasn't clear from the name. An easy way to fix this was to split calculating the price and assigning a seat. Once we changed the design to accommodate that, everyone felt comfortable about moving forward with it. So Pros-Cons-and-Fixes is not only for documenting decision, but also a collaborative modeling tool which you can use any time in your design flow.

TIPS AND TRICKS TO GET THE MOST OUT OF THE TECHNIQUE

When using the Pros-Cons-and-Fixes with our clients, we noticed some common mistakes people made when filling in the list. Following is a list of tips and tricks to avoid these mistakes:

- *Not every con has a fix*—You can't neutralize every con; sometimes, you have to learn to accept the negative side of an alternative. When you split a monolith into services, the global complexity increases because those services have to communicate with each other. We designed the architecture in such a way that we don't push all the complexity in the communication between services, but we'll have to live with some global complexity.
- *A fix has to be actionable*—The term *actionable* means that you have to be able to do something when you read a fix. For example, "Find out if" or "Encourage people to" are not actionable steps. They point to missing information that we need to

make a decision. Find out if your fix is possible, make it concrete, and write that down. In figure 11.2, you'll notice that our fixes are actionable. We aren't wondering if we could hire extra developers, we know management is willing to give us a budget to hire the extra developers that we'll need. The list *is* the research moment; the research doesn't come after creating the list. You can't make an informed decision if you're not sure a fix is possible.

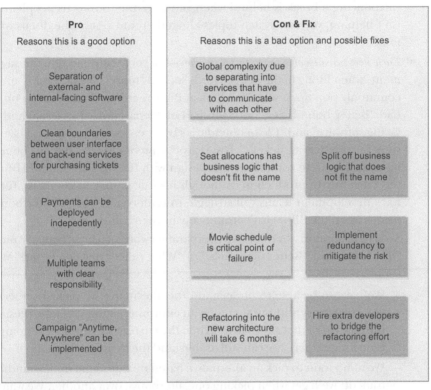

Purchasing tickets and scheduling domain separated, user interface and API separated

Pro	Con & Fix
Reasons this is a good option	Reasons this is a bad option and possible fixes
Separation of external- and internal-facing software	Global complexity due to separating into services that have to communicate with each other
Clean boundaries between user interface and back-end services for purchasing tickets	Seat allocations has business logic that doesn't fit the name	Split off business logic that does not fit the name
Payments can be deployed indepedently		
Multiple teams with clear responsibility	Movie schedule is critical point of failure	Implement redundancy to mitigate the risk
Campaign "Anytime, Anywhere" can be implemented	Refactoring into the new architecture will take 6 months	Hire extra developers to bridge the refactoring effort

(cc) Licensed under https://creativecommons.org/licenses/by-sa/4.0/

Figure 11.2   The Pros-Cons-and-Fixes list of the new architecture that enables the "Anytime, Anywhere" campaign

- *Understand the tradeoff when making decisions*—At BigScreen, we didn't create a Pros-Cons-and-Fixes list for the current architecture because we already knew it was no longer sufficient. We also had a majority on the third design, so we didn't dig deeper into those other designs that were created. If there's a lot of doubt between two designs, you need find the tradeoff to aid your decision:
  - Alternative A will give us x, y, and z with downsides a and b.
  - Alternative B will give us a, b, and z with downsides b and c.

If you pick A, you won't get certain pros and cons from alternative B, and vice versa. *That* is your tradeoff.

- *Focus on all of the consequences*—Something we've noticed when working with a Pros-Cons-and-Fixes list, is that it's very tempting to fixate on a couple of items on a list, instead of talking about the list as a whole. If you start doing that, you're just back to a pointless discussion that won't result in a decision with actionable steps to move forward. As a facilitator, it's important to stop the pointless discussion. You can try to refocus people on the entire list by giving out a climate report. Introducing a break is helpful when you're trying to refocus people. If a break isn't helping, you can switch topics altogether and restart the discussion after a few days.

- *Each item must be able to stand on its own*—It's very tempting to write vague statements when filling in the items. Words such as "more," "less," "faster," and "extra" commonly pop up. If we take a look at BigScreen, our first iteration on the pros had "Better boundaries" on it, instead of "Separation of external and internal facing software" and "Clean boundaries between user interface and backend services for purchasing tickets." The reason someone wrote "Better boundaries" is because they were comparing this design with the big ball of mud (BBoM) that was currently in production. Although it's our nature to compare, future software development teams will struggle to understand what "Better boundaries" means when the BBoM isn't around anymore to compare.

  So, as a facilitator, when you see comparative words such as "better," "more," and "less," always ask "Better than what?" or "What exactly makes it faster?" We do this for two reasons:

  - We have to be able to understand the alternative we picked on its own two years from now, without spending an enormous amount of time reestablishing the context of that alternative. When the current situation we're comparing to is no longer there, we can still understand the items on the list.

  - We don't want to pick an alternative based on our vague understanding of the tradeoff we'll get when picking one alternative over another. We want to have concrete information when we're making our decision.

GUIDING HEURISTIC   When doing Pros-Cons-and-Fixes, words such as "better," "more," "less," and "extra" are triggers to dig deeper so that we understand the real consequences.

- *Some consequences are just neutral*—Whether or not a consequence is positive or negative is subjective and context-specific information. Therefore, not all consequences can be categorized as positive or negative; some are just neutral.

  For example, you want to make a decision on which programming language to use for a prototype of a microservice. There are two options on the table: C# (current programming language) and Python (very good for prototyping). Nobody on the team knows Python. In a company that doesn't invest in educating their people, this is a downside. But, if you work in a company that invests a lot in education, learning Python can be seen as neutral. It's something we'll have to do that will take time, so that isn't immediately positive, but it's not a downside either because we're supported in this. So "Learning python" is neutral (neither a pro nor a con).

You can adapt the Pros-Cons-and-Fixes list, as shown in figure 11.3, to capture the neutral consequences of an alternative.

<< alternative 1 >>

Pro	Con & Fix	Neutral
Reasons to take this alternative	Reasons against this alternative and possible fixes	Neutral consequences of this alternative

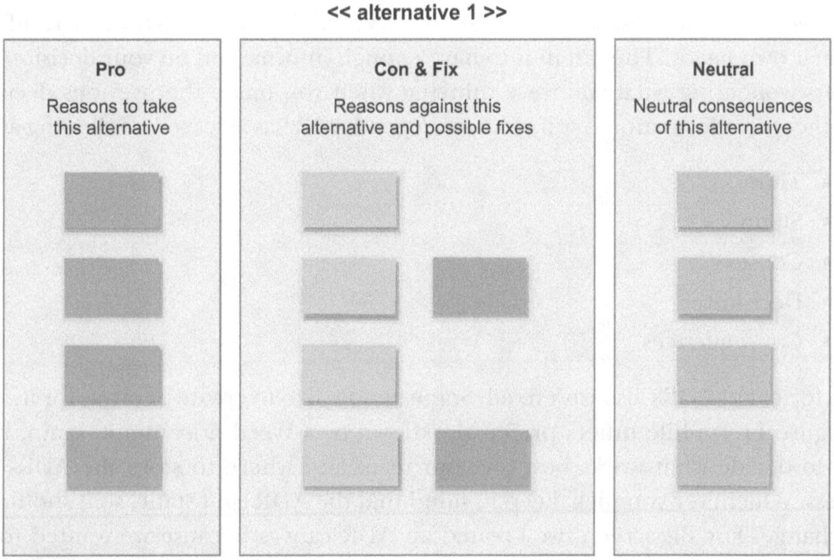

Licensed under https://creativecommons.org/licenses/by-sa/4.0/

Figure 11.3 Extend the Pros-Cons-and-Fixes list to capture the neutral consequences of an alternative. Whether something is pro, con, or neutral depends on the context because what is neutral for one team can be a con for another.

- *Individual brainstorming before team collaboration*—If you're creating the Pros-Cons-and-Fixes list in a team, it's better to divide each step into two steps:
  - Write down all your pros individually.
  - Group them together, and merge the individual items into one pro column.

  The same goes for summing up cons and their fixes. Note there can be differences of opinion in a team when writing down pros (and cons and their fixes) individually first. It's important to have a conversation about these pros and decide together as a team what the pros are for the team as a whole. Instead of brainstorming cons and fixes at the same time, we recommend making it a two-pass process that allows everyone to consider fixes for all cons, not just the ones they thought of themselves.

11.1.2   *Capturing the decision*

If we want to stop wondering what were they thinking, we need to capture more than just the outcome of a decision. The good news is that there already is a documentation tool available—the *architectural decision record* (ADR)—to capture architectural decisions. ADRs were first mentioned by Michael Nygard in 2011 (https://mng.bz/4JPD) and have gained more popularity over the years. The purpose of the tool is to create clarity on previous decisions that were made. It's an investment you make now, so you don't have to be confused in the future about prior decisions that were made.

There are some recommendations on how to create ADRs and what information is valuable to add, but besides that, ADRs are very flexible, and teams are free to adapt them to their own needs. The intent is to have enough information on your decision to avoid others wondering what you were thinking when you made the previous decision and whether the information is still accurate. A good ADR has at least the following attributes:

- Title
- Status
- Context
- Decision
- Consequences

The format of ADRs also isn't fixed. Some people like to create a canvas for it, as shown in figure 11.4, while others prefer Markdown or a Word document. Again, it's up to you to decide what works best for your team and where to store the ADRs for easy access. Whichever you pick, keep in mind that the ADR isn't static, so it should be easy to change. For BigScreen, we created an ADR canvas because we wanted to keep it close to our design efforts, which happen on Miro.

TITLE

The title describes the architectural decision we're making. We're designing a new architecture to enable the "Anytime, Anywhere" campaign. We also added a reference number, ADR #1, so that we can refer to this specific record in other ADRs.

STATUS

When reading about ADRs, the three most commonly used statuses are Proposed, Accepted, and Superseded. Of course, it's up to you to extend the statuses to capture what's important to your team. For example, Rejected is sometimes added as a status. When an ADR has the Proposed status, it means that we're actively discussing it, and no conclusion has been reached yet. When a conclusion is reached, meaning we know which alternative we want, the status changes to Accepted. So, for BigScreen, the current status is Accepted. We also added the date on which the decision was accepted at BigScreen.

Until a design is tested in production, we can never be 100% sure that it's a good design. In addition, the world doesn't stand still while you're refactoring your designs. As mentioned in chapter 9, we're making decisions under uncertainty, and sustainable

ADR #1 - Redesigning the monolithic big ball of mud (BBoM) to enable the "Anytime, Anywhere" campaign	**Accepted** on 2023-06-20

Decision makers
Kala, Jack, Rose, Caledon, Rick, Rodney, Caelan, Ralph, Amir

Context
The application has been around for 15 years, and the modularity has heavily decreased over that period of time. The business wants to add a mobile app, which currently is not possible due to that decrease in modularity.
The business has difficulty making informed decisions because the internal- and external-facing parts of the software system are intertwined and adding the features they need has proven difficult.

Consequences

Decision
We will extract the back office into the Planning and Scheduling service to disentangle internal- and external-facing parts of the software system. This way, we can create and iterate on the models specifically designed for the business to make informed decisions.

We will create a service Movie Schedule that contains all the information on movies. This allows us to eliminate dependencies between Purchasing Tickets and the PaS.
We will refactor Purchasing Tickets into client and server, with clear boundaries for Price Calculation, payments, and seat allocations. This enables the creation of a mobile app.

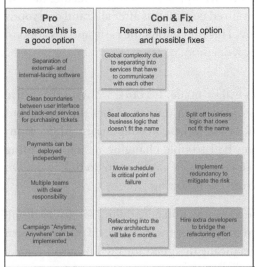

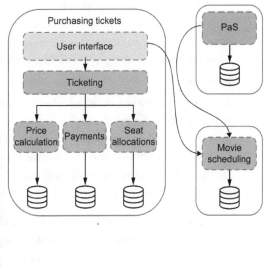

Figure 11.4   The ADR for redesigning the BBoM into clear boundaries to enable the "Anytime, Anywhere" campaign. It contains the new architecture for the system and the Pros-Cons-and-Fixes list.

decision-making means reevaluating your design when new information becomes available. This is why an ADR can be superseded. Instead of adapting the ADR, we create a new one and mark the previous one as in Superseded status with a reference to the new ADR. We want to have a historical understanding of the design decisions we made and how we adapted them.

CONTEXT

The context of a decision is important because we'll select different alternatives as more desirable based on that context:

- How much budget is there to implement the decision?
- Who is supportive of this, and who is opposed?

- What is the time constraint?
- What are the technical constraints?
- What other political, technical, or social constraints need to be taken into account?

We described the context of the ADR for BigScreen (refer to figure 11.4) as follows: The application has been around for 15 years, and the modularity has heavily decreased over that period of time. The business wants to add a mobile app, which currently isn't possible due to that decrease in modularity. The business has difficulty making informed decisions because the internal and external facing parts of the software system are intertwined, and adding the features they need has proven difficult.

At BigScreen, we were very lucky. Everybody was supportive of rearchitecting the current design, money was not a problem (they hired consultants after all), and everybody agreed that this was critical for the company. This isn't always the case, and it's good to understand everything at play when making a decision.

DECISION

The decision is a summary of what changes will be made. It's often written in an active voice: we will, Kala will, and so on. The summary not only describes the "what" but also the "why." As you can see on the ADR of BigScreen, making informed decisions became difficult because the software team had trouble changing or implementing features. Separating internal- and external-facing logic enables us to do this again. On the ADR for BigScreen (figure 11.4), we wrote the following:

- We'll extract the back office into the Planning and Scheduling service to disentangle internal- and external-facing parts of the software system. This way, we can create and iterate on the models specifically designed for the business to make informed decisions.
- We'll create a service called Movie Schedule that contains all the information on movies. This allows us to eliminate dependencies between Purchasing Tickets and planning and scheduling (PaS).
- We'll refactor Purchasing Tickets into client and server, with clear boundaries for Price Calculation, Payments, and Seat Allocations. This enables the creation of a mobile app.

CONSEQUENCES

The consequences explain the effect this will have on your project or product. This section tackles the future "What were they thinking?" questions. If you're using the Pros-Cons-and-Fixes list, as we did at BigScreen, you can add it here.

Some teams also like to add the other alternatives that were considered, together with the analysis of those consequences and the reason they selected a certain alternative. If you want to capture the tradeoff clearly, this is a good practice.

11.2 *Spreading the knowledge through the company*

Now that we've formalized a decision, we'll delve deeper into propagating these decisions and their accompanying knowledge throughout the company. This is crucial because not everyone can always be present at each of these collaborative modeling sessions. Furthermore, involving everyone in each meeting would be expensive, time-consuming, and, honestly, rather boring for many.

11.2.1 *Communicating decisions*

The most important action to take when decisions are made is to update those who either weren't present but could be affected by the decision or possess relevant expertise. We learned this heuristic from Andrew Harmel-Law's "architecture advice process,"[2] which shifts architectural decision-making toward the team constructing the software.

> **VALUE-BASED HEURISTIC**   Communicate the decision to the people who weren't there but are either affected by that decision or have expertise involved in that decision.

But who exactly are these individuals within an organization? How can we pinpoint them? Referring back to chapter 4, we should have already identified these stakeholders using the essential categories from chapter 2 during the preparation of our collaborative modeling session. However, new stakeholders might be discovered during the session itself.

Therefore, it's crucial during a session to ascertain we have consent of these stakeholders and whether we can proceed with a decision in the absence of certain stakeholders. This is a sensemaking task that requires ongoing attention. We must strike a balance—while we don't want to involve everyone all the time, it's possible that people excluded from smaller design groups might be affected by the decisions made. What we ought to do then is to generate options in an ADR and subsequently involve these individuals. This can be done asynchronously, such as updating everyone via email or messaging app about a new ADR. When doing so, it's important to consider levels of buy-in from chapter 9. Be explicit about how you communicate the ad based on the levels of buy-in. Alternatively, involvement of people who are affected by the decision could occur during the architecture advice process[3] mentioned earlier or the weekly Architecture Advisory Forum, or it might necessitate scheduling a new meeting.

COMMUNICATING ASYNCHRONOUSLY

When we communicate asynchronously with people, the ADR format is a structured way to do so. However, during collaborative modeling, a lot of the conversation is still lost, and people might lack context or make assumptions if we only present them with the outcome of the collaborative modeling. We should then either clean up the

---

[2] Harmel-Law, A. "Scaling the Practice of Architecture, Conversationally," 2021. https://mng.bz/Ad4Q
[3] Ibid.

outcome or distill it into a clear diagram. The most essential pattern here is what Jacqui Read calls "know your audience" in her book *Communication Patterns* (O'Reilly, 2024).

For instance, with the team at BigScreen, we engaged in a lot of EventStorming, Example Mapping, and domain storytelling. So, after a session, to allow the team to asynchronously review what happened, we cleaned up the outcome on a virtual board. Cleaning up the outcome means structuring and making the model complete with a good legend, as discussed during the session. Most of the time, the model after such a session isn't clear enough to show to others. The model itself is also not the artifact or outcome of such a session—it's the transformative capabilities of the shared understanding we get from collaborative modeling. So, we also don't focus on having a clear model as the outcome. However, to get more people on board, we want to make the model more exact. That way, the team became familiar with these collaborative modeling tools, which began to serve as a language for communicating these sessions, ensuring that everyone understood what had transpired.

DISTILLING DIAGRAMS

Some tools, however, such as all the EventStorming color coding, might be confusing to people who have never experienced such a session. We prefer to create domain storytelling diagrams combined with a visualized Example Mapping, like the one in figure 11.5, especially for people on the business side to understand better. These diagrams express a much clearer functional understanding without the need for extensive knowledge of the legend.

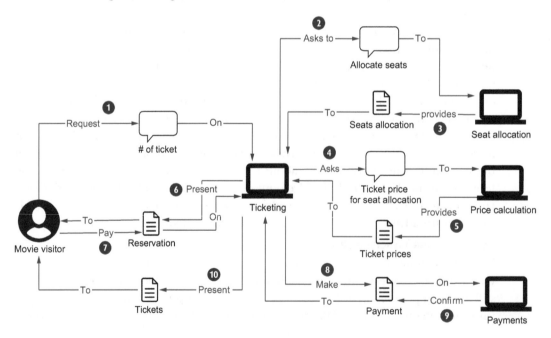

Figure 11.5   Domain storytelling diagram distilled from one of the collaborative modeling sessions to get the message across to the business of what the end flow might look like.

Sometimes, you need to communicate and distill different tools and show varied levels of abstraction to give all the unique perspectives to a decision. For example, if you want to communicate how your architecture changed, you can distill that to a C4 diagram like the one you see in figure 11.6. Be sure to remain consistent in the diagrams, especially regarding language.

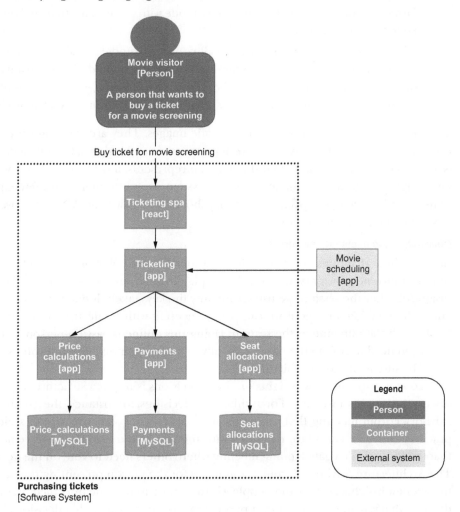

Figure 11.6 C4 Container diagram explaining how the architecture might look in the new design

One crucial aspect to comprehend regarding distilling diagrams is that despite their clarity, there's always room for misinterpretation. This can lead to assumptions and misconceptions. Therefore, it's pivotal to have a system where individuals can provide feedback asynchronously. We advocate for two effective methods:

- *Diagramming as code*—Think of this as generating visual diagrams from textual descriptions using specific coding languages. These textual descriptions generate the visual diagrams for you. A few examples are Mermaid JS, PlantUML, and some specific tools such as Structurizr for modeling C4. These coded diagrams can be stored in a repository so that team members and anyone with access can critique, modify, or comment directly on the code. The diagrams can also be integrated with ticketing systems so you don't need the work to be planned first. However, don't confuse diagramming as code with a generator that analyzes your code and creates a diagram from it.

- *Virtual tools*—Platforms such as Miro allow users to model and showcase their diagrams. Here, participants can seamlessly comment on and discuss various parts of the illustration, fostering collaboration. These online whiteboard tools can often be easily integrated into other documentation platforms, such as wikis.

Ultimately, diagrams are more than just static images. They are evolving representations of ideas that continually reveal fresh perspectives and insights. Because a diagram is a perspective on the reality that the diagram represents, a fresh pair of eyes will get new insights on improving the model or the system. However, there are a few expectations, specifically when the diagram is a snapshot in time as with an ADR, when we want to keep that diagram immutable!

COMMUNICATING DECISIONS BY PROXY

Because these diagrams, as well as the decisions from a collaborative modeling session, can give new insights, we find that explaining the session by proxy is the most insightful. After the session, we usually identify the key stakeholders who weren't present at the meeting and see if we can plan a meeting with them. In that meeting, we go through the outcome of the session. Doing this online is easy; in-person meetings mean you need to roll up the paper carefully in hopes nothing falls off if you use stickies, so be sure to always take pictures.

A good way to gain new insights on these decisions is to put a structure in place to discuss the insights and share. For architecture decisions, for instance, the Architecture Advisory Forum meeting that we mentioned earlier is a good structure to scale that practice. Here, we can share decisions with the rest of the company. But remember that the forum isn't a gatekeeping meeting where others need to vote on the decision. The Architecture Advisory Forum in essence is for the person presenting the decision to gain new insights and for the people who are there to become informed. Because a decision that is made is almost never permanent, we need to keep that decision alive.

11.3 *Keeping the decision alive*

Now that you've created ADRs to capture your entire decision and communicated in the right way, you might think that will do the trick. Unfortunately, the journey doesn't end here. Actually, the journey is a collection of feedback loops that will have you iterate on your model and design continuously. These iterations are needed to challenge your model and design to make relevant adjustments as you go. Because we're making decisions under uncertainty, we need feedback loops that provide us with information to make an informed decision. You could see the modeling process as a whirlpool, which we'll explain in this section.

This nonlinear modeling process includes iterations, feedback loops, and living documentation, which means you'll have to throw away a model every once in a while. We've seen many people fall in love with a model, which ended up in terrible heartbreaks. One of the best pieces of advice we can give you is to not fall in love with any model, design, or decision because they aren't static and are highly likely to change with every iteration. Spare yourself the heartache by not setting your heart on it.

11.3.1 *The modeling process as a whirlpool*

Now that you've made it to the documentation part, it might seem that you're almost there. The heavy lifting part is done, you've dealt with conflicts and polarities, and made a decision or two. The ADR is filled in, and the Pros-Cons-and-Fixes list provided some valuable insights. Let's wrap it up, right? Well, not quite. Software design isn't a linear process. You should consider it a loop, or multiple loops within one loop— almost like a whirlpool. The key is to keep challenging your software model. New insights, new people, time passing, new requirements, market changes, budget costs, and technical decisions that have social consequences are just some of the complexities of the environment that the software model and the system will be implemented in. All of these factors should motivate you to adapt your model continuously.

From our experience, the modeling process is sometimes considered, or at least experienced, in a linear manner. Starting with understanding and discovering, eventually strategizing and organizing ourselves based on modeling endeavors, and eventually realizing all of this effort into code. This isn't where it should stop. The modeling process consists of multiple loops that provide new insights and require changes to your model. The starting point, for example, which is often about discovering and understanding, requires multiple iterations and feedback loops. Trying to fully understand the current state by, for example, doing EventStorming just once, won't complete the discovery of your current state. You need iterations with new or different people who add their perspective, knowledge, and wisdom to the EventStorm, for example. New insights always pop up after an EventStorming session because you let it sink in for a while. Then, when the model is being shared with others outside the modeling bubble, you can expect an additional iteration or two. The real value of these collaborative modeling sessions is in the modeling itself, not the output. You can iterate on your model based on the conversations that take place, the people you speak to, the conflicts that pop up, and the biases that becomes explicit during a session. This means you'll go around in loops, which is exactly what you need.

In his Whirlpool Process of Model Exploration diagram (figure 11.7), Eric Evans presents a whirlpool model designed to aid in exploring models and iterating on their design. This approach isn't linear; instead, it promotes challenging one's understanding and examining models from various angles. This process bears similarities to the approach taken in Behavior-Driven Development (BDD). We touched on BDD in chapter 2, specifically discussing Example Mapping. In BDD, we select a story from the backlog, identify the requirements, formalize them into acceptance criteria, and perhaps automate these criteria into automated acceptance tests. Each of these steps incorporates feedback loops. The stages of discovery, formalization, and automation mirror the pattern of scenario, model, and code probe, emphasizing the necessity to close the feedback loop in each phase.

This is exactly what we aim for with collaborative modeling, while also taking in the social and cognitive perspectives that we described in previous chapters, such as ranking, bias, conflict, and polarities.

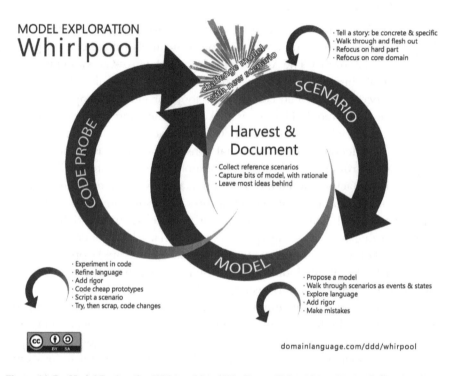

Figure 11.7   Model Exploration Whirlpool from Eric Evans. This whirlpool helps in considering collaborative modeling as a collection of feedback loops, rather than a linear process. (Source: www.domainlanguage.com/ddd/whirlpool/)

The whirlpool in figure 11.7 starts with Harvest & Document to capture the current state. BigPicture EventStorming, Business Model Canvas, and Wardley Mapping are excellent tools to gather the relevant information and knowledge here. These collaborative modeling tools can provide relevant scenarios and will enable you to propose a model after a while. The whirlpool allows exploring multiple scenarios and models, instead of going through a linear process. It's about experimenting in code based on the proposed model, then challenging that model with new scenarios, and rolling your way through the whirlpool again. In this way, you keep challenging your model continuously, which will make it more valuable. In other words, when you arrive at the part where you can fill in ADRs and Pros-Cons-and-Fixes lists, it might actually be the start of a new loop! Isn't that an exciting idea?! Let's illustrate this with an example of our friends at BigScreen:

- BigScreen started off with Big Picture EventStorming to visualize their current state with all relevant domain experts. This exercise provided highly valuable insights, and emerging bounded contexts were popping up.
- Smaller parts of the EventStorm, for example, Purchasing a Ticket and Movie Scheduling, can become bounded contexts that allow BigScreen to start design activities. Instead of wanting to get all the possible bounded contexts right, they picked these and started a second iteration.
- In that next iteration, they noticed domain events around Payment happen in the system of their payment provider, meaning there needs to be communication with that external system.
- Then we went back to our emerging bounded context design and make sure we capture that.

The preceding example is a simple illustration of how these feedback loops work by creating smaller iterations that trigger feedback and challenge our assumptions and perspectives. We can't really prescribe how to design these feedback loops. From our experience, it helps to have different tools in your toolbox that you can use to create these feedback loops. All the tools we mentioned in earlier chapters—Event-Storming, Business Model Canvas, Example Mapping, and sensemaking—can help you create valuable feedback loops. If you want to understand more on how the whirlpool works, or how to start a modeling process, check out the Domain-Driven Design Starter Modelling Process by the DDD Crew: https://github.com/ddd-crew/ddd-starter-modelling-process.

THE IMPORTANCE OF FEEDBACK LOOPS

If you ask a random person about feedback loops, they will probably confirm that having those loops in place is crucial. The real question is why they are so important. We've learned that they are important, and we're conditioned to at least consider them in a lot of our activities, but the "why" of feedback loops sometimes remains ambiguous. For us, it's pretty clear: we need feedback loops because we make decisions under uncertainty and use heuristics when making decisions. Both uncertainty and heuristics don't guarantee success, so we need feedback loops to gather information—not only once, but during multiple loops.

Chapter 9 helped us understand that information is crucial to make an informed decision. What makes a decision easy or hard is how well informed you feel about the decision you have to make. The more information we have, the better we can evaluate available alternatives and make an informed decision. You want to get the level of uncertainty down, so the decision will be easier to make. You can never be 100% informed, but you can be as informed as possible.

Creating feedback loops will help you in gathering the necessary information to evaluate alternatives and eventually make an informed decision. You must use the information you're getting from the feedback loops to adjust your model when necessary. When your models aren't functioning as you hoped, you need to make adjustments instead of continuing on your stubborn path.

The other reason feedback loops are important is related to the uncertainty that comes with making decisions and how using heuristics can help you deal with that. As explained in chapter 3, heuristics are simple rules to help you make decisions. Heuristics are based on experience and knowledge, and help us to progress forward when a decision is needed. Are we putting this boundary here or there? Are we going to split up to design bounded contexts or do that collectively? These are both situations where you could use heuristics, but these heuristics don't guarantee solutions or success as Billy Vaughn Koen points out in his book *Discussion of The Method: Conducting the Engineer's Approach to Problem Solving*, heuristics are ultimately unjustified, impossible to fully justify, and inherently fallible. So, you need feedback loops that will provide you with more information. Maybe split up for now, but come back together after two days to do a walkthrough and adjust the model collectively. Then, go back into (reshuffled) subgroups, and come back together again after two days. These iterations and feedback loops will help you discover what works well and what doesn't.

The thing is, you don't know if something works until it's in production. The same goes for architecture. You need these feedback loops to lower uncertainty by gathering information you need to make an important decision. So, the next time someone asks you why feedback loops are important, you know the answer: uncertainty.

EMERGING LIVING DOCUMENTATION

Documentation is part of your feedback loops. The way you document your models, thought processes, decisions, and design is crucial to get that information from your feedback loops you need to make an informed decision. This documentation preferably is alive and emerging, meaning this documentation emerges and changes every time you're in a (new) feedback loop. Based on new information you gathered in a loop, you may need to add something to your documentation. For example, from your Big Picture EventStorm, you take smaller parts to do some process EventStorming on. Or, based on your Example Mapping, you add a Pros-Cons-and-Fixes list.

There are different ways to deal with this emerging living documentation. With online whiteboards such as Miro and Mural, it's relatively easy to keep track of what you're doing. You could start with one big Miro board that contains all of your information: EventStorming, context maps, Pros-Cons-and-Fixes lists, and polarity maps. But maybe you'll realize that your board is getting very big by continuing to add new information and iterations, so you might want to go with separate boards for all bounded contexts, for example. You might also start a separate polarity board that captures all relevant maps and polarities within the group. Then you come to the point where you want to start documenting ADRs. Although this will be easier in Git, for example, you might want to add links to it on your Miro board.

GUIDING HEURISTIC   When your online whiteboard gets too big, find a way to split the board up based on your teams, or architecture.

This is how you end up with emerging living documentation, which will keep decisions alive and allow you to make relevant adjustments to your models based on information from your feedback loops. Note that it's up to the people working on the models and designs to decide how you deal with this documentation, such as when it's preferred to start a separate board or who the board owners will be, for example. The choices you make regarding this emerging living documentation are design decisions as well.

Note that with the use of Miro, we see people continuing on versions they started with, which means in following iterations, the model is being adjusted or extended during new collaborative modeling sessions. By doing this, you're losing the previous version. This could be a downside because you also might lose important thought processes or small design decisions you've made along the way. In that light, it's important to consciously make a distinction between reusing collaborative models and immutable collaborative models in which the immutable models are frozen at a point in time, let's say. As a group, you decide when to freeze the model, and if you want to start iterations, you make a copy of that immutable model and start working on that copy. In that way, you keep important information on your board so you can keep track of adjustments. To decide when to freeze a model, you could use ADRs. ADRs capture significant design decisions, so every time you create an ADR, that might be a natural moment to freeze a model and make a copy for further iterations, superseding the model.

GUIDING HEURISTIC   Whenever you create an ADR, freeze your model and use copies for following iterations.

11.3.2 Don't fall in love with your model

Remember, as beautiful and brilliant as your model might be, don't fall in love with it! When you fall in love with something, it's hard to look at it objectively, let alone throw it away when necessary. With the feedback loops comes new information that helps you make an informed decision. The new information you gathered might require you to make adjustments to your model or design, or even throw it away completely. When you're already madly in love with a model, you'll be tempted to make extensions to the existing model, rather than redesigning it so that it will be a better fit for purpose. That's what you want to avoid.

VALUE-BASED HEURISTIC   Tell yourself not to fall in love with a model every now and then and that it's okay to throw your model away when needed.

In chapter 7, we talked about the availability bias and model fitting. The availability bias pops up when we're trying to make decisions or assess information, and we add more value to information that can be recalled easily or at least find it more important than alternative solutions not as readily recalled. When we do collaborative modeling, we might favor our first design over later designs because we substitute "good" for "easy." So due to the availability bias, we already have a strong preference for the first model we came up with and that will only grow over time. We feed our love for that model and get emotionally attached to it, so when we then get challenged on our assumptions and perspectives in a feedback loop, we might be hesitant to completely redesign our first model. This can be true even though the new information indicates that this is the best way forward.

What we then often see is that people start to make extensions of that first model, thereby compromising on its quality. This is called model fitting, where we deform, add, or leave out elements from the problem domain to force it into an already existing model just because we got emotionally attached to it. This is why it's important to design your models in different ways, so you get more information, reduce uncertainty, and prevent the availability bias from feeding too much love to your initial model.

Two other biases that are related to emotional attachment to an existing model and model fitting are loss aversion and sunk cost fallacy. *Loss aversion* was explained in chapter 9, which is about the tendency to avoid losses over gaining wins. Throwing away an existing model, however strong the arguments may be, feels like a loss. Because we want to avoid that, we'll be more likely to start model fitting instead of doing a redesign. *Sunk cost fallacy* is about our tendency to follow through on an endeavor if we've already invested time, effort, or money into it, whether or not the current costs outweigh the benefits. So, we might stick with an existing model because we've been working on it for months, it has cost a lot of frustration and iterations to finally get somewhere, and we won't throw it away just because we got some new piece of information that might contradict our previous endeavors. The more you invest in a model, the more emotionally attached you'll be, the harder it will be to throw it away. It might feel like you're throwing away all the hard work you and your team put into it over the past months. And that's a horrible feeling.

Note that all these biases can be at play at the same time, reinforcing each other. Due to the availability bias, we prefer the existing model, and our tendency to avoid loss will make it very hard to throw that existing model away. At the same time, thanks to the sunk cost fallacy, we are heavily emotionally attached to that existing model. Note that these biases—just like other biases—are working mainly unconsciously. We're often not aware of our emotional attachment and the behavior that follows from it. This is where a facilitator can come in to observe and recognize the biases at hand, making them explicit. Either way, all these forces may lead you toward model fitting, instead of doing what's necessary: face your breakup and part ways with your model, or as writers would say, "Kill your darlings."

To conclude this chapter and our attempt to convince you that you shouldn't fall in love with your model, we understand that we might not succeed—or at least not with everyone. Our words of advice might resonate with you, but there are other ways to make important messages stick. In that light, we asked ChatGPT to write a song about not falling in love with your model. We proudly present the lyrics to you here!

Verse 1:

Blueprints and sketches, lines on the page

A designer's vision, a world to create

The structure's design, it's so alluring

But don't get too caught up, it's just a drawing

Chorus:

Don't fall in love with the model

It's just a concept, not something to hold

Don't let the plans consume your soul

Remember it's just a vision, not a reality to behold

Verse 2:

The curves and angles, they may entice

But don't forget, it's not a living device

It's just a model, a representation

Not something to build your life's foundation

Chorus:

Don't fall in love with the model

It's just an idea, not something to touch

Don't let the design control your role

Remember it's just a blueprint, not something you can clutch

11.4   Collaborative software design catalysts

- When there are different options to a decision, start experimenting with a Pros-Cons-and-Fixes list. Try out one for yourself first, and then see if you can use one together with your team.
- After using a Pros-Cons-and-Fixes list, reflect on its benefits and downsides. How can it help you? How or in which situations could it be valuable to you and/or your team to use the list?
- Start experimenting with ADRs. Don't start too big; consider something more lightweight to assess if this tool is something that would be of value to your team.

11.5   Chapter heuristics

Guiding heuristics

- When doing Pros-Cons-and-Fixes, words such as "better," "more," "less," and "extra" are triggers to dig deeper so that we understand the real consequences
- When your online whiteboard gets too big, find a way to split the board up based on your teams, or architecture.
- Whenever you create an ADR, freeze your model and use copies for following iterations.

Value-based heuristics

- Communicate the decision to the people who weren't there but are either affected by that decision or have expertise involved in that decision.
- Tell yourself to not fall in love with a model every now and then and that it's okay to throw your model away when needed.

11.6   Further reading

- *Communication Patterns* by Jacqui Read (O'Reilly, 2024)
- "Scaling the Practice of Architecture, Conversationally" by Andrew Harmel-Law (https://mng.bz/Ad4Q)

Summary

- Formalizing decisions is essential for future reference and understanding. This involves finding the consequences of chosen alternatives and capturing them.
- The Pros-Cons-and-Fixes list is a powerful technique to visualize the benefits and drawbacks of alternatives. It helps identify actionable fixes for disadvantages, aiding decision-making.
- When faced with multiple options, it's crucial to assess tradeoffs to make informed decisions. Each item in the Pros-Cons-and-Fixes list should stand on its own, avoiding vague statements and focusing on all consequences.
- The Architectural Decision Record (ADR) is a flexible documentation tool for capturing entire architectural decisions, including context, decision, and consequences, to avoid future misunderstandings and enable sustainable decision-making.
- A well-structured ADR includes essential attributes such as title, context, decision, status, and consequences. It allows teams to record decisions effectively and adapt as needed to account for changing circumstances.
- Updating absent stakeholders and experts by using ADR format and asynchronous methods on decisions is crucial for transparency and inclusivity.

- Distill diagrams such as C4 models, domain storytelling, and Example Mapping to enhance understanding, allowing asynchronous comments for insights.

- You can facilitate discussions in forums such as the Architecture Advisory Forum to share decisions, keep them alive, and gain further insights for ongoing improvement.

- Design isn't linear but a loop; challenge and iterate on the model to accommodate new insights, perspectives, and requirements.

- Use feedback loops to gather information, lower uncertainty, and make informed decisions. Adopt emerging living documentation to keep models alive and allow relevant adjustments based on feedback.

- Avoid Emotional Attachment and don't fall in love with your model to maintain objectivity and prevent biases such as availability bias, model fitting, loss aversion, and sunk cost fallacy.

- Embrace redesign, and be open to throwing away or redesigning your model based on new information to reduce uncertainty and make better decisions.

Collaborative modeling beyond software design

12

This chapter covers

- Understanding the context through collaborative modeling with managing roles
- Collaborating with user researchers and product and engineering managers
- Moving toward implementation through collaborative modeling

We hope you've gotten a good understanding of why designing software requires collaborative software design with stakeholders. We also hope this book has been helpful as you take the first steps and understand how to do so. We discussed the different stages you'll go through during collaborative modeling and what facilitation skills are needed to help the group move past certain blockers. We covered the social dynamics that come into play when bringing a diverse group of people together in a room, especially how to manage conflicts and include everyone when making software design decisions. We also demonstrated how to incorporate insights and onboard people who weren't present during the collaboration. Additionally, we highlighted the importance of building in feedback loops to keep the decision-making process alive.

However, the knowledge we shared isn't just useful in the domain of software design; in fact, much of the information came from the diverse fields of anthropology, behavioral science, and complexity science. So, you can imagine these skills have applications beyond software design. In this final chapter, we'll provide examples of how collaborative modeling can be used for understanding context, mapping out strategies, and collaborating with user researchers, product owners, and engineering managers. We'll conclude with a clear example of how to progress toward implementation.

12.1 *Moving toward understanding the context*

In chapter 2, we already introduced you to the Business Model Canvas as a way for a team to align with the business objectives. While many Business Model Canvases are created by management and product managers to explore their business, it also helps to include the development teams in this process. A very good example that shows the power of including teams in this process comes from Javier Fernández's talk, "Black Ops DDD Using the Business Model Canvas" (www.youtube.com/watch?v =M5CbbWmdsFU). He conducted separate sessions with his CEO and the development team, and then compared outcomes. This approach gave the CEO new insights into value proposition opportunities.

12.1.1 *Focusing on customer needs*

Many times, we see people focusing on solutions when doing collaborative modeling. I hope this isn't a new insight for you, but we often find ourselves falling into this same anti-pattern. When you conduct a Business Model Canvas, as explained in chapter 2, with either business stakeholders or teams, you should be wary of this anti-pattern, as it can divert your discovery away from understanding the context.

Organizations often jump to solutions based on initial perceptions. For example, they might deduce that a client wants a chatbot feature in their app. However, this approach can be restrictive—don't get lured into that trap! It's crucial to first understand the "value proposition" of a Business Model Canvas, which means identifying the primary benefits or unique offerings your product or service brings to the market. Simultaneously, it's equally important to identify the "customer segment" on the Business Model Canvas, which highlights the specific demographic or group you're aiming to serve. A deeper dive into these elements can be achieved through a Value Proposition Canvas, as illustrated in figure 12.1, ensuring you cater directly to customer needs.

The same can happen when doing Domain Storytelling or EventStorming. When we model the process as it currently exists, the process may be designed to revolve around the current software systems. Businesses often buy software that might fit at the time, but as businesses change with the market, those software systems might wear them down. As a result, they start working around the problems with several patch processes to fix them—and don't forget that Excel export that everyone wants! By removing the systems from EventStorming and Domain Storytelling, you'll be able to refocus on customer needs and gain a deeper understanding of the context and business problems.

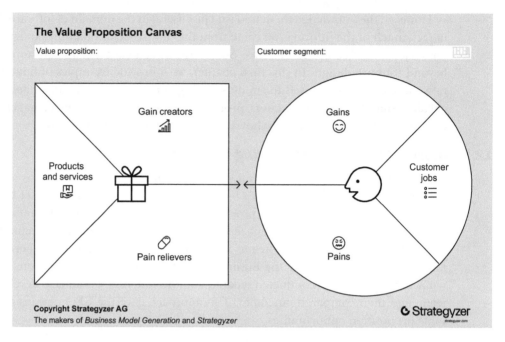

Figure 12.1   The Value Proposition Canvas from Strategyzer. You start by filling in the customer segment before moving to the value proposition. This can be used as a base in your Business Model Canvas.

12.1.2 *Connecting business strategy, product, and software architecture*

In the IT industry, there's a common problem with aligning our solutions with the overall business strategy. Tools such as the Business Model Canvas can provide some guidance, but they don't show us how our software architecture fits with the strategy. They also don't help us adjust our software to see if it still aligns with our goals.

This misalignment often leads to software systems that don't adapt to meet the company's strategy. When we build new systems on top of the existing ones without proper alignment, it only complicates the situation further. The systems become more intertwined and less adaptable to strategic changes. Strategies in the business world are often put into words that seem logical but don't really help us grasp the entire situation. This leads to software systems that don't effectively align with our strategic goals, resulting in a very rigid software architecture that is unable to accommodate business changes.

WARDLEY MAPPING

Simon Wardley (who created Wardley Mapping) faced this problem years ago when he was a CEO. Once, an executive asked him if his strategy made sense, and he realized he didn't know what a genuine strategy should look like. Although his strategy seemed fine and resembled others he'd seen, with familiar diagrams and wording, he later discovered that no one really understood it. Wardley compared most boardroom strategies and strategic consultancy decisions to playing chess without a chessboard. Without seeing the board, people often end up mimicking others' moves. In business, when there's no clear understanding of the landscape of an organization, companies tend to adopt generic strategies that have worked for others. Common examples might include embracing microservices, the cloud, the Spotify model, or a digital-first approach.

But it's difficult to discern what's truly important for an organization without a clear view of its landscape or to know how to act based on a strategy that lacks context. How can development teams, often facing complex situations, be expected to move in the right direction? Wardley recognized this problem and created a strategy cycle, as illustrated in figure 12.2. Inspired by Sun Tzu's *The Art of War* and John Boyd's OODA loop, the cycle begins with mapping out the current organizational landscape. This approach seeks to provide a clearer understanding of the organizational environment, so strategies can be more tailored, relevant, and effective.

> **DEFINITION** The *OODA loop (Observe, Orient, Decide, Act)* is a decision-making framework developed by military strategist John Boyd, emphasizing rapid, continuous cycles of observation, orientation, decision-making, and action to outmaneuver opponents or adapt to changing environments. It's widely used in military, business, and other strategic fields to enhance responsiveness and effectiveness.

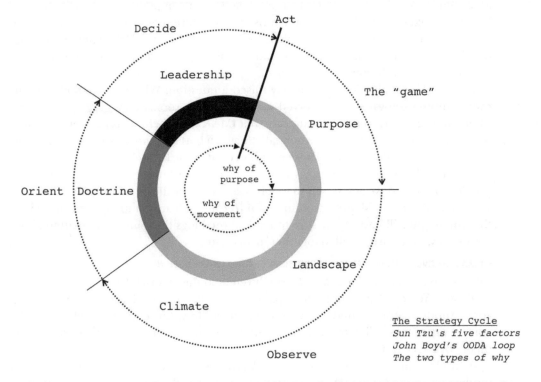

Figure 12.2 Wardley Mapping Strategy Cycle, based on Sun Tzu's five factors and John Boyd's OODA loop. It includes mapping the landscape, introducing climate patterns, adding doctrine, and making decisions that create a purpose. (Source: https://mng.bz/67PZ. Licensed by Simon Wardley under a Creative Commons Attribution-ShareAlike 4.0 license)

Wardley Mapping is effective not only in the boardroom but also for other strategic decisions such as product, teams, and software architecture. It's a powerful storytelling tool that creates a shared understanding of the current landscape and climate, where we can orient what principles to use and make collaborative decisions together. So, what exactly does Wardley mean by "landscape" in this cycle?

In chapter 10, we introduced you to the initial phase of mapping the landscape, which is the value chain as a vertical axis. We identified the users as an anchor on the map to start from. These users have needs that are fulfilled by the capabilities required to meet those needs in the organization. For user needs mapping we dived deeper in streamlets and team boundaries. For Wardley Mapping we go to the horizontal axis where we place each capability on the map in a stage of evolution. The four evolution stages are Genesis, Custom Build, Product & Rental, and Commodity & Utility. For each capability in the value chain, we collaborate on which evolution stage that capability is in based on the context of our organization.

Determining evolutionary stages collaboratively is pivotal for informed strategy and resource allocation. Different stages signal varied competitive advantages, risks, and required management practices. Recognizing a component's stage aids in predicting its natural progression, optimizing supply chains, and tailoring operational approaches accordingly, ensuring organizations remain agile and competitive in their landscape. Different stages have different characteristics, so different approaches are needed to handle them. Let's look at an example from BigScreen in figure 12.3 where we continued from the value chain; however, instead of looking for streamlets, we now place each capability in an evolutionary stage.

Placing the capabilities immediately raised a question: Why were we building our own planning software? We observed specific cinema rooms emerging on the map, where management could communicate that IMAX was reaching its market cap, while 4DX (movies shown with environmental effects such as seat movement) seemed to be maturing into a solid product. These insights could guide future design decisions.

Wardley Mapping involves many more steps than we cannot explain in a few paragraphs. Therefore, we advise you to visit https://learnwardleymapping.com. This website offers all Wardley Mapping resources for free and will answer many of the questions that you might still have. Make sure to read all the blogs that Simon has written about his journey, which are bundled together in an e-pub.

COLLABORATIVE STRESSOR ANALYSIS FOR RESILIENT SOFTWARE DESIGN

Another topic to consider is *climate*, which refers to the external forces acting on your landscape. You can learn about these patterns as well at https://learnwardleymapping.com. Another tool we find useful for understanding the contextual effect of the complexity of these climate patterns is a *stressor analysis*, which comes from residuality theory by Barry M. O'Reilly.

A fundamental idea in this theory is *hyperliminality*,[1] which is an ordered system inside a disordered system. Software systems are ordered systems that are predictable,

---

[1] O'Reilly, B. M. "Residuality Theory, Random Simulation, and Attractor Networks," 2022. Procedia Computer Science, 201:639–645.

mappable, and testable, and they operate in our organization, which is the disordered system. In chapter 3, we already mentioned that a more fitting job title would be clairvoyant, because we can't predict what will happen in that organization and the market it's operating in. When we collaboratively design software, we're forced to work toward

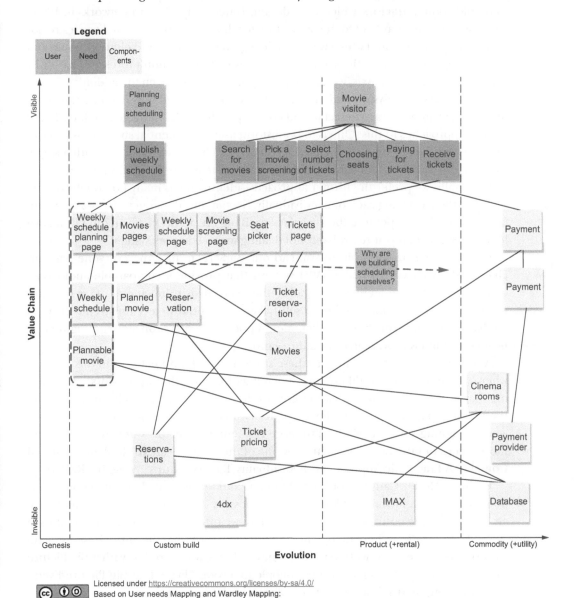

Licensed under https://creativecommons.org/licenses/by-sa/4.0/
Based on User needs Mapping and Wardley Mapping:
https://teamtopologies.com/key-concepts-content/exploring-team-and-service-boundaries-with-user-needs-mapping

Figure 12.3 Step 2 of Wardley Mapping performed with the management and development teams of BigScreen. In this case, we placed each capability where the group believes the capability is in the context of BigScreen. We observed that people wondered why we will build the planning software ourselves, so we circled that with an arrow to the right and a red sticky to indicate that.

an unknown future. Any event that arises in that unknown future, which the system isn't designed for, is known as a *stressor*.[2]

These stressors all lead to something called an *attractor*, a limited number of states in the network's state space to which the system will repeatedly return.[3] There is more to unfold about attractors, which were demonstrated by Kaufmann networks in 1969.[4] Different stressors may lead to the same attractor that affects our system. Even a stressor that seems irrelevant, and which we might disregard due to its low likelihood, could end up affecting the system in the same way as a stressor that we didn't foresee. That's why when doing stressor analysis, we ignore probability. Heck, it's even forbidden!

With a stressor analysis, we identify the stressor, understand how it affects the architecture, determine ways to detect it, and come up with ways to mitigate its effect. There are two approaches to this: One is to brainstorm as many potential stressors as you can think of and then outline their characteristics. The alternative is to start with a single stressor, fully define it, and allow additional stressors to emerge organically.

Personally, we prefer the former approach—identifying as many potential stressors first, and then assessing each one individually. Keep in mind that new stressors may surface as you delve deeper into the analysis of each one. In addition, if you can't think of a lot of stressors, then you're probably not dealing with a complex system.

Let's consider an example relevant to our BigScreen: imagine everyone has purchased advanced virtual reality (VR) systems that provide a comparable audiovisual experience to that of a cinema, negating the need to visit the cinema. This scenario would affect the cinema's ability to sell tickets. We could detect this trend through media reports and a decline in ticket sales. A potential mitigation strategy might be to begin offering VR movies on our online platform.

At some point when working out these stressors, you'll find patterns in the stressors when a lot of the times you'll use the same mitigation for different stressors. The stressors that lead to the same mitigation are considered attractors, which can be seen in the Wardley Mapping sense as climate patterns. Taking these mitigations into account when designing software will lead to more resilient architectures. If you want to read more, check out the blog post written by one of the authors called "Resilient Bounded Contexts: A Pragmatic Approach with Residuality Theory" (https://mng.bz/RZWa).

Business Model Canvas, Wardley Mapping, and stressor analysis all require your domain experts and stakeholders to actually possess the expertise required and have an overview of the entire system. Unfortunately, we often observe companies that have a siloed organization where no one has the full picture of what the entire business actually does. If you're faced with that situation, we always advise to start with a Big Picture EventStorming by putting all of these people in a room. From that Big Picture Event-Storming, you can distill several aspects of your business.

---

[2]   O'Reilly, "Residuality Theory," 639–645.
[3]   Ibid.
[4]   Ibid.

12.2   *Collaborative modeling beyond software design*

As mentioned before, software design is not all there is when it comes to collaborative modeling. In section 12.1, we zoomed out a bit to get a clear overview of the entire context we're working in. The modeling part can really drag you down potential rabbit holes, so it's good to zoom out every now and then and reconsider what it was that you wanted to achieve in the first place.

As far as context goes, it doesn't stop there. It's also important to consider that software design is only a small part of the entire cycle of teams and organizations. There are lots of different roles and people that are part of that bigger cycle who could also benefit from collaborative modeling. In this section, we want to zoom in on them and their needs a little bit.

12.2.1   *Different roles, different modeling needs*

What we talked about so far in this book mainly focuses on software design. But, as mentioned, there's more to that story. It's just a small part of the bigger picture that we call an organization. Plus, the things we talked about so far aren't limited to software design as they also apply to organizational change in a more general sense. Collaborative modeling implies a variety of stakeholders together in the same room. Big Picture EventStorms can be very useful for product managers and product owners to improve the requirements gathering process, for CTOs to optimize the (global) strategy, and for UX designers to improve user journeys and customer journeys, just to name a few. One of the authors even successfully used EventStorming to plan their wedding (check out https://mng.bz/2Kxw). When a tool can even help you manage your in-laws, you can't deny that it's more broadly applicable than software design.

Long story short, the different people and roles that are part of the entire context will have to do some form of collaborative modeling. They might have different needs than software developers, but they can still benefit from collaborative modeling tools. We'll highlight a few of them to give you an idea of how to apply other forms of collaborative modeling to meet different needs.

THE CUSTOMER JOURNEY

You may have noticed how we've casually referred to customer journeys and user journeys. We introduced both customer and user journeys in chapter 2. These two tools are often used interchangeably, but there are some nuances. What they have in common is that they are both visual representations of the stages that customers go through and how they interact with the company and its products. Another important similarity is that they take the perspective of the customer as the starting point.

The difference we see is that a customer journey is a more holistic representation of the broader customer experience, including touch points and channels. So, interaction with marketing, customer service, and company employees (both digital and physical) are important aspects. In the case of BigScreen, the *customer journey* represents the entire experience of customers from searching a movie to going home and reviewing the movie. A *user journey*, on the other hand, is something we more often see in product design and development. The focus in a user journey map is more on the product itself and the user's experience with that product, that is, understanding the different steps a user takes when using the product, what their needs are, and where they can run into challenges. To us, the main difference lies thus in the focus of the different maps: the entire customer journey versus the interaction of users with a product. For now, we'll dive more into the customer journey that BigScreen created.

A customer journey can be an excellent starting point for various collaborative modeling sessions, including User Story Mapping, EventStorming, and Wardley Mapping. It tells you, from the perspective of your customer, what happens from start to finish. Apart from technical opportunities, linked (external) systems, and software design challenges, it provides insights into what's important to your customer, which is a great addition to or starting point for your software architecture.

Our friends at BigScreen were very aware of that, and they created a customer journey themselves. It's a work in progress, and based on iterative updates, it represents the general customer journey of people who are visiting BigScreen. Figure 12.4 shows the customer journey of BigScreen.

For the purpose of this chapter and book, we don't show all the details because they aren't crucial in understanding the journey. This customer journey provides an overview of the main stages and the type of information that is required in a typical

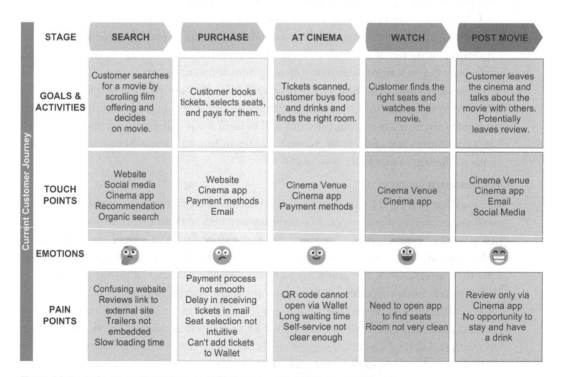

Current Customer Journey	STAGE	SEARCH	PURCHASE	AT CINEMA	WATCH	POST MOVIE
	GOALS & ACTIVITIES	Customer searches for a movie by scrolling film offering and decides on movie.	Customer books tickets, selects seats, and pays for them.	Tickets scanned, customer buys food and drinks and finds the right room.	Customer finds the right seats and watches the movie.	Customer leaves the cinema and talks about the movie with others. Potentially leaves review.
	TOUCH POINTS	Website Social media Cinema app Recommendation Organic search	Website Cinema app Payment methods Email	Cinema Venue Cinema app Payment methods	Cinema Venue Cinema app	Cinema Venue Cinema app Email Social Media
	EMOTIONS	😧	🙁	😐	😃	😁
	PAIN POINTS	Confusing website Reviews link to external site Trailers not embedded Slow loading time	Payment process not smooth Delay in receiving tickets in mail Seat selection not intuitive Can't add tickets to Wallet	QR code cannot open via Wallet Long waiting time Self-service not clear enough	Need to open app to find seats Room not very clean	Review only via Cinema app No opportunity to stay and have a drink

Figure 12.4   A simple customer journey of BigScreen, with details removed from it

customer journey. We'll use this journey to further explain some of the collaborative modeling tools that you can use.

USER STORY MAPPING

To map your user stories to the customer journey, you must have a customer journey in the first place. In the customer journey of BigScreen just shown in figure 12.4, let's take product managers or product owners as an example here. There is a product that needs to be managed, and User Story Mapping is an excellent collaborative modeling tool that you can use here. From a product management perspective, you want to create solutions that focus on the needs and desires of the actual users. It would also be great if everyone involved had the same understanding of what those needs are and which solutions (products) they are building.

User Story Mapping can help you out with that! It's a well-established tool coming from the Agile community and focuses on telling a story with the user perspective in mind. At the end of a User Story Mapping session, you have a visualized representation of the context of the customer journey, and you'll be able to make your product backlog more transparent based on that visualization. As mentioned, User Story Mapping is a collaborative modeling tool. To create the best user experience, everyone who contributes to the delivery of customer value should be in the session, so you can expect product management, engineers, UX/design, sales, marketing, customer support, and legal to be represented.

The narrative is central here: it's about the user experience. Taking that perspective prevents you from getting caught up in your own perspectives of what you believe would add value. If you take this too far, you'll end up with a monstrous product backlog full of potentially irrelevant user stories. The goal is to map your user stories to the customer journey to make sure all your stories are relevant. By doing this, it will become easier to discover product increments and stay aligned with everyone involved. Based on that, you'll be able to create a transparent and focused backlog with user stories that are relevant to your customers. As a bonus, writing user stories will also become much easier because they flow from the narrative you all follow. More guidance on how to run this exercise is extensively described in *Visual Collaboration Tools: For Teams Building Software* (https://leanpub.com/visualcollaborationtools/).

IMPACT MAPPING

Whatever product you're building, eventually you need to deliver business value. Impact Mapping is another well-established visualization tool that focuses on aligning user stories with business objectives. Together with relevant stakeholders, four questions will be answered (we'll delve into these in detail later in this section):

- *Why?*—Goals
- *Who?*—Actors
- *How?*—Impact
- *What?*—Deliverables

Because it all starts with the intended goal of the product (milestone), everything that will be identified after will have a direct effect on achieving that goal. It's a great tool to get a mutual understanding of the goals, visualize assumptions, set priorities, and discuss delivery options. Impact Mapping was introduced by Gojko Adzic in *Impact Mapping* (Provoking Thoughts, 2012).

There are several reasons to create an Impact Map. As mentioned, focus, prioritization, and business value are important benefits. We see lots of companies and teams that get so caught up in building a solution that they forget what problem they were trying to solve or if the solution they're building is (still) in line with business requirements. The map is visualized and simple, which makes it an excellent tool to have meaningful discussions with other stakeholders, including customers. It explains why certain features are being prioritized and why others aren't, which is all linked back to that initial goal.

Impact Mapping can also be a way to detect cognitive bias and manage it when necessary. Availability bias, for example (as explained in chapter 7), can hinder us from taking on new perspectives and thinking creatively. With Impact Mapping, you can explore various options to reach a goal early on when no one has fallen deeply in love with any solution yet, and you're still flexible enough to change course. You can visualize different options and pick the one that seems best.

Let's briefly consider the steps that you go through when creating an Impact Map. As mentioned, it all starts with describing the goal of a product (milestone). That might sound easy, but formulating a good goal is challenging. "Creating a mobile Cinema app," for example, isn't a good goal, although it could be a means to an end. What do you want to achieve with this app? More early bird reservations, enhanced client satisfaction, increased mobile advertising revenue, and/or stronger customer loyalty? These are all examples that would work well. The first step is to decide on what the real goal is together with your relevant stakeholders:

- *Step 1: Goal.* Why are you doing this? The preceding examples provide inspiration for this step. Don't take it lightly. Spend significant time on specifying your goal and creating alignment.

- *Step 2: Actors.* Who has an effect on achieving the aforementioned goal? To answer this question, consider the following questions: Who can obstruct achieving the goal? For whom are we building this product; identifying our users and customers? Who will be affected by our product? There's a strong link to behavior here: potential required behavioral change for the actors to achieve the goal determines step 3.

- *Step 3: Impact.* This is where we relate actors to our business goal: What behavior is required from our actors to achieve our goal? Do we need a behavioral change? What is the current undesired behavior we see? How does that negatively affect achieving our goal? What behavior that is currently there should not change? These questions should be answered for all actors identified in step 2.

- *Step 4: Deliverables.* Now that we know which role each actor plays in achieving our goal and which behavior is needed to get there, we can define deliverables such as features and organizational activities that support the impact we identified in step 3 and that are needed to achieve our goal.

Figure 12.5 is an example of an Impact Map from Adzic's book. As you can see, it's a simple visualization that provides a lot of insights and knowledge.

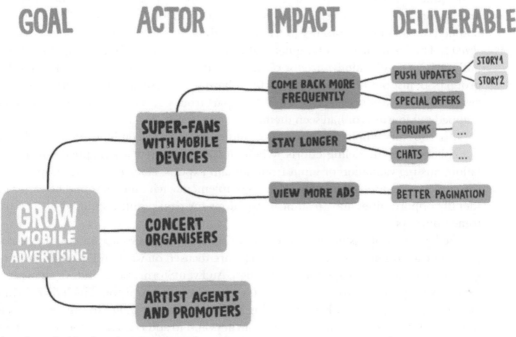

Impact mapping https://www.impactmapping.org/

Figure 12.5　An example of an Impact Map

12.2.2　*Customer journeys and EventStorming: A love story*

Different roles have unique needs and can benefit from different collaborative modeling tools, but the whole point of collaborative modeling is to do the modeling part together, meaning that there might be mutual value in different collaborative modeling efforts. From our experience, there definitely can be! Let's take a look at a potential love story, specifically the one between customer journeys and EventStorming.

Imagine our situation at BigScreen. Several customer journeys have been mapped out by the UX designers, aiming at visualizing their needs and opportunities for BigScreen in terms of pain points and touch points. At the same time, a group of people visualized the bigger picture during a Big Picture EventStorming session as input for their software architecture. It doesn't take a rocket scientist to see there is mutual value in these efforts. User journeys should fit the current software architecture, if we want to deliver the most value to our customers. What we often see happening, however, is that customer journeys are being mapped out in (partial) isolation and are mainly used for marketing efforts.

Here's one example we've encountered: We once facilitated a Big Picture Event-Storming session where both UX and developers were present, among others, of course. At one point, the architect wondered aloud if it would be useful to have customer journeys, so they could map that on the EventStorm to identify potential hotspots and opportunities. All of a sudden, someone stated (mildly frustrated), "Obviously, we mapped out all of our customer journeys already, and they are all available on *<shared drive>*!" The room turned a bit quiet and was wondering what to do next. One of the authors here—we'll anonymize for obvious reasons—raised their hand and asked the group: "So, just out of curiosity, who of you have seen these customer journeys or are aware of their existence?" Turned out that apart from UX, no one was aware of these mapped-out journeys or had seen them.

This side story emphasizes the opportunities available to combine and align different collaborative modeling efforts. When customer journeys are mapped out in isolation, missing validation or input from domain experts, chances are they won't fit in the current software architecture. If they complement each other, it would be easier to identify opportunities and (technical) solutions for pain points identified in the customer journeys.

The love story of customer journeys and EventStorming is rooted in how they complement each other. The customer journeys are focused on what end users or customers have to do and the stages they go through. An EventStorm also includes systems and how they support the process. To strengthen collaboration, you could include existing customer journeys in your EventStorming session, adding existing wireframes or mock ups. It's a way to validate your customer journeys and to add crucial wisdom from a customer perspective to your EventStorm.

If you take another look at the customer journey shown earlier in figure 12.4, you can see how it maps to (parts of) the Big Picture EventStorm. The Purchase stage, for example, is also visualized in the EventStorm. When we were designing boundaries in chapter 3, figure 3.6 showed a small part of the Big Picture EventStorm that captures the Payments part. As shown in that figure, external systems are mapped on two different bounded contexts: Movie Scheduling and Ticketing. By combining your customer journey and EventStorm, you can validate both and let them complement each other. In that way, you also allow all the present wisdom and knowledge to be part of the bigger picture.

12.2.3 *Aligning capabilities with your strategy*

Once you understand your entire context, you can take it one step further. If you know what you want to achieve, and you know what your context looks like, you can assess your current capabilities and discover if and which new capabilities you might need to reach your goals. We want to highlight two tools that we use to dive into understanding team processes and capabilities. With those outcomes, you can further strategize for the future and implementation.

TEAM TOPOLOGIES

We've already briefly discussed how the value chain of Wardley Mapping can be used to identify streamlets with user needs mapping. However, an important aspect we haven't covered yet is cognitive load, a concept characterized by psychologist John Sweller in 1988 as "the total amount of mental effort being used in the working memory."[5]

Engineering managers need to consider the cognitive load their teams are dealing with. For example, a software architecture that, theoretically, might be the most decoupled—such as a large number of small microservices—might result in teams grappling with a multitude of cross-cutting concerns. Alternatively, if the software architecture isn't intentionally structured, it could result in excessive collaboration among teams, which can not only be costly but also cognitively demanding.

Team together with management, we can use Team Topologies as a collaborative modeling tool to map out teams and their interactions. The goal is to consider these independent business flows and the teams' cognitive loads. It's essential to keep in mind that when you begin collaborative software design, particularly with complex systems, circumstances can change quickly. This fluidity means you might need to adjust the teams and reevaluate their collaborations. Don't apply Team Topologies once and then forget about it; instead, decide how you can strategize over time to transition teams from high collaboration to what Team Topologies calls "as-a-service." Team Topologies is meant to be used as a collaborative modeling tool and dynamically changing teams over time to accommodate for changing business needs and problems.

For those keen to delve deeper into the theoretical integration of Domain-Driven Design (DDD), Wardley Mapping, and Team Topologies, we highly recommend exploring the insightful resources provided by Susanne Kaiser. Her videos and the upcoming book offer a valuable exploration of these ideas. We've included her blog post on this topic in the further reading list in section 12.6 for a more comprehensive understanding.

CHANGE/MATURITY MAPPING

In Team Topologies, we can design an enabling team to infuse new knowledge into the Stream-aligned team. When modernizing your architecture, as we did at BigScreen, the team may require new capabilities to implement that architecture. For example, transitioning toward a microservice architecture necessitates many new capabilities to handle cross-cutting concerns and introduces a plethora of methods for observability.

Traditionally, many managers resort to using a skills matrix, or worse, a maturity model. The problem with these methods is that they don't account for the context in which a team operates. Each team may require different capabilities and find themselves in unique contextual situations regarding their abilities. That's why we can

---

[5]   Skelton, M., & Pais, M. "Team Cognitive Load," 2021, https://itrevolution.com/articles/cognitive-load/.

employ a variant of Wardley Mapping, created by Marc Burgauer and Chris McDermott, known as Maturity Mapping (https://maturitymapping.com/).

The concept is similar to Wardley Mapping, but we map out Capabilities as practices, which evolve from Novel, to Emerging, to Good, and finally to Best. However, it's crucial to understand the team's objective: What problem are they solving? From there, we can create a value chain and align every practice with the problem they are addressing for the business. This top anchor provides the context the team needs to map their maturity and understand their position.

This map empowers the team to decide how they should develop their capabilities. They can initiate experiments by having one or two people investigate a new capability. Once that capability has emerged and seems to work, the team can then advance it to a "good practice" and perhaps document the way of working. This map also provides the engineering manager with information for discussions about how individuals' personal growth can align with the team's goals. It can also inform decisions about whether to hire specialists, or if several teams are experiencing the same capability problem, whether to create an enabling team. Collaborative modeling and mapping out a landscape together serve as powerful tools for collaboration between management and teams!

12.3 *Moving toward implementation*

The end goal of collaborative modeling is to create a functioning software system that fits the user needs. To do that, there are a few questions left, which we'll answer in this section:

- When do we know it's time to start coding?
- Now that we have our EventStorm, what do we do with it?

12.3.1 *When to go from collaborative modeling to coding*

Let's start with the first one: When do we know it's time to start coding? We can also ask ourselves the reverse: How do we know we haven't modeled enough yet? Collaborative Modeling versus Coding is another polarity that needs to be managed, which we spoke about in chapter 10. A design stays a design, until it's tested in production—only then do we know the feasibility of our models. On the other hand, modeling with stickies is cheaper than having to refactor.

As a facilitator, it's interesting to map out this polarity together with the group you're facilitating to understand the signals and actions of the polarity. In figure 12.6, you can see some examples of the positive and negative effects of staying too long in both poles. We called the positive effects of coding and collaborative modeling, L+ and R+, Domain-Oriented Modeling. We named the negative effects, L– and R–, Shallow Technical Programming.

Next, you can ask the group for signals that they have been modeling too long or not long enough. If you start coding, and you have to add a lot of comments in the code to

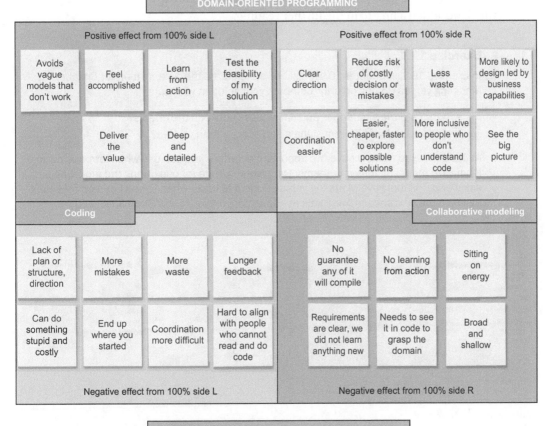

DOMAIN-ORIENTED PROGRAMMING

Positive effect from 100% side L				Positive effect from 100% side R			
Avoids vague models that don't work	Feel accomplished	Learn from action	Test the feasibility of my solution	Clear direction	Reduce risk of costly decision or mistakes	Less waste	More likely to design led by business capabilities
	Deliver the value	Deep and detailed		Coordination easier	Easier, cheaper, faster to explore possible solutions	More inclusive to people who don't understand code	See the big picture

Coding / Collaborative modeling

Lack of plan or structure, direction	More mistakes	More waste	Longer feedback	No guarantee any of it will compile	No learning from action	Sitting on energy
Can do something stupid and costly	End up where you started	Coordination more difficult	Hard to align with people who cannot read and do code	Requirements are clear, we did not learn anything new	Needs to see it in code to grasp the domain	Broad and shallow

Negative effect from 100% side L	Negative effect from 100% side R

SHALLOW TECHNICAL PROGRAMMING

Licensed under https://creativecommons.org/licenses/by- sa/4.0/
Based on Barry Johnson's Polarity map

Figure 12.6 The positive and negative effects of the polarity "coding versus collaborative modeling"

explain what's happening, it's time to go back to the virtual drawing board together with your team and dig a bit deeper into this part of the business logic. Ask the group questions such as the following: Can we introduce a new concept in our ubiquitous language that will make the code more readable?

Then, you fill in the actions that the group can take when they notice one of the signals. If you have too many comments in your code, you can model that specific scenario in detail. If you're mainly discussing technical aspects of the model, it's time to implement those technical aspects into the code. In figure 12.7, you can see our signals and actions.

As you may have noticed, those are fairly generic. Signals and heuristics are context dependent, and what is a signal or a possible action in one group of people, won't be there in another group. We wrote more in details about this polarity for EventStore which we added a link to in the further reading.

Exercise 12.1

In exercise 10.1 in chapter 10, we asked you to create the polarity map for Collaborative Modeling versus Coding polarity. Compare your solution with ours:

- What are the similarities and differences between the effects?
- Did we think of different signals and actions than you did?

At this point, you already have two important polarities you can use when introducing collaborative modeling into your teams: Deep versus Wide for use during the modeling sessions and Collaborative Modeling versus Coding to know when to start or stop modeling again. In the next section, we'll look at how to convert your EventStorm into code.

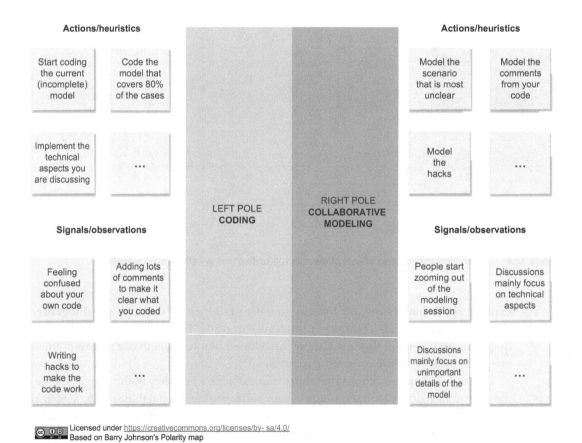

Licensed under https://creativecommons.org/licenses/by-sa/4.0/
Based on Barry Johnson's Polarity map

Figure 12.7   Signals and actions that you can use to move between collaborative modeling and implementing the solution

12.3.2 *From collaborative modeling to code*

Now that we know when to go from collaborative modeling to code, let's dive a bit deeper into how to do that. In chapter 2, we showed a piece of the EventStorm that we did together with the business at BigScreen. You can see a portion of this in figure 12.8. Where we want to end up is functionality implemented in the software. In this section, we'll walk you through our approach to get there. We'll leave the customer changing seats out of scope, and we'll focus on purchasing tickets.

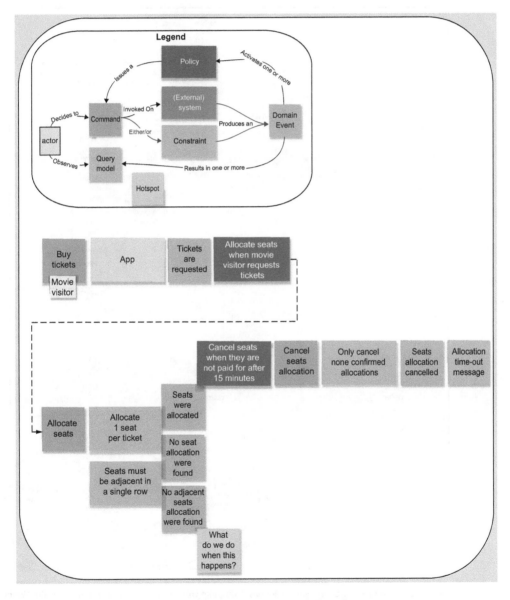

Figure 12.8 A small part of the process for buying a ticket and allocating a seat

We've already designed the bounded contexts here, but that doesn't mean we can just start implementing. We're going to walk through the EventStorm again and add questions we still have that prevent us from implementing this (figure 12.9).

One of the questions we still have is around the cancellation policy: we're trying to buy a ticket, but something with the seat allocation can go wrong. We said that this cancellation policy needs to deallocate the seat, but we also already requested the ticket. So, we also need to release the reserved tickets when their reservation has expired.

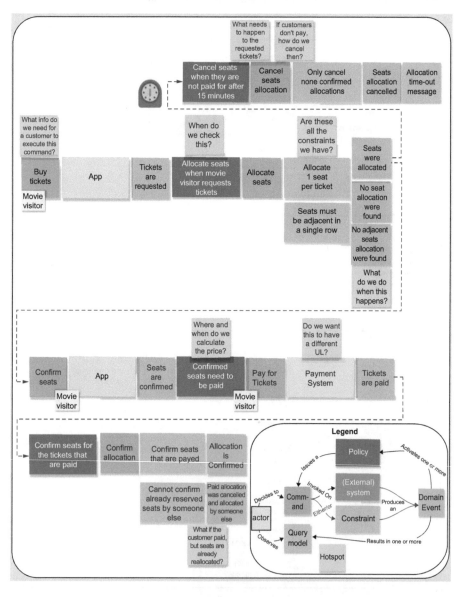

Figure 12.9   Your EventStorm will look something like this after you've iterated on it again. We now have added the questions we still need answered to start implementing them explicitly.

DIVING INTO CONSTRAINTS

In chapter 2, we demonstrated Example Mapping. To go from collaborative modeling to implementation, we need to understand the constraints best of all. Those are stickies that will turn into code. We had a hotspot sticky next to the event that said "What do we do when this happens?" We can find that hotspot in our examples too. If you look at figure 12.10, there are still some cases in which we don't allocate seats. It was conflicting with other information that we received, stating that seats always need to have an initial allocation.

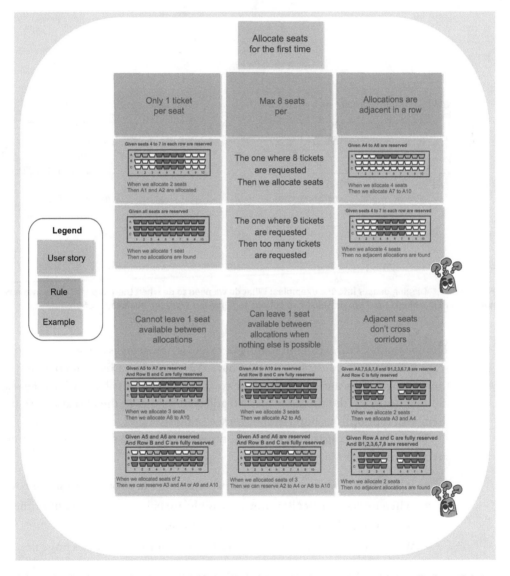

Figure 12.10 Some constraints result in not allocating seats when customers are purchasing a ticket. These are clues that we don't fully understand the constraints yet.

We went back to the business with some concrete examples of how we could allocate seats when we still had availability, but it didn't match any of the constraints we discussed before. You can see the result of this in figure 12.11. We gave the business possible options and asked which one they preferred. When there are still seats available, but not in a single row, the business wanted us to balance the seats over multiple rows.

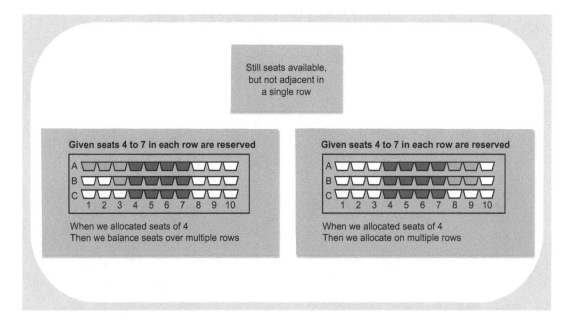

Figure 12.11   Digging deeper into the examples: What do we need to do when there are still seats available, but not adjacent in a single row? We provided two options to figure out what the business preferred.

The constraint "Only adjacent seating per row" is now seen as a first attempt to allocate seats, not the only constraint that we have. We also have a backup constraint to continue trying to allocate: when no single row allocation is possible, we balance seats over multiple rows. We did the same for "No adjacent seats over the corridor." We provided them with four options here, as you can see in figure 12.12.

Our initial two constraints have now transformed into a series of constraints with a specific order:

- When allocating for the first time, we should try to allocate in a single row.
- When no single row allocation is possible, we balance seats over multiple rows.
- When we can't balance in a column, we balance over corridors.
- When there are only scattered seats left, we allocate as close as possible.

Digging deeper into the seat allocation constraints gave us very valuable information. There always should be a seat allocation, unless we don't have the capacity anymore.

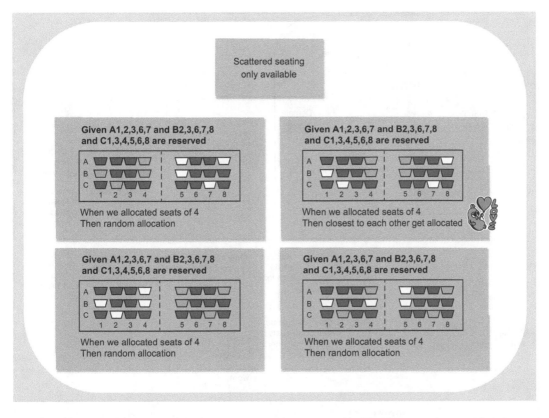

Figure 12.12 Examining the "No adjacent seats over corridor" constraint. What happens when we only have scattered seats available? We discovered that we're allowed to allocate seats with a corridor in between, but we should try this only when we can't balance seats in a column.

DESIGNING FOR IMPLEMENTATION

After digging deeper into the constraints and resolving some hotspots from figure 12.9, we have a much clearer idea already of how to implement the functionality of the EventStorm. There are still some pieces missing right now, however:

- Where are the consistency boundaries?
- How can we glue commands together with the events the system is supposed to respond to?
- Which bounded context has the information to answer the queries that our customers need to make a decision?

Most of the functionality is part of the Seat Allocations bounded context, but as you can see in figure 12.13, we have two commands and events that are in a different boundary: Price Calculation and Payments. We're going to leave those as is for now and focus on Seat Allocations.

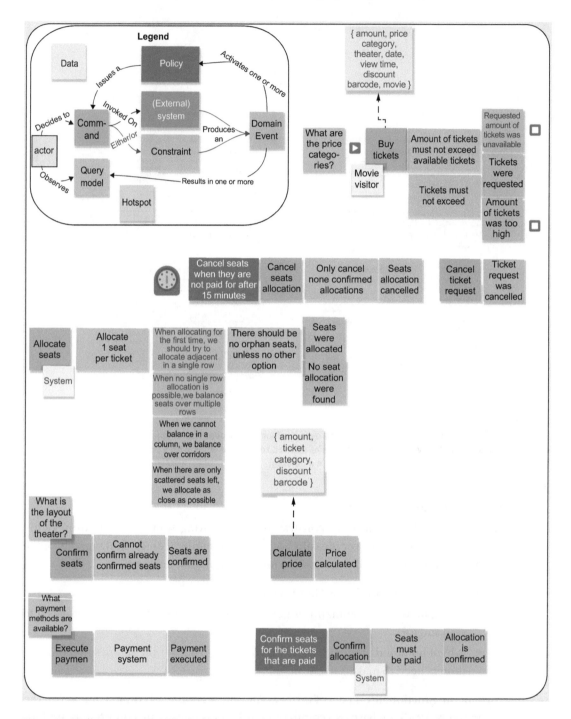

Figure 12.13   The end result of digging deeper into the constraints and resolving the hotspots. By resolving the hotspots, we came to the conclusion that we need to not only cancel or confirm seat allocations but also do the same for the ticket reservation.

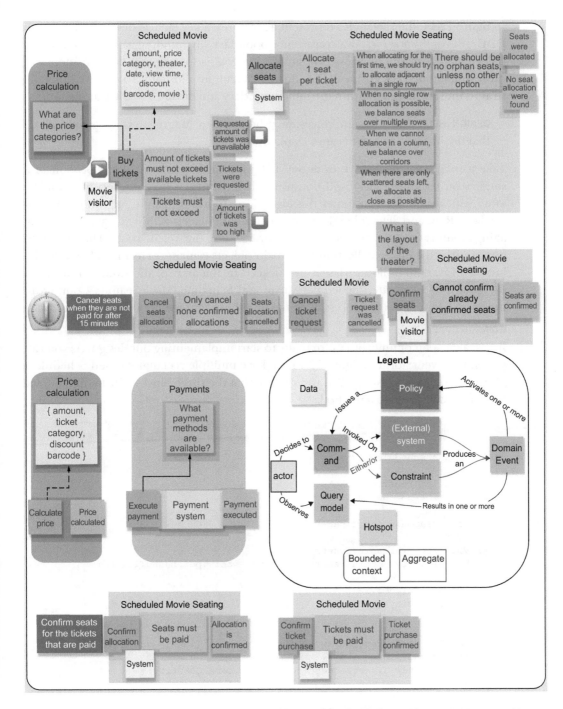

Figure 12.14 Our EventStorm is divided into consistency boundaries (rectangles). Most of the events reside within the Seat allocations context. Two commands and events are from different bounded contexts (rounded corners): Price Calculation and Payments.

In figure 12.14, the rectangles represent aggregates, a key tactical design pattern from DDD. An *aggregate* serves as a consistency boundary surrounding a cluster of domain objects, safeguarding business invariants. Our goal is to maintain the consistency of these domain objects, ensuring they don't reach an invalid state. To achieve this, constraints must be applied within the same boundary and during a single transaction.

DESIGN HEURISTIC   Design consistency boundaries (aggregates) to guarantee that the business invariants aren't violated.

Take a simple yet illustrative example: It's important to prevent the allocation of a single seat to multiple tickets. If not, two individual tickets hold a reservation for the same seat, resulting in customer dissatisfaction. To avoid this, we might encapsulate the Seat, Row, and ScheduledMovieSeating domain objects within an aggregate, managing modifications through ScheduledMovieSeating (aggregate root). This approach ensures that the entire collection of domain objects remain correct in relation to the business invariant "Allocate 1 seat per ticket." In this part of the EventStorm, we've designed two aggregates: ScheduledMovie and ScheduledMovieSeating. Coming up next, we'll delve into the process of converting these aggregates into executable code.

GOING TO CODE

It has taken a bit of time, but we're ready to start implementing our design! As you can see on the EventStorm in figure 12.14, we have multiple rectangles called Scheduled-Movie. If you look at listing 12.1, you can see that the three blocks of ScheduledMovie have been converted to a method.

Listing 12.1   Simplified aggregate ScheduledMovie

```
public class ScheduledMovie {

   private int reservedTickets;
   private int purchasedTickets;

   private readonly int capacity;

   private int AvailableTickets =>
     this.capacity - this.reservedTickets - this.purchasedTickets;

   public ScheduledMovie() {
      this.capacity = 200;
   }

   public TicketsRequested RequestTickets(RequestTickets command) {
      if(command.Amount > 8) {
         throw new TicketRequestTooLarge(command.Quantity);
      }

      if(this.AvailableTickets < command.Quantity) {
         throw new TicketRequestExceedsCapacity(
            command.Amount, this.capacity);
      }
```

```
        this.reservedTickets += command.Quantity;
        return new TicketsRequested(command.Quantity);
    }

    public TicketsCancelled CancelReservedTickets(CancelTickets command) {
        this.reservedTickets -= command.Quantity;
        return new TicketsCancelled(command.Quantity);
    }

    public TicketsConfirmed ConfirmTicketPurchase(ConfirmTickets command) {
        this.reservedTickets -= command.Quantity;
        this.purchasedTickets += command.Quantity;
        return new TicketsConfirmed(command.Quantity);
    }
}
```

If we take a closer look at the RequestTickets method, we can see two if statements there. Those are the constraints from our EventStorm "amount of tickets must not exceed available tickets" and "tickets must not exceed 8." This aggregate and code design is far from finished, and it only serves as a simplified example to show how those constraints ended up in code. We also only looked at a very small piece of the EventStorm in this section. As mentioned in chapter 11, section 11.3, software design is nonlinear, which can be best described as a whirlpool, and that includes the coding part. However, this gives you a good idea of how to go from collaborative modeling to code:

- A block on your EventStorm is a method in your aggregate.
- The method has an input parameter, which is the command.
- The method has a return type, which is the event.
- The constraints get implemented in the method.

There are a lot of ways to go from collaborative modeling to code, and a lot of books in the DDD community go a lot deeper into that. So be sure to go to https://virtualddd .com and join the community to learn more about it.

12.4 Collaborative software design catalysts

- When the team needs to implement a new feature, create a customer journey for this feature.
- Organize a "Lunch and Learn" session within your company to explore the Impact Map.
- With your team, create your own Collaborative Modeling versus Coding polarity map.
- Go back to the business logic of your code: Take a large piece of code and create an EventStorm out of it. If applicable, draw the consistency boundaries.

12.5   Chapter heuristics

Design heuristic

- Design consistency boundaries (aggregates) to guarantee that the business invariants aren't violated.

12.6   Further reading

- *Adaptive Systems with Domain-Driven Design, Wardley Mapping, and Team Topologies: Architecture for Flow* by Susanne Kaiser (Pearson Education, 2024)
- "Architecture for Flow with Wardley Mapping, DDD, and Team Topologies" by Susanne Kaiser (QCon Plus conference video), https://mng.bz/ZE59
- "Black Ops DDD Using the Business Model Canvas" by Javier Fernández (Explore DDD conference video), www.youtube.com/watch?v=M5CbbWmdsFU
- "DDD, Wardley Mapping, & Team Topologies" by Susanne Kaiser (InfoQ podcast), https://mng.bz/1GxR_
- "EventStorming the Perfect Wedding" by Kenny Baas-Schwegler, https://mng.bz/2Kxw
- *Impact Mapping: Making a Big Impact with Software Products and Projects* by Gojko Adzic (Provoking Thoughts, 2012)
- "Resilient Bounded Contexts: A Pragmatic Approach with Residuality Theory" by Kenny Baas-Schwegler, https://mng.bz/RZWa
- *User Story Mapping: Discover the Whole Story, Build the Right Product* by Jeff Patton (O'Reilly, 2014)
- *Residues: Time, Change, and Uncertainty in Software Architecture*, Barry M. O'Reilly (Leanpub, 2024)
- *Team Topologies: Organizing for fast flow of value*, by Manuel Pais and Matthew Skelton (It Revolution Press, 2019)
- "When to go from collaborative modelling to coding? Part 1" by Kenny Baas-Schwegler, Evelyn van Kelle, and Gien Verschatse, https://www.eventstore.com/blog/when-to-go-from-collaborative-modelling-to-coding-part-1

Summary

- Avoid the trap of preconceived solutions; prioritize understanding customer needs and context in collaborative modeling tools such as Business Model Canvas and EventStorming. Refocus on value proposition and customer segment, eliminating software-centric biases to gain deeper insights.
- By mapping the business landscape, introducing climate patterns, and using evolution stages, Wardley Mapping provides a clear view for tailored, effective strategies, aiding decisions in product, teams, and software design areas.

- Stressor analysis, derived from residuality theory, uncovers hidden stressors in complex systems, guiding mitigation strategies and fostering resilient software architectures through shared approaches.

- Collaborative modeling, applicable beyond software design, benefits product manager and UX designer roles through techniques such as Big Picture EventStorming.

- Customer journeys encompass overall experiences, while user journeys focus on product interactions; both enhance sessions such as User Story Mapping and EventStorming, enriching software architecture with customer-centric insights.

- Impact Mapping, introduced by Gojko Adzic, visually aligns user stories with business goals by clarifying why, who, how, and what. This technique aids prioritization, fosters discussions, detects cognitive bias, and guides product development by connecting behavior change with deliverables.

- Integrating mapped customer journeys into EventStorming sessions validates and enhances understanding, helping identify pain points, opportunities, and solutions for a more comprehensive perspective.

- Consider cognitive load when designing software architecture, as the most decoupled architecture may lead to cross-cutting concerns or excessive collaboration. Team Topologies, when combined with Maturity Mapping, offers a collaborative modeling approach to strategically structure teams, manage capabilities, and foster adaptive development in evolving contexts.

- Address the balance between collaborative modeling and coding by recognizing signals and actions. Domain-Oriented Modeling (L+ and R+) supports meaningful design, while Shallow Technical Programming (L– and R–) leads to inefficiencies.

- Transitioning from collaborative modeling to code implementation involves transforming EventStorm blocks into aggregate methods.

- Constraints identified in the EventStorm guide the implementation process and are incorporated into the body of the methods of the aggregate.

- Deeper analysis and discussions with the business refine constraints, leading to a clearer implementation plan.

- Aggregates define consistency boundaries around domain objects, maintaining internal consistency.

appendix A

Appendix A illustrates a collaborative modeling session, capturing both its technical and social aspects. Figure A.1 shows the modeling space, where participants work together on software models using a variety of tools. The facilitator directs the process, guiding the group toward making sustainable design decisions that fulfill the session's goals.

On the table, the facilitator's toolbox is visible, containing all the necessary items for a productive session: various modeling tools, styles, ingredients, and heuristics. This toolbox is crucial, allowing the facilitator to effectively blend these elements while managing the social dynamics within the group. These dynamics are represented by text balloons and shadows in the image. The shadows symbolize the unconscious dynamics within the group, such as ranking, cognitive biases, conflicts, and polarities, which can disrupt the session and prevent the group from moving forward.

The facilitator shines a metaphorical flashlight on these shadows, making them visible and manageable. If left unaddressed, these shadows can grow into larger obstacles—depicted as demons—that hinder the group from reaching a shared understanding and achieving their goals.

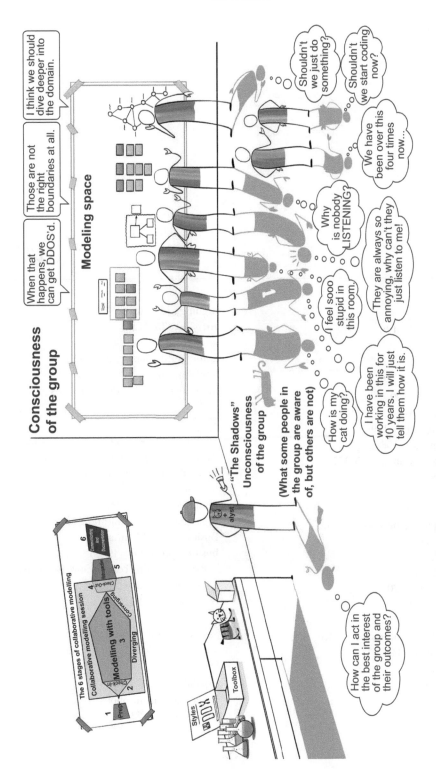

Figure A.1   The full visual representation of our mental model of a collaborative modeling session

index